The Word of the Lord – Year B

The Word of the Lord

YEAR B

Readings
for the Principal, Second and Third Services

on
Sundays, Principal Feasts
and Principal Holy Days
(Temporale),

as authorized by the Church of England

CANTERBURY
PRESS
Norwich

The Word of the Lord - Year B
is published by **Canterbury Press Norwich**
a publishing imprint of Hymns Ancient & Modern Limited,
a registered charity,
St Mary's Works, St Mary's Plain, Norwich, Norfolk, NR3 3BH

Edited by Brother Tristam SSF

Published 1999

A catalogue record for this book is available
from the British Library.

ISBN 1 85311 222 4

Printed and bound in Great Britain by Biddles Ltd, Guildford and King's Lynn

Contents

Notes

ORDERING THE SERVICE

Notes for ordering the service can be found in *The Christian Year: Calendar, Lectionary and Collects*, published by Church House Publishing.

THE LECTIONARY

The readings are taken from the Church of England three-year lectionary which has been adapted from *The Revised Common Lectionary*.

The **references** give book, chapter and verse, in that order.

Three sets of psalms and readings are provided for each Sunday. The **Principal Service lectionary** is intended for use at the principal service of the day (whether this service is Holy Communion or some other authorized form). In most church communities, this is likely to be the mid-morning service, but the minister is free to decide which service time normally constitutes the principal service of the day.

The **Second Service lectionary** is intended for a second main service. In many churches, this lectionary will be the appropriate provision for a Sunday afternoon or evening service. A Gospel reading is always provided so that this lectionary can, if necessary, be used at the Holy Communion.

The **Third Service lectionary**, with shorter readings, is intended where a third set of psalms and readings is needed and is most appropriate for use at an office. A Gospel reading is not always provided, so this lectionary is not suitable for use at the Holy Communion.

If only **two readings** are used at the Principal Service and that service is Holy Communion, the second reading must always be the Gospel reading. When the Principal Service lectionary is used at a service other than Holy Communion, the Gospel reading need not always be chosen.

If there are only two readings at the Principal Service on the Sundays in Eastertide, Ascension Day and Pentecost, the reading from the Acts of the Apostles must always be used.

In the choice of **readings other than the Gospel** reading, the minister should ensure that, in any year, a balance is maintained between readings from the Old and New Testaments and that, where a particular biblical book is appointed to be read over several weeks, the choice ensures that this continuity of one book is not lost.

Where a reading from the **Apocrypha** is offered, an alternative Old

Testament reading is provided.

On the Sundays after Trinity, the Principal Service lectionary provides **alternative** Old Testament **readings and psalms**. The first reading provides a continuous reading of a particular book of the Old Testament; the second reading provides a related reading to the Gospel of the day. If beginning on the continuous course of reading the Old Testament, serious consideration should be given before diverting from this for the remainder of that Christian Year.

ROUND BRACKETS ( ) which are included in the text of the NRSV are repeated here. Such text should always be read.

SQUARE BRACKETS [ ] indicate that the text within them may be omitted. Such brackets are used very occasionally in the text of the NRSV usually to indicate text which not all ancient authorities include, and these are sometimes repeated here. However, in the vast majority of cases in this book, they indicate the verses which may be omitted as suggested by the compilers of the Lectionaries.

SUPERSCRIPT VERSE NUMBERS
Where some verses have been omitted, the verse number at which the text resumes is noted in superscript. This may be quietly announced if others are following the text in their own Bibles. Otherwise, no announcement is necessary.

SISTER VOLUMES
Two further volumes, entitled *The Word of the Lord – Year A* and The *Word of the Lord – Year C* accompany this book.
A book containing all the **Gospel readings** for use at the Principal Service is called *The Gospel of The Lord*.
A slimmer volume of readings for use on **Special Occasions**, such as Guidance of the Holy Spirit, Harvest Thanksgiving, Ministry (Ember Days), Mission & Evangelism, Peace, Rogation Days, Social Justice, Unity, For the Sovereign, In Time of Trouble, is entitled *The Word of the Lord – Readings for Special Occasions*.
The final sister volume to this series of books is *Exciting Holiness* and is published by Canterbury Press Norwich. It contains the Scripture readings necessary for use on **Festivals and Lesser Festivals**, together with brief biographies of all those included in the Calendar. All these books follow the authorised lectionaries.
Celebrating the Saints & *Celebrating the Seasons*, by Robert Atwell, also published by Canterbury Press Norwich, provide non-scriptural readings for use with **Common Worship**.

Table of Moveable Feasts

Year	Ash Wednesday	EASTER DAY	Ascension Day	Pentecost	Trinity 1	Advent Sunday
1999	17 February	4 April	13 May	23 May	Proper 5	28 November (Year B begins)
2000	8 March	23 April	1 June	11 June	Proper 7	3 December (Year C begins)
2001	28 February	15 April	24 May	3 June	Proper 6	2 December (Year A begins)
2002	13 February	31 March	9 May	19 May	Proper 4	1 December (Year B begins)
2003	5 March	20 April	29 May	8 June	Proper 7	30 November (Year C begins)
2004	25 February	11 April	20 May	30 May	Proper 6	28 November (Year A begins)
2005	9 February	27 March	5 May	15 May	Proper 4	27 November (Year B begins)
2006	1 March	16 April	25 May	4 June	Proper 6	3 December (Year C begins)
2007	21 February	8 April	17 May	27 May	Proper 5	2 December (Year A begins)
2008	6 February	23 March	1 May	11 May	Proper 3	30 November (Year B begins)
2009	25 February	12 April	21 May	31 May	Proper 6	29 November (Year C begins)
2010	17 February	4 April	13 May	23 May	Proper 5	28 November (Year A begins)
2011	9 March	24 April	2 June	12 June	Proper 8	27 November (Year B begins)
2012	22 February	8 April	17 May	27 May	Proper 5	2 December (Year C begins)
2013	13 February	31 March	9 May	19 May	Proper 4	1 December (Year A begins)
2014	5 March	20 April	29 May	8 June	Proper 7	30 November (Year B begins)
2015	18 February	5 April	14 May	24 May	Proper 5	29 November (Year C begins)
2016	10 February	27 March	5 May	15 May	Proper 4	27 November (Year A begins)
2017	1 March	16 April	25 May	4 June	Proper 6	3 December (Year B begins)
2018	14 February	1 April	10 May	20 May	Proper 4	2 December (Year C begins)
2019	6 March	21 April	30 May	9 June	Proper 7	1 December (Year A begins)
2020	26 February	12 April	21 May	31 May	Proper 6	29 November (Year B begins)
2021	17 February	4 April	13 May	23 May	Proper 5	28 November (Year C begins)
2022	2 March	17 April	26 May	5 June	Proper 7	27 November (Year A begins)
2023	22 February	9 April	18 May	28 May	Proper 5	3 December (Year B begins)
2024	14 February	31 March	9 May	19 May	Proper 4	1 December (Year C begins)
2025	5 March	20 April	29 May	8 June	Proper 7	30 November (Year A begins)

Advent

The First Sunday of Advent

Principal Service
Isaiah 64.1-9; Ps 80.1-7 [17-19]; 1 Corinthians 1.3-9; Mark 13.24-37

A reading from the prophecy of Isaiah. *(64.1-9)*

O that you would tear open the heavens and come down,
  so that the mountains would quake at your presence –
as when fire kindles brushwood
  and the fire causes water to boil –
to make your name known to your adversaries,
  so that the nations might tremble at your presence!
When you did awesome deeds that we did not expect,
  you came down, the mountains quaked at your presence.
From ages past no one has heard,
  no ear has perceived,
no eye has seen any God besides you,
  who works for those who wait for him.
You meet those who gladly do right,
  those who remember you in your ways.
But you were angry, and we sinned;
  because you hid yourself we transgressed.
We have all become like one who is unclean,
  and all our righteous deeds are like a filthy cloth.
We all fade like a leaf,
  and our iniquities, like the wind, take us away.
There is no one who calls on your name,
  or attempts to take hold of you;
for you have hidden your face from us,
  and have delivered us into the hand of our iniquity.
Yet, O Lord, you are our Father;
  we are the clay, and you are our potter;
  we are all the work of your hand.
Do not be exceedingly angry, O Lord,
  and do not remember iniquity for ever.
Now consider, we are all your people.

This is the word of the Lord.

A reading from the First Letter of Paul to the Corinthians. (1.3-9)

Grace to you and peace from God our Father and the Lord Jesus Christ.

I give thanks to my God always for you because of the grace of God that has been given you in Christ Jesus, for in every way you have been enriched in him, in speech and knowledge of every kind – just as the testimony of Christ has been strengthened among you – so that you are not lacking in any spiritual gift as you wait for the revealing of our Lord Jesus Christ. He will also strengthen you to the end, so that you may be blameless on the day of our Lord Jesus Christ. God is faithful; by him you were called into the fellowship of his Son, Jesus Christ our Lord.

This is the word of the Lord.

Hear the gospel of our Lord Jesus Christ according to Mark. (13.24-37)

Jesus said to Peter, James, John and Andrew,
'In those days, after that suffering,
   the sun will be darkened,
     and the moon will not give its light,
  and the stars will be falling from heaven,
     and the powers in the heavens will be shaken.
Then they will see "the Son of Man coming in clouds" with great power and glory. Then he will send out the angels, and gather his elect from the four winds, from the ends of the earth to the ends of heaven.

'From the fig tree learn its lesson: as soon as its branch becomes tender and puts forth its leaves, you know that summer is near. So also, when you see these things taking place, you know that he is near, at the very gates. Truly I tell you, this generation will not pass away until all these things have taken place. Heaven and earth will pass away, but my words will not pass away.

'But about that day or hour no one knows, neither the angels in heaven, nor the Son, but only the Father. Beware, keep alert; for you do not know when the time will come. It is like a man going on a journey, when he leaves home and puts his slaves in charge, each with his work, and commands the doorkeeper to be on the watch. Therefore, keep awake – for you do not know when the master of the house will come, in the evening, or at midnight, or at cockcrow, or at dawn, or else he may find you asleep when he comes suddenly. And what I say to you I say to all: Keep awake.'

This is the gospel of the Lord.

Second Service

Ps 25 *or* 25.1-10; Isaiah 1.1-20; Matthew 21.1-13

A reading from the prophecy of Isaiah. (1.1-20)

The vision of Isaiah son of Amoz, which he saw concerning Judah and Jerusalem in the days of Uzziah, Jotham, Ahaz, and Hezekiah, kings of Judah.
>Hear, O heavens, and listen, O earth;
>>for the Lord has spoken:
>I reared children and brought them up,
>>but they have rebelled against me.
>The ox knows its owner,
>>and the donkey its master's crib;
>but Israel does not know,
>>my people do not understand.

>Ah, sinful nation,
>>people laden with iniquity,
>offspring who do evil,
>>children who deal corruptly,
>who have forsaken the Lord,
>>who have despised the Holy One of Israel,
>>who are utterly estranged!

>Why do you seek further beatings?
>>Why do you continue to rebel?
>The whole head is sick,
>>and the whole heart faint.
>From the sole of the foot even to the head,
>>there is no soundness in it,
>but bruises and sores
>>and bleeding wounds;
>they have not been drained, or bound up,
>>or softened with oil.

>Your country lies desolate,
>>your cities are burned with fire;
>in your very presence
>>aliens devour your land;
>>it is desolate, as overthrown by foreigners.
>And daughter Zion is left
>>like a booth in a vineyard,
>like a shelter in a cucumber field,
>>like a besieged city.

If the Lord of hosts
>had not left us a few survivors,
we would have been like Sodom,
>and become like Gomorrah.

Hear the word of the Lord,
>you rulers of Sodom!
Listen to the teaching of our God,
>you people of Gomorrah!
What to me is the multitude of your sacrifices?
>says the Lord;
I have had enough of burnt-offerings of rams
>and the fat of fed beasts;
I do not delight in the blood of bulls,
or of lambs, or of goats.

When you come to appear before me,
>who asked this from your hand?
>Trample my courts no more;
bringing offerings is futile;
>incense is an abomination to me.
New moon and sabbath and calling of convocation –
>I cannot endure solemn assemblies with iniquity.
Your new moons and your appointed festivals
>my soul hates;
they have become a burden to me,
>I am weary of bearing them.
When you stretch out your hands,
>I will hide my eyes from you;
even though you make many prayers,
>I will not listen; your hands are full of blood.
Wash yourselves; make yourselves clean;
>remove the evil of your doings
>from before my eyes;
cease to do evil,
>learn to do good;
seek justice,
>rescue the oppressed,
defend the orphan,
>plead for the widow.

Come now, let us argue it out,
>says the Lord:
though your sins are like scarlet,

they shall be like snow;
though they are red like crimson,
    they shall become like wool.
If you are willing and obedient,
    you shall eat the good of the land;
but if you refuse and rebel,
    you shall be devoured by the sword;
    for the mouth of the Lord has spoken.

A reading from the gospel according to Matthew. (21.1-13)

When Jesus and his disciples had come near Jerusalem and had
reached Bethphage, at the Mount of Olives, Jesus sent two disciples,
saying to them, 'Go into the village ahead of you, and immediately
you will find a donkey tied, and a colt with her; untie them and bring
them to me. If anyone says anything to you, just say this, "The Lord
needs them." And he will send them immediately.' This took place
to fulfil what had been spoken through the prophet, saying,
    'Tell the daughter of Zion,
    Look, your king is coming to you,
        humble, and mounted on a donkey,
    and on a colt, the foal of a donkey.'
The disciples went and did as Jesus had directed them; they brought
the donkey and the colt, and put their cloaks on them, and he sat on
them. A very large crowd spread their cloaks on the road, and others cut branches from the trees and spread them on the road. The
crowds that went ahead of him and that followed were shouting,
    'Hosanna to the Son of David!
    Blessèd is the one who comes in the name of the Lord!
    Hosanna in the highest heaven!'
When he entered Jerusalem, the whole city was in turmoil, asking,
'Who is this?' The crowds were saying, 'This is the prophet Jesus
from Nazareth in Galilee.'
    Then Jesus entered the temple and drove out all who were selling
and buying in the temple, and he overturned the tables of the money-
changers and the seats of those who sold doves. He said to them, 'It
is written,
    "My house shall be called a house of prayer";
        but you are making it a den of robbers.'

Third Service
Ps 44; Isaiah 2.1-5; Luke 12.35-48

A reading from the prophecy of Isaiah. (2.1-5)

The word that Isaiah son of Amoz saw concerning Judah and Jerusalem.

In days to come
the mountain of the Lord's house
shall be established as the highest of the mountains,
and shall be raised above the hills;
all the nations shall stream to it.
Many peoples shall come and say,
'Come, let us go up to the mountain of the Lord,
to the house of the God of Jacob;
that he may teach us his ways
and that we may walk in his paths.'
For out of Zion shall go forth instruction,
and the word of the Lord from Jerusalem.
He shall judge between the nations,
and shall arbitrate for many peoples;
they shall beat their swords into ploughshares,
and their spears into pruning-hooks;
nation shall not lift up sword against nation,
neither shall they learn war any more.
O house of Jacob,
come, let us walk
in the light of the Lord!

A reading from the gospel according to Luke. (12.35-48)

Jesus said to his disciples, 'Be dressed for action and have your lamps lit; be like those who are waiting for their master to return from the wedding banquet, so that they may open the door for him as soon as he comes and knocks. Blessèd are those slaves whom the master finds alert when he comes; truly I tell you, he will fasten his belt and have them sit down to eat, and he will come and serve them. If he comes during the middle of the night, or near dawn, and finds them so, blessèd are those slaves.

'But know this: if the owner of the house had known at what hour the thief was coming, he would not have let his house be broken into. You also must be ready, for the Son of Man is coming at an unexpected hour.'

Peter said, 'Lord, are you telling this parable for us or for everyone?'

And the Lord said, 'Who then is the faithful and prudent manager whom his master will put in charge of his slaves, to give them their allowance of food at the proper time? Blessèd is that slave whom his master will find at work when he arrives. Truly I tell you, he will put that one in charge of all his possessions. But if that slave says to himself, "My master is delayed in coming", and if he begins to beat the other slaves, men and women, and to eat and drink and get drunk, the master of that slave will come on a day when he does not expect him and at an hour that he does not know, and will cut him in pieces, and put him with the unfaithful. That slave who knew what his master wanted, but did not prepare himself or do what was wanted, will receive a severe beating. But one who did not know and did what deserved a beating will receive a light beating. From everyone to whom much has been given, much will be required; and from one to whom much has been entrusted, even more will be demanded. '

The Second Sunday of Advent

Principal Service
Isaiah 40.1-11; Ps 85.[1-2] 8-13; 2 Peter 3.8-15a; Mark 1.1-8

A reading from the prophecy of Isaiah. (40.1-11)

> Comfort, O comfort my people,
>   says your God.
> Speak tenderly to Jerusalem,
>   and cry to her
> that she has served her term,
> that her penalty is paid,
> that she has received from the Lord's hand
>   double for all her sins.
>
> A voice cries out:
> 'In the wilderness prepare the way of the Lord,
>   make straight in the desert a highway for our God.
> Every valley shall be lifted up,
>   and every mountain and hill be made low;
> the uneven ground shall become level,
>   and the rough places a plain.
> Then the glory of the Lord shall be revealed,
>   and all people shall see it together,
>   for the mouth of the Lord has spoken.'

A voice says, 'Cry out!'
    And I said, 'What shall I cry?'
All people are grass,
    their constancy is like the flower of the field.
The grass withers, the flower fades,
    when the breath of the Lord blows upon it;
    surely the people are grass.
The grass withers, the flower fades;
    but the word of our God will stand for ever.
Get you up to a high mountain,
    O Zion, herald of good tidings;
lift up your voice with strength,
    O Jerusalem, herald of good tidings,
    lift it up, do not fear;
say to the cities of Judah,
    'Here is your God!'
See, the Lord God comes with might,
    and his arm rules for him;
his reward is with him,
    and his recompense before him.
He will feed his flock like a shepherd;
    he will gather the lambs in his arms,
and carry them in his bosom,
    and gently lead the mother sheep.

This is the word of the Lord.

A reading from the Second Letter of Peter. (3.8-15a)

Do not ignore this one fact, belovèd, that with the Lord one day is like
a thousand years, and a thousand years are like one day. The Lord is
not slow about his promise, as some think of slowness, but is patient
with you, not wanting any to perish, but all to come to repentance.
But the day of the Lord will come like a thief, and then the heavens
will pass away with a loud noise, and the elements will be dissolved
with fire, and the earth and everything that is done on it will be disclosed.

  Since all these things are to be dissolved in this way, what sort of
people ought you to be in leading lives of holiness and godliness,
waiting for and hastening the coming of the day of God, because of
which the heavens will be set ablaze and dissolved, and the elements
will melt with fire? But, in accordance with his promise, we wait for
new heavens and a new earth, where righteousness is at home.

  Therefore, belovèd, while you are waiting for these things, strive to be found by him at peace, without spot or blemish; and regard the patience of our Lord as salvation.

This is the word of the Lord.

Hear the gospel of our Lord Jesus Christ according to Mark. (1.1-8)

The beginning of the good news of Jesus Christ, the Son of God.
As it is written in the prophet Isaiah,
    'See, I am sending my messenger ahead of you,
        who will prepare your way;
    the voice of one crying out in the wilderness:
        "Prepare the way of the Lord,
        make his paths straight"',
John the baptizer appeared in the wilderness, proclaiming a baptism of repentance for the forgiveness of sins. And people from the whole Judean countryside and all the people of Jerusalem were going out to him, and were baptized by him in the river Jordan, confessing their sins. Now John was clothed with camel's hair, with a leather belt around his waist, and he ate locusts and wild honey. He proclaimed, 'The one who is more powerful than I is coming after me; I am not worthy to stoop down and untie the thong of his sandals. I have baptized you with water; but he will baptize you with the Holy Spirit.'

This is the gospel of the Lord.

Second Service
Ps 40 *or* 40.11-17; 1 Kings 22.1-28; Romans 15.4-13;
if a Eucharist: Matthew 11.2-11

A reading from the First Book of the Kings. (22.1-28)

For three years Aram and Israel continued without war. But in the third year King Jehoshaphat of Judah came down to the king of Israel. The king of Israel said to his servants, 'Do you know that Ramoth-gilead belongs to us, yet we are doing nothing to take it out of the hand of the king of Aram?' He said to Jehoshaphat, 'Will you go with me to battle at Ramoth-gilead?' Jehoshaphat replied to the king of Israel, 'I am as you are; my people are your people, my horses are your horses.'

But Jehoshaphat also said to the king of Israel, 'Inquire first for the word of the Lord.' Then the king of Israel gathered the prophets together, about four hundred of them, and said to them, 'Shall I go to battle against Ramoth-gilead, or shall I refrain?' They said, 'Go up; for the Lord will give it into the hand of the king.' But Jehoshaphat said, 'Is there no other prophet of the Lord here of whom we may inquire?' The king of Israel said to Jehoshaphat, 'There is still one other by whom we may inquire of the Lord, Micaiah son of Imlah; but I hate him, for he never prophesies anything favourable about me, but only disaster.' Jehoshaphat said, 'Let the king not say such a thing.' Then the king of Israel summoned an officer and said, 'Bring quickly Micaiah son of Imlah.' Now the king of Israel and King Jehoshaphat of Judah were sitting on their thrones, arrayed in their robes, at the threshing-floor at the entrance of the gate of Samaria; and all the prophets were prophesying before them. Zedekiah son of Chenaanah made for himself horns of iron, and he said, 'Thus says the Lord: With these you shall gore the Arameans until they are destroyed.' All the prophets were prophesying the same and saying, 'Go up to Ramoth-gilead and triumph; the Lord will give it into the hand of the king.'

The messenger who had gone to summon Micaiah said to him, 'Look, the words of the prophets with one accord are favourable to the king; let your word be like the word of one of them, and speak favourably.' But Micaiah said, 'As the Lord lives, whatever the Lord says to me, that I will speak.'

When he had come to the king, the king said to him, 'Micaiah, shall we go to Ramoth-gilead to battle, or shall we refrain?' He answered him, 'Go up and triumph; the Lord will give it into the hand of the king.' But the king said to him, 'How many times must I make you swear to tell me nothing but the truth in the name of the Lord?' Then Micaiah said, 'I saw all Israel scattered on the mountains, like sheep that have no shepherd; and the Lord said, "These have no master; let each one go home in peace."' The king of Israel said to Jehoshaphat, 'Did I not tell you that he would not prophesy anything favourable about me, but only disaster?'

Then Micaiah said, 'Therefore hear the word of the Lord: I saw the Lord sitting on his throne, with all the host of heaven standing beside him to the right and to the left of him. And the Lord said, "Who will entice Ahab, so that he may go up and fall at Ramoth-gilead?" Then one said one thing, and another said another, until a spirit came forward and stood before the Lord, saying, "I will entice him." "How?" the Lord asked him. He replied, "I will go out and be a lying spirit in the mouth of all his prophets." Then the Lord said, "You are to entice him, and you shall succeed; go out and do it." So you see, the Lord has put a lying spirit in the mouth of all these your prophets; the Lord has decreed disaster for you.'

Then Zedekiah son of Chenaanah came up to Micaiah, slapped him on the cheek, and said, 'Which way did the spirit of the Lord pass from me to speak to you?' Micaiah replied, 'You will find out on that day when you go in to hide in an inner chamber.' The king of Israel then ordered, 'Take Micaiah, and return him to Amon the governor of the city and to Joash the king's son, and say, "Thus says the king: Put this fellow in prison, and feed him on reduced rations of bread and water until I come in peace."' Micaiah said, 'If you return in peace, the Lord has not spoken by me.' And he said, 'Hear, you peoples, all of you!'

A reading from the Letter of Paul to the Romans. (15.4-13)

Whatever was written in former days was written for our instruction, so that by steadfastness and by the encouragement of the scriptures we might have hope. May the God of steadfastness and encouragement grant you to live in harmony with one another, in accordance with Christ Jesus, so that together you may with one voice glorify the God and Father of our Lord Jesus Christ.

Welcome one another, therefore, just as Christ has welcomed you, for the glory of God. For I tell you that Christ has become a servant of the circumcised on behalf of the truth of God in order that he might confirm the promises given to the patriarchs, and in order that the Gentiles might glorify God for his mercy. As it is written,
'Therefore I will confess you among the Gentiles,
    and sing praises to your name';
and again he says,
'Rejoice, O Gentiles, with his people';
and again,
'Praise the Lord, all you Gentiles,
    and let all the peoples praise him';
and again Isaiah says,
'The root of Jesse shall come,
    the one who rises to rule the Gentiles;
    in him the Gentiles shall hope.'
May the God of hope fill you with all joy and peace in believing, so that you may abound in hope by the power of the Holy Spirit.

If a Eucharist:
Hear the gospel of our Lord Jesus Christ according to Matthew.
(11.2-11)

When John heard in prison what the Messiah was doing, he sent word by his disciples and said to him, 'Are you the one who is to come, or are we to wait for another?' Jesus answered them, 'Go and tell John what you hear and see: the blind receive their sight, the lame walk, the lepers are cleansed, the deaf hear, the dead are raised, and the poor have good news brought to them. And blessèd is anyone who takes no offence at me.'

As they went away, Jesus began to speak to the crowds about John: 'What did you go out into the wilderness to look at? A reed shaken by the wind? What then did you go out to see? Someone dressed in soft robes? Look, those who wear soft robes are in royal palaces. What then did you go out to see? A prophet? Yes, I tell you, and more than a prophet. This is the one about whom it is written,

"See, I am sending my messenger ahead of you,
who will prepare your way before you."

Truly I tell you, among those born of women no one has arisen greater than John the Baptist; yet the least in the kingdom of heaven is greater than he.'

This is the gospel of the Lord.

Third Service
Ps 80; Baruch 5.1-9 *or* Zephaniah 3.14-20; Luke 1.5-20

A reading from the Book of Baruch. (5.1-9)

Take off the garment of your sorrow and affliction, O Jerusalem,
and put on for ever the beauty of the glory from God.
Put on the robe of the righteousness that comes from God;
put on your head the diadem of the glory of the Everlasting;
for God will show your splendour everywhere under heaven.
For God will give you evermore the name
'Righteous Peace, Godly Glory'.

Arise, O Jerusalem, stand upon the height;
look towards the east,
and see your children gathered from west and east
at the word of the Holy One,
rejoicing that God has remembered them.

For they went out from you on foot,
led away by their enemies;
but God will bring them back to you,
carried in glory, as on a royal throne.

For God has ordered that every high mountain
and the everlasting hills be made low
and the valleys filled up, to make level ground,
so that Israel may walk safely in the glory of God.
The woods and every fragrant tree

have shaded Israel at God's command.
For God will lead Israel with joy,
    in the light of his glory,
with the mercy and righteousness that come from him.

Or:

A reading from the prophecy of Zephaniah. *(3.14-20)*

Sing aloud, O daughter Zion;
    shout, O Israel!
Rejoice and exult with all your heart,
    O daughter Jerusalem!
The Lord has taken away the judgements against you,
    he has turned away your enemies.
The king of Israel, the Lord, is in your midst;
    you shall fear disaster no more.
On that day it shall be said to Jerusalem:
Do not fear, O Zion;
    do not let your hands grow weak.
The Lord, your God, is in your midst,
    a warrior who gives victory;
he will rejoice over you with gladness,
    he will renew you in his love;
he will exult over you with loud singing
    as on a day of festival.
I will remove disaster from you,
    so that you will not bear reproach for it.
I will deal with all your oppressors
    at that time.
And I will save the lame
    and gather the outcast,
and I will change their shame
    into praise and renown in all the earth.
At that time I will bring you home,
    at the time when I gather you;
for I will make you renowned and praised
    among all the peoples of the earth,
when I restore your fortunes
    before your eyes, says the Lord.

A reading from the gospel according to Luke. *(1.5-20)*

In the days of King Herod of Judea, there was a priest named
Zechariah, who belonged to the priestly order of Abijah. His wife

was a descendant of Aaron, and her name was Elizabeth. Both of them were righteous before God, living blamelessly according to all the commandments and regulations of the Lord. But they had no children, because Elizabeth was barren, and both were getting on in years.

Once when he was serving as priest before God and his section was on duty, he was chosen by lot, according to the custom of the priesthood, to enter the sanctuary of the Lord and offer incense. Now at the time of the incense-offering, the whole assembly of the people was praying outside. Then there appeared to him an angel of the Lord, standing at the right side of the altar of incense. When Zechariah saw him, he was terrified; and fear overwhelmed him. But the angel said to him, 'Do not be afraid, Zechariah, for your prayer has been heard. Your wife Elizabeth will bear you a son, and you will name him John. You will have joy and gladness, and many will rejoice at his birth, for he will be great in the sight of the Lord. He must never drink wine or strong drink; even before his birth he will be filled with the Holy Spirit. He will turn many of the people of Israel to the Lord their God. With the spirit and power of Elijah he will go before him, to turn the hearts of parents to their children, and the disobedient to the wisdom of the righteous, to make ready a people prepared for the Lord.' Zechariah said to the angel, 'How will I know that this is so? For I am an old man, and my wife is getting on in years.' The angel replied, 'I am Gabriel. I stand in the presence of God, and I have been sent to speak to you and to bring you this good news. But now, because you did not believe my words, which will be fulfilled in their time, you will become mute, unable to speak, until the day these things occur.'

The Third Sunday of Advent

Principal Service
Isaiah 61.1-4,8-11; Ps 126 *or* Magnificat; 1 Thessalonians 5.16-24; John 1.6-8,19-28

A reading from the prophecy of Isaiah. (61.1-4,8-11)

The spirit of the Lord God is upon me,
    because the Lord has anointed me;
he has sent me to bring good news to the oppressed,
    to bind up the broken-hearted,
to proclaim liberty to the captives,
    and release to the prisoners;
to proclaim the year of the Lord's favour,

and the day of vengeance of our God;
to comfort all who mourn;
to provide for those who mourn in Zion –
to give them a garland instead of ashes,
the oil of gladness instead of mourning,
the mantle of praise instead of a faint spirit.
They will be called oaks of righteousness,
the planting of the Lord, to display his glory.
They shall build up the ancient ruins,
they shall raise up the former devastations;
they shall repair the ruined cities,
the devastations of many generations.

8   For I the Lord love justice,
I hate robbery and wrongdoing;
I will faithfully give them their recompense,
and I will make an everlasting covenant with them.
Their descendants shall be known among the nations,
and their offspring among the peoples;
all who see them shall acknowledge
that they are a people whom the Lord has blessed.
I will greatly rejoice in the Lord,
my whole being shall exult in my God;
for he has clothed me with the garments of salvation,
he has covered me with the robe of righteousness,
as a bridegroom decks himself with a garland,
and as a bride adorns herself with her jewels.
For as the earth brings forth its shoots,
and as a garden causes what is sown in it to spring up,
so the Lord God will cause righteousness and praise
to spring up before all the nations.

This is the word of the Lord.

A reading from the First Letter of Paul to the Thessalonians. (5.16-24)

Rejoice always, pray without ceasing, give thanks in all circum-stances; for this is the will of God in Christ Jesus for you. Do not quench the Spirit. Do not despise the words of prophets, but test everything; hold fast to what is good; abstain from every form of evil. May the God of peace himself sanctify you entirely; and may your spirit and soul and body be kept sound and blameless at the coming of our Lord Jesus Christ. The one who calls you is faithful, and he will do this.

This is the word of the Lord.

Hear the gospel of our Lord Jesus Christ according to John.

(1.6-8,19-28)

There was a man sent from God, whose name was John. He came as a witness to testify to the light, so that all might believe through him. He himself was not the light, but he came to testify to the light. [19] This is the testimony given by John when the Jews sent priests and Levites from Jerusalem to ask him, 'Who are you?' He confessed and did not deny it, but confessed, 'I am not the Messiah.' And they asked him, 'What then? Are you Elijah?' He said, 'I am not.' 'Are you the prophet?' He answered, 'No.' Then they said to him, 'Who are you? Let us have an answer for those who sent us. What do you say about yourself?' He said, 'I am the voice of one crying out in the wilderness, "Make straight the way of the Lord"', as the prophet Isaiah said. Now they had been sent from the Pharisees. They asked him, 'Why then are you baptizing if you are neither the Messiah, nor Elijah, nor the prophet?' John answered them, 'I baptize with water. Among you stands one whom you do not know, the one who is coming after me; I am not worthy to untie the thong of his sandal.' This took place in Bethany across the Jordan where John was baptizing.

This is the gospel of the Lord.

Second Service
Ps 68.1-8 [9-20]; Malachi 3.1-4 & 4; Philippians 4.4-7;
if a Eucharist: Matthew 14.1-12

A reading from the prophecy of Malachi. (3.1-4 & 4)

See, I am sending my messenger to prepare the way before me, and the Lord whom you seek will suddenly come to his temple. The messenger of the covenant in whom you delight – indeed, he is coming, says the Lord of hosts. But who can endure the day of his coming, and who can stand when he appears?

For he is like a refiner's fire and like fullers' soap; he will sit as a refiner and purifier of silver, and he will purify the descendants of Levi and refine them like gold and silver, until they present offerings to the Lord in righteousness. Then the offering of Judah and Jerusalem will be pleasing to the Lord as in the days of old and as in former years. [4.1] See, the day is coming, burning like an oven, when all the arrogant and all evildoers will be stubble; the day that comes shall burn them up, says the Lord of hosts, so that it will leave them neither root nor branch. But for you who revere my name the sun of righteousness shall rise, with healing in its wings. You shall go out leaping like calves from the stall. And you shall tread down the wicked, for they will be ashes under the soles of your feet, on the day when I act, says the Lord of hosts.

Remember the teaching of my servant Moses, the statutes and ordinances that I commanded him at Horeb for all Israel.

Lo, I will send you the prophet Elijah before the great and terrible day of the Lord comes. He will turn the hearts of parents to their children and the hearts of children to their parents, so that I will not come and strike the land with a curse.

A reading from the Letter of Paul to the Philippians. (4.4-7)

Rejoice in the Lord always; again I will say, Rejoice. Let your gentleness be known to everyone. The Lord is near. Do not worry about anything, but in everything by prayer and supplication with thanksgiving let your requests be made known to God. And the peace of God, which surpasses all understanding, will guard your hearts and your minds in Christ Jesus.

If a Eucharist:
Hear the gospel of our Lord Jesus Christ according to Matthew.
(14.1-12)

Herod the ruler heard reports about Jesus; and he said to his servants, 'This is John the Baptist; he has been raised from the dead, and for this reason these powers are at work in him.' For Herod had arrested John, bound him, and put him in prison on account of Herodias, his brother Philip's wife, because John had been telling him, 'It is not lawful for you to have her.' Though Herod wanted to put him to death, he feared the crowd, because they regarded him as a prophet. But when Herod's birthday came, the daughter of Herodias danced before the company, and she pleased Herod so much that he promised on oath to grant her whatever she might ask. Prompted by her mother, she said, 'Give me the head of John the Baptist here on a platter.' The king was grieved, yet out of regard for his oaths and for the guests, he commanded it to be given; he sent and had John beheaded in the prison. The head was brought on a platter and given to the girl, who brought it to her mother. His disciples came and took the body and buried it; then they went and told Jesus.

This is the gospel of the Lord.

Third Service

Pss 50.1-6, 62; Isaiah 12; Luke 1.57-66

A reading from the prophecy of Isaiah. (Chapter 12)

> You will say on that day:
> > I will give thanks to you, O Lord,
> for though you were angry with me,
> > your anger turned away, and you comforted me.
>
> Surely God is my salvation;
> > I will trust, and will not be afraid,
> for the Lord God is my strength and my might;
> > he has become my salvation.

With joy you will draw water from the wells of salvation. And you will say on that day:

> Give thanks to the Lord,
> > call on his name;
> make known his deeds among the nations;
> > proclaim that his name is exalted.
>
> Sing praises to the Lord, for he has done gloriously;
> > let this be known in all the earth.
> Shout aloud and sing for joy, O royal Zion,
> > for great in your midst is the Holy One of Israel.

A reading from the gospel according to Luke. (1.57-66)

The time came for Elizabeth to give birth, and she bore a son. Her neighbours and relatives heard that the Lord had shown his great mercy to her, and they rejoiced with her.

On the eighth day they came to circumcise the child, and they were going to name him Zechariah after his father. But his mother said, 'No; he is to be called John.' They said to her, 'None of your relatives has this name.' Then they began motioning to his father to find out what name he wanted to give him. He asked for a writing-tablet and wrote, 'His name is John.' And all of them were amazed. Immediately his mouth was opened and his tongue freed, and he began to speak, praising God. Fear came over all their neighbours, and all these things were talked about throughout the entire hill country of Judea. All who heard them pondered them and said, 'What then will this child become?' For, indeed, the hand of the Lord was with him.

The Fourth Sunday of Advent

Principal Service
2 Samuel 7.1-11,16; Magnificat *or* Ps 89.1-4,19-26 *or* 89.1-8;
Romans 16.25-27; Luke 1.26-38

A reading from the Second Book of Samuel. (7.1-11,16)

When King David was settled in his house, and the Lord had given him rest from all his enemies around him, the king said to the prophet Nathan, 'See now, I am living in a house of cedar, but the ark of God stays in a tent.' Nathan said to the king, 'Go, do all that you have in mind; for the Lord is with you.'

But that same night the word of the Lord came to Nathan: Go and tell my servant David: Thus says the Lord: Are you the one to build me a house to live in? I have not lived in a house since the day I brought up the people of Israel from Egypt to this day, but I have been moving about in a tent and a tabernacle. Wherever I have moved about among all the people of Israel, did I ever speak a word with any of the tribal leaders of Israel, whom I commanded to shepherd my people Israel, saying, 'Why have you not built me a house of cedar?' Now therefore thus you shall say to my servant David: Thus says the Lord of hosts: I took you from the pasture, from following the sheep to be prince over my people Israel; and I have been with you wherever you went, and have cut off all your enemies from before you; and I will make for you a great name, like the name of the great ones of the earth. And I will appoint a place for my people Israel and will plant them, so that they may live in their own place, and be disturbed no more; and evildoers shall afflict them no more, as formerly, from the time that I appointed judges over my people Israel; and I will give you rest from all your enemies. Moreover, the Lord declares to you that the Lord will make you a house. [16] Your house and your kingdom shall be made sure for ever before me; your throne shall be established for ever.

This is the word of the Lord.

A reading from the Letter of Paul to the Romans. (16.25-27)

Now to God who is able to strengthen you according to my gospel and the proclamation of Jesus Christ, according to the revelation of the mystery that was kept secret for long ages but is now disclosed, and through the prophetic writings is made known to all the Gentiles, according to the command of the eternal God, to bring about the obedience of faith – to the only wise God, through Jesus Christ, to whom be the glory for ever! Amen.

This is the word of the Lord.

Hear the gospel of our Lord Jesus Christ according to Luke. (1.26-38)

In the sixth month the angel Gabriel was sent by God to a town in Galilee called Nazareth, to a virgin engaged to a man whose name was Joseph, of the house of David. The virgin's name was Mary. And he came to her and said, 'Greetings, favoured one! The Lord is with you.' But she was much perplexed by his words and pondered what sort of greeting this might be. The angel said to her, 'Do not be afraid, Mary, for you have found favour with God. And now, you will conceive in your womb and bear a son, and you will name him Jesus. He will be great, and will be called the Son of the Most High, and the Lord God will give to him the throne of his ancestor David. He will reign over the house of Jacob for ever, and of his kingdom there will be no end.' Mary said to the angel, 'How can this be, since I am a virgin?' The angel said to her, 'The Holy Spirit will come upon you, and the power of the Most High will overshadow you; therefore the child to be born will be holy; he will be called Son of God. And now, your relative Elizabeth in her old age has also conceived a son; and this is the sixth month for her who was said to be barren. For nothing will be impossible with God.' Then Mary said, 'Here am I, the servant of the Lord; let it be with me according to your word.' Then the angel departed from her.

This is the gospel of the Lord.

Second Service
Pss 113 [131]; Zechariah 2.10-13; Luke 1.39-55

A reading from the prophecy of Zechariah. (2.10-13)

Sing and rejoice, O daughter Zion! For lo, I will come and dwell in your midst, says the Lord. Many nations shall join themselves to the Lord on that day, and shall be my people; and I will dwell in your midst. And you shall know that the Lord of hosts has sent me to you. The Lord will inherit Judah as his portion in the holy land, and will again choose Jerusalem.

  Be silent, all people, before the Lord; for he has roused himself from his holy dwelling.

A reading from the gospel according to Luke. (1.39-55)

Mary set out and went with haste to a Judean town in the hill country, where she entered the house of Zechariah and greeted Elizabeth. When Elizabeth heard Mary's greeting, the child leapt in her womb. And Elizabeth was filled with the Holy Spirit and exclaimed with a loud cry, 'Blessèd are you among women, and blessèd is the fruit of your womb. And why has this happened to me, that the mother of my Lord comes to me? For as soon as I heard the sound of your greeting, the child in my womb leapt for joy. And blessèd is she who believed that there would be a fulfilment of what was spoken to her by the Lord.'

And Mary said,

'My soul magnifies the Lord,
and my spirit rejoices in God my Saviour,
for he has looked with favour on the lowliness of his servant.
Surely, from now on all generations will call me blessèd;
for the Mighty One has done great things for me,
and holy is his name.
His mercy is for those who fear him
from generation to generation.
He has shown strength with his arm;
he has scattered the proud in the thoughts of their hearts.
He has brought down the powerful from their thrones,
and lifted up the lowly;
he has filled the hungry with good things,
and sent the rich away empty.
He has helped his servant Israel,
in remembrance of his mercy,
according to the promise he made to our ancestors,
to Abraham and to his descendants for ever.'

Third Service
Ps 144; Isaiah 7.10-16; Romans 1.1-7

A reading from the prophecy of Isaiah. (7.10-16)

The Lord spoke to Ahaz, saying, Ask a sign of the Lord your God; let it be deep as Sheol or high as heaven. But Ahaz said, I will not ask, and I will not put the Lord to the test. Then Isaiah said: 'Hear then, O house of David! Is it too little for you to weary mortals, that you weary my God also? Therefore the Lord himself will give you a sign. Look, the young woman is with child and shall bear a son, and shall name him Immanuel. He shall eat curds and honey by the time he knows how to refuse the evil and choose the good. For before the child knows how to refuse the evil and choose the good, the land before whose two kings you are in dread will be deserted.

A reading from the Letter of Paul to the Romans. (1.1-7)

Paul, a servant of Jesus Christ, called to be an apostle, set apart for the gospel of God, which he promised beforehand through his prophets in the holy scriptures, the gospel concerning his Son, who was descended from David according to the flesh and was declared to be Son of God with power according to the spirit of holiness by resurrection from the dead, Jesus Christ our Lord, through whom we have received grace and apostleship to bring about the obedience of faith among all the Gentiles for the sake of his name, including yourselves who are called to belong to Jesus Christ,

To all God's belovèd in Rome, who are called to be saints:

Grace to you and peace from God our Father and the Lord Jesus Christ.

Christmas Eve

Morning Eucharist
2 Samuel 7.1-5,8-11,16; Ps 89.2,21-27; Acts 13.16-26; Luke 1.67-79

A reading from the Second Book of Samuel. (7.1-5,8-11,16)

When King David was settled in his house, and the Lord had given him rest from all his enemies around him, the king said to the prophet Nathan, 'See now, I am living in a house of cedar, but the ark of God stays in a tent.' Nathan said to the king, 'Go, do all that you have in mind; for the Lord is with you.'

But that same night the word of the Lord came to Nathan: Go and tell my servant David: Thus says the Lord: Are you the one to build me a house to live in? I took you from the pasture, from following the sheep to be prince over my people Israel; and I have been with you wherever you went, and have cut off all your enemies from before you; and I will make for you a great name, like the name of the great ones of the earth. And I will appoint a place for my people Israel and will plant them, so that they may live in their own place, and be disturbed no more; and evildoers shall afflict them no more, as formerly, from the time that I appointed judges over my people Israel; and I will give you rest from all your enemies. Moreover, the Lord declares to you that the Lord will make you a house. Your house and your kingdom shall be made sure for ever before me; your throne shall be established for ever.

This is the word of the Lord.

A reading from the Acts of the Apostles. (13.16-26)

Paul stood up in the synagogue and with a gesture began to speak: 'You Israelites, and others who fear God, listen. The God of this people Israel chose our ancestors and made the people great during their stay in the land of Egypt, and with uplifted arm he led them out of it. For about forty years he put up with them in the wilderness. After he had destroyed seven nations in the land of Canaan, he gave them their land as an inheritance for about four hundred and fifty years. After that he gave them judges until the time of the prophet Samuel. Then they asked for a king; and God gave them Saul son of Kish, a man of the tribe of Benjamin, who reigned for forty years. When he had removed him, he made David their king. In his testimony about him he said, "I have found David, son of Jesse, to be a man after my heart, who will carry out all my wishes." Of this man's posterity God has brought to Israel a Saviour, Jesus, as he promised; before his coming John had already proclaimed a baptism of repentance to all the people of Israel. And as John was finishing his work, he said, "What do you suppose that I am? I am not he. No, but one is coming after me; I am not worthy to untie the thong of the sandals on his feet."

'My brothers, you descendants of Abraham's family, and others who fear God, to us the message of this salvation has been sent.'

This is the word of the Lord.

Hear the gospel of our Lord Jesus Christ according to Luke. (1.67-79)

The child's father, Zechariah, was filled with the Holy Spirit and spoke this prophecy:
'Blessèd be the Lord God of Israel,
    for he has looked favourably on his people and redeemed them.
He has raised up a mighty saviour for us
        in the house of his servant David,
as he spoke through the mouth of his holy prophets from of old,
        that we would be saved from our enemies
        and from the hand of all who hate us.
Thus he has shown the mercy promised to our ancestors,
        and has remembered his holy covenant,
the oath that he swore to our ancestor Abraham,
        to grant us that we,
        being rescued from the hands of our enemies,
might serve him without fear,
        in holiness and righteousness before him all our days.
    'And you, child,

will be called the prophet of the Most High;
for you will go before the Lord to prepare his ways,
to give knowledge of salvation to his people
    by the forgiveness of their sins.
By the tender mercy of our God,
    the dawn from on high will break upon us,
to give light to those who sit in darkness
    and in the shadow of death,
to guide our feet into the way of peace.'

This is the gospel of the Lord.

Christmas

Christmas Eve *(24 December)*

Evening Prayer

Ps 85; Zechariah 2; Revelation 1.1-8

A reading from the prophecy of Zechariah. (Chapter 2)

I looked up and saw a man with a measuring line in his hand. Then I asked, 'Where are you going?' He answered me, 'To measure Jerusalem, to see what is its width and what is its length.' Then the angel who talked with me came forward, and another angel came forward to meet him, and said to him, 'Run, say to that young man: Jerusalem shall be inhabited like villages without walls, because of the multitude of people and animals in it. For I will be a wall of fire all round it, says the Lord, and I will be the glory within it.'

Up, up! Flee from the land of the north, says the Lord; for I have spread you abroad like the four winds of heaven, says the Lord. Up! Escape to Zion, you that live with daughter Babylon. For thus said the Lord of hosts (after his glory sent me) regarding the nations that plundered you: Truly, one who touches you touches the apple of my eye. See now, I am going to raise my hand against them, and they shall become plunder for their own slaves. Then you will know that the Lord of hosts has sent me. Sing and rejoice, O daughter Zion! For lo, I will come and dwell in your midst, says the Lord. Many nations shall join themselves to the Lord on that day, and shall be my people; and I will dwell in your midst. And you shall know that the Lord of hosts has sent me to you. The Lord will inherit Judah as his portion in the holy land, and will again choose Jerusalem.

Be silent, all people, before the Lord; for he has roused himself from his holy dwelling.

A reading from the Revelation to John. (1.1-8)

The revelation of Jesus Christ, which God gave him to show his servants what must soon take place; he made it known by sending his angel to his servant John, who testified to the word of God and to the testimony of Jesus Christ, even to all that he saw.

Blessèd is the one who reads aloud the words of the prophecy, and blessèd are those who hear and who keep what is written in it; for the time is near.

John to the seven churches that are in Asia: Grace to you and peace from him who is and who was and who is to come, and from the seven spirits who are before his throne, and from Jesus Christ, the faithful witness, the firstborn of the dead, and the ruler of the kings of the earth.

To him who loves us and freed us from our sins by his blood, and made us to be a kingdom, priests serving his God and Father, to him be glory and dominion for ever and ever. Amen.

Look! He is coming with the clouds; every eye will see him, even those who pierced him; and on his account all the tribes of the earth will wail. So it is to be. Amen.

'I am the Alpha and the Omega', says the Lord God, who is and who was and who is to come, the Almighty.

Christmas Day *(25 December)*

Any of the following sets of readings may be used on the evening of Christmas Eve and on Christmas Day. Set III should be used at some service during the celebration.

I	II	III
Isaiah 9.2-7	Isaiah 62.6-12	Isaiah 52.7-10
Ps 96	Ps 97	Ps 98
Titus 2.11-14	Titus 3.4-7	Hebrews 1.1-4 [5-12]
Luke 2.1-14 [15-20]	Luke 2.[1-7] 8-20	John 1.1-14

Set I
A reading from the prophecy of Isaiah. (9.2-7)

The people who walked in darkness
    have seen a great light;
those who lived in a land of deep darkness –
    on them light has shined.
You have multiplied the nation,
    you have increased its joy;
they rejoice before you as with joy at the harvest,
    as people exult when dividing plunder.
For the yoke of their burden,
    and the bar across their shoulders, the rod of their oppressor,
    you have broken as on the day of Midian.
For all the boots of the tramping warriors
    and all the garments rolled in blood
    shall be burned as fuel for the fire.
For a child has been born for us,
    a son given to us;

authority rests upon his shoulders;
    and he is named
Wonderful Counsellor, Mighty God,
    Everlasting Father, Prince of Peace.
His authority shall grow continually,
    and there shall be endless peace
for the throne of David and his kingdom.
    He will establish and uphold it
with justice and with righteousness
    from this time onwards and for evermore.
The zeal of the Lord of hosts will do this.

This is the word of the Lord.

A reading from the Letter of Paul to Titus. (2.11-14)

The grace of God has appeared, bringing salvation to all, training us to renounce impiety and worldly passions, and in the present age to live lives that are self-controlled, upright, and godly, while we wait for the blessèd hope and the manifestation of the glory of our great God and Saviour, Jesus Christ. He it is who gave himself for us that he might redeem us from all iniquity and purify for himself a people of his own who are zealous for good deeds.

This is the word of the Lord.

Hear the gospel of our Lord Jesus Christ according to Luke.
(2.1-14 [15-20])

In those days a decree went out from Emperor Augustus that all the world should be registered. This was the first registration and was taken while Quirinius was governor of Syria. All went to their own towns to be registered. Joseph also went from the town of Nazareth in Galilee to Judea, to the city of David called Bethlehem, because he was descended from the house and family of David. He went to be registered with Mary, to whom he was engaged and who was expecting a child. While they were there, the time came for her to deliver her child. And she gave birth to her firstborn son and wrapped him in bands of cloth, and laid him in a manger, because there was no place for them in the inn.

In that region there were shepherds living in the fields, keeping watch over their flock by night. Then an angel of the Lord stood before them, and the glory of the Lord shone around them, and they were terrified. But the angel said to them, 'Do not be afraid; for see – I am bringing you good news of great joy for all the people: to you is born this day in the city of David a Saviour, who is the Messiah, the Lord. This will be a sign for you: you will find a child wrapped in bands of cloth and lying in a manger.'

And suddenly there was with the angel a multitude of the heavenly host, praising God and saying, 'Glory to God in the highest heaven, and on earth peace among those whom he favours!'

[15 When the angels had left them and gone into heaven, the shepherds said to one another, 'Let us go now to Bethlehem and see this thing that has taken place, which the Lord has made known to us.' So they went with haste and found Mary and Joseph, and the child lying in the manger. When they saw this, they made known what had been told them about this child; and all who heard it were amazed at what the shepherds told them. But Mary treasured all these words and pondered them in her heart. The shepherds returned, glorifying and praising God for all they had heard and seen, as it had been told them.]

This is the gospel of the Lord.

Set II
A reading from the prophecy of Isaiah. (62.6-12)

Upon your walls, O Jerusalem,
    I have posted sentinels;
all day and all night
    they shall never be silent.
You who remind the Lord,
    take no rest,
and give him no rest
    until he establishes Jerusalem
    and makes it renowned throughout the earth.
The Lord has sworn by his right hand
    and by his mighty arm:
I will not again give your grain
    to be food for your enemies,
and foreigners shall not drink the wine
    for which you have laboured;
but those who garner it shall eat it
    and praise the Lord,
and those who gather it
    shall drink it in my holy courts.

Go through, go through the gates,
    prepare the way for the people;

build up, build up the highway,
    clear it of stones,
    lift up an ensign over the peoples.
The Lord has proclaimed
    to the end of the earth:
Say to daughter Zion,
    'See, your salvation comes;
his reward is with him,
    and his recompense before him.'
They shall be called,
    'The Holy People,
    The Redeemed of the Lord';
and you shall be called,
    'Sought Out,
    A City Not Forsaken.'

This is the word of the Lord.

A reading from the Letter of Paul to Titus. (3.4-7)

When the goodness and loving-kindness of God our Saviour appeared, he saved us, not because of any works of righteousness that we had done, but according to his mercy, through the water of rebirth and renewal by the Holy Spirit. This Spirit he poured out on us richly through Jesus Christ our Saviour, so that, having been justified by his grace, we might become heirs according to the hope of eternal life.

This is the word of the Lord.

Hear the gospel of our Lord Jesus Christ according to Luke
(2.[1-7] 8-20)

[In those days a decree went out from Emperor Augustus that all the world should be registered. This was the first registration and was taken while Quirinius was governor of Syria. All went to their own towns to be registered. Joseph also went from the town of Nazareth in Galilee to Judea, to the city of David called Bethlehem, because he was descended from the house and family of David. He went to be registered with Mary, to whom he was engaged and who was expecting a child. While they were there, the time came for her to deliver her child. And she gave birth to her firstborn son and wrapped him in bands of cloth, and laid him in a manger, because there was no place for them in the inn.]
⁸ In that region there were shepherds living in the fields, keeping

watch over their flock by night. Then an angel of the Lord stood before them, and the glory of the Lord shone around them, and they were terrified. But the angel said to them, 'Do not be afraid; for see – I am bringing you good news of great joy for all the people: to you is born this day in the city of David a Saviour, who is the Messiah, the Lord. This will be a sign for you: you will find a child wrapped in bands of cloth and lying in a manger.'

And suddenly there was with the angel a multitude of the heavenly host, praising God and saying, 'Glory to God in the highest heaven, and on earth peace among those whom he favours!'

When the angels had left them and gone into heaven, the shepherds said to one another, 'Let us go now to Bethlehem and see this thing that has taken place, which the Lord has made known to us.' So they went with haste and found Mary and Joseph, and the child lying in the manger. When they saw this, they made known what had been told them about this child; and all who heard it were amazed at what the shepherds told them. But Mary treasured all these words and pondered them in her heart. The shepherds returned, glorifying and praising God for all they had heard and seen, as it had been told them.

This is the gospel of the Lord.

Set III
A reading from the prophecy of Isaiah. (52.7-10)

How beautiful upon the mountains
    are the feet of the messenger who announces peace,
who brings good news,
    who announces salvation,
    who says to Zion, 'Your God reigns.'
Listen! Your sentinels lift up their voices,
    together they sing for joy;
for in plain sight
    they see the return of the Lord to Zion.
Break forth together into singing,
    you ruins of Jerusalem;
for the Lord has comforted his people,
    he has redeemed Jerusalem.
The Lord has bared his holy arm
    before the eyes of all the nations;
and all the ends of the earth
shall see the salvation of our God.

This is the word of the Lord.

A reading from the Letter to the Hebrews. (1.1-4 [5-12])

Long ago God spoke to our ancestors in many and various ways by the prophets, but in these last days he has spoken to us by a Son, whom he appointed heir of all things, through whom he also created the worlds. He is the reflection of God's glory and the exact imprint of God's very being, and he sustains all things by his powerful word. When he had made purification for sins, he sat down at the right hand of the Majesty on high, having become as much superior to angels as the name he has inherited is more excellent than theirs.

[5 For to which of the angels did God ever say, 'You are my Son; today I have begotten you'? Or again, 'I will be his Father, and he will be my Son'? And again, when he brings the firstborn into the world, he says, 'Let all God's angels worship him.'

Of the angels he says, 'He makes his angels winds, and his servants flames of fire.'

But of the Son he says, 'Your throne, O God, is for ever and ever, and the righteous sceptre is the sceptre of your kingdom. You have loved righteousness and hated wickedness; therefore God, your God, has anointed you with the oil of gladness beyond your companions.' And, 'In the beginning, Lord, you founded the earth, and the heavens are the work of your hands; they will perish, but you remain; they will all wear out like clothing; like a cloak you will roll them up, and like clothing they will be changed. But you are the same, and your years will never end.']

This is the word of the Lord.

Hear the gospel of our Lord Jesus Christ according to John. (1.1-14)

In the beginning was the Word, and the Word was with God, and the Word was God. He was in the beginning with God. All things came into being through him, and without him not one thing came into being. What has come into being in him was life, and the life was the light of all people. The light shines in the darkness, and the darkness did not overcome it.

There was a man sent from God, whose name was John. He came as a witness to testify to the light, so that all might believe through him. He himself was not the light, but he came to testify to the light. The true light, which enlightens everyone, was coming into the world.

He was in the world, and the world came into being through him; yet the world did not know him. He came to what was his own, and his own people did not accept him. But to all who received him, who believed in his name, he gave power to become children of God, who were born, not of blood or of the will of the flesh or of the will of man, but of God.

And the Word became flesh and lived among us, and we have seen his glory, the glory as of a father's only son, full of grace and truth.

This is the gospel of the Lord.

Second Service

Ps 8; Isaiah 65.17-25; Philippians 2.5-11 ; *or* Luke 2.1-20 *if it has not been used at the Principal Service of the day.*

A reading from the prophecy of Isaiah. (65.17-25)

I am about to create new heavens and a new earth;
    the former things shall not be remembered or come to mind.
But be glad and rejoice for ever in what I am creating;
        for I am about to create Jerusalem as a joy,
        and its people as a delight.
I will rejoice in Jerusalem,
        and delight in my people;
no more shall the sound of weeping be heard in it,
        or the cry of distress.
No more shall there be in it an infant that lives but a few days,
        or an old person who does not live out a lifetime;
for one who dies at a hundred years will be considered a youth,
        and one who falls short of a hundred
        will be considered accursed.
They shall build houses and inhabit them;
        they shall plant vineyards and eat their fruit.
They shall not build and another inhabit;
        they shall not plant and another eat;
for like the days of a tree shall the days of my people be,
        and my chosen shall long enjoy the work of their hands.
They shall not labour in vain,
        or bear children for calamity;
for they shall be offspring blessed by the Lord –
        and their descendants as well.
Before they call I will answer,
        while they are yet speaking I will hear.
The wolf and the lamb shall feed together,
        the lion shall eat straw like the ox;
but the serpent – its food shall be dust!
They shall not hurt or destroy
        on all my holy mountain, says the Lord.

A reading from the Letter of Paul to the Philippians. (2.5-11)

Let the same mind be in you that was in Christ Jesus, who, though he was in the form of God, did not regard equality with God as something to be exploited, but emptied himself, taking the form of a slave, being born in human likeness. And being found in human form, he humbled himself and became obedient to the point of death – even death on a cross.

Therefore God also highly exalted him and gave him the name that is above every name, so that at the name of Jesus every knee should bend, in heaven and on earth and under the earth, and every tongue should confess that Jesus Christ is Lord, to the glory of God the Father.

Or:
A reading from the gospel according to Luke. (2.1-20; *see page 27*).

Third Service
Ps 110; Isaiah 62.1-5; Matthew 1.18-25

A reading from the prophecy of Isaiah. (62.1-5)

> For Zion's sake I will not keep silent,
>> and for Jerusalem's sake I will not rest,
> until her vindication shines out like the dawn,
>> and her salvation like a burning torch.
> The nations shall see your vindication,
>> and all the kings your glory;
> and you shall be called by a new name
>> that the mouth of the Lord will give.
> You shall be a crown of beauty in the hand of the Lord,
>> and a royal diadem in the hand of your God.
> You shall no more be termed Forsaken,
>> and your land shall no more be termed Desolate;
> but you shall be called My Delight Is in Her,
>> and your land Married;
> for the Lord delights in you,
>> and your land shall be married.
> For as a young man marries a young woman,
>> so shall your builder marry you,
> and as the bridegroom rejoices over the bride,
>> so shall your God rejoice over you.

A reading from the gospel according to Matthew. (1.18-25)

Now the birth of Jesus the Messiah took place in this way. When his mother Mary had been engaged to Joseph, but before they lived together, she was found to be with child from the Holy Spirit.

Her husband Joseph, being a righteous man and unwilling to expose her to public disgrace, planned to dismiss her quietly. But just when he had resolved to do this, an angel of the Lord appeared to him in a dream and said, 'Joseph, son of David, do not be afraid to take Mary as your wife, for the child conceived in her is from the Holy Spirit. She will bear a son, and you are to name him Jesus, for he will save his people from their sins.' All this took place to fulfil what had been spoken by the Lord through the prophet: 'Look, the virgin shall conceive and bear a son, and they shall name him Emmanuel', which means, 'God is with us.'

When Joseph awoke from sleep, he did as the angel of the Lord commanded him; he took her as his wife, but had no marital relations with her until she had borne a son; and he named him Jesus.

The First Sunday of Christmas

Principal Service
Isaiah 61.10 - 62.3; Ps 148.[1-6] 7-14; Galatians 4.4-7; Luke 2.15-21

A reading from the prophecy of Isaiah. (61.10 - 62.3)

I will greatly rejoice in the Lord,
    my whole being shall exult in my God;
for he has clothed me with the garments of salvation,
    he has covered me with the robe of righteousness,
as a bridegroom decks himself with a garland,
    and as a bride adorns herself with her jewels.

For as the earth brings forth its shoots,
    and as a garden causes what is sown in it to spring up,
so the Lord God will cause righteousness and praise
    to spring up before all the nations.

For Zion's sake I will not keep silent,
    and for Jerusalem's sake I will not rest,
until her vindication shines out like the dawn,
    and her salvation like a burning torch.
The nations shall see your vindication,
    and all the kings your glory;

and you shall be called by a new name
   that the mouth of the Lord will give.
You shall be a crown of beauty in the hand of the Lord,
   and a royal diadem in the hand of your God.

This is the word of the Lord.

A reading from the Letter of Paul to the Galatians. (4.4-7)

When the fullness of time had come, God sent his Son, born of a woman, born under the law, in order to redeem those who were under the law, so that we might receive adoption as children. And because you are children, God has sent the Spirit of his Son into our hearts, crying, 'Abba! Father!' So you are no longer a slave but a child, and if a child then also an heir, through God.

This is the word of the Lord.

Hear the gospel of our Lord Jesus Christ according to Luke. (2.15-21)

When the angels had left them and gone into heaven, the shepherds said to one another, 'Let us go now to Bethlehem and see this thing that has taken place, which the Lord has made known to us.' So they went with haste and found Mary and Joseph, and the child lying in the manger. When they saw this, they made known what had been told them about this child; and all who heard it were amazed at what the shepherds told them. But Mary treasured all these words and pondered them in her heart. The shepherds returned, glorifying and praising God for all they had heard and seen, as it had been told them.

   After eight days had passed, it was time to circumcise the child; and he was called Jesus, the name given by the angel before he was conceived in the womb.

This is the gospel of the Lord.

Second Service
Ps 132; Isaiah 35; Colossians 1.9-20 *or* Luke 2.41-52

A reading from the prophecy of Isaiah. (Chapter 35)

The wilderness and the dry land shall be glad,
   the desert shall rejoice and blossom;
like the crocus it shall blossom abundantly,
   and rejoice with joy and singing.
The glory of Lebanon shall be given to it,

the majesty of Carmel and Sharon.
They shall see the glory of the Lord,
   the majesty of our God.

Strengthen the weak hands,
   and make firm the feeble knees.
Say to those who are of a fearful heart,
   'Be strong, do not fear!
Here is your God.
   He will come with vengeance,
with terrible recompense.
   He will come and save you.'

Then the eyes of the blind shall be opened,
   and the ears of the deaf unstopped;
then the lame shall leap like a deer,
   and the tongue of the speechless sing for joy.
For waters shall break forth in the wilderness,
   and streams in the desert;
the burning sand shall become a pool,
   and the thirsty ground springs of water;
the haunt of jackals shall become a swamp,
   the grass shall become reeds and rushes.

A highway shall be there,
   and it shall be called the Holy Way;
the unclean shall not travel on it,
   but it shall be for God's people;
   no traveller, not even fools, shall go astray.
No lion shall be there,
   nor shall any ravenous beast come up on it;
they shall not be found there,
   but the redeemed shall walk there.
And the ransomed of the Lord shall return,
   and come to Zion with singing;
everlasting joy shall be upon their heads;
   they shall obtain joy and gladness,
   and sorrow and sighing shall flee away.

A reading from the Letter of Paul to the Colossians. (1.9-20)

[For this reason, since the day we heard it,] we have not ceased praying for you and asking that you may be filled with the knowledge of
God's will in all spiritual wisdom and understanding, so that you
may lead lives worthy of the Lord, fully pleasing to him, as you bear

fruit in every good work and as you grow in the knowledge of God. May you be made strong with all the strength that comes from his glorious power, and may you be prepared to endure everything with patience, while joyfully giving thanks to the Father, who has enabled you to share in the inheritance of the saints in the light. He has rescued us from the power of darkness and transferred us into the kingdom of his belovèd Son, in whom we have redemption, the forgiveness of sins.

He is the image of the invisible God, the firstborn of all creation; for in him all things in heaven and on earth were created, things visible and invisible, whether thrones or dominions or rulers or powers – all things have been created through him and for him. He himself is before all things, and in him all things hold together. He is the head of the body, the church; he is the beginning, the firstborn from the dead, so that he might come to have first place in everything. For in him all the fullness of God was pleased to dwell, and through him God was pleased to reconcile to himself all things, whether on earth or in heaven, by making peace through the blood of his cross.

Or:

A reading from the gospel according to Luke. (2.41-52)

Every year the parents of Jesus went to Jerusalem for the festival of the Passover. And when he was twelve years old, they went up as usual for the festival. When the festival was ended and they started to return, the boy Jesus stayed behind in Jerusalem, but his parents did not know it. Assuming that he was in the group of travellers, they went a day's journey. Then they started to look for him among their relatives and friends. When they did not find him, they returned to Jerusalem to search for him. After three days they found him in the temple, sitting among the teachers, listening to them and asking them questions. And all who heard him were amazed at his understanding and his answers. When his parents saw him they were astonished; and his mother said to him, 'Child, why have you treated us like this? Look, your father and I have been searching for you in great anxiety.' He said to them, 'Why were you searching for me? Did you not know that I must be in my Father's house?' But they did not understand what he said to them. Then he went down with them and came to Nazareth, and was obedient to them. His mother treasured all these things in her heart.

And Jesus increased in wisdom and in years, and in divine and human favour.

Third Service
Ps 105.1-9; Isaiah 63.7-9; Ephesians 3.5-12

A reading from the prophecy of Isaiah. (63.7-9)

> I will recount the gracious deeds of the Lord,
>   the praiseworthy acts of the Lord,
> because of all that the Lord has done for us,
>   and the great favour to the house of Israel
> that he has shown them according to his mercy,
>   according to the abundance of his steadfast love.
> For he said, 'Surely they are my people,
>   children who will not deal falsely';
> and he became their saviour
>   in all their distress.
> It was no messenger or angel
>   but his presence that saved them;
> in his love and in his pity he redeemed them;
>   he lifted them up and carried them all the days of old.

A reading from the Letter of Paul to the Ephesians. (3.5-12)

In former generations this mystery was not made known to humankind, as it has now been revealed to his holy apostles and prophets by the Spirit: that is, the Gentiles have become fellow-heirs, members of the same body, and sharers in the promise in Christ Jesus through the gospel.

Of this gospel I have become a servant according to the gift of God's grace that was given to me by the working of his power. Although I am the very least of all the saints, this grace was given to me to bring to the Gentiles the news of the boundless riches of Christ, and to make everyone see what is the plan of the mystery hidden for ages in God who created all things; so that through the church the wisdom of God in its rich variety might now be made known to the rulers and authorities in the heavenly places. This was in accordance with the eternal purpose that he has carried out in Christ Jesus our Lord, in whom we have access to God in boldness and confidence through faith in him.

The Second Sunday of Christmas

Principal Service

Jeremiah 31.7-14   *or*   Ecclesiasticus 24.1-12
Ps 147.12-20   *Cant:* Wisdom of Solomon 10.15-21
           Ephesians 1.3-14
           John 1.[1-9] 10-18

A reading from the prophecy of Jeremiah. (31.7-14)

Thus says the Lord:
Sing aloud with gladness for Jacob,
    and raise shouts for the chief of the nations;
proclaim, give praise, and say,
    'Save, O Lord, your people, the remnant of Israel.'
See, I am going to bring them from the land of the north,
    and gather them from the farthest parts of the earth,
among them the blind and the lame,
    those with child and those in labour, together;
    a great company, they shall return here.
With weeping they shall come,
    and with consolations I will lead them back,
I will let them walk by brooks of water,
    in a straight path in which they shall not stumble;
for I have become a father to Israel,
    and Ephraim is my firstborn.

Hear the word of the Lord, O nations,
    and declare it in the coastlands far away;
say, 'He who scattered Israel will gather him,
    and will keep him as a shepherd a flock.'
For the Lord has ransomed Jacob,
    and has redeemed him from hands too strong for him.
They shall come and sing aloud on the height of Zion,
    and they shall be radiant over the goodness of the Lord,
over the grain, the wine, and the oil,
    and over the young of the flock and the herd;
their life shall become like a watered garden,
    and they shall never languish again.
Then shall the young women rejoice in the dance,
    and the young men and the old shall be merry.
I will turn their mourning into joy,
    I will comfort them, and give them gladness for sorrow.
I will give the priests their fill of fatness,

and my people shall be satisfied with my bounty,
says the Lord.

This is the word of the Lord.

Or:
A reading from the book Ecclesiasticus. (24.1-12)

Wisdom praises herself, and tells of her glory in the midst of her people. In the assembly of the Most High she opens her mouth, and in the presence of his hosts she tells of her glory: 'I came forth from the mouth of the Most High, and covered the earth like a mist. I dwelt in the highest heavens, and my throne was in a pillar of cloud. Alone I compassed the vault of heaven and traversed the depths of the abyss. Over waves of the sea, over all the earth, and over every people and nation I have held sway. Among all these I sought a resting-place; in whose territory should I abide?

'Then the Creator of all things gave me a command, and my Creator chose the place for my tent. He said, "Make your dwelling in Jacob, and in Israel receive your inheritance." Before the ages, in the beginning, he created me, and for all the ages I shall not cease to be. In the holy tent I ministered before him, and so I was established in Zion. Thus in the belovèd city he gave me a resting-place, and in Jerusalem was my domain. I took root in an honoured people, in the portion of the Lord, his heritage.'

This is the word of the Lord.

A reading from the Letter of Paul to the Ephesians. (1.3-14)

Blessèd be the God and Father of our Lord Jesus Christ, who has blessed us in Christ with every spiritual blessing in the heavenly places, just as he chose us in Christ before the foundation of the world to be holy and blameless before him in love. He destined us for adoption as his children through Jesus Christ, according to the good pleasure of his will, to the praise of his glorious grace that he freely bestowed on us in the Belovèd. In him we have redemption through his blood, the forgiveness of our trespasses, according to the riches of his grace that he lavished on us. With all wisdom and insight he has made known to us the mystery of his will, according to his good pleasure that he set forth in Christ, as a plan for the fullness of time, to gather up all things in him, things in heaven and things on earth. In Christ we have also obtained an inheritance, having been destined according to the purpose of him who accomplishes all things according to his counsel and will, so that we, who were the first to set our hope on Christ, might live for the praise of his glory. In him you also, when you had heard the word of truth, the gospel of your salvation, and had believed in him, were marked with the seal of the promised Holy Spirit; this is the pledge of our inheritance towards redemption as God's own people, to the praise of his glory.

This is the word of the Lord.

Hear the gospel of our Lord Jesus Christ according to John.

(1.[1-9] 10-18)

[In the beginning was the Word, and the Word was with God, and the Word was God. He was in the beginning with God. All things came into being through him, and without him not one thing came into being. What has come into being in him was life, and the life was the light of all people. The light shines in the darkness, and the darkness did not overcome it.

There was a man sent from God, whose name was John. He came as a witness to testify to the light, so that all might believe through him. He himself was not the light, but he came to testify to the light. The true light, which enlightens everyone, was coming into the world.]

[10] He was in the world, and the world came into being through him; yet the world did not know him. He came to what was his own, and his own people did not accept him. But to all who received him, who believed in his name, he gave power to become children of God, who were born, not of blood or of the will of the flesh or of the will of man, but of God.

And the Word became flesh and lived among us, and we have seen his glory, the glory as of a father's only son, full of grace and truth. (John testified to him and cried out, 'This was he of whom I said, "He who comes after me ranks ahead of me because he was before me."') From his fullness we have all received, grace upon grace. The law indeed was given through Moses; grace and truth came through Jesus Christ. No one has ever seen God. It is God the only Son, who is close to the Father's heart, who has made him known.

This is the gospel of the Lord.

Second Service

Ps 135.1-14 [15-21]; Isaiah 46.3-13; Romans 12.1-8;
if a Eucharist: Matthew 2.13-23

A reading from the prophecy of Isaiah. (46.3-13)

Listen to me, O house of Jacob,
  all the remnant of the house of Israel,
who have been borne by me from your birth,
  carried from the womb;
even to your old age I am he,
  even when you turn grey I will carry you.
I have made, and I will bear;
  I will carry and will save.

To whom will you liken me and make me equal,
  and compare me, as though we were alike?
Those who lavish gold from the purse,
  and weigh out silver in the scales –
they hire a goldsmith, who makes it into a god;
  then they fall down and worship!
They lift it to their shoulders, they carry it,
  they set it in its place, and it stands there;
  it cannot move from its place.
If one cries out to it, it does not answer
  or save anyone from trouble.

Remember this and consider,
  recall it to mind, you transgressors,
  remember the former things of old;
for I am God, and there is no other;
  I am God, and there is no one like me,
declaring the end from the beginning
  and from ancient times things not yet done,
saying, 'My purpose shall stand,
  and I will fulfil my intention',
calling a bird of prey from the east,
  the man for my purpose from a far country.
I have spoken, and I will bring it to pass;
  I have planned, and I will do it.

Listen to me, you stubborn of heart,
  you who are far from deliverance:
I bring near my deliverance, it is not far off,
  and my salvation will not tarry;
I will put salvation in Zion,
  for Israel my glory.

A reading from the Letter of Paul to the Romans. (12.1-8)

I appeal to you, brothers and sisters, by the mercies of God, to present your bodies as a living sacrifice, holy and acceptable to God, which is your spiritual worship. Do not be conformed to this world, but be transformed by the renewing of your minds, so that you may discern what is the will of God – what is good and acceptable and perfect.

For by the grace given to me I say to everyone among you not to think of yourself more highly than you ought to think, but to think with sober judgement, each according to the measure of faith that God has assigned. For as in one body we have many members, and not all the members have the same function, so we, who are many, are one body in Christ, and individually we are members one of another. We have gifts that differ according to the grace given to us: prophecy, in proportion to faith; ministry, in ministering; the teacher, in teaching; the exhorter, in exhortation; the giver, in generosity; the leader, in diligence; the compassionate, in cheerfulness.

If a Eucharist:
Hear the gospel of our Lord Jesus Christ according to Matthew.
(2.13-23)

After the Magi had left, an angel of the Lord appeared to Joseph in a dream and said, 'Get up, take the child and his mother, and flee to Egypt, and remain there until I tell you; for Herod is about to search for the child, to destroy him.' Then Joseph got up, took the child and his mother by night, and went to Egypt, and remained there until the death of Herod. This was to fulfil what had been spoken by the Lord through the prophet, 'Out of Egypt I have called my son.'

When Herod saw that he had been tricked by the wise men, he was infuriated, and he sent and killed all the children in and around Bethlehem who were two years old or under, according to the time that he had learned from the wise men. Then was fulfilled what had been spoken through the prophet Jeremiah:

'A voice was heard in Ramah,
    wailing and loud lamentation,
Rachel weeping for her children;
    she refused to be consoled, because they are no more.'

When Herod died, an angel of the Lord suddenly appeared in a dream to Joseph in Egypt and said, 'Get up, take the child and his mother, and go to the land of Israel, for those who were seeking the child's life are dead.' Then Joseph got up, took the child and his mother, and went to the land of Israel. But when he heard that

Archelaus was ruling over Judea in place of his father Herod, he was afraid to go there. And after being warned in a dream, he went away to the district of Galilee. There he made his home in a town called Nazareth, so that what had been spoken through the prophets might be fulfilled, 'He will be called a Nazorean.'

This is the gospel of the Lord.

Third Service
Ps 87; Zechariah 8.1-8; Luke 2.41-52

A reading from the prophecy of Zechariah. (8.1-8)

The word of the Lord of hosts came to me, saying: Thus says the Lord of hosts: I am jealous for Zion with great jealousy, and I am jealous for her with great wrath. Thus says the Lord: I will return to Zion, and will dwell in the midst of Jerusalem; Jerusalem shall be called the faithful city, and the mountain of the Lord of hosts shall be called the holy mountain. Thus says the Lord of hosts: Old men and old women shall again sit in the streets of Jerusalem, each with staff in hand because of their great age. And the streets of the city shall be full of boys and girls playing in its streets. Thus says the Lord of hosts: Even though it seems impossible to the remnant of this people in these days, should it also seem impossible to me, says the Lord of hosts? Thus says the Lord of hosts: I will save my people from the east country and from the west country; and I will bring them to live in Jerusalem. They shall be my people and I will be their God, in faithfulness and in righteousness.

A reading from the gospel according to Luke. (2.41-52)

Every year, the parents of Jesus went to Jerusalem for the festival of the Passover. And when he was twelve years old, they went up as usual for the festival. When the festival was ended and they started to return, the boy Jesus stayed behind in Jerusalem, but his parents did not know it. Assuming that he was in the group of travellers, they went a day's journey. Then they started to look for him among their relatives and friends. When they did not find him, they returned to Jerusalem to search for him. After three days they found him in the temple, sitting among the teachers, listening to them and asking them questions. And all who heard him were amazed at his understanding and his answers. When his parents saw him they were astonished; and his mother said to him, 'Child, why have you treated us like this? Look, your father and I have been searching for you in great anxiety.' He said to them, 'Why were you searching for me? Did you not know that I must be in my Father's house?' But they did not understand what he said to them. Then he went down with them and came to Nazareth, and was obedient to them. His mother treasured all these things in her heart.

And Jesus increased in wisdom and in years, and in divine and human favour.

Epiphany

The Epiphany *(6 January)*

Evening Prayer on the Eve *(5 January)*
Pss 96,97; Isaiah 49.1-13; John 4.7-26

A reading from the prophecy of Isaiah. (49.1-13)

Listen to me, O coastlands,
   pay attention, you peoples from far away!
The Lord called me before I was born,
   while I was in my mother's womb he named me.
He made my mouth like a sharp sword,
   in the shadow of his hand he hid me;
he made me a polished arrow,
   in his quiver he hid me away.
And he said to me, 'You are my servant,
   Israel, in whom I will be glorified.'
But I said, 'I have laboured in vain,
   I have spent my strength for nothing and vanity;
   yet surely my cause is with the Lord,
and my reward with my God.'

And now the Lord says,
   who formed me in the womb to be his servant,
to bring Jacob back to him,
   and that Israel might be gathered to him,
for I am honoured in the sight of the Lord,
   and my God has become my strength –
he says, 'It is too light a thing that you should be my servant
   to raise up the tribes of Jacob
   and to restore the survivors of Israel;
I will give you as a light to the nations,
   that my salvation may reach to the end of the earth.'

Thus says the Lord,
   the Redeemer of Israel and his Holy One,
to one deeply despised, abhorred by the nations,
   the slave of rulers,
'Kings shall see and stand up,
   princes, and they shall prostrate themselves,
because of the Lord, who is faithful,
   the Holy One of Israel, who has chosen you.'

Thus says the Lord:
In a time of favour I have answered you,
    on a day of salvation I have helped you;
I have kept you and given you as a covenant to the people,
    to establish the land, to apportion the desolate heritages;
saying to the prisoners, 'Come out',
    to those who are in darkness, 'Show yourselves.'
They shall feed along the ways,
    on all the bare heights shall be their pasture;
they shall not hunger or thirst,
    neither scorching wind nor sun shall strike them down,
for he who has pity on them will lead them,
    and by springs of water will guide them.
And I will turn all my mountains into a road,
    and my highways shall be raised up.
Lo, these shall come from far away,
    and lo, these from the north and from the west,
    and these from the land of Syene.

Sing for joy, O heavens, and exult, O earth;
    break forth, O mountains, into singing!
For the Lord has comforted his people,
    and will have compassion on his suffering ones.

A reading from the gospel according to John. (4.7-26)
A Samaritan woman came to draw water, and Jesus said to her, 'Give me a drink' (his disciples had gone to the city to buy food). The Samaritan woman said to him, 'How is it that you, a Jew, ask a drink of me, a woman of Samaria?' (Jews do not share things in common with Samaritans.) Jesus answered her, 'If you knew the gift of God, and who it is that is saying to you, "Give me a drink", you would have asked him, and he would have given you living water.' The woman said to him, 'Sir, you have no bucket, and the well is deep. Where do you get that living water? Are you greater than our ancestor Jacob, who gave us the well, and with his sons and his flocks drank from it?' Jesus said to her, 'Everyone who drinks of this water will be thirsty again, but those who drink of the water that I will give them will never be thirsty. The water that I will give will become in them a spring of water gushing up to eternal life.' The woman said to him, 'Sir, give me this water, so that I may never be thirsty or have to keep coming here to draw water.'

Jesus said to her, 'Go, call your husband, and come back.' The woman answered him, 'I have no husband.' Jesus said to her, 'You

are right in saying, "I have no husband"; for you have had five husbands, and the one you have now is not your husband. What you
have said is true!' The woman said to him, 'Sir, I see that you are a
prophet. Our ancestors worshipped on this mountain, but you say
that the place where people must worship is in Jerusalem.' Jesus said
to her, 'Woman, believe me, the hour is coming when you will worship the Father neither on this mountain nor in Jerusalem. You worship what you do not know; we worship what we know, for salvation is from the Jews. But the hour is coming, and is now here, when
the true worshippers will worship the Father in spirit and truth, for
the Father seeks such as these to worship him. God is spirit, and
those who worship him must worship in spirit and truth.' The
woman said to him, 'I know that Messiah is coming' (who is called
Christ). 'When he comes, he will proclaim all things to us.' Jesus said
to her, 'I am he, the one who is speaking to you.'

Principal Service

Isaiah 60.1-6; Ps 72.[1-9] 10-15; Ephesians 3.1-12; Matthew 2.1-12

A reading from the prophecy of Isaiah. (60. 1-6)

Arise, shine; for your light has come,
    and the glory of the Lord has risen upon you.
For darkness shall cover the earth,
    and thick darkness the peoples;
but the Lord will arise upon you,
    and his glory will appear over you.
Nations shall come to your light,
    and kings to the brightness of your dawn.

Lift up your eyes and look around;
    they all gather together, they come to you;
your sons shall come from far away,
    and your daughters shall be carried on their nurses' arms.
Then you shall see and be radiant;
    your heart shall thrill and rejoice,
    because the abundance of the sea shall be brought to you,
    the wealth of the nations shall come to you.
A multitude of camels shall cover you,
    the young camels of Midian and Ephah;
    all those from Sheba shall come.
They shall bring gold and frankincense,
and shall proclaim the praise of the Lord.

This is the word of the Lord.

A reading from the Letter of Paul to the Ephesians. (3.1-12)

This is the reason that I Paul am a prisoner for Christ Jesus for the sake of you Gentiles – for surely you have already heard of the commission of God's grace that was given to me for you, and how the mystery was made known to me by revelation, as I wrote above in a few words, a reading of which will enable you to perceive my understanding of the mystery of Christ. In former generations this mystery was not made known to humankind, as it has now been revealed to his holy apostles and prophets by the Spirit: that is, the Gentiles have become fellow-heirs, members of the same body, and sharers in the promise in Christ Jesus through the gospel.

Of this gospel I have become a servant according to the gift of God's grace that was given to me by the working of his power. Although I am the very least of all the saints, this grace was given to me to bring to the Gentiles the news of the boundless riches of Christ, and to make everyone see what is the plan of the mystery hidden for ages in God who created all things; so that through the church the wisdom of God in its rich variety might now be made known to the rulers and authorities in the heavenly places. This was in accordance with the eternal purpose that he has carried out in Christ Jesus our Lord, in whom we have access to God in boldness and confidence through faith in him.

This is the word of the Lord.

Hear the gospel of our Lord Jesus Christ according to Matthew.

(2.1-12)

In the time of King Herod, after Jesus was born in Bethlehem of Judea, wise men from the East came to Jerusalem, asking, 'Where is the child who has been born king of the Jews? For we observed his star at its rising, and have come to pay him homage.' When King Herod heard this, he was frightened, and all Jerusalem with him; and calling together all the chief priests and scribes of the people, he inquired of them where the Messiah was to be born. They told him, 'In Bethlehem of Judea; for so it has been written by the prophet:
    "And you, Bethlehem, in the land of Judah,
        are by no means least among the rulers of Judah;
    for from you shall come a ruler
        who is to shepherd my people Israel."'
    Then Herod secretly called for the wise men and learnèd from them the exact time when the star had appeared. Then he sent them to Bethlehem, saying, 'Go and search diligently for the child; and when you have found him, bring me word so that I may also go and pay

him homage.' When they had heard the king, they set out; and there, ahead of them, went the star that they had seen at its rising, until it stopped over the place where the child was. When they saw that the star had stopped, they were overwhelmed with joy. On entering the house, they saw the child with Mary his mother; and they knelt down and paid him homage. Then, opening their treasure-chests, they offered him gifts of gold, frankincense, and myrrh. And having been warned in a dream not to return to Herod, they left for their own country by another road.

This is the gospel of the Lord.

Second Service
Pss 98,100; Baruch 4.36 - 5.9 *or* Isaiah 60.1-9; John 2.1-11

A reading from the Book of Baruch. (4.36 - 5.9)

Look towards the east, O Jerusalem,
    and see the joy that is coming to you from God.
Look, your children are coming, whom you sent away;
    they are coming, gathered from east and west,
        at the word of the Holy One, rejoicing in the glory of God.

Take off the garment of your sorrow and affliction, O Jerusalem,
    and put on for ever the beauty of the glory from God.
Put on the robe of the righteousness that comes from God;
    put on your head the diadem of the glory of the Everlasting;
for God will show your splendour everywhere under heaven.
For God will give you evermore the name
    'Righteous Peace, Godly Glory'.

Arise, O Jerusalem, stand upon the height;
    look towards the east,
and see your children gathered from west and east
    at the word of the Holy One,
    rejoicing that God has remembered them.
For they went out from you on foot, led away by their enemies;
    but God will bring them back to you,
    carried in glory, as on a royal throne.
For God has ordered that every high mountain
    and the everlasting hills be made low
and the valleys filled up, to make level ground,
    so that Israel may walk safely in the glory of God.
The woods and every fragrant tree have shaded Israel
    at God's command.

For God will lead Israel with joy, in the light of his glory,
    with the mercy and righteousness that come from him.

Or:

A reading from the prophecy of Isaiah. (60.1-9)

Arise, shine; for your light has come,
    and the glory of the Lord has risen upon you.
For darkness shall cover the earth,
    and thick darkness the peoples;
but the Lord will arise upon you,
    and his glory will appear over you.
Nations shall come to your light,
    and kings to the brightness of your dawn.

Lift up your eyes and look around;
    they all gather together, they come to you;
your sons shall come from far away,
    and your daughters shall be carried on their nurses' arms.
Then you shall see and be radiant;
    your heart shall thrill and rejoice,
    because the abundance of the sea shall be brought to you,
    the wealth of the nations shall come to you.
A multitude of camels shall cover you,
    the young camels of Midian and Ephah;
    all those from Sheba shall come.
They shall bring gold and frankincense,
and shall proclaim the praise of the Lord.
All the flocks of Kedar shall be gathered to you,
    the rams of Nebaioth shall minister to you;
they shall be acceptable on my altar,
    and I will glorify my glorious house.

Who are these that fly like a cloud,
    and like doves to their windows?
For the coastlands shall wait for me,
    the ships of Tarshish first,
    to bring your children from far away,
    their silver and gold with them,
for the name of the Lord your God,
    and for the Holy One of Israel, because he has glorified you.

A reading from the gospel according to John (2.1-11)

On the third day there was a wedding in Cana of Galilee, and the
mother of Jesus was there. Jesus and his disciples had also been

invited to the wedding. When the wine gave out, the mother of Jesus said to him, 'They have no wine.' And Jesus said to her, 'Woman, what concern is that to you and to me? My hour has not yet come.' His mother said to the servants, 'Do whatever he tells you.' Now standing there were six stone water-jars for the Jewish rites of purification, each holding twenty or thirty gallons. Jesus said to them, 'Fill the jars with water.' And they filled them up to the brim. He said to them,' Now draw some out, and take it to the chief steward.' So they took it. When the steward tasted the water that had become wine, and did not know where it came from (though the servants who had drawn the water knew), the steward called the bridegroom and said to him, 'Everyone serves the good wine first, and then the inferior wine after the guests have become drunk. But you have kept the good wine until now.' Jesus did this, the first of his signs, in Cana of Galilee, and revealed his glory; and his disciples believed in him.

Third Service
Pss 113,132; Jeremiah 31.7-14; John 1.29-34

A reading from the prophecy of Jeremiah. (31.7-14)

Thus says the Lord:
    Sing aloud with gladness for Jacob,
    and raise shouts for the chief of the nations;
proclaim, give praise, and say,
    'Save, O Lord, your people, the remnant of Israel.'
See, I am going to bring them from the land of the north,
    and gather them from the farthest parts of the earth,
among them the blind and the lame,
    those with child and those in labour, together;
    a great company, they shall return here.
With weeping they shall come,
    and with consolations I will lead them back,
I will let them walk by brooks of water,
    in a straight path in which they shall not stumble;
for I have become a father to Israel, and Ephraim is my firstborn.

Hear the word of the Lord, O nations,
    and declare it in the coastlands far away;
say, 'He who scattered Israel will gather him,
    and will keep him as a shepherd a flock.'
For the Lord has ransomed Jacob,
    and has redeemed him from hands too strong for him.
They shall come and sing aloud on the height of Zion,

and they shall be radiant over the goodness of the Lord,
over the grain, the wine, and the oil,
    and over the young of the flock and the herd;
their life shall become like a watered garden,
    and they shall never languish again.
Then shall the young women rejoice in the dance,
    and the young men and the old shall be merry.
I will turn their mourning into joy, I will comfort them,
    and give them gladness for sorrow.
I will give the priests their fill of fatness,
    and my people shall be satisfied with my bounty,
    says the Lord.

A reading from the gospel according to John. (1.29-34)

John saw Jesus coming towards him and declared, 'Here is the Lamb of God who takes away the sin of the world! This is he of whom I said, "After me comes a man who ranks ahead of me because he was before me." I myself did not know him; but I came baptizing with water for this reason, that he might be revealed to Israel.' And John testified, 'I saw the Spirit descending from heaven like a dove, and it remained on him. I myself did not know him, but the one who sent me to baptize with water said to me, "He on whom you see the Spirit descend and remain is the one who baptizes with the Holy Spirit." And I myself have seen and have testified that this is the Son of God.'

The Baptism of Christ
(The First Sunday of Epiphany)

Evening Prayer of the Eve
Ps 36; Isaiah 61; Titus 2.11-14; 3.4-7

A reading from the prophecy of Isaiah. (Chapter 61)

The spirit of the Lord God is upon me,
    because the Lord has anointed me;
he has sent me to bring good news to the oppressed,
    to bind up the broken-hearted,
to proclaim liberty to the captives,
    and release to the prisoners;
to proclaim the year of the Lord's favour,
    and the day of vengeance of our God;
to comfort all who mourn;

to provide for those who mourn in Zion –
to give them a garland instead of ashes,
    the oil of gladness instead of mourning,
    the mantle of praise instead of a faint spirit.
They will be called oaks of righteousness,
    the planting of the Lord, to display his glory.
They shall build up the ancient ruins,
    they shall raise up the former devastations;
they shall repair the ruined cities,
    the devastations of many generations.

Strangers shall stand and feed your flocks,
    foreigners shall till your land and dress your vines;
but you shall be called priests of the Lord,
    you shall be named ministers of our God;
you shall enjoy the wealth of the nations,
    and in their riches you shall glory.
Because their shame was double,
    and dishonour was proclaimed as their lot,
therefore they shall possess a double portion;
    everlasting joy shall be theirs.

For I the Lord love justice,
    I hate robbery and wrongdoing;
I will faithfully give them their recompense,
    and I will make an everlasting covenant with them.
Their descendants shall be known among the nations,
    and their offspring among the peoples;
all who see them shall acknowledge
    that they are a people whom the Lord has blessed.
I will greatly rejoice in the Lord,
    my whole being shall exult in my God;
for he has clothed me with the garments of salvation,
    he has covered me with the robe of righteousness,
as a bridegroom decks himself with a garland,
    and as a bride adorns herself with her jewels.
For as the earth brings forth its shoots,
    and as a garden causes what is sown in it to spring up,
so the Lord God will cause righteousness and praise
    to spring up before all the nations.

A reading from the Letter of Paul to Titus. (2.11-14; 3.4-7)

The grace of God has appeared, bringing salvation to all, training us to renounce impiety and worldly passions, and in the present age to live lives that are self-controlled, upright, and godly, while we wait for the blessèd hope and the manifestation of the glory of our great God and Saviour, Jesus Christ. He it is who gave himself for us that he might redeem us from all iniquity and purify for himself a people of his own who are zealous for good deeds.

3.4 But when the goodness and loving-kindness of God our Saviour appeared, he saved us, not because of any works of righteousness that we had done, but according to his mercy, through the water of rebirth and renewal by the Holy Spirit. This Spirit he poured out on us richly through Jesus Christ our Saviour, so that, having been justified by his grace, we might become heirs according to the hope of eternal life.

Principal Service

Genesis 1.1-5; Ps 29; Acts 19.1-7; Mark 1.4-11

A reading from the book Genesis. (1.1-5)

In the beginning when God created the heavens and the earth, the earth was a formless void and darkness covered the face of the deep, while a wind from God swept over the face of the waters. Then God said, 'Let there be light'; and there was light. And God saw that the light was good; and God separated the light from the darkness. God called the light Day, and the darkness he called Night. And there was evening and there was morning, the first day.

This is the word of the Lord.

A reading from the Acts of the Apostles. (19.1-7)

While Apollos was in Corinth, Paul passed through the inland regions and came to Ephesus, where he found some disciples. He said to them, 'Did you receive the Holy Spirit when you became believers?' They replied, 'No, we have not even heard that there is a Holy Spirit.' Then he said, 'Into what then were you baptized?' They answered, 'Into John's baptism.' Paul said, 'John baptized with the baptism of repentance, telling the people to believe in the one who was to come after him, that is, in Jesus.' On hearing this, they were baptized in the name of the Lord Jesus. When Paul had laid his hands on them, the Holy Spirit came upon them, and they spoke in tongues and prophesied – altogether there were about twelve of them.

This is the word of the Lord.

Hear the gospel of our Lord Jesus Christ according to Mark. (1.4-11)

John the baptizer appeared in the wilderness, proclaiming a baptism of repentance for the forgiveness of sins. And people from the whole Judean countryside and all the people of Jerusalem were going out to him, and were baptized by him in the river Jordan, confessing their sins. Now John was clothed with camel's hair, with a leather belt around his waist, and he ate locusts and wild honey. He proclaimed, 'The one who is more powerful than I is coming after me; I am not worthy to stoop down and untie the thong of his sandals. I have baptized you with water; but he will baptize you with the Holy Spirit.'
  In those days Jesus came from Nazareth of Galilee and was baptized by John in the Jordan. And just as he was coming up out of the water, he saw the heavens torn apart and the Spirit descending like a dove on him. And a voice came from heaven, 'You are my Son, the Belovèd; with you I am well pleased.'

This is the gospel of the Lord.

Second Service
Pss 46 [47]; Isaiah 42.1-9; Ephesians 2.1-10;
if a Eucharist: Matthew 3.13-17

A reading from the prophecy of Isaiah. (42.1-9)

> Here is my servant, whom I uphold,
>   my chosen, in whom my soul delights;
> I have put my spirit upon him;
>   he will bring forth justice to the nations.
> He will not cry or lift up his voice,
>   or make it heard in the street;
> a bruised reed he will not break,
>   and a dimly burning wick he will not quench;
>   he will faithfully bring forth justice.
> He will not grow faint or be crushed
>   until he has established justice in the earth;
>   and the coastlands wait for his teaching.
>
> Thus says God, the Lord,
>   who created the heavens and stretched them out,
>   who spread out the earth and what comes from it,
> who gives breath to the people upon it
>   and spirit to those who walk in it:
> I am the Lord, I have called you in righteousness,
>   I have taken you by the hand and kept you;

I have given you as a covenant to the people,
    a light to the nations,
    to open the eyes that are blind,
to bring out the prisoners from the dungeon,
    from the prison those who sit in darkness.
I am the Lord, that is my name;
    my glory I give to no other,
    nor my praise to idols.
See, the former things have come to pass,
    and new things I now declare;
before they spring forth,
    I tell you of them.

A reading from the Letter of Paul to the Ephesians. (2.1-10)

You were dead through the trespasses and sins in which you once lived, following the course of this world, following the ruier of the power of the air, the spirit that is now at work among those who are disobedient. All of us once lived among them in the passions of our flesh, following the desires of flesh and senses, and we were by nature children of wrath, like everyone else. But God, who is rich in mercy, out of the great love with which he loved us even when we were dead through our trespasses, made us alive together with Christ – by grace you have been saved – and raised us up with him and seated us with him in the heavenly places in Christ Jesus, so that in the ages to come he might show the immeasurable riches of his grace in kindness towards us in Christ Jesus. For by grace you have been saved through faith, and this is not your own doing; it is the gift of God – not the result of works, so that no one may boast. For we are what he has made us, created in Christ Jesus for good works, which God prepared beforehand to be our way of life.

If a Eucharist:

Hear the gospel of our Lord Jesus Christ according to Matthew. (3.13-17)
Jesus came from Galilee to John at the Jordan, to be baptized by him. John would have prevented him, saying, 'I need to be baptized by you, and do you come to me?' But Jesus answered him, 'Let it be so now; for it is proper for us in this way to fulfil all righteousness.' Then he consented. And when Jesus had been baptized, just as he came up from the water, suddenly the heavens were opened to him and he saw the Spirit of God descending like a dove and alighting on him. And a voice from heaven said, 'This is my Son, the Belovèd, with whom I am well pleased.'

This is the gospel of the Lord.

Third Service
Ps 89.20-29; 1 Samuel 16.1-3,13; John 1.29-34

A reading from the First Book of Samuel. (16.1-3,13)

The Lord said to Samuel, 'How long will you grieve over Saul? I have rejected him from being king over Israel. Fill your horn with oil and set out; I will send you to Jesse the Bethlehemite, for I have provided for myself a king among his sons.' Samuel said, 'How can I go? If Saul hears of it, he will kill me.' And the Lord said, 'Take a heifer with you, and say, "I have come to sacrifice to the Lord." Invite Jesse to the sacrifice, and I will show you what you shall do; and you shall anoint for me the one whom I name to you.'
[13] Then Samuel took the horn of oil, and anointed David in the presence of his brothers; and the spirit of the Lord came mightily upon David from that day forward. Samuel then set out and went to Ramah.

A reading from the gospel according to John. (1.29-34)

John saw Jesus coming towards him and declared, 'Here is the Lamb of God who takes away the sin of the world! This is he of whom I said, "After me comes a man who ranks ahead of me because he was before me." I myself did not know him; but I came baptizing with water for this reason, that he might be revealed to Israel.' And John testified, 'I saw the Spirit descending from heaven like a dove, and it remained on him. I myself did not know him, but the one who sent me to baptize with water said to me, "He on whom you see the Spirit descend and remain is the one who baptizes with the Holy Spirit." And I myself have seen and have testified that this is the Son of God.'

The Second Sunday of Epiphany

Principal Service
1 Samuel 3.1-10[11-20]; Ps 139.1-6,13-18 *or* 139.1-10;
Revelation 5.1-10; John 1.43-51

A reading from the First Book of Samuel. (3.1-10 [11-20])

The boy Samuel was ministering to the Lord under Eli. The word of the Lord was rare in those days; visions were not widespread.

   At that time Eli, whose eyesight had begun to grow dim so that he could not see, was lying down in his room; the lamp of God had not yet gone out, and Samuel was lying down in the temple of the Lord, where the ark of God was. Then the Lord called, 'Samuel! Samuel!' and he said, 'Here I am!' and ran to Eli, and said, 'Here I am, for you called me.' But he said, 'I did not call; lie down again.' So he went and lay down. The Lord called again, 'Samuel!' Samuel got up and went to Eli, and said, 'Here I am, for you called me.' But he said, 'I did not call, my son; lie down again.' Now Samuel did not yet know the Lord, and the word of the Lord had not yet been revealed to him. The Lord called Samuel again, a third time. And he got up and went to Eli, and said, 'Here I am, for you called me.' Then Eli perceived that the Lord was calling the boy. Therefore Eli said to Samuel, 'Go, lie down; and if he calls you, you shall say, "Speak, Lord, for your servant is listening."' So Samuel went and lay down in his place.

Now the Lord came and stood there, calling as before, 'Samuel! Samuel!' And Samuel said, 'Speak, for your servant is listening.' [¹¹ Then the Lord said to Samuel, 'See, I am about to do something in Israel that will make both ears of anyone who hears of it tingle. On that day I will fulfil against Eli all that I have spoken concerning his house, from beginning to end. For I have told him that I am about to punish his house for ever, for the iniquity that he knew, because his sons were blaspheming God, and he did not restrain them. Therefore I swear to the house of Eli that the iniquity of Eli's house shall not be expiated by sacrifice or offering for ever.'

Samuel lay there until morning; then he opened the doors of the house of the Lord. Samuel was afraid to tell the vision to Eli. But Eli called Samuel and said, 'Samuel, my son.' He said, 'Here I am.' Eli said, 'What was it that he told you? Do not hide it from me. May God do so to you and more also, if you hide anything from me of all that he told you.' So Samuel told him everything and hid nothing from him. Then he said, 'It is the Lord; let him do what seems good to him.'

As Samuel grew up, the Lord was with him and let none of his words fall to the ground. And all Israel from Dan to Beer-sheba knew that Samuel was a trustworthy prophet of the Lord.]

This is the word of the Lord.

A reading from the Revelation to John. (5.1-10)

I saw in the right hand of the one seated on the throne a scroll written on the inside and on the back, sealed with seven seals; and I saw a mighty angel proclaiming with a loud voice, 'Who is worthy to open the scroll and break its seals?' And no one in heaven or on earth or under the earth was able to open the scroll or to look into it. And I began to weep bitterly because no one was found worthy to open the scroll or to look into it. Then one of the elders said to me, 'Do not weep. See, the Lion of the tribe of Judah, the Root of David, has conquered, so that he can open the scroll and its seven seals.'

Then I saw between the throne and the four living creatures and among the elders a Lamb standing as if it had been slaughtered, having seven horns and seven eyes, which are the seven spirits of God sent out into all the earth. He went and took the scroll from the right hand of the one who was seated on the throne. When he had taken the scroll, the four living creatures and the twenty-four elders fell before the Lamb, each holding a harp and golden bowls full of incense, which are the prayers of the saints. They sing a new song:
'You are worthy to take the scroll
    and to open its seals,
for you were slaughtered and by your blood
        you ransomed for God
    saints from every tribe and language and people and nation;
you have made them to be a kingdom
        and priests serving our God,
    and they will reign on earth.'

This is the word of the Lord.

Hear the gospel of our Lord Jesus Christ according to John. (1.43-51)

Jesus decided to go to Galilee. He found Philip and said to him, 'Follow me.' Now Philip was from Bethsaida, the city of Andrew and Peter. Philip found Nathanael and said to him, 'We have found him about whom Moses in the law and also the prophets wrote, Jesus son of Joseph from Nazareth.' Nathanael said to him, 'Can anything good come out of Nazareth?' Philip said to him, 'Come and see.' When Jesus saw Nathanael coming towards him, he said of him, 'Here is truly an Israelite in whom there is no deceit!' Nathanael asked him, 'Where did you come to know me?' Jesus answered, 'I saw you under the fig tree before Philip called you.' Nathanael replied, 'Rabbi, you are the Son of God! You are the King of Israel!' Jesus answered, 'Do you believe because I told you that I saw you under the fig tree? You will see greater things than these.' And he said to him, 'Very truly, I tell you, you will see heaven opened and the angels of God ascending and descending upon the Son of Man.'

This is the gospel of the Lord.

Second Service
Ps 96; Isaiah 60.9-22; Hebrews 6.17 - 7.10;
if a Eucharist: Matthew 8.5-13

A reading from the prophecy of Isaiah. (60.9-22)

The coastlands shall wait for me,
    the ships of Tarshish first,
to bring your children from far away,
    their silver and gold with them,
for the name of the Lord your God,
    and for the Holy One of Israel,
    because he has glorified you.
Foreigners shall build up your walls,
    and their kings shall minister to you;
for in my wrath I struck you down,
    but in my favour I have had mercy on you.
Your gates shall always be open;
    day and night they shall not be shut,
so that nations shall bring you their wealth,
    with their kings led in procession.
For the nation and kingdom
    that will not serve you shall perish;
    those nations shall be utterly laid waste.
The glory of Lebanon shall come to you,
    the cypress, the plane, and the pine,
to beautify the place of my sanctuary;
    and I will glorify where my feet rest.
The descendants of those who oppressed you
    shall come bending low to you,
and all who despised you
    shall bow down at your feet;
they shall call you the City of the Lord,
    the Zion of the Holy One of Israel.
Whereas you have been forsaken and hated,
    with no one passing through,
I will make you majestic for ever,
    a joy from age to age.
You shall suck the milk of nations,
    you shall suck the breasts of kings;
and you shall know that I, the Lord, am your Saviour
    and your Redeemer, the Mighty One of Jacob.

Instead of bronze I will bring gold,
    instead of iron I will bring silver;
instead of wood, bronze,
    instead of stones, iron.
I will appoint Peace as your overseer
    and Righteousness as your taskmaster.
Violence shall no more be heard in your land,
    devastation or destruction within your borders;
you shall call your walls Salvation,
    and your gates Praise.
The sun shall no longer be
    your light by day,
nor for brightness shall the moon
    give light to you by night;
but the Lord will be your everlasting light,
    and your God will be your glory.
Your sun shall no more go down,
    or your moon withdraw itself;
for the Lord will be your everlasting light,
    and your days of mourning shall be ended.
Your people shall all be righteous;
    they shall possess the land for ever.
They are the shoot that I planted,
    the work of my hands, so that I might be glorified.
The least of them shall become a clan,
    and the smallest one a mighty nation;
I am the Lord;
    in its time I will accomplish it quickly.

A reading from the Letter to the Hebrews. (6.17 - 7.10)

When God desired to show even more clearly to the heirs of the promise the unchangeable character of his purpose, he guaranteed it by an oath, so that through two unchangeable things, in which it is impossible that God would prove false, we who have taken refuge might be strongly encouraged to seize the hope set before us. We have this hope, a sure and steadfast anchor of the soul, a hope that enters the inner shrine behind the curtain, where Jesus, a forerunner on our behalf, has entered, having become a high priest for ever according to the order of Melchizedek.

This 'King Melchizedek of Salem, priest of the Most High God, met Abraham as he was returning from defeating the kings and blessed him'; and to him Abraham apportioned 'one-tenth of everything'.

His name, in the first place, means 'king of righteousness'; next he is also king of Salem, that is, 'king of peace'. Without father, without mother, without genealogy, having neither beginning of days nor end of life, but resembling the Son of God, he remains a priest for ever.

See how great he is! Even Abraham the patriarch gave him a tenth of the spoils. And those descendants of Levi who receive the priestly office have a commandment in the law to collect tithes from the people, that is, from their kindred, though these also are descended from Abraham. But this man, who does not belong to their ancestry, collected tithes from Abraham and blessed him who had received the promises. It is beyond dispute that the inferior is blessed by the superior. In the one case, tithes are received by those who are mortal; in the other, by one of whom it is testified that he lives. One might even say that Levi himself, who receives tithes, paid tithes through Abraham, for he was still in the loins of his ancestor when Melchizedek met him.

If a Eucharist:
Hear the gospel of our Lord Jesus Christ according to Matthew.

(8.5-13)

When Jesus entered Capernaum, a centurion came to him, appealing to him and saying, 'Lord, my servant is lying at home paralysed, in terrible distress.' And he said to him, 'I will come and cure him.' The centurion answered, 'Lord, I am not worthy to have you come under my roof; but only speak the word, and my servant will be healed. For I also am a man under authority, with soldiers under me; and I say to one, "Go", and he goes, and to another, "Come", and he comes, and to my slave, "Do this", and the slave does it.' When Jesus heard him, he was amazed and said to those who followed him, 'Truly I tell you, in no one in Israel have I found such faith. I tell you, many will come from east and west and will eat with Abraham and Isaac and Jacob in the kingdom of heaven, while the heirs of the kingdom will be thrown into the outer darkness, where there will be weeping and gnashing of teeth.' And to the centurion Jesus said, 'Go; let it be done for you according to your faith.' And the servant was healed in that hour.

This is the gospel of the Lord.

Third Service
Ps 145.1-12; Isaiah 62.1-5; 1 Corinthians 6.11-20

A reading from the prophecy of Isaiah. (62.1-5)

For Zion's sake I will not keep silent,
    and for Jerusalem's sake I will not rest,
until her vindication shines out like the dawn,
    and her salvation like a burning torch.
The nations shall see your vindication,
    and all the kings your glory;
and you shall be called by a new name
    that the mouth of the Lord will give.
You shall be a crown of beauty in the hand of the Lord,
    and a royal diadem in the hand of your God.
You shall no more be termed Forsaken,
    and your land shall no more be termed Desolate;
but you shall be called My Delight Is in Her,
    and your land Married;
for the Lord delights in you,
    and your land shall be married.
For as a young man marries a young woman,
    so shall your builder marry you,
and as the bridegroom rejoices over the bride,
    so shall your God rejoice over you.

A reading from the First Letter of Paul to the Corinthians. (6.11-20)

Some of you used to be wrongdoers. But you were washed, you were sanctified, you were justified in the name of the Lord Jesus Christ and in the Spirit of our God.

'All things are lawful for me', but not all things are beneficial. 'All things are lawful for me', but I will not be dominated by anything. 'Food is meant for the stomach and the stomach for food', and God will destroy both one and the other. The body is meant not for fornication but for the Lord, and the Lord for the body. And God raised the Lord and will also raise us by his power. Do you not know that your bodies are members of Christ? Should I therefore take the members of Christ and make them members of a prostitute? Never! Do you not know that whoever is united to a prostitute becomes one body with her? For it is said, 'The two shall be one flesh.' But anyone united to the Lord becomes one spirit with him. Shun fornication! Every sin that a person commits is outside the body; but the fornicator sins against the body itself. Or do you not know that your body is a temple of the Holy Spirit within you, which you have from God, and that you are not your own? For you were bought with a price; therefore glorify God in your body.

The Third Sunday of Epiphany

Principal Service

Genesis 14.17-20; Ps 128; Revelation 19.6-10; John 2.1-11

A reading from the book Genesis. (14.17-20)

After Abram's return from the defeat of Chedorlaomer and the kings who were with him, the king of Sodom went out to meet him at the Valley of Shaveh (that is, the King's Valley). And King Melchizedek of Salem brought out bread and wine; he was priest of God Most High. He blessed him and said,
     'Blessèd be Abram by God Most High,
        maker of heaven and earth;
     and blessèd be God Most High,
        who has delivered your enemies into your hand!'
And Abram gave him one-tenth of everything.

This is the word of the Lord.

A reading from the Revelation to John. (19.6-10)

I heard what seemed to be the voice of a great multitude, like the sound of many waters and like the sound of mighty thunder-peals, crying out,
     'Hallelujah!
     For the Lord our God the Almighty reigns.
        Let us rejoice and exult and give him the glory,
     for the marriage of the Lamb has come,
        and his bride has made herself ready;
     to her it has been granted to be clothed
        with fine linen, bright and pure' –
for the fine linen is the righteous deeds of the saints.
     And the angel said to me, 'Write this: Blessèd are those who are invited to the marriage supper of the Lamb.' And he said to me, 'These are true words of God.' Then I fell down at his feet to worship him, but he said to me, 'You must not do that! I am a fellow-servant with you and your comrades who hold the testimony of Jesus. Worship God! For the testimony of Jesus is the spirit of prophecy.'

This is the word of the Lord.

Hear the gospel of our Lord Jesus Christ according to John. (2.1-11)

On the third day there was a wedding in Cana of Galilee, and the mother of Jesus was there. Jesus and his disciples had also been invited to the wedding. When the wine gave out, the mother of Jesus said to him, 'They have no wine.' And Jesus said to her, 'Woman, what concern is that to you and to me? My hour has not yet come.' His mother said to the servants, 'Do whatever he tells you.' Now standing there were six stone water-jars for the Jewish rites of purification, each holding twenty or thirty gallons. Jesus said to them, 'Fill the jars with water.' And they filled them up to the brim. He said to them, 'Now draw some out, and take it to the chief steward.' So they took it. When the steward tasted the water that had become wine, and did not know where it came from (though the servants who had drawn the water knew), the steward called the bridegroom and said to him, 'Everyone serves the good wine first, and then the inferior wine after the guests have become drunk. But you have kept the good wine until now.' Jesus did this, the first of his signs, in Cana of Galilee, and revealed his glory; and his disciples believed in him.

This is the gospel of the Lord.

Second Service
Ps 33 or 33.1-12; Jeremiah 3.21 - 4.2; Titus 2.1-8, 11-14;
if a Eucharist: Matthew 4.12-23

A reading from the prophecy of Jeremiah. (3.21 - 4.2)

A voice on the bare heights is heard,
    the plaintive weeping of Israel's children,
because they have perverted their way,
    they have forgotten the Lord their God:
Return, O faithless children,
    I will heal your faithlessness.

'Here we come to you;
    for you are the Lord our God.
Truly the hills are a delusion,
    the orgies on the mountains.
Truly in the Lord our God
    is the salvation of Israel.
'But from our youth the shameful thing has devoured all for which our ancestors had laboured, their flocks and their herds, their sons and their daughters. Let us lie down in our shame, and let our dishonour cover us; for we have sinned against the Lord our God, we

and our ancestors, from our youth even to this day; and we have not
obeyed the voice of the Lord our God.'

> If you return, O Israel, says the Lord,
>   if you return to me,
> if you remove your abominations from my presence,
>   and do not waver,
> and if you swear, 'As the Lord lives!'
>   in truth, in justice, and in uprightness,
> then nations shall be blessed by him,
>   and by him they shall boast.

A reading from the Letter of Paul to Titus. (2.1-8,11-14)

As for you, teach what is consistent with sound doctrine. Tell the
older men to be temperate, serious, prudent, and sound in faith, in
love, and in endurance.

Likewise, tell the older women to be reverent in behaviour, not to be
slanderers or slaves to drink; they are to teach what is good, so that
they may encourage the young women to love their husbands, to
love their children, to be self-controlled, chaste, good managers of the
household, kind, being submissive to their husbands, so that the
word of God may not be discredited.

Likewise, urge the younger men to be self-controlled. Show yourself in all respects a model of good works, and in your teaching show
integrity, gravity, and sound speech that cannot be censured; then
any opponent will be put to shame, having nothing evil to say of us.
[11] For the grace of God has appeared, bringing salvation to all, training us to renounce impiety and worldly passions, and in the present
age to live lives that are self-controlled, upright, and godly, while we
wait for the blessèd hope and the manifestation of the glory of our
great God and Saviour, Jesus Christ. He it is who gave himself for us
that he might redeem us from all iniquity and purify for himself a
people of his own who are zealous for good deeds.

If a Eucharist:
Hear the gospel of our Lord Jesus Christ according to Matthew.
(4.12-23)

When Jesus heard that John had been arrested, he withdrew to
Galilee. He left Nazareth and made his home in Capernaum by the
lake, in the territory of Zebulun and Naphtali, so that what had been
spoken through the prophet Isaiah might be fulfilled:

> 'Land of Zebulun, land of Naphtali,
>   on the road by the sea, across the Jordan,

Galilee of the Gentiles –
the people who sat in darkness
have seen a great light,
and for those who sat in the region and shadow of death
light has dawned.'
From that time Jesus began to proclaim, 'Repent, for the kingdom of heaven has come near.'

As he walked by the Sea of Galilee, he saw two brothers, Simon, who is called Peter, and Andrew his brother, casting a net into the lake – for they were fishermen. And he said to them, 'Follow me, and I will make you fish for people.' Immediately they left their nets and followed him. As he went from there, he saw two other brothers, James son of Zebedee and his brother John, in the boat with their father Zebedee, mending their nets, and he called them. Immediately they left the boat and their father, and followed him.

Jesus went throughout Galilee, teaching in their synagogues and proclaiming the good news of the kingdom and curing every disease and every sickness among the people.

This is the gospel of the Lord.

Third Service
Ps 113; Jonah 3.1-5,10; John 3.16-21

A reading from the Book of Jonah. (3.1-5,10)

The word of the Lord came to Jonah a second time, saying, 'Get up, go to Nineveh, that great city, and proclaim to it the message that I tell you.' So Jonah set out and went to Nineveh, according to the word of the Lord. Now Nineveh was an exceedingly large city, a three days' walk across. Jonah began to go into the city, going a day's walk. And he cried out, 'Forty days more, and Nineveh shall be overthrown!' And the people of Nineveh believed God; they proclaimed a fast, and everyone, great and small, put on sackcloth.
¹⁰ When God saw what they did, how they turned from their evil ways, God changed his mind about the calamity that he had said he would bring upon them; and he did not do it.

A reading from the gospel according to John. (3.16-21)

Jesus said to a Pharisee named Nicodemus, a leader of the Jews, who had come to him, 'God so loved the world that he gave his only Son, so that everyone who believes in him may not perish but may have eternal life.

'Indeed, God did not send the Son into the world to condemn the world, but in order that the world might be saved through him. Those who believe in him are not condemned; but those who do not believe are condemned already, because they have not believed in the name of the only Son of God. And this is the judgement, that the light has come into the world, and people loved darkness rather than light because their deeds were evil. For all who do evil hate the light and do not come to the light, so that their deeds may not be exposed. But those who do what is true come to the light, so that it may be clearly seen that their deeds have been done in God.'

The Fourth Sunday of Epiphany

Principal Service
Deuteronomy 18.15-20; Ps 111; Revelation 12.1-5a; Mark 1.21-28

A reading from the book Deuteronomy. (18.15-20)

Moses said to all Israel: The Lord your God will raise up for you a prophet like me from among your own people; you shall heed such a prophet. This is what you requested of the Lord your God at Horeb on the day of the assembly when you said: 'If I hear the voice of the Lord my God any more, or ever again see this great fire, I will die.' Then the Lord replied to me: 'They are right in what they have said. I will raise up for them a prophet like you from among their own people; I will put my words in the mouth of the prophet, who shall speak to them everything that I command. Anyone who does not heed the words that the prophet shall speak in my name, I myself will hold accountable. But any prophet who speaks in the name of other gods, or who presumes to speak in my name a word that I have not commanded the prophet to speak – that prophet shall die.'

This is the word of the Lord.

A reading from the Revelation to John. (12.1-5a)

A great portent appeared in heaven: a woman clothed with the sun, with the moon under her feet, and on her head a crown of twelve stars. She was pregnant and was crying out in birth pangs, in the agony of giving birth. Then another portent appeared in heaven: a great red dragon, with seven heads and ten horns, and seven diadems on his heads. His tail swept down a third of the stars of heaven and threw them to the earth. Then the dragon stood before the woman who was about to bear a child, so that he might devour her child as soon as it was born. And she gave birth to a son, a male child, who is to rule all the nations with a rod of iron.

This is the word of the Lord.

Hear the gospel of our Lord Jesus Christ according to Mark. (1.21-28)

Jesus and his disciples went to Capernaum; and when the sabbath came, he entered the synagogue and taught. They were astounded at his teaching, for he taught them as one having authority, and not as the scribes. Just then there was in their synagogue a man with an unclean spirit, and he cried out, 'What have you to do with us, Jesus of Nazareth? Have you come to destroy us? I know who you are, the Holy One of God.' But Jesus rebuked him, saying, 'Be silent, and come out of him!' And the unclean spirit, throwing him into convulsions and crying with a loud voice, came out of him. They were all amazed, and they kept on asking one another, 'What is this? A new teaching – with authority! He commands even the unclean spirits, and they obey him.' At once his fame began to spread throughout the surrounding region of Galilee.

This is the gospel of the Lord.

Second Service
Ps 34 or 34.1-10; 1 Samuel 3.1-20; 1 Corinthians 14.12-20;
if a Eucharist: Matthew 13.10-17

A reading from the First Book of Samuel. (3.1-20)

The boy Samuel was ministering to the Lord under Eli. The word of the Lord was rare in those days; visions were not widespread.

At that time Eli, whose eyesight had begun to grow dim so that he could not see, was lying down in his room; the lamp of God had not yet gone out, and Samuel was lying down in the temple of the Lord, where the ark of God was. Then the Lord called, 'Samuel! Samuel!' and he said, 'Here I am!' and ran to Eli, and said, 'Here I am, for you called me.' But he said, 'I did not call; lie down again.' So he went and lay down. The Lord called again, 'Samuel!' Samuel got up and went to Eli, and said, 'Here I am, for you called me.' But he said, 'I did not call, my son; lie down again.' Now Samuel did not yet know the Lord, and the word of the Lord had not yet been revealed to him. The Lord called Samuel again, a third time. And he got up and went to Eli, and said, 'Here I am, for you called me.' Then Eli perceived that the Lord was calling the boy. Therefore Eli said to Samuel, 'Go, lie down; and if he calls you, you shall say, "Speak, Lord, for your servant is listening."' So Samuel went and lay down in his place.

Now the Lord came and stood there, calling as before, 'Samuel! Samuel!' And Samuel said, 'Speak, for your servant is listening.' Then the Lord said to Samuel, 'See, I am about to do something in Israel that will make both ears of anyone who hears of it tingle. On that day I will fulfil against Eli all that I have spoken concerning his house, from beginning to end. For I have told him that I am about to punish his house for ever, for the iniquity that he knew, because his sons were blaspheming God, and he did not restrain them. Therefore I swear to the house of Eli that the iniquity of Eli's house shall not be expiated by sacrifice or offering for ever.'

Samuel lay there until morning; then he opened the doors of the house of the Lord. Samuel was afraid to tell the vision to Eli. But Eli called Samuel and said, 'Samuel, my son.' He said, 'Here I am.' Eli said, 'What was it that he told you? Do not hide it from me. May God do so to you and more also, if you hide anything from me of all that he told you.' So Samuel told him everything and hid nothing from him. Then he said, 'It is the Lord; let him do what seems good to him.'

As Samuel grew up, the Lord was with him and let none of his words fall to the ground. And all Israel from Dan to Beer-sheba knew that Samuel was a trustworthy prophet of the Lord.

A reading from the First Letter of Paul to the Corinthians. (14.12-20)

Since you are eager for spiritual gifts, strive to excel in them for building up the church.

Therefore, one who speaks in a tongue should pray for the power to interpret. For if I pray in a tongue, my spirit prays but my mind is unproductive. What should I do then? I will pray with the spirit, but I will pray with the mind also; I will sing praise with the spirit, but I will sing praise with the mind also. Otherwise, if you say a blessing with the spirit, how can anyone in the position of an outsider say the 'Amen' to your thanksgiving, since the outsider does not know what you are saying? For you may give thanks well enough, but the other person is not built up. I thank God that I speak in tongues more than all of you; nevertheless, in church I would rather speak five words with my mind, in order to instruct others also, than ten thousand words in a tongue.

Brothers and sisters, do not be children in your thinking; rather, be infants in evil, but in thinking be adults.

If a Eucharist:
Hear the gospel of our Lord Jesus Christ according to Matthew.
(13.10-17)

The disciples asked Jesus, 'Why do you speak to the crowds in parables?' He answered, 'To you it has been given to know the secrets of the kingdom of heaven, but to them it has not been given. For to those who have, more will be given, and they will have an abundance; but from those who have nothing, even what they have will be taken away. The reason I speak to them in parables is that "seeing they do not perceive, and hearing they do not listen, nor do they understand." With them indeed is fulfilled the prophecy of Isaiah that says:

> "You will indeed listen, but never understand,
>> and you will indeed look, but never perceive.
> For this people's heart has grown dull,
>> and their ears are hard of hearing,
>>> and they have shut their eyes;
>>> so that they might not look with their eyes,
>> and listen with their ears,
> and understand with their heart and turn –
> and I would heal them."

But blessèd are your eyes, for they see, and your ears, for they hear. Truly I tell you, many prophets and righteous people longed to see what you see, but did not see it, and to hear what you hear, but did not hear it.'

This is the gospel of the Lord.

Third Service
Ps 71.1-6,15-17; Jeremiah 1.4-10; Mark 1.40-45

A reading from the prophecy of Jeremiah. (1.4-10)

The word of the Lord came to me saying,

> 'Before I formed you in the womb I knew you,
> and before you were born I consecrated you;
> I appointed you a prophet to the nations.'

Then I said, 'Ah, Lord God! Truly I do not know how to speak, for I am only a boy.' But the Lord said to me,

> 'Do not say, "I am only a boy";
>> for you shall go to all to whom I send you,
>> and you shall speak whatever I command you.
> Do not be afraid of them,
>> for I am with you to deliver you, says the Lord.'

Then the Lord put out his hand and touched my mouth; and the Lord said to me,

'Now I have put my words in your mouth.
See, today I appoint you over nations and over kingdoms,
to pluck up and to pull down,
to destroy and to overthrow,
to build and to plant.'

A reading from the gospel according to Mark. (1.40-45)

A leper came to Jesus begging him, and kneeling he said to him, 'If you choose, you can make me clean.' Moved with pity, Jesus stretched out his hand and touched him, and said to him, 'I do choose. Be made clean!' Immediately the leprosy left him, and he was made clean. After sternly warning him he sent him away at once, saying to him, 'See that you say nothing to anyone; but go, show yourself to the priest, and offer for your cleansing what Moses commanded, as a testimony to them.' But he went out and began to proclaim it freely, and to spread the word, so that Jesus could no longer go into a town openly, but stayed out in the country; and people came to him from every quarter.

The Presentation of Christ in the Temple – Candlemas (2 February)

Evening Prayer on the Eve (1 February)
Ps 118; 1 Samuel 1.19b-28; Hebrews 4.12-16

A reading from the First Book of Samuel. (1.19b-28)

Elkanah knew his wife Hannah, and the Lord remembered her. In due time Hannah conceived and bore a son. She named him Samuel, for she said, 'I have asked him of the Lord.'

The man Elkanah and all his household went up to offer to the Lord the yearly sacrifice, and to pay his vow. But Hannah did not go up, for she said to her husband, 'As soon as the child is weaned, I will bring him, that he may appear in the presence of the Lord, and remain there for ever; I will offer him as a nazirite for all time.' Her husband Elkanah said to her, 'Do what seems best to you, wait until you have weaned him; only – may the Lord establish his word.' So the woman remained and nursed her son, until she weaned him. When she had weaned him, she took him up with her, along with a three-year-old bull, an ephah of flour, and a skin of wine. She brought him to the house of the Lord at Shiloh; and the child was young. Then they slaughtered the bull, and they brought the child to Eli. And she said, 'Oh, my lord! As you live, my lord, I am the woman who was standing here in your presence, praying to the Lord. For this child I prayed; and the Lord has granted me the petition that I made to him. Therefore I have lent him to the Lord; as long as he lives, he is given to the Lord.' She left him there for the Lord.

A reading from the Letter to the Hebrews. (4.12-16)

The word of God is living and active, sharper than any two-edged sword, piercing until it divides soul from spirit, joints from marrow; it is able to judge the thoughts and intentions of the heart. And before him no creature is hidden, but all are naked and laid bare to the eyes of the one to whom we must render an account.

Since, then, we have a great high priest who has passed through the heavens, Jesus, the Son of God, let us hold fast to our confession. For we do not have a high priest who is unable to sympathize with our weaknesses, but we have one who in every respect has been tested as we are, yet without sin. Let us therefore approach the throne of grace with boldness, so that we may receive mercy and find grace to help in time of need.

Principal Service
Malachi 3.1-5; Ps 24.[1-6]7-10; Hebrews 2.14-18; Luke 2.22-40

A reading from the prophecy of Malachi. (3.1-5)

See, I am sending my messenger to prepare the way before me, and the Lord whom you seek will suddenly come to his temple. The messenger of the covenant in whom you delight – indeed, he is coming, says the Lord of hosts. But who can endure the day of his coming, and who can stand when he appears?

For he is like a refiner's fire and like fullers' soap; he will sit as a refiner and purifier of silver, and he will purify the descendants of Levi and refine them like gold and silver, until they present offerings to the Lord in righteousness. Then the offering of Judah and Jerusalem will be pleasing to the Lord as in the days of old and as in former years.

Then I will draw near to you for judgement; I will be swift to bear witness against the sorcerers, against the adulterers, against those who swear falsely, against those who oppress the hired workers in their wages, the widow, and the orphan, against those who thrust aside the alien, and do not fear me, says the Lord of hosts.

This is the word of the Lord.

A reading from the Letter to the Hebrews. (2.14-18)

Since the children share flesh and blood, Jesus himself likewise shared the same things, so that through death he might destroy the one who has the power of death, that is, the devil, and free those who all their lives were held in slavery by the fear of death. For it is clear that he did not come to help angels, but the descendants of Abraham. Therefore he had to become like his brothers and sisters in every respect, so that he might be a merciful and faithful high priest in the service of God, to make a sacrifice of atonement for the sins of the people. Because he himself was tested by what he suffered, he is able to help those who are being tested.

This is the word of the Lord.

Hear the gospel of our Lord Jesus Christ according to Luke. (2.22-40)

When the time came for their purification according to the law of Moses, Mary and Joseph brought Jesus up to Jerusalem to present him to the Lord (as it is written in the law of the Lord, 'Every first-born male shall be designated as holy to the Lord'), and they offered a sacrifice according to what is stated in the law of the Lord, 'a pair of turtle-doves or two young pigeons.'

Now there was a man in Jerusalem whose name was Simeon; this man was righteous and devout, looking forward to the consolation of Israel, and the Holy Spirit rested on him. It had been revealed to him by the Holy Spirit that he would not see death before he had seen the Lord's Messiah. Guided by the Spirit, Simeon came into the temple; and when the parents brought in the child Jesus, to do for him what was customary under the law, Simeon took him in his arms and praised God, saying,

'Master, now you are dismissing your servant in peace,
      according to your word;
   for my eyes have seen your salvation,
      which you have prepared in the presence of all peoples,
   a light for revelation to the Gentiles
      and for glory to your people Israel.'

And the child's father and mother were amazed at what was being said about him. Then Simeon blessed them and said to his mother Mary, 'This child is destined for the falling and the rising of many in Israel, and to be a sign that will be opposed so that the inner thoughts of many will be revealed – and a sword will pierce your own soul too.'

There was also a prophet, Anna the daughter of Phanuel, of the tribe of Asher. She was of a great age, having lived with her husband for seven years after her marriage, then as a widow to the age of eighty-four. She never left the temple but worshipped there with fasting and prayer night and day. At that moment she came, and began to praise God and to speak about the child to all who were looking for the redemption of Jerusalem.

When they had finished everything required by the law of the Lord, they returned to Galilee, to their own town of Nazareth. The child grew and became strong, filled with wisdom; and the favour of God was upon him.

This is the gospel of the Lord.

Second Service
Pss 122,132; Haggai 2.1-9; John 2.13-22

A reading from the Book of Haggai. (2.1-9)

In the second year of King Darius, in the seventh month, on the twenty-first day of the month, the word of the Lord came by the prophet Haggai, saying: Speak now to Zerubbabel son of Shealtiel, governor of Judah, and to Joshua son of Jehozadak, the high priest, and to the remnant of the people, and say, Who is left among you that saw this house in its former glory? How does it look to you now? Is it not in your sight as nothing? Yet now take courage, O Zerubbabel, says the Lord; take courage, O Joshua, son of Jehozadak, the high priest; take courage, all you people of the land, says the Lord; work, for I am with you, says the Lord of hosts, according to the promise that I made you when you came out of Egypt. My spirit abides among you; do not fear. For thus says the Lord of hosts: Once again, in a little while, I will shake the heavens and the earth and the sea and the dry land; and I will shake all the nations, so that the treasure of all nations shall come, and I will fill this house with splendour, says the Lord of hosts. The silver is mine, and the gold is mine, says the Lord of hosts. The latter splendour of this house shall be greater than the former, says the Lord of hosts; and in this place I will give prosperity, says the Lord of hosts.

A reading from the gospel according to John. (2.13-22)

The Passover of the Jews was near, and Jesus went up to Jerusalem. In the temple he found people selling cattle, sheep, and doves, and the money changers seated at their tables. Making a whip of cords, he drove all of them out of the temple, both the sheep and the cattle. He also poured out the coins of the money changers and overturned their tables. He told those who were selling the doves, 'Take these things out of here! Stop making my Father's house a marketplace!' His disciples remembered that it was written, 'Zeal for your house will consume me.' The Jews said to him, 'What sign can you show us for doing this?' Jesus answered them, 'Destroy this temple, and in three days I will raise it up.' The Jews then said, 'This temple has been under construction for forty-six years, and will you raise it up in three days?' But he was speaking of the temple of his body. After he was raised from the dead, his disciples remembered that he had said this; and they believed the scripture and the word that Jesus had spoken.

Third Service
Pss 42,43,48; Exodus 13.1-16; Romans 12.1-5

A reading from the Book of the Exodus. (13.1-16)

The Lord said to Moses: Consecrate to me all the firstborn; whatever is the first to open the womb among the Israelites, of human beings and animals, is mine.

Moses said to the people, 'Remember this day on which you came out of Egypt, out of the house of slavery, because the Lord brought you out from there by strength of hand; no leavened bread shall be eaten. Today, in the month of Abib, you are going out. When the Lord brings you into the land of the Canaanites, the Hittites, the Amorites, the Hivites, and the Jebusites, which he swore to your ancestors to give you, a land flowing with milk and honey, you shall keep this observance in this month. For seven days you shall eat unleavened bread, and on the seventh day there shall be a festival to the Lord. Unleavened bread shall be eaten for seven days; no leavened bread shall be seen in your possession, and no leaven shall be seen among you in all your territory. You shall tell your child on that day, "It is because of what the Lord did for me when I came out of Egypt." It shall serve for you as a sign on your hand and as a reminder on your forehead, so that the teaching of the Lord may be on your lips; for with a strong hand the Lord brought you out of Egypt. You shall keep this ordinance at its proper time from year to year.

'When the Lord has brought you into the land of the Canaanites, as he swore to you and your ancestors, and has given it to you, you shall set apart to the Lord all that first opens the womb. All the firstborn of your livestock that are males shall be the Lord's. But every first-born donkey you shall redeem with a sheep; if you do not redeem it, you must break its neck. Every firstborn male among your children you shall redeem. When in the future your child asks you, "What does this mean?" you shall answer, "By strength of hand the Lord brought us out of Egypt, from the house of slavery. When Pharaoh stubbornly refused to let us go, the Lord killed all the firstborn in the land of Egypt, from human firstborn to the firstborn of animals. Therefore I sacrifice to the Lord every male that first opens the womb, but every firstborn of my sons I redeem." It shall serve as a sign on your hand and as an emblem on your forehead that by strength of hand the Lord brought us out of Egypt.'

A reading from the Letter of Paul to the Romans. (12.1-5)

I appeal to you, brothers and sisters, by the mercies of God, to present your bodies as a living sacrifice, holy and acceptable to God, which is your spiritual worship. Do not be conformed to this world, but be transformed by the renewing of your minds, so that you may discern what is the will of God – what is good and acceptable and perfect.

   For by the grace given to me I say to everyone among you not to think of yourself more highly than you ought to think, but to think with sober judgement, each according to the measure of faith that God has assigned. For as in one body we have many members, and not all the members have the same function, so we, who are many, are one body in Christ, and individually we are members one of another.

Ordinary Time - Spring

Proper 1

Sunday between 3 and 9 February inclusive
(if earlier than the Second Sunday before Lent)

Principal Service
Isaiah 40.21-31; Ps 147.1-11[20c]; 1 Corinthians 9.16-23;
Mark 1.29-39

A reading from the prophecy of Isaiah. (40.21-31)

Have you not known? Have you not heard?
　　Has it not been told you from the beginning?
　　Have you not understood from the foundations of the earth?
It is he who sits above the circle of the earth,
　　and its inhabitants are like grasshoppers;
who stretches out the heavens like a curtain,
　　and spreads them like a tent to live in;
who brings princes to naught,
　　and makes the rulers of the earth as nothing.

Scarcely are they planted, scarcely sown,
　　scarcely has their stem taken root in the earth,
when he blows upon them, and they wither,
　　and the tempest carries them off like stubble.

To whom then will you compare me,
　　or who is my equal? says the Holy One.
Lift up your eyes on high and see:
　　Who created these?
He who brings out their host and numbers them,
　　calling them all by name;
because he is great in strength, mighty in power,
　　not one is missing.

Why do you say, O Jacob,
　　and speak, O Israel,
'My way is hidden from the Lord,
　　and my right is disregarded by my God'?
Have you not known? Have you not heard?
The Lord is the everlasting God,
　　the Creator of the ends of the earth.
He does not faint or grow weary;
　　his understanding is unsearchable.

He gives power to the faint,
and strengthens the powerless.
Even youths will faint and be weary,
and the young will fall exhausted;
but those who wait for the Lord shall renew their strength,
they shall mount up with wings like eagles,
they shall run and not be weary,
they shall walk and not faint.

This is the word of the Lord.

A reading from the First Letter of Paul to the Corinthians.

(9.16-23)

If I proclaim the gospel, this gives me no ground for boasting, for an obligation is laid on me, and woe betide me if I do not proclaim the gospel! For if I do this of my own will, I have a reward; but if not of my own will, I am entrusted with a commission. What then is my reward? Just this: that in my proclamation I may make the gospel free of charge, so as not to make full use of my rights in the gospel.

For though I am free with respect to all, I have made myself a slave to all, so that I might win more of them. To the Jews I became as a Jew, in order to win Jews. To those under the law I became as one under the law (though I myself am not under the law) so that I might win those under the law. To those outside the law I became as one outside the law (though I am not free from God's law but am under Christ's law) so that I might win those outside the law. To the weak I became weak, so that I might win the weak. I have become all things to all people, so that I might by any means save some. I do it all for the sake of the gospel, so that I may share in its blessings.

This is the word of the Lord.

Hear the gospel of our Lord Jesus Christ according to Mark. (1.29-39)

As soon as Jesus and his disciples left the synagogue, they entered the house of Simon and Andrew, with James and John. Now Simon's mother-in-law was in bed with a fever, and they told him about her at once. He came and took her by the hand and lifted her up. Then the fever left her, and she began to serve them.

That evening, at sundown, they brought to him all who were sick or possessed with demons. And the whole city was gathered around the door. And he cured many who were sick with various diseases, and cast out many demons; and he would not permit the demons to speak, because they knew him.

In the morning, while it was still very dark, he got up and went out to a deserted place, and there he prayed. And Simon and his companions hunted for him. When they found him, they said to him, 'Everyone is searching for you.' He answered, 'Let us go on to the neighbouring towns, so that I may proclaim the message there also; for that is what I came out to do.' And he went throughout Galilee, proclaiming the message in their synagogues and casting out demons.

This is the gospel of the Lord.

Second Service
Ps 5; Numbers 13.1-2,27-33; Philippians 2.12-28;
if a Eucharist: Luke 5.1-11

A reading from the the book Numbers. (13.1-2,27-33)

The Lord said to Moses, 'Send men to spy out the land of Canaan, which I am giving to the Israelites; from each of their ancestral tribes you shall send a man, every one a leader among them.'
^{27} And when they returned from spying out the land, they told Moses, 'We came to the land to which you sent us; it flows with milk and honey, and this is its fruit. Yet the people who live in the land are strong, and the towns are fortified and very large; and besides, we saw the descendants of Anak there. The Amalekites live in the land of the Negeb; the Hittites, the Jebusites, and the Amorites live in the hill country; and the Canaanites live by the sea, and along the Jordan.'

But Caleb quieted the people before Moses, and said, 'Let us go up at once and occupy it, for we are well able to overcome it.' Then the men who had gone up with him said, 'We are not able to go up against this people, for they are stronger than we are.' So they brought to the Israelites an unfavourable report of the land that they had spied out, saying, 'The land that we have gone through as spies is a land that devours its inhabitants; and all the people that we saw in it are of great size. There we saw the Nephilim (the Anakites come from the Nephilim); and to ourselves we seemed like grasshoppers, and so we seemed to them.'

A reading from the Letter of Paul to the Philippians. (2.12-28)

My belovèd, just as you have always obeyed me, not only in my presence, but much more now in my absence, work out your own salvation with fear and trembling; for it is God who is at work in you, enabling you both to will and to work for his good pleasure.

Do all things without murmuring and arguing, so that you may be blameless and innocent, children of God without blemish in the midst of a crooked and perverse generation, in which you shine like stars in the world. It is by your holding fast to the word of life that I can boast on the day of Christ that I did not run in vain or labour in vain. But even if I am being poured out as a libation over the sacrifice and the offering of your faith, I am glad and rejoice with all of you – and in the same way you also must be glad and rejoice with me.

I hope in the Lord Jesus to send Timothy to you soon, so that I may be cheered by news of you. I have no one like him who will be genuinely concerned for your welfare. All of them are seeking their own interests, not those of Jesus Christ. But Timothy's worth you know, how like a son with a father he has served with me in the work of the gospel. I hope therefore to send him as soon as I see how things go with me; and I trust in the Lord that I will also come soon.

Still, I think it necessary to send to you Epaphroditus – my brother and co-worker and fellow-soldier, your messenger and minister to my need; for he has been longing for all of you, and has been distressed because you heard that he was ill. He was indeed so ill that he nearly died. But God had mercy on him, and not only on him but on me also, so that I would not have one sorrow after another. I am the more eager to send him, therefore, in order that you may rejoice at seeing him again, and that I may be less anxious.

If a Eucharist:
Hear the gospel of our Lord Jesus Christ according to Luke. *(5.1-11)*

Once while Jesus was standing beside the lake of Gennesaret, and the crowd was pressing in on him to hear the word of God, he saw two boats there at the shore of the lake; the fishermen had gone out of them and were washing their nets. He got into one of the boats, the one belonging to Simon, and asked him to put out a little way from the shore. Then he sat down and taught the crowds from the boat. When he had finished speaking, he said to Simon, 'Put out into the deep water and let down your nets for a catch.' Simon answered, 'Master, we have worked all night long but have caught nothing. Yet if you say so, I will let down the nets.' When they had done this, they caught so many fish that their nets were beginning to break. So they signalled to their partners in the other boat to come and help them. And they came and filled both boats, so that they began to sink. But when Simon Peter saw it, he fell down at Jesus' knees, saying, 'Go away from me, Lord, for I am a sinful man!' For he and all who were with him were amazed at the catch of fish that they had taken; and so also were James and John, sons of Zebedee, who were partners with Simon. Then Jesus said to Simon, 'Do not be afraid; from now on you will be catching people.' When they had brought their boats to shore, they left everything and followed him.

This is the gospel of the Lord.

Third Service
Pss 2,3; Jeremiah 26.1-16; Acts 3.1-10

A reading from the prophecy of Jeremiah. (26.1-16)

At the beginning of the reign of King Jehoiakim son of Josiah of Judah, this word came from the Lord: Thus says the Lord: Stand in the court of the Lord's house, and speak to all the cities of Judah that come to worship in the house of the Lord; speak to them all the words that I command you; do not hold back a word. It may be that they will listen, all of them, and will turn from their evil way, that I may change my mind about the disaster that I intend to bring on them because of their evil doings. You shall say to them: Thus says the Lord: If you will not listen to me, to walk in my law that I have set before you, and to heed the words of my servants the prophets whom I send to you urgently – though you have not heeded – then I will make this house like Shiloh, and I will make this city a curse for all the nations of the earth.

The priests and the prophets and all the people heard Jeremiah speaking these words in the house of the Lord. And when Jeremiah had finished speaking all that the Lord had commanded him to speak to all the people, then the priests and the prophets and all the people laid hold of him, saying, 'You shall die! Why have you prophesied in the name of the Lord, saying, "This house shall be like Shiloh, and this city shall be desolate, without inhabitant"?' And all the people gathered around Jeremiah in the house of the Lord.

When the officials of Judah heard these things, they came up from the king's house to the house of the Lord and took their seat in the entry of the New Gate of the house of the Lord. Then the priests and the prophets said to the officials and to all the people, 'This man deserves the sentence of death because he has prophesied against this city, as you have heard with your own ears.'

Then Jeremiah spoke to all the officials and all the people, saying, 'It is the Lord who sent me to prophesy against this house and this city all the words you have heard. Now therefore amend your ways and your doings, and obey the voice of the Lord your God, and the Lord will change his mind about the disaster that he has pronounced against you. But as for me, here I am in your hands. Do with me as seems good and right to you. Only know for certain that if you put me to death, you will be bringing innocent blood upon yourselves and upon this city and its inhabitants, for in truth the Lord sent me to you to speak all these words in your ears.'

Then the officials and all the people said to the priests and the prophets, 'This man does not deserve the sentence of death, for he has spoken to us in the name of the Lord our God.'

A reading from the Acts of the Apostles. (3.1-10)

One day Peter and John were going up to the temple at the hour of prayer, at three o'clock in the afternoon. And a man lame from birth was being carried in. People would lay him daily at the gate of the temple called the Beautiful Gate so that he could ask for alms from those entering the temple. When he saw Peter and John about to go into the temple, he asked them for alms. Peter looked intently at him, as did John, and said, 'Look at us.' And he fixed his attention on them, expecting to receive something from them. But Peter said, 'I have no silver or gold, but what I have I give you; in the name of Jesus Christ of Nazareth, stand up and walk.' And he took him by the right hand and raised him up; and immediately his feet and ankles were made strong. Jumping up, he stood and began to walk, and he entered the temple with them, walking and leaping and praising God. All the people saw him walking and praising God, and they recognized him as the one who used to sit and ask for alms at the Beautiful Gate of the temple; and they were filled with wonder and amazement at what had happened to him.

Proper 2

Sunday between 10 and 16 February inclusive
(if earlier than the Second Sunday before Lent)

Principal Service
2 Kings 5.1-14; Ps 30; 1 Corinthians 9.24-27; Mark 1.40-45

A reading from the Second Book of the Kings. (5.1-14)

Naaman, commander of the army of the king of Aram, was a great man and in high favour with his master, because by him the Lord had given victory to Aram. The man, though a mighty warrior, suffered from leprosy. Now the Arameans on one of their raids had taken a young girl captive from the land of Israel, and she served

Naaman's wife. She said to her mistress, 'If only my lord were with the prophet who is in Samaria! He would cure him of his leprosy.' So Naaman went in and told his lord just what the girl from the land of Israel had said. And the king of Aram said, 'Go then, and I will send along a letter to the king of Israel.'

He went, taking with him ten talents of silver, six thousand shekels of gold, and ten sets of garments. He brought the letter to the king of Israel, which read, 'When this letter reaches you, know that I have sent to you my servant Naaman, that you may cure him of his leprosy.' When the king of Israel read the letter, he tore his clothes and said, 'Am I God, to give death or life, that this man sends word to me to cure a man of his leprosy? Just look and see how he is trying to pick a quarrel with me.'

But when Elisha the man of God heard that the king of Israel had torn his clothes, he sent a message to the king, 'Why have you torn your clothes? Let him come to me, that he may learn that there is a prophet in Israel.' So Naaman came with his horses and chariots, and halted at the entrance of Elisha's house. Elisha sent a messenger to him, saying, 'Go, wash in the Jordan seven times, and your flesh shall be restored and you shall be clean.' But Naaman became angry and went away, saying, 'I thought that for me he would surely come out, and stand and call on the name of the Lord his God, and would wave his hand over the spot, and cure the leprosy! Are not Abana and Pharpar, the rivers of Damascus, better than all the waters of Israel? Could I not wash in them, and be clean?' He turned and went away in a rage. But his servants approached and said to him, 'Father, if the prophet had commanded you to do something difficult, would you not have done it? How much more, when all he said to you was, "Wash, and be clean"?' So he went down and immersed himself seven times in the Jordan, according to the word of the man of God; his flesh was restored like the flesh of a young boy, and he was clean.

This is the word of the Lord.

A reading from the First Letter of Paul to the Corinthians. (9.24-27)

Do you not know that in a race the runners all compete, but only one receives the prize? Run in such a way that you may win it. Athletes exercise self-control in all things; they do it to receive a perishable garland, but we an imperishable one. So I do not run aimlessly, nor do I box as though beating the air; but I punish my body and enslave it, so that after proclaiming to others I myself should not be disqualified.

This is the word of the Lord.

Hear the gospel of our Lord Jesus Christ according to Mark. (1.40-45)

A leper came to Jesus begging him, and kneeling he said to him, 'If you choose, you can make me clean.' Moved with pity, Jesus stretched out his hand and touched him, and said to him, 'I do choose. Be made clean!' Immediately the leprosy left him, and he was made clean. After sternly warning him he sent him away at once, saying to him, 'See that you say nothing to anyone; but go, show yourself to the priest, and offer for your cleansing what Moses commanded, as a testimony to them.' But he went out and began to proclaim it freely, and to spread the word, so that Jesus could no longer go into a town openly, but stayed out in the country; and people came to him from every quarter.

This is the gospel of the Lord.

Second Service
Ps 6; Numbers 20.2-13; Philippians 3.7-21;
if a Eucharist: Luke 6.17-26

A reading from the book Numbers. (20.2-13)

In the wilderness of Zin there was no water for the congregation of Israel; so they gathered together against Moses and against Aaron. The people quarrelled with Moses and said, 'Would that we had died when our kindred died before the Lord! Why have you brought the assembly of the Lord into this wilderness for us and our livestock to die here? Why have you brought us up out of Egypt, to bring us to this wretched place? It is no place for grain, or figs, or vines, or pomegranates; and there is no water to drink.' Then Moses and Aaron went away from the assembly to the entrance of the tent of meeting; they fell on their faces, and the glory of the Lord appeared to them. The Lord spoke to Moses, saying: Take the staff, and assemble the congregation, you and your brother Aaron, and command the rock before their eyes to yield its water. Thus you shall bring water out of the rock for them; thus you shall provide drink for the congregation and their livestock.

So Moses took the staff from before the Lord, as he had commanded him. Moses and Aaron gathered the assembly together before the rock, and he said to them, 'Listen, you rebels, shall we bring water for you out of this rock?' Then Moses lifted up his hand and struck the rock twice with his staff; water came out abundantly, and the congregation and their livestock drank. But the Lord said to Moses and Aaron, 'Because you did not trust in me, to show my holiness before the eyes of the Israelites, therefore you shall not bring this assembly into the land that I have given them.' These are the waters of Meribah, where the people of Israel quarrelled with the Lord, and by which he showed his holiness.

A reading from the Letter of Paul to the Philippians. (3.7-21)

Whatever gains I had, these I have come to regard as loss because of Christ. More than that, I regard everything as loss because of the surpassing value of knowing Christ Jesus my Lord. For his sake I have suffered the loss of all things, and I regard them as rubbish, in order that I may gain Christ and be found in him, not having a righteousness of my own that comes from the law, but one that comes through faith in Christ, the righteousness from God based on faith. I want to know Christ and the power of his resurrection and the sharing of his sufferings by becoming like him in his death, if somehow I may attain the resurrection from the dead.

Not that I have already obtained this or have already reached the goal; but I press on to make it my own, because Christ Jesus has made me his own. Belovèd, I do not consider that I have made it my own; but this one thing I do: forgetting what lies behind and straining forward to what lies ahead, I press on towards the goal for the prize of the heavenly call of God in Christ Jesus. Let those of us then who are mature be of the same mind; and if you think differently about anything, this too God will reveal to you. Only let us hold fast to what we have attained.

Brothers and sisters, join in imitating me, and observe those who live according to the example you have in us. For many live as enemies of the cross of Christ; I have often told you of them, and now I tell you even with tears. Their end is destruction; their god is the belly; and their glory is in their shame; their minds are set on earthly things. But our citizenship is in heaven, and it is from there that we are expecting a Saviour, the Lord Jesus Christ. He will transform the body of our humiliation so that it may be conformed to the body of his glory, by the power that also enables him to make all things subject to himself.

If a Eucharist:
Hear the gospel of our Lord Jesus Christ according to Luke. (6.17-26)

Jesus came down with his apostles and stood on a level place, with a great crowd of his disciples and a great multitude of people from all Judea, Jerusalem, and the coast of Tyre and Sidon. They had come to hear him and to be healed of their diseases; and those who were troubled with unclean spirits were cured. And all in the crowd were trying to touch him, for power came out from him and healed all of them.

Then he looked up at his disciples and said:

'Blessèd are you who are poor,
    for yours is the kingdom of God.
'Blessèd are you who are hungry now,
    for you will be filled.
'Blessèd are you who weep now,
    for you will laugh.

'Blessèd are you when people hate you, and when they exclude you, revile you, and defame you on account of the Son of Man. Rejoice on that day and leap for joy, for surely your reward is great in heaven; for that is what their ancestors did to the prophets.

'But woe to you who are rich,
    for you have received your consolation.
'Woe to you who are full now,
    for you will be hungry.
'Woe to you who are laughing now,
    for you will mourn and weep.

'Woe to you when all speak well of you, for that is what their ancestors did to the false prophets.'

This is the gospel of the Lord.

Third Service
Ps 7; Jeremiah 30.1-3,10-22; Acts 6

A reading from the prophecy of Jeremiah. (30.1-3,10-22)

The word that came to Jeremiah from the Lord: Thus says the Lord, the God of Israel: Write in a book all the words that I have spoken to you. For the days are surely coming, says the Lord, when I will restore the fortunes of my people, Israel and Judah, says the Lord, and I will bring them back to the land that I gave to their ancestors and they shall take possession of it.

[10] Have no fear, my servant Jacob, says the Lord,
    and do not be dismayed, O Israel;
for I am going to save you from far away,
    and your offspring from the land of their captivity.
Jacob shall return and have quiet and ease,
    and no one shall make him afraid.
For I am with you, says the Lord, to save you;
    I will make an end of all the nations

among which I scattered you,
but of you I will not make an end.
I will chastise you in just measure,
and I will by no means leave you unpunished.
For thus says the Lord:
Your hurt is incurable, your wound is grievous.
There is no one to uphold your cause,
no medicine for your wound, no healing for you.
All your lovers have forgotten you; they care nothing for you;
for I have dealt you the blow of an enemy,
the punishment of a merciless foe,
because your guilt is great, because your sins are so numerous.
Why do you cry out over your hurt? Your pain is incurable.
Because your guilt is great, because your sins are so numerous,
I have done these things to you.
Therefore all who devour you shall be devoured,
and all your foes, every one of them,
shall go into captivity;
those who plunder you shall be plundered,
and all who prey on you I will make a prey.
For I will restore health to you,
and your wounds I will heal, says the Lord,
because they have called you an outcast:
'It is Zion; no one cares for her!'
Thus says the Lord:
I am going to restore the fortunes of the tents of Jacob,
and have compassion on his dwellings;
the city shall be rebuilt upon its mound,
and the citadel set on its rightful site.
Out of them shall come thanksgiving,
and the sound of merrymakers.
I will make them many, and they shall not be few;
I will make them honoured, and they shall not be disdained.
Their children shall be as of old,
their congregation shall be established before me;
and I will punish all who oppress them.
Their prince shall be one of their own,
their ruler shall come from their midst;
I will bring him near, and he shall approach me,
for who would otherwise dare to approach me?
says the Lord.
And you shall be my people, and I will be your God.

A reading from the Acts of the Apostles. (Chapter 6)

During the days when the disciples were increasing in number, the Hellenists complained against the Hebrews because their widows were being neglected in the daily distribution of food. And the twelve called together the whole community of the disciples and said, 'It is not right that we should neglect the word of God in order to wait at tables. Therefore, friends, select from among yourselves seven men of good standing, full of the Spirit and of wisdom, whom we may appoint to this task, while we, for our part, will devote ourselves to prayer and to serving the word.' What they said pleased the whole community, and they chose Stephen, a man full of faith and the Holy Spirit, together with Philip, Prochorus, Nicanor, Timon, Parmenas, and Nicolaus, a proselyte of Antioch. They had these men stand before the apostles, who prayed and laid their hands on them.

The word of God continued to spread; the number of the disciples increased greatly in Jerusalem, and a great many of the priests became obedient to the faith.

Stephen, full of grace and power, did great wonders and signs among the people. Then some of those who belonged to the synagogue of the Freedmen (as it was called), Cyrenians, Alexandrians, and others of those from Cilicia and Asia, stood up and argued with Stephen. But they could not withstand the wisdom and the Spirit with which he spoke. Then they secretly instigated some men to say, 'We have heard him speak blasphemous words against Moses and God.' They stirred up the people as well as the elders and the scribes; then they suddenly confronted him, seized him, and brought him before the council. They set up false witnesses who said, 'This man never stops saying things against this holy place and the law; for we have heard him say that this Jesus of Nazareth will destroy this place and will change the customs that Moses handed on to us.' And all who sat in the council looked intently at him, and they saw that his face was like the face of an angel.

Proper 3

*Sunday between 17 and 23 February inclusive
(if earlier than the Second Sunday before Lent)*

Principal Service

Isaiah 43.18-25; Ps 41; 2 Corinthians 1.18-22; Mark 2.1-12

A reading from the prophecy of Isaiah. (43.18-25)

Do not remember the former things,
    or consider the things of old.
I am about to do a new thing;
    now it springs forth, do you not perceive it?
I will make a way in the wilderness
    and rivers in the desert.
The wild animals will honour me,
    the jackals and the ostriches;
for I give water in the wilderness,
    rivers in the desert,
to give drink to my chosen people,
    the people whom I formed for myself
so that they might declare my praise.

Yet you did not call upon me, O Jacob;
    but you have been weary of me, O Israel!
You have not brought me your sheep for burnt-offerings,
    or honoured me with your sacrifices.
I have not burdened you with offerings,
    or wearied you with frankincense.
You have not bought me sweet cane with money,
    or satisfied me with the fat of your sacrifices.
But you have burdened me with your sins;
    you have wearied me with your iniquities.
I, I am He
    who blots out your transgressions for my own sake,
    and I will not remember your sins.

This is the word of the Lord.

A reading from the Second Letter of Paul to the Corinthians. (1.18-22)

As surely as God is faithful, our word to you has not been 'Yes and
No.' For the Son of God, Jesus Christ, whom we proclaimed among
you, Silvanus and Timothy and I, was not 'Yes and No'; but in him it
is always 'Yes.' For in him every one of God's promises is a 'Yes.'

For this reason it is through him that we say the 'Amen', to the glory of God. But it is God who establishes us with you in Christ and has anointed us, by putting his seal on us and giving us his Spirit in our hearts as a first instalment.

This is the word of the Lord.

Hear the gospel of our Lord Jesus Christ according to Mark. (2.1-12)

When Jesus returned to Capernaum after some days, it was reported that he was at home. So many gathered around that there was no longer room for them, not even in front of the door; and he was speaking the word to them. Then some people came, bringing to him a paralysed man, carried by four of them. And when they could not bring him to Jesus because of the crowd, they removed the roof above him; and after having dug through it, they let down the mat on which the paralytic lay. When Jesus saw their faith, he said to the paralytic, 'Son, your sins are forgiven.' Now some of the scribes were sitting there, questioning in their hearts, 'Why does this fellow speak in this way? It is blasphemy! Who can forgive sins but God alone?' At once Jesus perceived in his spirit that they were discussing these questions among themselves; and he said to them, 'Why do you raise such questions in your hearts? Which is easier, to say to the paralytic, "Your sins are forgiven", or to say, "Stand up and take your mat and walk"? But so that you may know that the Son of Man has authority on earth to forgive sins' – he said to the paralytic – 'I say to you, stand up, take your mat and go to your home.' And he stood up, and immediately took the mat and went out before all of them; so that they were all amazed and glorified God, saying, 'We have never seen anything like this!'

This is the gospel of the Lord.

Second Service
Ps 10; Numbers 22.21 - 23.12; Philippians 4.10-20;
if a Eucharist: Luke 6.27-38

A reading from the book Numbers. (22.21 - 23.12)

Balaam got up in the morning, saddled his donkey, and went with the officials of Moab.

God's anger was kindled because he was going, and the angel of the Lord took his stand in the road as his adversary. Now he was riding on the donkey, and his two servants were with him. The donkey saw the angel of the Lord standing in the road, with a drawn sword in his hand; so the donkey turned off the road, and went into the field; and

Balaam struck the donkey, to turn it back on to the road. Then the angel of the Lord stood in a narrow path between the vineyards, with a wall on either side. When the donkey saw the angel of the Lord, it scraped against the wall, and scraped Balaam's foot against the wall; so he struck it again. Then the angel of the Lord went ahead, and stood in a narrow place, where there was no way to turn either to the right or to the left. When the donkey saw the angel of the Lord, it lay down under Balaam; and Balaam's anger was kindled, and he struck the donkey with his staff. Then the Lord opened the mouth of the donkey, and it said to Balaam, 'What have I done to you, that you have struck me these three times?' Balaam said to the donkey, 'Because you have made a fool of me! I wish I had a sword in my hand! I would kill you right now!' But the donkey said to Balaam, 'Am I not your donkey, which you have ridden all your life to this day? Have I been in the habit of treating you in this way?' And he said, 'No.'

Then the Lord opened the eyes of Balaam, and he saw the angel of the Lord standing in the road, with his drawn sword in his hand; and he bowed down, falling on his face. The angel of the Lord said to him, 'Why have you struck your donkey these three times? I have come out as an adversary, because your way is perverse before me. The donkey saw me, and turned away from me these three times. If it had not turned away from me, surely I would by now have killed you and let it live.' Then Balaam said to the angel of the Lord, 'I have sinned, for I did not know that you were standing in the road to oppose me. Now therefore, if it is displeasing to you, I will return home.' The angel of the Lord said to Balaam, 'Go with the men; but speak only what I tell you to speak.' So Balaam went on with the officials of Balak.

When Balak heard that Balaam had come, he went out to meet him at Ir-moab, on the boundary formed by the Arnon, at the farthest point of the boundary. Balak said to Balaam, 'Did I not send to summon you? Why did you not come to me? Am I not able to honour you?' Balaam said to Balak, 'I have come to you now, but do I have power to say just anything? The word God puts in my mouth, that is what I must say.' Then Balaam went with Balak, and they came to Kiriath-huzoth. Balak sacrificed oxen and sheep, and sent them to Balaam and to the officials who were with him.

On the next day Balak took Balaam and brought him up to Bamoth-baal; and from there he could see part of the people of Israel. Then Balaam said to Balak, 'Build me seven altars here, and prepare seven bulls and seven rams for me.' Balak did as Balaam had said; and

Balak and Balaam offered a bull and a ram on each altar. Then Balaam said to Balak, 'Stay here beside your burnt-offerings while I go aside. Perhaps the Lord will come to meet me. Whatever he shows me I will tell you.' And he went to a bare height.

Then God met Balaam; and Balaam said to him, 'I have arranged the seven altars, and have offered a bull and a ram on each altar.' The Lord put a word in Balaam's mouth, and said, 'Return to Balak, and this is what you must say.' So he returned to Balak, who was standing beside his burnt-offerings with all the officials of Moab. Then Balaam uttered his oracle, saying:

'Balak has brought me from Aram,
    the king of Moab from the eastern mountains:
"Come, curse Jacob for me;
    Come, denounce Israel!"
How can I curse whom God has not cursed?
    How can I denounce those
       whom the Lord has not denounced?
For from the top of the crags I see him,
    from the hills I behold him;
Here is a people living alone,
    and not reckoning itself among the nations!
Who can count the dust of Jacob,
    or number the dust-cloud of Israel?
Let me die the death of the upright,
    and let my end be like his!'

Then Balak said to Balaam, 'What have you done to me? I brought you to curse my enemies, but now you have done nothing but bless them.' He answered, 'Must I not take care to say what the Lord puts into my mouth?'

A reading from the Letter of Paul to the Philippians. (4.10-20)

I rejoice in the Lord greatly that now at last you have revived your concern for me; indeed, you were concerned for me, but had no opportunity to show it. Not that I am referring to being in need; for I have learned to be content with whatever I have. I know what it is to have little, and I know what it is to have plenty. In any and all circumstances I have learned the secret of being well-fed and of going hungry, of having plenty and of being in need. I can do all things through him who strengthens me. In any case, it was kind of you to share my distress.

You Philippians indeed know that in the early days of the gospel, when I left Macedonia, no church shared with me in the matter of giving and receiving, except you alone. For even when I was in Thessalonica, you sent me help for my needs more than once. Not that I seek the gift, but I seek the profit that accumulates to your account. I have been paid in full and have more than enough; I am fully satisfied, now that I have received from Epaphroditus the gifts you sent, a fragrant offering, a sacrifice acceptable and pleasing to God. And my God will fully satisfy every need of yours according to his riches in glory in Christ Jesus. To our God and Father be glory for ever and ever. Amen.

If a Eucharist:
***Hear the gospel of our Lord Jesus Christ according to Luke.** (6.27-38)*

Jesus said to his disciples, 'I say to you that listen, Love your enemies, do good to those who hate you, bless those who curse you, pray for those who abuse you. If anyone strikes you on the cheek, offer the other also; and from anyone who takes away your coat do not withhold even your shirt. Give to everyone who begs from you; and if anyone takes away your goods, do not ask for them again. Do to others as you would have them do to you.

'If you love those who love you, what credit is that to you? For even sinners love those who love them. If you do good to those who do good to you, what credit is that to you? For even sinners do the same. If you lend to those from whom you hope to receive, what credit is that to you? Even sinners lend to sinners, to receive as much again. But love your enemies, do good, and lend, expecting nothing in return. Your reward will be great, and you will be children of the Most High; for he is kind to the ungrateful and the wicked. Be merciful, just as your Father is merciful.

'Do not judge, and you will not be judged; do not condemn, and you will not be condemned. Forgive, and you will be forgiven; give, and it will be given to you. A good measure, pressed down, shaken together, running over, will be put into your lap; for the measure you give will be the measure you get back.'

This is the gospel of the Lord.

Third Service
Ps 9; Jeremiah 33.1-11; Acts 8.4-25

A reading from the prophecy of Jeremiah. (33.1-11)

The word of the Lord came to Jeremiah a second time, while he was still confined in the court of the guard: Thus says the Lord who made the earth, the Lord who formed it to establish it – the Lord is his name: Call to me and I will answer you, and will tell you great and hidden things that you have not known. For thus says the Lord, the God of Israel, concerning the houses of this city and the houses of the kings of Judah that were torn down to make a defence against the siege-ramps and before the sword: The Chaldeans are coming in to fight and to fill them with the dead bodies of those whom I shall strike down in my anger and my wrath, for I have hidden my face from this city because of all their wickedness. I am going to bring it recovery and healing; I will heal them and reveal to them abundance of prosperity and security. I will restore the fortunes of Judah and the fortunes of Israel, and rebuild them as they were at first. I will cleanse them from all the guilt of their sin against me, and I will forgive all the guilt of their sin and rebellion against me. And this city shall be to me a name of joy, a praise and a glory before all the nations of the earth who shall hear of all the good that I do for them; they shall fear and tremble because of all the good and all the prosperity I provide for it.

Thus says the Lord: In this place of which you say, 'It is a waste without human beings or animals', in the towns of Judah and the streets of Jerusalem that are desolate, without inhabitants, human or animal, there shall once more be heard the voice of mirth and the voice of gladness, the voice of the bridegroom and the voice of the bride, the voices of those who sing, as they bring thank-offerings to the house of the Lord:

'Give thanks to the Lord of hosts,
　　for the Lord is good,
　for his steadfast love endures for ever!'
For I will restore the fortunes of the land as at first, says the Lord.

A reading from the Acts of the Apostles. (8.4-25)

Those disciples who were scattered went from place to place, proclaiming the word. Philip went down to the city of Samaria and proclaimed the Messiah to them. The crowds with one accord listened eagerly to what was said by Philip, hearing and seeing the signs that he did, for unclean spirits, crying with loud shrieks, came out of many who were possessed; and many others who were paralysed or lame were cured. So there was great joy in that city.

Now a certain man named Simon had previously practised magic in the city and amazed the people of Samaria, saying that he was someone great. All of them, from the least to the greatest, listened to him eagerly, saying, 'This man is the power of God that is called Great.' And they listened eagerly to him because for a long time he had amazed them with his magic. But when they believed Philip, who was proclaiming the good news about the kingdom of God and the name of Jesus Christ, they were baptized, both men and women. Even Simon himself believed. After being baptized, he stayed constantly with Philip and was amazed when he saw the signs and great miracles that took place.

Now when the apostles at Jerusalem heard that Samaria had accepted the word of God, they sent Peter and John to them. The two went down and prayed for them that they might receive the Holy Spirit (for as yet the Spirit had not come upon any of them; they had only been baptized in the name of the Lord Jesus). Then Peter and John laid their hands on them, and they received the Holy Spirit. Now when Simon saw that the Spirit was given through the laying on of the apostles' hands, he offered them money, saying, 'Give me also this power so that anyone on whom I lay my hands may receive the Holy Spirit.' But Peter said to him, 'May your silver perish with you, because you thought you could obtain God's gift with money! You have no part or share in this, for your heart is not right before God. Repent therefore of this wickedness of yours, and pray to the Lord that, if possible, the intent of your heart may be forgiven you. For I see that you are in the gall of bitterness and the chains of wickedness.' Simon answered, 'Pray for me to the Lord, that nothing of what you have said may happen to me.'

Now after Peter and John had testified and spoken the word of the Lord, they returned to Jerusalem, proclaiming the good news to many villages of the Samaritans.

The Second Sunday before Lent

Principal Service
Proverbs 8.1,22-31; Ps 104.24-35; Colossians 1.15-20; John 1.1-14

A reading from the book Proverbs. (8.1,22-31)

Does not wisdom call,
    and does not understanding raise her voice?

²² The Lord created me at the beginning of his work,
    the first of his acts of long ago.
Ages ago I was set up,
    at the first, before the beginning of the earth.
When there were no depths I was brought forth,
    when there were no springs abounding with water.
Before the mountains had been shaped,
    before the hills, I was brought forth –
when he had not yet made earth and fields,
    or the world's first bits of soil.
When he established the heavens, I was there,
    when he drew a circle on the face of the deep,
when he made firm the skies above,
    when he established the fountains of the deep,
when he assigned to the sea its limit,
    so that the waters might not transgress his command,
when he marked out the foundations of the earth,
    then I was beside him, like a master worker;
and I was daily his delight,
    rejoicing before him always,
rejoicing in his inhabited world
    and delighting in the human race.

This is the word of the Lord.

A reading from the Letter of Paul to the Colossians. (1.15-20)

Christ Jesus is the image of the invisible God, the firstborn of all creation; for in him all things in heaven and on earth were created, things visible and invisible, whether thrones or dominions or rulers or powers – all things have been created through him and for him. He himself is before all things, and in him all things hold together. He is the head of the body, the church; he is the beginning, the firstborn from the dead, so that he might come to have first place in everything. For in him all the fullness of God was pleased to dwell, and through him God was pleased to reconcile to himself all things, whether on earth or in heaven, by making peace through the blood of his cross.

This is the word of the Lord.

Hear the gospel of our Lord Jesus Christ according to John. (1.1-14)

In the beginning was the Word, and the Word was with God, and the Word was God. He was in the beginning with God. All things came into being through him, and without him not one thing came into being. What has come into being in him was life, and the life was the light of all people. The light shines in the darkness, and the darkness did not overcome it.

There was a man sent from God, whose name was John. He came as a witness to testify to the light, so that all might believe through him. He himself was not the light, but he came to testify to the light. The true light, which enlightens everyone, was coming into the world.

He was in the world, and the world came into being through him; yet the world did not know him. He came to what was his own, and his own people did not accept him. But to all who received him, who believed in his name, he gave power to become children of God, who were born, not of blood or of the will of the flesh or of the will of man, but of God.

And the Word became flesh and lived among us, and we have seen his glory, the glory as of a father's only son, full of grace and truth.

This is the gospel of the Lord.

Second Service
Ps 65; Genesis 2.4b-25; Luke 8.22-35

A reading from the book Genesis. (2.4b-25)

In the day that the Lord God made the earth and the heavens, when no plant of the field was yet in the earth and no herb of the field had yet sprung up – for the Lord God had not caused it to rain upon the earth, and there was no one to till the ground; but a stream would rise from the earth, and water the whole face of the ground – then the Lord God formed man from the dust of the ground, and breathed into his nostrils the breath of life; and the man became a living being. And the Lord God planted a garden in Eden, in the east; and there he put the man whom he had formed. Out of the ground the Lord God made to grow every tree that is pleasant to the sight and good for food, the tree of life also in the midst of the garden, and the tree of the knowledge of good and evil.

A river flows out of Eden to water the garden, and from there it divides and becomes four branches. The name of the first is Pishon; it is the one that flows around the whole land of Havilah, where there is gold; and the gold of that land is good; bdellium and onyx stone are there. The name of the second river is Gihon; it is the one that flows around the whole land of Cush. The name of the third river is Tigris, which flows east of Assyria. And the fourth river is the Euphrates.

The Lord God took the man and put him in the garden of Eden to till it and keep it. And the Lord God commanded the man, 'You may freely eat of every tree of the garden; but of the tree of the knowledge of good and evil you shall not eat, for in the day that you eat of it you shall die.'

Then the Lord God said, 'It is not good that the man should be alone; I will make him a helper as his partner.' So out of the ground the Lord God formed every animal of the field and every bird of the air, and brought them to the man to see what he would call them; and whatever the man called each living creature, that was its name. The man gave names to all cattle, and to the birds of the air, and to every animal of the field; but for the man there was not found a helper as his partner. So the Lord God caused a deep sleep to fall upon the man, and he slept; then he took one of his ribs and closed up its place with flesh. And the rib that the Lord God had taken from the man he made into a woman and brought her to the man. Then the man said,

'This at last is bone of my bones
    and flesh of my flesh;
this one shall be called Woman,
    for out of Man this one was taken.'

Therefore a man leaves his father and his mother and clings to his wife, and they become one flesh. And the man and his wife were both naked, and were not ashamed.

A reading from the gospel according to Luke. (8.22-35)

One day Jesus got into a boat with his disciples, and he said to them, 'Let us go across to the other side of the lake.' So they put out, and while they were sailing he fell asleep. A gale swept down on the lake, and the boat was filling with water, and they were in danger. They went to him and woke him up, shouting, 'Master, Master, we are perishing!' And he woke up and rebuked the wind and the raging waves; they ceased, and there was a calm. He said to them, 'Where is your faith?' They were afraid and amazed, and said to one another, 'Who then is this, that he commands even the winds and the water, and they obey him?'

Then they arrived at the country of the Gerasenes, which is opposite Galilee. As he stepped out on land, a man of the city who had demons met him. For a long time he had worn no clothes, and he did not live in a house but in the tombs. When he saw Jesus, he fell down before him and shouted at the top of his voice, 'What have you to do with me, Jesus, Son of the Most High God? I beg you, do not torment me' – for Jesus had commanded the unclean spirit to come out of the man (for many times it had seized him; he was kept under guard and bound with chains and shackles, but he would break the bonds and be driven by the demon into the wilds). Jesus then asked him, 'What is your name?' He said, 'Legion'; for many demons had entered him. They begged him not to order them to go back into the abyss.

Now there on the hillside a large herd of swine was feeding; and the demons begged Jesus to let them enter these. So he gave them permission. Then the demons came out of the man and entered the swine, and the herd rushed down the steep bank into the lake and was drowned.

When the swineherds saw what had happened, they ran off and told it in the city and in the country. Then people came out to see what had happened, and when they came to Jesus, they found the man from whom the demons had gone sitting at the feet of Jesus, clothed and in his right mind. And they were afraid.

Third Service
Pss 29,67; Deuteronomy 8.1-10; Matthew 6.25-34

A reading from the book Deuteronomy. (8.1-10)

Moses said to all Israel: This entire commandment that I command you today you must diligently observe, so that you may live and increase, and go in and occupy the land that the Lord promised on oath to your ancestors. Remember the long way that the Lord your God has led you these forty years in the wilderness, in order to humble you, testing you to know what was in your heart, whether or not you would keep his commandments. He humbled you by letting you hunger, then by feeding you with manna, with which neither you nor your ancestors were acquainted, in order to make you understand that one does not live by bread alone, but by every word that comes from the mouth of the Lord. The clothes on your back did not wear out and your feet did not swell these forty years. Know then in your heart that as a parent disciplines a child so the Lord your

God disciplines you. Therefore keep the commandments of the Lord your God, by walking in his ways and by fearing him. For the Lord your God is bringing you into a good land, a land with flowing streams, with springs and underground waters welling up in valleys and hills, a land of wheat and barley, of vines and fig trees and pome-granates, a land of olive trees and honey, a land where you may eat bread without scarcity, where you will lack nothing, a land whose stones are iron and from whose hills you may mine copper. You shall eat your fill and bless the Lord your God for the good land that he has given you.

A reading from the gospel according to Matthew. (6.25-34)

Jesus said to the crowd, 'I tell you, do not worry about your life, what you will eat or what you will drink, or about your body, what you will wear. Is not life more than food, and the body more than cloth-ing? Look at the birds of the air; they neither sow nor reap nor gath-er into barns, and yet your heavenly Father feeds them. Are you not of more value than they? And can any of you by worrying add a sin-gle hour to your span of life? And why do you worry about cloth-ing? Consider the lilies of the field, how they grow; they neither toil nor spin, yet I tell you, even Solomon in all his glory was not clothed like one of these. But if God so clothes the grass of the field, which is alive today and tomorrow is thrown into the oven, will he not much more clothe you – you of little faith? Therefore do not worry, saying, "What will we eat?" or "What will we drink?" or "What will we wear?" For it is the Gentiles who strive for all these things; and indeed your heavenly Father knows that you need all these things. But strive first for the kingdom of God and his righteousness, and all these things will be given to you as well.

'So do not worry about tomorrow, for tomorrow will bring worries of its own. Today's trouble is enough for today.'

The Sunday next before Lent

Principal Service
2 Kings 2.1-12; Ps 50.1-6; 2 Corinthians 4.3-6; Mark 9.2-9

A reading from the Second Book of the Kings. (2.1-12)

Now when the Lord was about to take Elijah up to heaven by a whirl-wind, Elijah and Elisha were on their way from Gilgal. Elijah said to Elisha, 'Stay here; for the Lord has sent me as far as Bethel.' But Elisha said, 'As the Lord lives, and as you yourself live, I will not leave you.' So they went down to Bethel. The company of prophets who were in Bethel came out to Elisha, and said to him, 'Do you know that today the Lord will take your master away from you?' And he said, 'Yes, I know; keep silent.'

Elijah said to him, 'Elisha, stay here; for the Lord has sent me to Jeri-cho.' But he said, 'As the Lord lives, and as you yourself live, I will not leave you.' So they came to Jericho. The company of prophets who were at Jericho drew near to Elisha, and said to him, 'Do you know that today the Lord will take your master away from you?' And he answered, 'Yes, I know; be silent.'

Then Elijah said to him, 'Stay here; for the Lord has sent me to the Jordan.' But he said, 'As the Lord lives, and as you yourself live, I will not leave you.' So the two of them went on. Fifty men of the company of prophets also went, and stood at some distance from them, as they both were standing by the Jordan. Then Elijah took his mantle and rolled it up, and struck the water; the water was parted to the one side and to the other, until the two of them crossed on dry ground.

When they had crossed, Elijah said to Elisha, 'Tell me what I may do for you, before I am taken from you.' Elisha said, 'Please let me inherit a double share of your spirit.' He responded, 'You have asked a hard thing; yet, if you see me as I am being taken from you, it will be granted you; if not, it will not.' As they continued walking and talking, a chariot of fire and horses of fire separated the two of them, and Elijah ascended in a whirlwind into heaven. Elisha kept watch-ing and crying out, 'Father, father! The chariots of Israel and its horsemen!' But when he could no longer see him, he grasped his own clothes and tore them in two pieces.

This is the word of the Lord.

A reading from the Second Letter of Paul to the Corinthians. (4.3-6)

Even if our gospel is veiled, it is veiled to those who are perishing. In their case the god of this world has blinded the minds of the unbelievers, to keep them from seeing the light of the gospel of the glory of Christ, who is the image of God. For we do not proclaim ourselves; we proclaim Jesus Christ as Lord and ourselves as your slaves for Jesus' sake. For it is the God who said, 'Let light shine out of darkness', who has shone in our hearts to give the light of the knowledge of the glory of God in the face of Jesus Christ.

This is the word of the Lord.

Hear the gospel of our Lord Jesus Christ according to Mark. (9.2-9)

Jesus took with him Peter and James and John, and led them up a high mountain apart, by themselves. And he was transfigured before them, and his clothes became dazzling white, such as no one on earth could bleach them. And there appeared to them Elijah with Moses, who were talking with Jesus. Then Peter said to Jesus, 'Rabbi, it is good for us to be here; let us make three dwellings, one for you, one for Moses, and one for Elijah.' He did not know what to say, for they were terrified. Then a cloud overshadowed them, and from the cloud there came a voice, 'This is my Son, the Belovèd; listen to him!' Suddenly when they looked around, they saw no one with them any more, but only Jesus.

  As they were coming down the mountain, he ordered them to tell no one about what they had seen, until after the Son of Man had risen from the dead.

This is the gospel of the Lord.

Second Service
Pss 2 [99]; 1 Kings 19.1-16; 2 Peter 1.16-21;
if a Eucharist: Mark 9.[2-8]9-13

A reading from the First Book of the Kings. (19.1-16)

Ahab told Jezebel all that Elijah had done, and how he had killed all the prophets with the sword. Then Jezebel sent a messenger to Elijah, saying, 'So may the gods do to me, and more also, if I do not make your life like the life of one of them by this time tomorrow.' Then he was afraid; he got up and fled for his life, and came to Beersheba, which belongs to Judah; he left his servant there.

  But he himself went a day's journey into the wilderness, and came and sat down under a solitary broom tree. He asked that he might die: 'It is enough; now, O Lord, take away my life, for I am no better than my ancestors.' Then he lay down under the broom tree and fell asleep. Suddenly an angel touched him and said to him, 'Get up and eat.' He looked, and there at his head was a cake baked on hot stones, and a jar of water. He ate and drank, and lay down again. The angel of the Lord came a second time, touched him, and said, 'Get up and eat, otherwise the journey will be too much for you.' He got up, and ate and drank; then he went in the strength of that food for forty days and forty nights to Horeb the mount of God. At that place he came to a cave, and spent the night there.

Then the word of the Lord came to him, saying, 'What are you doing here, Elijah?' He answered, 'I have been very zealous for the Lord, the God of hosts; for the Israelites have forsaken your covenant, thrown down your altars, and killed your prophets with the sword. I alone am left, and they are seeking my life, to take it away.'

He said, 'Go out and stand on the mountain before the Lord, for the Lord is about to pass by.' Now there was a great wind, so strong that it was splitting mountains and breaking rocks in pieces before the Lord, but the Lord was not in the wind; and after the wind an earthquake, but the Lord was not in the earthquake; and after the earthquake a fire, but the Lord was not in the fire; and after the fire a sound of sheer silence.

When Elijah heard it, he wrapped his face in his mantle and went out and stood at the entrance of the cave. Then there came a voice to him that said, 'What are you doing here, Elijah?' He answered, 'I have been very zealous for the Lord, the God of hosts; for the Israelites have forsaken your covenant, thrown down your altars, and killed your prophets with the sword. I alone am left, and they are seeking my life, to take it away.' Then the Lord said to him, 'Go, return on your way to the wilderness of Damascus; when you arrive, you shall anoint Hazael as king over Aram. Also you shall anoint Jehu son of Nimshi as king over Israel; and you shall anoint Elisha son of Shaphat of Abel-meholah as prophet in your place.

A reading from the Second Letter of Peter. (1.16-21)

We did not follow cleverly devised myths when we made known to you the power and coming of our Lord Jesus Christ, but we had been eyewitnesses of his majesty. For he received honour and glory from God the Father when that voice was conveyed to him by the Majestic Glory, saying, 'This is my Son, my Belovèd, with whom I am well pleased.' We ourselves heard this voice come from heaven, while we were with him on the holy mountain.

So we have the prophetic message more fully confirmed. You will do well to be attentive to this as to a lamp shining in a dark place, until the day dawns and the morning star rises in your hearts. First of all you must understand this, that no prophecy of scripture is a matter of one's own interpretation, because no prophecy ever came by human will, but men and women moved by the Holy Spirit spoke from God.

If a Eucharist:
Hear the gospel of our Lord Jesus Christ according to Mark.

(9.[2-8] 9-13)

[Jesus took with him Peter and James and John, and led them up a high mountain apart, by themselves. And he was transfigured before them, and his clothes became dazzling white, such as no one on earth could bleach them. And there appeared to them Elijah with Moses, who were talking with Jesus. Then Peter said to Jesus, 'Rabbi, it is good for us to be here; let us make three dwellings, one for you, one for Moses, and one for Elijah.' He did not know what to say, for they were terrified. Then a cloud overshadowed them, and from the cloud there came a voice, 'This is my Son, the Belovèd; listen to him!' Suddenly when they looked around, they saw no one with them any more, but only Jesus.]

⁹ As they were coming down the mountain, Jesus ordered Peter, James and John to tell no one about what they had seen, until after the Son of Man had risen from the dead. So they kept the matter to themselves, questioning what this rising from the dead could mean. Then they asked him, 'Why do the scribes say that Elijah must come first?' He said to them, 'Elijah is indeed coming first to restore all things. How then is it written about the Son of Man, that he is to go through many sufferings and be treated with contempt? But I tell you that Elijah has come, and they did to him whatever they pleased, as it is written about him.'

This is the gospel of the Lord.

Third Service
Pss 27,150; Exodus 24.12-18; 2 Corinthians 3.12-18

A reading from the Book of the Exodus. (24.12-18)

The Lord said to Moses, 'Come up to me on the mountain, and wait there; and I will give you the tablets of stone, with the law and the commandment, which I have written for their instruction.' So Moses set out with his assistant Joshua, and Moses went up into the mountain of God. To the elders he had said, 'Wait here for us, until we come to you again; for Aaron and Hur are with you; whoever has a dispute may go to them.'

Then Moses went up on the mountain, and the cloud covered the mountain. The glory of the Lord settled on Mount Sinai, and the cloud covered it for six days; on the seventh day he called to Moses out of the cloud. Now the appearance of the glory of the Lord was like a devouring fire on the top of the mountain in the sight of the people of Israel. Moses entered the cloud, and went up on the mountain. Moses was on the mountain for forty days and forty nights.

A reading from the Second Letter of Paul to the Corinthians. (3.12-18)

Since, then, we have such a hope, we act with great boldness, not like Moses, who put a veil over his face to keep the people of Israel from gazing at the end of the glory that was being set aside. But their minds were hardened. Indeed, to this very day, when they hear the reading of the old covenant, that same veil is still there, since only in Christ is it set aside. Indeed, to this very day whenever Moses is read, a veil lies over their minds; but when one turns to the Lord, the veil is removed. Now the Lord is the Spirit, and where the Spirit of the Lord is, there is freedom. And all of us, with unveiled faces, seeing the glory of the Lord as though reflected in a mirror, are being transformed into the same image from one degree of glory to another; for this comes from the Lord, the Spirit.

Lent

Ash Wednesday

Principal Service
Joel 2.1-2,12-17 *or* Isaiah 58.1-12; Ps 51. 1-17; 2 Corinthians 5.20*b* - 6.10;
Matthew 6.1-6,16-21 *or* John 8.1-11

A reading from the prophecy of Joel. (2.1-2,12-17)

Blow the trumpet in Zion;
  sound the alarm on my holy mountain!
Let all the inhabitants of the land tremble,
  for the day of the Lord is coming, it is near –
a day of darkness and gloom,
  a day of clouds and thick darkness!
Like blackness spread upon the mountains
  a great and powerful army comes;
their like has never been from of old,
  nor will be again after them in ages to come.

[12] Yet even now, says the Lord,
  return to me with all your heart,
with fasting, with weeping, and with mourning;
  rend your hearts and not your clothing.
Return to the Lord, your God,
  for he is gracious and merciful,
slow to anger, and abounding in steadfast love,
  and relents from punishing.
Who knows whether he will not turn and relent,
  and leave a blessing behind him,
a grain-offering and a drink-offering
  for the Lord, your God?

Blow the trumpet in Zion;
  sanctify a fast;
call a solemn assembly;
  gather the people.
Sanctify the congregation;
  assemble the aged;
gather the children,
  even infants at the breast.
Let the bridegroom leave his room,
  and the bride her canopy.

Between the vestibule and the altar
> let the priests, the ministers of the Lord, weep.
Let them say, 'Spare your people, O Lord,
> and do not make your heritage a mockery,
> a byword among the nations.
Why should it be said among the peoples,
> "Where is their God?"'

This is the word of the Lord.

Or:

A reading from the prophecy of Isaiah. (58.1-12)

Shout out, do not hold back!
> Lift up your voice like a trumpet!
Announce to my people their rebellion,
> to the house of Jacob their sins.
Yet day after day they seek me
> and delight to know my ways,
as if they were a nation that practised righteousness
> and did not forsake the ordinance of their God;
they ask of me righteous judgements,
> they delight to draw near to God.
'Why do we fast, but you do not see?
> Why humble ourselves, but you do not notice?'
Look, you serve your own interest on your fast-day,
> and oppress all your workers.
Look, you fast only to quarrel and to fight
> and to strike with a wicked fist.
Such fasting as you do today
> will not make your voice heard on high.
Is such the fast that I choose,
> a day to humble oneself?
Is it to bow down the head like a bulrush,
> and to lie in sackcloth and ashes?
Will you call this a fast,
> a day acceptable to the Lord?

Is not this the fast that I choose:
> to loose the bonds of injustice,
> to undo the thongs of the yoke,
to let the oppressed go free,
> and to break every yoke?
Is it not to share your bread with the hungry,
> and bring the homeless poor into your house;

when you see the naked, to cover them,
   and not to hide yourself from your own kin?
Then your light shall break forth like the dawn,
   and your healing shall spring up quickly;
your vindicator shall go before you,
   the glory of the Lord shall be your rearguard.
Then you shall call, and the Lord will answer;
   you shall cry for help, and he will say, Here I am.

If you remove the yoke from among you,
   the pointing of the finger, the speaking of evil,
if you offer your food to the hungry
   and satisfy the needs of the afflicted,
then your light shall rise in the darkness
   and your gloom be like the noonday.
The Lord will guide you continually,
   and satisfy your needs in parched places,
   and make your bones strong;
and you shall be like a watered garden,
   like a spring of water, whose waters never fail.
Your ancient ruins shall be rebuilt;
   you shall raise up the foundations of many generations;
you shall be called the repairer of the breach,
   the restorer of streets to live in.

This is the word of the Lord.

A reading from the Second Letter of Paul to the Corinthians.
                                                    (5.20b - 6.10)
We entreat you on behalf of Christ, be reconciled to God. For our
sake he made him to be sin who knew no sin, so that in him we might
become the righteousness of God.
   As we work together with him, we urge you also not to accept the
grace of God in vain. For he says,
   'At an acceptable time I have listened to you,
      and on a day of salvation I have helped you.'
See, now is the acceptable time; see, now is the day of salvation! We
are putting no obstacle in anyone's way, so that no fault may be
found with our ministry, but as servants of God we have commended ourselves in every way: through great endurance, in afflictions,
hardships, calamities, beatings, imprisonments, riots, labours, sleepless nights, hunger; by purity, knowledge, patience, kindness, holiness of spirit, genuine love, truthful speech, and the power of God;
with the weapons of righteousness for the right hand and for the left;

in honour and dishonour, in ill repute and good repute. We are treated as impostors, and yet are true; as unknown, and yet are well known; as dying, and see – we are alive; as punished, and yet not killed; as sorrowful, yet always rejoicing; as poor, yet making many rich; as having nothing, and yet possessing everything.

This is the word of the Lord.

Hear the gospel of our Lord Jesus Christ according to Matthew.
                                                          (6.1-6,16-21)

Jesus said to the crowds, 'Beware of practising your piety before others in order to be seen by them; for then you have no reward from your Father in heaven.

 'So whenever you give alms, do not sound a trumpet before you, as the hypocrites do in the synagogues and in the streets, so that they may be praised by others. Truly I tell you, they have received their reward. But when you give alms, do not let your left hand know what your right hand is doing, so that your alms may be done in secret; and your Father who sees in secret will reward you.

 'And whenever you pray, do not be like the hypocrites; for they love to stand and pray in the synagogues and at the street corners, so that they may be seen by others. Truly I tell you, they have received their reward. But whenever you pray, go into your room and shut the door and pray to your Father who is in secret; and your Father who sees in secret will reward you.

¹⁶ 'And whenever you fast, do not look dismal, like the hypocrites, for they disfigure their faces so as to show others that they are fasting. Truly I tell you, they have received their reward. But when you fast, put oil on your head and wash your face, so that your fasting may be seen not by others but by your Father who is in secret; and your Father who sees in secret will reward you.

 'Do not store up for yourselves treasures on earth, where moth and rust consume and where thieves break in and steal; but store up for yourselves treasures in heaven, where neither moth nor rust consumes and where thieves do not break in and steal. For where your treasure is, there your heart will be also.'

This is the gospel of the Lord.

Or:

Hear the gospel of our Lord Jesus Christ according to John. *(8.1-11)*

Jesus went to the Mount of Olives. Early in the morning he came again to the temple. All the people came to him and he sat down and began to teach them. The scribes and the Pharisees brought a woman who had been caught in adultery; and making her stand before all of them, they said to him, 'Teacher, this woman was caught in the very act of committing adultery. Now in the law Moses commanded us to stone such women. Now what do you say?' They said this to test him, so that they might have some charge to bring against him. Jesus bent down and wrote with his finger on the ground. When they kept on questioning him, he straightened up and said to them, 'Let anyone among you who is without sin be the first to throw a stone at her.' And once again he bent down and wrote on the ground. When they heard it, they went away, one by one, beginning with the elders; and Jesus was left alone with the woman standing before him. Jesus straightened up and said to her, 'Woman, where are they? Has no one condemned you?' She said, 'No one, sir.' And Jesus said, 'Neither do I condemn you. Go your way, and from now on do not sin again.'

This is the gospel of the Lord.

Second Service
Ps 102.1-17 [18-28]; Isaiah 1.10-18; Luke 15.11-32

A reading from the prophecy of Isaiah. (1.10-18)

Hear the word of the Lord,
     you rulers of Sodom!
Listen to the teaching of our God,
     you people of Gomorrah!
What to me is the multitude of your sacrifices?
     says the Lord;
I have had enough of burnt-offerings of rams
     and the fat of fed beasts;
I do not delight in the blood of bulls,
     or of lambs, or of goats.

When you come to appear before me,
     who asked this from your hand?
Trample my courts no more;
     bringing offerings is futile;
     incense is an abomination to me.
New moon and sabbath and calling of convocation –
     I cannot endure solemn assemblies with iniquity.
Your new moons and your appointed festivals
     my soul hates;
they have become a burden to me,
     I am weary of bearing them.
When you stretch out your hands,

I will hide my eyes from you;
even though you make many prayers, I will not listen;
   your hands are full of blood.
Wash yourselves; make yourselves clean;
   remove the evil of your doings from before my eyes;
cease to do evil,
   learn to do good;
seek justice,
   rescue the oppressed,
defend the orphan,
   plead for the widow.

Come now, let us argue it out,
   says the Lord:
though your sins are like scarlet,
   they shall be like snow;
though they are red like crimson,
   they shall become like wool.

A reading from the gospel according to Luke. (15.11-32)

Jesus said to the scribes and Pharisees, 'There was a man who had two sons. The younger of them said to his father, "Father, give me the share of the property that will belong to me." So he divided his property between them. A few days later the younger son gathered all he had and travelled to a distant country, and there he squandered his property in dissolute living. When he had spent everything, a severe famine took place throughout that country, and he began to be in need. So he went and hired himself out to one of the citizens of that country, who sent him to his fields to feed the pigs. He would gladly have filled himself with the pods that the pigs were eating; and no one gave him anything. But when he came to himself he said, "How many of my father's hired hands have bread enough and to spare, but here I am dying of hunger! I will get up and go to my father, and I will say to him, 'Father, I have sinned against heaven and before you; I am no longer worthy to be called your son; treat me like one of your hired hands.'" So he set off and went to his father. But while he was still far off, his father saw him and was filled with compassion; he ran and put his arms around him and kissed him. Then the son said to him, "Father, I have sinned against heaven and before you; I am no longer worthy to be called your son." But the father said to his slaves, "Quickly, bring out a robe – the best one – and put it on him; put a ring on his finger and sandals on his feet. And get the fatted calf and kill it, and let us eat and celebrate; for this

son of mine was dead and is alive again; he was lost and is found!"
And they began to celebrate.

'Now his elder son was in the field; and when he came and
approached the house, he heard music and dancing. He called one
of the slaves and asked what was going on. He replied, "Your brother has come, and your father has killed the fatted calf, because he has
got him back safe and sound." Then he became angry and refused to
go in. His father came out and began to plead with him. But he
answered his father, "Listen! For all these years I have been working
like a slave for you, and I have never disobeyed your command; yet
you have never given me even a young goat so that I might celebrate
with my friends. But when this son of yours came back, who has
devoured your property with prostitutes, you killed the fatted calf
for him!" Then the father said to him, "Son, you are always with me,
and all that is mine is yours. But we had to celebrate and rejoice,
because this brother of yours was dead and has come to life; he was
lost and has been found."'

Third Service
Ps 38; Daniel 9.3-6,17-19; 1 Timothy 6.6-19

A reading from the Book of Daniel. (9.3-6,17-19)

I, Daniel, turned to the Lord God, to seek an answer by prayer and
supplication with fasting and sackcloth and ashes. I prayed to the
Lord my God and made confession, saying,

'Ah, Lord, great and awesome God, keeping covenant and steadfast
love with those who love you and keep your commandments, we
have sinned and done wrong, acted wickedly and rebelled, turning
aside from your commandments and ordinances. We have not listened to your servants the prophets, who spoke in your name to our
kings, our princes, and our ancestors, and to all the people of the
land.
¹⁷ 'Now therefore, O our God, listen to the prayer of your servant and
to his supplication, and for your own sake, Lord, let your face shine
upon your desolated sanctuary. Incline your ear, O my God, and
hear. Open your eyes and look at our desolation and the city that
bears your name. We do not present our supplication before you on
the ground of our righteousness, but on the ground of your great
mercies. O Lord, hear; O Lord, forgive; O Lord, listen and act and do
not delay! For your own sake, O my God, because your city and your
people bear your name!'

A reading from the First Letter of Paul to Timothy. (6.6-19)

Of course, there is great gain in godliness combined with contentment; for we brought nothing into the world, so that we can take nothing out of it; but if we have food and clothing, we will be content with these. But those who want to be rich fall into temptation and are trapped by many senseless and harmful desires that plunge people into ruin and destruction. For the love of money is a root of all kinds of evil, and in their eagerness to be rich some have wandered away from the faith and pierced themselves with many pains.

But as for you, man of God, shun all this; pursue righteousness, godliness, faith, love, endurance, gentleness. Fight the good fight of the faith; take hold of the eternal life, to which you were called and for which you made the good confession in the presence of many witnesses. In the presence of God, who gives life to all things, and of Christ Jesus, who in his testimony before Pontius Pilate made the good confession, I charge you to keep the commandment without spot or blame until the manifestation of our Lord Jesus Christ, which he will bring about at the right time – he who is the blessèd and only Sovereign, the King of kings and Lord of lords. It is he alone who has immortality and dwells in unapproachable light, whom no one has ever seen or can see; to him be honour and eternal dominion. Amen.

As for those who in the present age are rich, command them not to be haughty, or to set their hopes on the uncertainty of riches, but rather on God who richly provides us with everything for our enjoyment. They are to do good, to be rich in good works, generous, and ready to share, thus storing up for themselves the treasure of a good foundation for the future, so that they may take hold of the life that really is life.

The First Sunday of Lent

Principal Service
Genesis 9.8-17; Ps 25.1-10; 1 Peter 3.18-22; Mark 1.9-15

A reading from the book Genesis. (9.8-17)

God said to Noah and to his sons with him, 'As for me, I am establishing my covenant with you and your descendants after you, and with every living creature that is with you, the birds, the domestic animals, and every animal of the earth with you, as many as came out of the ark. I establish my covenant with you, that never again shall all flesh be cut off by the waters of a flood, and never again shall there be a flood to destroy the earth.' God said, 'This is the sign of the covenant that I make between me and you and every living creature that is with you, for all future generations: I have set my bow in the clouds, and it shall be a sign of the covenant between me and the earth. When I bring clouds over the earth and the bow is seen in the clouds, I will remember my covenant that is between me and you and every living creature of all flesh; and the waters shall never again become a flood to destroy all flesh. When the bow is in the clouds, I will see it and remember the everlasting covenant between God and every living creature of all flesh that is on the earth.' God said to Noah, 'This is the sign of the covenant that I have established between me and all flesh that is on the earth.'

This is the word of the Lord.

A reading from the First Letter of Peter. (3.18-22)

Christ also suffered for sins once for all, the righteous for the unrighteous, in order to bring you to God. He was put to death in the flesh, but made alive in the spirit, in which also he went and made a proclamation to the spirits in prison, who in former times did not obey, when God waited patiently in the days of Noah, during the building of the ark, in which a few, that is, eight people, were saved through water. And baptism, which this prefigured, now saves you – not as a removal of dirt from the body, but as an appeal to God for a good conscience, through the resurrection of Jesus Christ, who has gone into heaven and is at the right hand of God, with angels, authorities, and powers made subject to him.

This is the word of the Lord.

Hear the gospel of our Lord Jesus Christ according to Mark. (1.9-15)

Jesus came from Nazareth of Galilee and was baptized by John in the Jordan. And just as he was coming up out of the water, he saw the heavens torn apart and the Spirit descending like a dove on him. And a voice came from heaven, 'You are my Son, the Belovèd; with you I am well pleased.'

And the Spirit immediately drove him out into the wilderness. He was in the wilderness for forty days, tempted by Satan; and he was with the wild beasts; and the angels waited on him.

Now after John was arrested, Jesus came to Galilee, proclaiming the good news of God, and saying, 'The time is fulfilled, and the kingdom of God has come near; repent, and believe in the good news.'

This is the gospel of the Lord.

Second Service
Ps 119.17-32; Genesis 2.15-17 & 3.1-7;
Romans 5.12-19 *or* Luke 13.31-35

A reading from the book Genesis. (2.15-17 & 3.1-7)

The Lord God took the man and put him in the garden of Eden to till it and keep it. And the Lord God commanded the man, 'You may freely eat of every tree of the garden; but of the tree of the knowledge of good and evil you shall not eat, for in the day that you eat of it you shall die.'
[3.1] Now the serpent was more crafty than any other wild animal that the Lord God had made. He said to the woman, 'Did God say, "You shall not eat from any tree in the garden"?' The woman said to the serpent, 'We may eat of the fruit of the trees in the garden; but God said, "You shall not eat of the fruit of the tree that is in the middle of the garden, nor shall you touch it, or you shall die."' But the serpent said to the woman, 'You will not die; for God knows that when you eat of it your eyes will be opened, and you will be like God, knowing good and evil.' So when the woman saw that the tree was good for food, and that it was a delight to the eyes, and that the tree was to be desired to make one wise, she took of its fruit and ate; and she also gave some to her husband, who was with her, and he ate. Then the eyes of both were opened, and they knew that they were naked; and they sewed fig leaves together and made loincloths for themselves.

A reading from the Letter of Paul to the Romans. (5.12-19)

Just as sin came into the world through one man, and death came through sin, and so death spread to all because all have sinned – sin was indeed in the world before the law, but sin is not reckoned when there is no law. Yet death exercised dominion from Adam to Moses, even over those whose sins were not like the transgression of Adam, who is a type of the one who was to come.
 But the free gift is not like the trespass. For if the many died through the one man's trespass, much more surely have the grace of God and the free gift in the grace of the one man, Jesus Christ, abounded for the many. And the free gift is not like the effect of the one man's sin. For the judgement following one trespass brought condemnation, but the free gift following many trespasses brings justification. If, because of the one man's trespass, death exercised dominion through that one, much more surely will those who receive the abundance of grace and the free gift of righteousness exercise dominion in life through the one man, Jesus Christ.

Therefore just as one man's trespass led to condemnation for all, so one man's act of righteousness leads to justification and life for all. For just as by the one man's disobedience the many were made sinners, so by the one man's obedience the many will be made righteous.

Or:

A reading from the gospel according to Luke. (13.31-35)

Some Pharisees came and said to Jesus, 'Get away from here, for Herod wants to kill you.' He said to them, 'Go and tell that fox for me, "Listen, I am casting out demons and performing cures today and tomorrow, and on the third day I finish my work. Yet today, tomorrow, and the next day I must be on my way, because it is impossible for a prophet to be killed away from Jerusalem."

'Jerusalem, Jerusalem, the city that kills the prophets and stones those who are sent to it! How often have I desired to gather your children together as a hen gathers her brood under her wings, and you were not willing! See, your house is left to you. And I tell you, you will not see me until the time comes when you say, "Blessèd is the one who comes in the name of the Lord."'

Third Service
Ps 77; Exodus 34.1-10; Romans 10. 8*b*-13

A reading from the Book of the Exodus. (34.1-10)

The Lord said to Moses, 'Cut two tablets of stone like the former ones, and I will write on the tablets the words that were on the former tablets, which you broke. Be ready in the morning, and come up in the morning to Mount Sinai and present yourself there to me, on the top of the mountain. No one shall come up with you, and do not let anyone be seen throughout all the mountain; and do not let flocks or herds graze in front of that mountain.' So Moses cut two tablets of stone like the former ones; and he rose early in the morning and went up on Mount Sinai, as the Lord had commanded him, and took in his hand the two tablets of stone. The Lord descended in the cloud and stood with him there, and proclaimed the name, 'The Lord.' The Lord passed before him, and proclaimed,

'The Lord, the Lord,
a God merciful and gracious,
slow to anger
and abounding in steadfast love and faithfulness,
keeping steadfast love for the thousandth generation,
forgiving iniquity and transgression and sin,

yet by no means clearing the guilty,
but visiting the iniquity of the parents
upon the children
and the children's children,
to the third and the fourth generation.'
And Moses quickly bowed his head towards the earth, and worshipped. He said, 'If now I have found favour in your sight, O Lord, I pray, let the Lord go with us. Although this is a stiff-necked people, pardon our iniquity and our sin, and take us for your inheritance.'

He said: I hereby make a covenant. Before all your people I will perform marvels, such as have not been performed in all the earth or in any nation; and all the people among whom you live shall see the work of the Lord; for it is an awesome thing that I will do with you.

A reading from the Letter of Paul to the Romans. (10. 8b-13)

Moses writes,
'The word is near you,
on your lips and in your heart'
(that is, the word of faith that we proclaim); because if you confess with your lips that Jesus is Lord and believe in your heart that God raised him from the dead, you will be saved. For one believes with the heart and so is justified, and one confesses with the mouth and so is saved. The scripture says, 'No one who believes in him will be put to shame.' For there is no distinction between Jew and Greek; the same Lord is Lord of all and is generous to all who call on him. For,
'Everyone who calls on the name of the Lord
shall be saved.'

The Second Sunday of Lent

Principal Service
Genesis 17.1-7,15-16; Ps 22.23-31; Romans 4.13-25; Mark 8.31-38

A reading from the book Genesis. (17.1-7,15-16)

When Abram was ninety-nine years old, the Lord appeared to Abram, and said to him, 'I am God Almighty; walk before me, and be blameless. And I will make my covenant between me and you, and will make you exceedingly numerous.' Then Abram fell on his face; and God said to him, 'As for me, this is my covenant with you: You shall be the ancestor of a multitude of nations. No longer shall your name be Abram, but your name shall be Abraham; for I have made you the ancestor of a multitude of nations. I will make you exceedingly fruitful; and I will make nations of you, and kings shall come from you. I will establish my covenant between me and you, and your offspring after you throughout their generations, for an everlasting covenant, to be God to you and to your offspring after you. [15] 'As for Sarai your wife, you shall not call her Sarai, but Sarah shall be her name. I will bless her, and moreover I will give you a son by her. I will bless her, and she shall give rise to nations; kings of peoples shall come from her.'

This is the word of the Lord.

A reading from the Letter of Paul to the Romans. (4.13-25)

The promise that he would inherit the world did not come to Abraham or to his descendants through the law but through the righteousness of faith. If it is the adherents of the law who are to be the heirs, faith is null and the promise is void. For the law brings wrath; but where there is no law, neither is there violation.

For this reason it depends on faith, in order that the promise may rest on grace and be guaranteed to all his descendants, not only to the adherents of the law but also to those who share the faith of Abraham (for he is the father of all of us, as it is written, 'I have made you the father of many nations') – in the presence of the God in whom he believed, who gives life to the dead and calls into existence the things that do not exist. Hoping against hope, he believed that he would become 'the father of many nations', according to what was said, 'So numerous shall your descendants be.' He did not weaken in faith when he considered his own body, which was already as good as dead (for he was about a hundred years old), or when he considered the barrenness of Sarah's womb. No distrust made him waver concerning the promise of God, but he grew strong in his faith as he gave glory to God, being fully convinced that God was able to do what he had promised. Therefore his faith 'was reckoned to him as righteousness.' Now the words, 'it was reckoned to him', were written not for his sake alone, but for ours also. It will be reckoned to us who believe in him who raised Jesus our Lord from the dead, who was handed over to death for our trespasses and was raised for our justification.

This is the word of the Lord.

Hear the gospel of our Lord Jesus Christ according to Mark. (8.31-38)

Jesus began to teach his disciples that the Son of Man must undergo great suffering, and be rejected by the elders, the chief priests, and the scribes, and be killed, and after three days rise again. He said all this quite openly. And Peter took him aside and began to rebuke him. But turning and looking at his disciples, he rebuked Peter and said, 'Get behind me, Satan! For you are setting your mind not on divine things but on human things.'

He called the crowd with his disciples, and said to them, 'If any want to become my followers, let them deny themselves and take up their cross and follow me. For those who want to save their life will lose it, and those who lose their life for my sake, and for the sake of the gospel, will save it. For what will it profit them to gain the whole world and forfeit their life? Indeed, what can they give in return for their life? Those who are ashamed of me and of my words in this adulterous and sinful generation, of them the Son of Man will also be ashamed when he comes in the glory of his Father with the holy angels.'

This is the gospel of the Lord.

Second Service
Ps 135.1-14[15-21]; Genesis 12.1-9; Hebrews 11.1-3,8-16;
if a Eucharist: Luke 14.27-33

A reading from the book Genesis. (12.1-9)

The Lord said to Abram, 'Go from your country and your kindred and your father's house to the land that I will show you. I will make of you a great nation, and I will bless you, and make your name great, so that you will be a blessing. I will bless those who bless you, and the one who curses you I will curse; and in you all the families of the earth shall be blessed.'

So Abram went, as the Lord had told him; and Lot went with him. Abram was seventy-five years old when he departed from Haran. Abram took his wife Sarai and his brother's son Lot, and all the possessions that they had gathered, and the persons whom they had acquired in Haran; and they set forth to go to the land of Canaan. Then they had come to the land of Canaan, Abram passed through the land to the place at Shechem, to the oak of Moreh. At that time the Canaanites were in the land. Then the Lord appeared to Abram, and said, 'To your offspring I will give this land.' So he built there an altar to the Lord, who had appeared to him. From there he moved on to the hill country on the east of Bethel, and pitched his tent, with Bethel on the west and Ai on the east; and there he built an altar to the Lord and invoked the name of the Lord. And Abram journeyed on by stages towards the Negeb.

A reading from the Letter to the Hebrews. (11.1-3,8-16)

Faith is the assurance of things hoped for, the conviction of things not seen. Indeed, by faith our ancestors received approval. By faith we understand that the worlds were prepared by the word of God, so that what is seen was made from things that are not visible.

⁸ By faith Abraham obeyed when he was called to set out for a place that he was to receive as an inheritance; and he set out, not knowing where he was going. By faith he stayed for a time in the land he had been promised, as in a foreign land, living in tents, as did Isaac and Jacob, who were heirs with him of the same promise. For he looked forward to the city that has foundations, whose architect and builder is God. By faith he received power of procreation, even though he was too old – and Sarah herself was barren – because he considered him faithful who had promised. Therefore from one person, and this one as good as dead, descendants were born, 'as many as the stars of heaven and as the innumerable grains of sand by the seashore.'

All of these died in faith without having received the promises, but from a distance they saw and greeted them. They confessed that they were strangers and foreigners on the earth, for people who speak in this way make it clear that they are seeking a homeland. If they had been thinking of the land that they had left behind, they would have had opportunity to return. But as it is, they desire a better country, that is, a heavenly one. Therefore God is not ashamed to be called their God; indeed, he has prepared a city for them.

If a Eucharist:
Hear the gospel of our Lord Jesus Christ according to Luke. *(14.27-33)*

Jesus said to the crowd, 'Whoever does not carry the cross and follow me cannot be my disciple. For which of you, intending to build a tower, does not first sit down and estimate the cost, to see whether he has enough to complete it? Otherwise, when he has laid a foundation and is not able to finish, all who see it will begin to ridicule him, saying, "This fellow began to build and was not able to finish." Or what king, going out to wage war against another king, will not sit down first and consider whether he is able with ten thousand to oppose the one who comes against him with twenty thousand? If he cannot, then, while the other is still far away, he sends a delegation and asks for the terms of peace. So therefore, none of you can become my disciple if you do not give up all your possessions.'

This is the gospel of the Lord.

Third Service
Ps 105. 1-6,37-45; Isaiah 51.1-11; Galatians 3.1-9,23-29

A reading from the prophecy of Isaiah. (51.1-11)

Listen to me, you that pursue righteousness,
　　you that seek the Lord.
Look to the rock from which you were hewn,
　　and to the quarry from which you were dug.
Look to Abraham your father
　　and to Sarah who bore you;
for he was but one when I called him,
　　but I blessed him and made him many.
For the Lord will comfort Zion;
　　he will comfort all her waste places,
and will make her wilderness like Eden,
　　her desert like the garden of the Lord;
joy and gladness will be found in her,
　　thanksgiving and the voice of song.

Listen to me, my people,
　　and give heed to me, my nation;
for a teaching will go out from me,
　　and my justice for a light to the peoples.
I will bring near my deliverance swiftly,
　　my salvation has gone out
　　and my arms will rule the peoples;
the coastlands wait for me,
　　and for my arm they hope.
Lift up your eyes to the heavens,
　　and look at the earth beneath;
for the heavens will vanish like smoke,
　　the earth will wear out like a garment,
　　and those who live on it will die like gnats;
but my salvation will be for ever,
　　and my deliverance will never be ended.

Listen to me, you who know righteousness,
　　you people who have my teaching in your hearts;
do not fear the reproach of others,
　　and do not be dismayed when they revile you.

For the moth will eat them up like a garment,
    and the worm will eat them like wool;
but my deliverance will be for ever,
    and my salvation to all generations.

Awake, awake, put on strength,
    O arm of the Lord!
Awake, as in days of old,
    the generations of long ago!
Was it not you who cut Rahab in pieces,
    who pierced the dragon?
Was it not you who dried up the sea,
    the waters of the great deep;
who made the depths of the sea
    a way for the redeemed to cross over?
So the ransomed of the Lord shall return,
    and come to Zion with singing;
everlasting joy shall be upon their heads;
    they shall obtain joy and gladness,
    and sorrow and sighing shall flee away.

A reading from the Letter of Paul to the Galatians. (3.1-9,23-29)

You foolish Galatians! Who has bewitched you? It was before your eyes that Jesus Christ was publicly exhibited as crucified! The only thing I want to learn from you is this: Did you receive the Spirit by doing the works of the law or by believing what you heard? Are you so foolish? Having started with the Spirit, are you now ending with the flesh? Did you experience so much for nothing? – if it really was for nothing. Well then, does God supply you with the Spirit and work miracles among you by your doing the works of the law, or by your believing what you heard?

Just as Abraham 'believed God, and it was reckoned to him as righteousness', so, you see, those who believe are the descendants of Abraham. And the scripture, foreseeing that God would justify the Gentiles by faith, declared the gospel beforehand to Abraham, saying, 'All the Gentiles shall be blessed in you.' For this reason, those who believe are blessed with Abraham who believed.

[23] Now before faith came, we were imprisoned and guarded under the law until faith would be revealed. Therefore the law was our disciplinarian until Christ came, so that we might be justified by faith. But now that faith has come, we are no longer subject to a disciplinarian, for in Christ Jesus you are all children of God through faith. As many of you as were baptized into Christ have clothed yourselves

with Christ. There is no longer Jew or Greek, there is no longer slave or free, there is no longer male and female; for all of you are one in Christ Jesus. And if you belong to Christ, then you are Abraham's offspring, heirs according to the promise.

The Third Sunday of Lent

Principal Service
Exodus 20.1-17; Ps 19 or 19.7-14; 1 Corinthians 1.18-25; John 2.13-22

A reading from the Book of the Exodus. (20.1-17)

God spoke all these words:

I am the Lord your God, who brought you out of the land of Egypt, out of the house of slavery; you shall have no other gods before me.

You shall not make for yourself an idol, whether in the form of anything that is in heaven above, or that is on the earth beneath, or that is in the water under the earth. You shall not bow down to them or worship them; for I the Lord your God am a jealous God, punishing children for the iniquity of parents, to the third and the fourth generation of those who reject me, but showing steadfast love to the thousandth generation of those who love me and keep my commandments.

You shall not make wrongful use of the name of the Lord your God, for the Lord will not acquit anyone who misuses his name.

Remember the sabbath day, and keep it holy. For six days you shall labour and do all your work. But the seventh day is a sabbath to the Lord your God; you shall not do any work - you, your son or your daughter, your male or female slave, your livestock, or the alien resident in your towns. For in six days the Lord made heaven and earth, the sea, and all that is in them, but rested the seventh day; therefore the Lord blessed the sabbath day and consecrated it.

Honour your father and your mother, so that your days may be long in the land that the Lord your God is giving you.

You shall not murder.

You shall not commit adultery.

You shall not steal.

You shall not bear false witness against your neighbour.

You shall not covet your neighbour's house; you shall not covet your neighbour's wife, or male or female slave, or ox, or donkey, or anything that belongs to your neighbour.

This is the word of the Lord.

A reading from the First Letter of Paul to the Corinthians. (1.18-25)

The message about the cross is foolishness to those who are perishing, but to us who are being saved it is the power of God. For it is written,

'I will destroy the wisdom of the wise,
  and the discernment of the discerning I will thwart.'

Where is the one who is wise? Where is the scribe? Where is the debater of this age? Has not God made foolish the wisdom of the world? For since, in the wisdom of God, the world did not know God through wisdom, God decided, through the foolishness of our proclamation, to save those who believe. For Jews demand signs and Greeks desire wisdom, but we proclaim Christ crucified, a stumbling-block to Jews and foolishness to Gentiles, but to those who are the called, both Jews and Greeks, Christ the power of God and the wisdom of God. For God's foolishness is wiser than human wisdom, and God's weakness is stronger than human strength.

This is the word of the Lord.

Hear the gospel of our Lord Jesus Christ according to John. (2.13-22)

The Passover of the Jews was near, and Jesus went up to Jerusalem. In the temple he found people selling cattle, sheep, and doves, and the money-changers seated at their tables. Making a whip of cords, he drove all of them out of the temple, both the sheep and the cattle. He also poured out the coins of the money-changers and overturned their tables. He told those who were selling the doves, 'Take these things out of here! Stop making my Father's house a market-place!' His disciples remembered that it was written, 'Zeal for your house will consume me.' The Jews then said to him, 'What sign can you show us for doing this?' Jesus answered them, 'Destroy this temple, and in three days I will raise it up.' The Jews then said, 'This temple has been under construction for forty-six years, and will you raise it up in three days?' But he was speaking of the temple of his body. After he was raised from the dead, his disciples remembered that he had said this; and they believed the scripture and the word that Jesus had spoken.

This is the gospel of the Lord.

Second Service

Pss 11,12; Exodus 5.1 - 6.1;
Philippians 3.4*b*-14 *or* Matthew 10.16-22

A reading from the Book of the Exodus. (5.1 - 6.1)

Moses and Aaron went to Pharaoh and said, 'Thus says the Lord, the God of Israel, "Let my people go, so that they may celebrate a festival to me in the wilderness."' But Pharaoh said, 'Who is the Lord, that I should heed him and let Israel go? I do not know the Lord, and I will not let Israel go.' Then they said, 'The God of the Hebrews has revealed himself to us; let us go a three days' journey into the wilderness to sacrifice to the Lord our God, or he will fall upon us with pestilence or sword.' But the king of Egypt said to them, 'Moses and Aaron, why are you taking the people away from their work? Get to your labours!' Pharaoh continued, 'Now they are more numerous than the people of the land and yet you want them to stop working!' That same day Pharaoh commanded the taskmasters of the people, as well as their supervisors, 'You shall no longer give the people straw to make bricks, as before; let them go and gather straw for themselves. But you shall require of them the same quantity of bricks as they have made previously; do not diminish it, for they are lazy; that is why they cry, "Let us go and offer sacrifice to our God." Let heavier work be laid on them; then they will labour at it and pay no attention to deceptive words.'

So the taskmasters and the supervisors of the people went out and said to the people, 'Thus says Pharaoh, "I will not give you straw. Go and get straw yourselves, wherever you can find it; but your work will not be lessened in the least."' So the people scattered throughout the land of Egypt, to gather stubble for straw. The taskmasters were urgent, saying, 'Complete your work, the same daily assignment as when you were given straw.' And the supervisors of the Israelites, whom Pharaoh's taskmasters had set over them, were beaten, and were asked, 'Why did you not finish the required quantity of bricks yesterday and today, as you did before?'

Then the Israelite supervisors came to Pharaoh and cried, 'Why do you treat your servants like this? No straw is given to your servants, yet they say to us, "Make bricks!" Look how your servants are beaten! You are unjust to your own people.' He said, 'You are lazy, lazy; that is why you say, "Let us go and sacrifice to the Lord." Go now, and work; for no straw shall be given you, but you shall still deliver the same number of bricks.' The Israelite supervisors saw that they were in trouble when they were told, 'You shall not lessen your daily number of bricks.' As they left Pharaoh, they came upon Moses and Aaron who were waiting to meet them. They said to them, 'The Lord look upon you and judge! You have brought us into bad odour with Pharaoh and his officials, and have put a sword in their hand to kill us.'

Then Moses turned again to the Lord and said, 'O Lord, why have you mistreated this people? Why did you ever send me? Since I first came to Pharaoh to speak in your name, he has mistreated this people, and you have done nothing at all to deliver your people.'

Then the Lord said to Moses, 'Now you shall see what I will do to Pharaoh: Indeed, by a mighty hand he will let them go; by a mighty hand he will drive them out of his land.'

A reading from the Letter of Paul to the Philippians. (3.4b-14)

If anyone else has reason to be confident in the flesh, I have more: circumcised on the eighth day, a member of the people of Israel, of the tribe of Benjamin, a Hebrew born of Hebrews; as to the law, a Pharisee; as to zeal, a persecutor of the church; as to righteousness under the law, blameless.

Yet whatever gains I had, these I have come to regard as loss because of Christ. More than that, I regard everything as loss because of the surpassing value of knowing Christ Jesus my Lord. For his sake I have suffered the loss of all things, and I regard them as rubbish, in order that I may gain Christ and be found in him, not having a righteousness of my own that comes from the law, but one that comes through faith in Christ, the righteousness from God based on faith. I want to know Christ and the power of his resurrection and the sharing of his sufferings by becoming like him in his death, if somehow I may attain the resurrection from the dead.

Not that I have already obtained this or have already reached the goal; but I press on to make it my own, because Christ Jesus has made me his own. Belovèd, I do not consider that I have made it my own; but this one thing I do: forgetting what lies behind and straining forward to what lies ahead, I press on towards the goal for the prize of the heavenly call of God in Christ Jesus.

Or:

A reading from the gospel according to Matthew. (10.16-22)

Jesus said to the twelve, 'See, I am sending you out like sheep into the midst of wolves; so be wise as serpents and innocent as doves. Beware of them, for they will hand you over to councils and flog you in their synagogues; and you will be dragged before governors and kings because of me, as a testimony to them and the Gentiles. When they hand you over, do not worry about how you are to speak or what you are to say; for what you are to say will be given to you at that time; for it is not you who speak, but the Spirit of your Father speaking through you. Brother will betray brother to death, and a father his child, and children will rise against parents and have them put to death; and you will be hated by all because of my name. But the one who endures to the end will be saved. '

Third Service
Ps 18.1-24; Jeremiah 38; Philippians 1.1-26

A reading from the prophecy of Jeremiah. (Chapter 38)

Shephatiah son of Mattan, Gedaliah son of Pashhur, Jucal son of Shelemiah, and Pashhur son of Malchiah heard the words that Jeremiah was saying to all the people, Thus says the Lord, Those who stay in this city shall die by the sword, by famine, and by pestilence; but those who go out to the Chaldeans shall live; they shall have their lives as a prize of war, and live. Thus says the Lord, This city shall surely be handed over to the army of the king of Babylon and be taken. Then the officials said to the king, 'This man ought to be put to death, because he is discouraging the soldiers who are left in this city, and all the people, by speaking such words to them. For this man is not seeking the welfare of this people, but their harm.' King Zedekiah said, 'Here he is; he is in your hands; for the king is powerless against you.' So they took Jeremiah and threw him into the cistern of Malchiah, the king's son, which was in the court of the guard, letting Jeremiah down by ropes. Now there was no water in the cistern, but only mud, and Jeremiah sank in the mud.

Ebed-melech the Ethiopian, a eunuch in the king's house, heard that they had put Jeremiah into the cistern. The king happened to be sitting at the Benjamin Gate, so Ebed-melech left the king's house and spoke to the king, 'My lord king, these men have acted wickedly in all they did to the prophet Jeremiah by throwing him into the cistern to die there of hunger, for there is no bread left in the city.' Then the king commanded Ebed-melech the Ethiopian, 'Take three men with you from here, and pull the prophet Jeremiah up from the cistern before he dies.' So Ebed-melech took the men with him and went to the house of the king, to a wardrobe of the storehouse, and took from there old rags and worn-out clothes, which he let down to Jeremiah in the cistern by ropes. So Ebed-melech took the men with him and went to the house of the king, to a wardrobe of the storehouse, and took from there old rags and worn-out clothes, which he let down to Jeremiah in the cistern by ropes. Then Ebed-melech the Ethiopian said to Jeremiah, 'Just put the rags and clothes between your armpits and the ropes.' Jeremiah did so. Then they drew Jeremiah up by the ropes and pulled him out of the cistern. And Jeremiah remained in the court of the guard.

King Zedekiah sent for the prophet Jeremiah and received him at the third entrance of the temple of the Lord. The king said to Jeremiah, 'I have something to ask you; do not hide anything from me.' Jeremiah said to Zedekiah, 'If I tell you, you will put me to death, will you not? And if I give you advice, you will not listen to me.' So King Zedekiah swore an oath in secret to Jeremiah, 'As the Lord lives, who gave us our lives, I will not put you to death or hand you over to these men who seek your life.'

Then Jeremiah said to Zedekiah, 'Thus says the Lord, the God of hosts, the God of Israel, If you will only surrender to the officials of the king of Babylon, then your life shall be spared, and this city shall not be burned with fire, and you and your house shall live. But if you do not surrender to the officials of the king of Babylon, then this city shall be handed over to the Chaldeans, and they shall burn it with fire, and you yourself shall not escape from their hand.' King Zedekiah said to Jeremiah, 'I am afraid of the Judeans who have deserted to the Chaldeans, for I might be handed over to them and they would abuse me.' Jeremiah said, 'That will not happen. Just obey the voice of the Lord in what I say to you, and it shall go well with you, and your life shall be spared. But if you are determined not to surrender, this is what the Lord has shown me – a vision of all the women remaining in the house of the king of Judah being led out to the officials of the king of Babylon and saying,

"Your trusted friends have seduced you
and have overcome you;
Now that your feet are stuck in the mud,
they desert you."

All your wives and your children shall be led out to the Chaldeans, and you yourself shall not escape from their hand, but shall be seized by the king of Babylon; and this city shall be burned with fire.'

Then Zedekiah said to Jeremiah, 'Do not let anyone else know of this conversation, or you will die. If the officials should hear that I have spoken with you, and they should come and say to you, "Just tell us what you said to the king; do not conceal it from us, or we will put you to death. What did the king say to you?" then you shall say to them, "I was presenting my plea to the king not to send me back to the house of Jonathan to die there."' All the officials did come to Jeremiah and questioned him; and he answered them in the very words the king had commanded. So they stopped questioning him, for the conversation had not been overheard. And Jeremiah remained in the court of the guard until the day that Jerusalem was taken.

A reading from the Letter of Paul to the Philippians. (1.1-26)

Paul and Timothy, servants of Christ Jesus,
To all the saints in Christ Jesus who are in Philippi, with the bishops and deacons:
Grace to you and peace from God our Father and the Lord Jesus Christ.

I thank my God every time I remember you, constantly praying with joy in every one of my prayers for all of you, because of your sharing in the gospel from the first day until now. I am confident of this, that the one who began a good work among you will bring it to completion by the day of Jesus Christ. It is right for me to think this way about all of you, because you hold me in your heart, for all of you share in God's grace with me, both in my imprisonment and in the defence and confirmation of the gospel. For God is my witness, how I long for all of you with the compassion of Christ Jesus. And this is my prayer, that your love may overflow more and more with knowledge and full insight to help you to determine what is best, so that on the day of Christ you may be pure and blameless, having produced the harvest of righteousness that comes through Jesus Christ for the glory and praise of God.

I want you to know, belovèd, that what has happened to me has actually helped to spread the gospel, so that it has become known throughout the whole imperial guard and to everyone else that my imprisonment is for Christ; and most of the brothers and sisters, having been made confident in the Lord by my imprisonment, dare to speak the word with greater boldness and without fear.

Some proclaim Christ from envy and rivalry, but others from goodwill. These proclaim Christ out of love, knowing that I have been put here for the defence of the gospel; the others proclaim Christ out of selfish ambition, not sincerely but intending to increase my suffering in my imprisonment. What does it matter? Just this, that Christ is proclaimed in every way, whether out of false motives or true; and in that I rejoice.

Yes, and I will continue to rejoice, for I know that through your prayers and the help of the Spirit of Jesus Christ this will result in my deliverance. It is my eager expectation and hope that I will not be put to shame in any way, but that by my speaking with all boldness, Christ will be exalted now as always in my body, whether by life or by death. For to me, living is Christ and dying is gain. If I am to live in the flesh, that means fruitful labour for me; and I do not know which I prefer. I am hard pressed between the two: my desire is to depart and be with Christ, for that is far better; but to remain in the flesh is more necessary for you. Since I am convinced of this, I know that I will remain and continue with all of you for your progress and joy in faith, so that I may share abundantly in your boasting in Christ Jesus when I come to you again.

The Fourth Sunday of Lent

Principal Service
Numbers 21.4-9; Ps 107.1-3,17-22 *or* 107.1-9; Ephesians 2.1-10; John 3.14-21

A reading from the book Numbers. (21.4-9)

From Mount Hor Israel set out by the way to the Red Sea, to go around the land of Edom; but the people became impatient on the way. The people spoke against God and against Moses, 'Why have you brought us up out of Egypt to die in the wilderness? For there is no food and no water, and we detest this miserable food.' Then the Lord sent poisonous serpents among the people, and they bit the people, so that many Israelites died. The people came to Moses and said, 'We have sinned by speaking against the Lord and against you; pray to the Lord to take away the serpents from us.' So Moses prayed for the people. And the Lord said to Moses, 'Make a poisonous serpent, and set it on a pole; and everyone who is bitten shall look at it and live.' So Moses made a serpent of bronze, and put it upon a pole; and whenever a serpent bit someone, that person would look at the serpent of bronze and live.

This is the word of the Lord.

A reading from the Letter of Paul to the Ephesians. (2.1-10)

You were dead through the trespasses and sins in which you once lived, following the course of this world, following the ruler of the power of the air, the spirit that is now at work among those who are disobedient. All of us once lived among them in the passions of our flesh, following the desires of flesh and senses, and we were by nature children of wrath, like everyone else. But God, who is rich in mercy, out of the great love with which he loved us even when we were dead through our trespasses, made us alive together with Christ – by grace you have been saved – and raised us up with him and seated us with him in the heavenly places in Christ Jesus, so that in the ages to come he might show the immeasurable riches of his grace in kindness towards us in Christ Jesus. For by grace you have been saved through faith, and this is not your own doing; it is the gift of God – not the result of works, so that no one may boast. For we are what he has made us, created in Christ Jesus for good works, which God prepared beforehand to be our way of life.

This is the word of the Lord.

Hear the gospel of our Lord Jesus Christ according to John. (3.14-21)

Jesus said to Nicodemus, 'Just as Moses lifted up the serpent in the wilderness, so must the Son of Man be lifted up, that whoever believes in him may have eternal life.

'For God so loved the world that he gave his only Son, so that every-one who believes in him may not perish but may have eternal life.

'Indeed, God did not send the Son into the world to condemn the world, but in order that the world might be saved through him. Those who believe in him are not condemned; but those who do not believe are condemned already, because they have not believed in the name of the only Son of God. And this is the judgement, that the light has come into the world, and people loved darkness rather than light because their deeds were evil. For all who do evil hate the light and do not come to the light, so that their deeds may not be exposed. But those who do what is true come to the light, so that it may be clearly seen that their deeds have been done in God.'

This is the gospel of the Lord.

Second Service

If the Principal Service readings have been displaced by Mothering Sunday provisions, the Principal Service readings may be used at this service.
Pss 13,14; Exodus 6.2-13; Romans 5.1-11; *if a Eucharist:* John 12.1-8

A reading from the Book of the Exodus. (6.2-13)

God spoke to Moses and said to him: 'I am the Lord. I appeared to Abraham, Isaac, and Jacob as God Almighty, but by my name "The Lord" I did not make myself known to them. I also established my covenant with them, to give them the land of Canaan, the land in which they resided as aliens. I have also heard the groaning of the Israelites, whom the Egyptians are holding as slaves, and I have remembered my covenant. Say therefore to the Israelites, "I am the Lord, and I will free you from the burdens of the Egyptians and deliver you from slavery to them. I will redeem you with an outstretched arm and with mighty acts of judgement. I will take you as my people, and I will be your God. You shall know that I am the Lord your God, who has freed you from the burdens of the Egyptians. I will bring you into the land that I swore to give to Abraham, Isaac, and Jacob; I will give it to you for a possession. I am the Lord."' Moses told this to the Israelites; but they would not listen to Moses, because of their broken spirit and their cruel slavery.

Then the Lord spoke to Moses, 'Go and tell Pharaoh king of Egypt to let the Israelites go out of his land.' But Moses spoke to the Lord, 'The Israelites have not listened to me; how then shall Pharaoh listen to me, poor speaker that I am?' Thus the Lord spoke to Moses and Aaron, and gave them orders regarding the Israelites and Pharaoh king of Egypt, charging them to free the Israelites from the land of Egypt.

A reading from the Letter of Paul to the Romans. (5.1-11)

Since we are justified by faith, we have peace with God through our Lord Jesus Christ, through whom we have obtained access to this grace in which we stand; and we boast in our hope of sharing the glory of God. And not only that, but we also boast in our sufferings, knowing that suffering produces endurance, and endurance produces character, and character produces hope, and hope does not disappoint us, because God's love has been poured into our hearts through the Holy Spirit that has been given to us.

For while we were still weak, at the right time Christ died for the ungodly. Indeed, rarely will anyone die for a righteous person – though perhaps for a good person someone might actually dare to die. But God proves his love for us in that while we still were sinners Christ died for us. Much more surely then, now that we have been justified by his blood, will we be saved through him from the wrath of God. For if while we were enemies, we were reconciled to God through the death of his Son, much more surely, having been reconciled, will we be saved by his life. But more than that, we even boast in God through our Lord Jesus Christ, through whom we have now received reconciliation.

If a Eucharist:
Hear the gospel of our Lord Jesus Christ according to John. (12.1-8)

Six days before the Passover Jesus came to Bethany, the home of Lazarus, whom he had raised from the dead. There they gave a dinner for him. Martha served, and Lazarus was one of those at the table with him. Mary took a pound of costly perfume made of pure nard, anointed Jesus' feet, and wiped them with her hair. The house was filled with the fragrance of the perfume. But Judas Iscariot, one of his disciples (the one who was about to betray him), said, 'Why was this perfume not sold for three hundred denarii and the money given to the poor?' (He said this not because he cared about the poor, but because he was a thief; he kept the common purse and used to steal what was put into it.) Jesus said, 'Leave her alone. She bought it so that she might keep it for the day of my burial. You always have the poor with you, but you do not always have me.'

This is the gospel of the Lord.

Third Service
Ps 27; 1 Samuel 16.1-13; John 9.1-25

A reading from the First Book of Samuel. (16.1-13)

The Lord said to Samuel, 'How long will you grieve over Saul? I have rejected him from being king over Israel. Fill your horn with oil and set out; I will send you to Jesse the Bethlehemite, for I have provided for myself a king among his sons.' Samuel said, 'How can I go? If Saul hears of it, he will kill me.' And the Lord said, 'Take a heifer with you, and say, "I have come to sacrifice to the Lord." Invite Jesse to the sacrifice, and I will show you what you shall do; and you shall anoint for me the one whom I name to you.' Samuel did what the Lord commanded, and came to Bethlehem. The elders of the city came to meet him trembling, and said, 'Do you come peaceably?' He said, 'Peaceably; I have come to sacrifice to the Lord; sanctify your-selves and come with me to the sacrifice.' And he sanctified Jesse and his sons and invited them to the sacrifice.

When they came, he looked on Eliab and thought, 'Surely the Lord's anointed is now before the Lord.' But the Lord said to Samuel, 'Do not look on his appearance or on the height of his stature, because I have rejected him; for the Lord does not see as mortals see; they look on the outward appearance, but the Lord looks on the heart.' Then Jesse called Abinadab, and made him pass before Samuel. He said, 'Neither has the Lord chosen this one.' Then Jesse made Shammah pass by. And he said, 'Neither has the Lord chosen this one.' Jesse made seven of his sons pass before Samuel, and Samuel said to Jesse, 'The Lord has not chosen any of these.' Samuel said to Jesse, 'Are all your sons here?' And he said, 'There remains yet the youngest, but he is keeping the sheep.' And Samuel said to Jesse, 'Send and bring him; for we will not sit down until he comes here.' He sent and brought him in. Now he was ruddy, and had beautiful eyes, and was handsome. The Lord said, 'Rise and anoint him; for this is the one.' Then Samuel took the horn of oil, and anointed him in the presence of his brothers; and the spirit of the Lord came mightily upon David from that day forward. Samuel then set out and went to Ramah.

A reading from the gospel according to John. (9.1-25)

As Jesus walked along, he saw a man blind from birth. His disciples asked him, 'Rabbi, who sinned, this man or his parents, that he was born blind?' Jesus answered, 'Neither this man nor his parents sinned; he was born blind so that God's works might be revealed in him. We must work the works of him who sent me while it is day; night is coming when no one can work. As long as I am in the world, I am the light of the world.' When he had said this, he spat on the ground and made mud with the saliva and spread the mud on the man's eyes, saying to him, 'Go, wash in the pool of Siloam' (which means Sent). Then he went and washed and came back able to see. The neighbours and those who had seen him before as a beggar began to ask, 'Is this not the man who used to sit and beg?' Some were saying, 'It is he.' Others were saying, 'No, but it is someone like him.' He kept saying, 'I am the man.' But they kept asking him, 'Then how were your eyes opened?' He answered, 'The man called Jesus made mud, spread it on my eyes, and said to me, "Go to Siloam and wash." Then I went and washed and received my sight.' They said to him, 'Where is he?' He said, 'I do not know.'

They brought to the Pharisees the man who had formerly been blind. Now it was a sabbath day when Jesus made the mud and opened his eyes. Then the Pharisees also began to ask him how he had received his sight. He said to them, 'He put mud on my eyes. Then I washed, and now I see.' Some of the Pharisees said, 'This man is not from God, for he does not observe the sabbath.' But others said, 'How can a man who is a sinner perform such signs? ' And they were divided. So they said again to the blind man, 'What do you say about him? It was your eyes he opened.' He said, 'He is a prophet.'

The Jews did not believe that he had been blind and had received his sight until they called the parents of the man who had received his sight and asked them, 'Is this your son, who you say was born blind? How then does he now see?' His parents answered, 'We know that this is our son, and that he was born blind; but we do not know how it is that now he sees, nor do we know who opened his eyes. Ask him; he is of age. He will speak for himself.' His parents said this because they were afraid of the Jews; for the Jews had already agreed that anyone who confessed Jesus to be the Messiah would be put out of the synagogue. Therefore his parents said, 'He is of age; ask him.'

So for the second time they called the man who had been blind, and they said to him, 'Give glory to God! We know that this man is a sinner.' He answered, 'I do not know whether he is a sinner. One thing I do know, that though I was blind, now I see.'

Or: *Mothering Sunday*

Principal Service

Exodus 2.1-10 *or* 1 Samuel 1.20-28;
Pss 34.11-20 *or* 127.1-4;
2 Corinthians 1.3-7 *or* Colossians 3.12-17;
Luke 2.33-35 *or* John 19.25-27

A reading from the Book of the Exodus. (2.1-10)

A man from the house of Levi married a Levite woman. The woman conceived and bore a son; and when she saw that he was a fine baby, she hid him for three months. When she could hide him no longer she got a papyrus basket for him, and plastered it with bitumen and pitch; she put the child in it and placed it among the reeds on the bank of the river. His sister stood at a distance, to see what would happen to him.

The daughter of Pharaoh came down to bathe at the river, while her attendants walked beside the river. She saw the basket among the reeds and sent her maid to bring it. When she opened it, she saw the child. He was crying, and she took pity on him. 'This must be one of the Hebrews' children,' she said. Then his sister said to Pharaoh's daughter, 'Shall I go and get you a nurse from the Hebrew women to nurse the child for you?' Pharaoh's daughter said to her, 'Yes.' So the girl went and called the child's mother. Pharaoh's daughter said to her, 'Take this child and nurse it for me, and I will give you your wages.' So the woman took the child and nursed it. When the child grew up, she brought him to Pharaoh's daughter, and she took him as her son. She named him Moses, 'because', she said, 'I drew him out of the water.'

This is the word of the Lord.

Or:
A reading from the First Book of Samuel. *(1.20-28)*

In due time Hannah, the wife of Elkanah, conceived and bore a son. She named him Samuel, for she said, 'I have asked him of the Lord.'

The man Elkanah and all his household went up to offer to the Lord the yearly sacrifice, and to pay his vow. But Hannah did not go up, for she said to her husband, 'As soon as the child is weaned, I will bring him, that he may appear in the presence of the Lord, and remain there for ever; I will offer him as a nazirite for all time.' Her husband Elkanah said to her, 'Do what seems best to you, wait until you have weaned him; only – may the Lord establish his word.' So the woman remained and nursed her son, until she weaned him. When she had weaned him, she took him up with her, along with a three-year-old bull, an ephah of flour, and a skin of wine. She brought him to the house of the Lord at Shiloh; and the child was young. Then they slaughtered the bull, and they brought the child to Eli. And she said, 'Oh, my lord! As you live, my lord, I am the woman who was standing here in your presence, praying to the Lord. For this child I prayed; and the Lord has granted me the petition that I made to him. Therefore I have lent him to the Lord; as long as he lives, he is given to the Lord.'

She left him there for the Lord.

This is the word of the Lord.

A reading from the Second Letter of Paul to the Corinthians. *(1.3-7)*

Blessèd be the God and Father of our Lord Jesus Christ, the Father of mercies and the God of all consolation, who consoles us in all our affliction, so that we may be able to console those who are in any affliction with the consolation with which we ourselves are consoled by God. For just as the sufferings of Christ are abundant for us, so also our consolation is abundant through Christ. If we are being afflicted, it is for your consolation and salvation; if we are being consoled, it is for your consolation, which you experience when you patiently endure the same sufferings that we are also suffering. Our hope for you is unshaken; for we know that as you share in our sufferings, so also you share in our consolation.

This is the word of the Lord.

Or:

A reading from the Letter of Paul to the Colossians. *(3.12-17)*

As God's chosen ones, holy and belovèd, clothe yourselves with compassion, kindness, humility, meekness, and patience. Bear with one another and, if anyone has a complaint against another, forgive each other; just as the Lord has forgiven you, so you also must forgive. Above all, clothe yourselves with love, which binds everything together in perfect harmony. And let the peace of Christ rule in your hearts, to which indeed you were called in the one body. And be thankful. Let the word of Christ dwell in you richly; teach and admonish one another in all wisdom; and with gratitude in your hearts sing psalms, hymns, and spiritual songs to God. And whatever you do, in word or deed, do everything in the name of the Lord Jesus, giving thanks to God the Father through him.

This is the word of the Lord.

Hear the gospel of our Lord Jesus Christ according to Luke. *(2.33-35)*

The father and mother of the child Jesus were amazed at what was being said about him. Then Simeon blessed them and said to his mother Mary, 'This child is destined for the falling and the rising of many in Israel, and to be a sign that will be opposed so that the inner thoughts of many will be revealed – and a sword will pierce your own soul too.'

This is the gospel of the Lord.

Or:

Hear the gospel of our Lord Jesus Christ according to John. *(19.25b-27)*

Standing near the cross of Jesus were his mother, and his mother's sister, Mary the wife of Clopas, and Mary Magdalene. When Jesus saw his mother and the disciple whom he loved standing beside her, he said to his mother, 'Woman, here is your son.' Then he said to the disciple, 'Here is your mother.' And from that hour the disciple took her into his own home.

This is the gospel of the Lord.

The Fifth Sunday of Lent

(Passiontide begins)

Principal Service

Jeremiah 31.31-34; Ps 51.1-12 *or* Ps 119.9-16; Hebrews 5.5-10;
John 12.20-33

A reading from the prophecy of Jeremiah. (31.31-34)

The days are surely coming, says the Lord, when I will make a new
covenant with the house of Israel and the house of Judah. It will not
be like the covenant that I made with their ancestors when I took
them by the hand to bring them out of the land of Egypt – a covenant
that they broke, though I was their husband, says the Lord. But this
is the covenant that I will make with the house of Israel after those
days, says the Lord: I will put my law within them, and I will write
it on their hearts; and I will be their God, and they shall be my people. No longer shall they teach one another, or say to each other,
'Know the Lord', for they shall all know me, from the least of them to
the greatest, says the Lord; for I will forgive their iniquity, and
remember their sin no more.

This is the word of the Lord.

A reading from the Letter to the Hebrews. (5.5-10)

Christ did not glorify himself in becoming a high priest, but was
appointed by the one who said to him,
    'You are my Son,
        today I have begotten you';
as he says also in another place,
    'You are a priest for ever,
        according to the order of Melchizedek.'
In the days of his flesh, Jesus offered up prayers and supplications,
with loud cries and tears, to the one who was able to save him from
death, and he was heard because of his reverent submission.
Although he was a Son, he learned obedience through what he suffered; and having been made perfect, he became the source of eternal
salvation for all who obey him, having been designated by God a
high priest according to the order of Melchizedek.

This is the word of the Lord.

Hear the gospel of our Lord Jesus Christ according to John. (12.20-33)

Among those who went up to worship at the Passover festival were some Greeks. They came to Philip, who was from Bethsaida in Galilee, and said to him, 'Sir, we wish to see Jesus.' Philip went and told Andrew; then Andrew and Philip went and told Jesus. Jesus answered them, 'The hour has come for the Son of Man to be glorified. Very truly, I tell you, unless a grain of wheat falls into the earth and dies, it remains just a single grain; but if it dies, it bears much fruit. Those who love their life lose it, and those who hate their life in this world will keep it for eternal life. Whoever serves me must follow me, and where I am, there will my servant be also. Whoever serves me, the Father will honour.

'Now my soul is troubled. And what should I say – "Father, save me from this hour"? No, it is for this reason that I have come to this hour. Father, glorify your name.' Then a voice came from heaven, 'I have glorified it, and I will glorify it again.' The crowd standing there heard it and said that it was thunder. Others said, 'An angel has spoken to him.' Jesus answered, 'This voice has come for your sake, not for mine. Now is the judgement of this world; now the ruler of this world will be driven out. And I, when I am lifted up from the earth, will draw all people to myself.' He said this to indicate the kind of death he was to die.

This is the gospel of the Lord.

Second Service
Ps 34 or 34.1-10; Exodus 7.8-24; Romans 5.12-21;
if a Eucharist: Luke 22.1-13

A reading from the Book of the Exodus. (7.8-24)

The Lord said to Moses and Aaron, 'When Pharaoh says to you, "Perform a wonder", then you shall say to Aaron, "Take your staff and throw it down before Pharaoh, and it will become a snake."' So Moses and Aaron went to Pharaoh and did as the Lord had commanded; Aaron threw down his staff before Pharaoh and his officials, and it became a snake. Then Pharaoh summoned the wise men and the sorcerers; and they also, the magicians of Egypt, did the same by their secret arts. Each one threw down his staff, and they became snakes; but Aaron's staff swallowed up theirs. Still Pharaoh's heart was hardened, and he would not listen to them, as the Lord had said.

Then the Lord said to Moses, 'Pharaoh's heart is hardened; he refuses to let the people go. Go to Pharaoh in the morning, as he is going out to the water; stand by at the river bank to meet him, and take in your hand the staff that was turned into a snake. Say to him, "The Lord, the God of the Hebrews, sent me to you to say, 'Let my people go, so that they may worship me in the wilderness.' But until now you have not listened. Thus says the Lord, 'By this you shall know that I am the Lord.' See, with the staff that is in my hand I will strike the water that is in the Nile, and it shall be turned to blood. The fish in the river shall die, the river itself shall stink, and the Egyptians shall be unable to drink water from the Nile."' The Lord said to Moses, 'Say to Aaron, "Take your staff and stretch out your hand over the waters of Egypt – over its rivers, its canals, and its ponds, and all its pools of water – so that they may become blood; and there shall be blood throughout the whole land of Egypt, even in vessels of wood and in vessels of stone."'

Moses and Aaron did just as the Lord commanded. In the sight of Pharaoh and of his officials he lifted up the staff and struck the water in the river, and all the water in the river was turned into blood, and the fish in the river died. The river stank so that the Egyptians could not drink its water, and there was blood throughout the whole land of Egypt. But the magicians of Egypt did the same by their secret arts; so Pharaoh's heart remained hardened, and he would not listen to them, as the Lord had said. Pharaoh turned and went into his house, and he did not take even this to heart. And all the Egyptians had to dig along the Nile for water to drink, for they could not drink the water of the river.

A reading from the Letter of Paul to the Romans. (5.12-21)

Just as sin came into the world through one man, and death came through sin, and so death spread to all because all have sinned – sin was indeed in the world before the law, but sin is not reckoned when there is no law. Yet death exercised dominion from Adam to Moses, even over those whose sins were not like the transgression of Adam, who is a type of the one who was to come.

But the free gift is not like the trespass. For if the many died through the one man's trespass, much more surely have the grace of God and the free gift in the grace of the one man, Jesus Christ, abounded for the many. And the free gift is not like the effect of the one man's sin. For the judgement following one trespass brought condemnation, but the free gift following many trespasses brings justification. If, because of the one man's trespass, death exercised dominion through that one, much more surely will those who receive the abundance of grace and the free gift of righteousness exercise dominion in life through the one man, Jesus Christ.

Therefore just as one man's trespass led to condemnation for all, so one man's act of righteousness leads to justification and life for all. For just as by the one man's disobedience the many were made sinners, so by the one man's obedience the many will be made righteous. But law came in, with the result that the trespass multiplied; but where sin increased, grace abounded all the more, so that, just as sin exercised dominion in death, so grace might also exercise dominion through justification leading to eternal life through Jesus Christ our Lord.

If a Eucharist:
Hear the gospel of our Lord Jesus Christ according to Luke. *(22.1-13)*

The festival of Unleavened Bread, which is called the Passover, was near. The chief priests and the scribes were looking for a way to put Jesus to death, for they were afraid of the people.

Then Satan entered into Judas called Iscariot, who was one of the twelve; he went away and conferred with the chief priests and officers of the temple police about how he might betray him to them. They were greatly pleased and agreed to give him money. So he consented and began to look for an opportunity to betray him to them when no crowd was present.

Then came the day of Unleavened Bread, on which the Passover lamb had to be sacrificed. So Jesus sent Peter and John, saying, 'Go and prepare the Passover meal for us that we may eat it.' They asked him, 'Where do you want us to make preparations for it?' 'Listen,' he said to them, 'when you have entered the city, a man carrying a jar of water will meet you; follow him into the house he enters and say to the owner of the house, "The teacher asks you, 'Where is the guest room, where I may eat the Passover with my disciples?'" He will show you a large room upstairs, already furnished. Make preparations for us there.' So they went and found everything as he had told them; and they prepared the Passover meal.

This is the word of the Lord.

Third Service
Ps 107.1-22; Exodus 24.3-8; Hebrews 12.18-29

A reading from the Book of the Exodus. *(24.3-8)*

Moses came and told the people all the words of the Lord and all the ordinances; and all the people answered with one voice, and said, 'All the words that the Lord has spoken we will do.' And Moses wrote down all the words of the Lord. He rose early in the morning, and built an altar at the foot of the mountain, and set up twelve pillars, corresponding to the twelve tribes of Israel. He sent young men of the people of Israel, who offered burnt-offerings and sacrificed oxen as offerings of well-being to the Lord. Moses took half of the blood and put it in basins, and half of the blood he dashed against the altar. Then he took the book of the covenant, and read it in the hearing of the people; and they said, 'All that the Lord has spoken we will do, and we will be obedient.' Moses took the blood and dashed it on the people, and said, 'See the blood of the covenant that the Lord has made with you in accordance with all these words.'

A reading from the Letter to the Hebrews. (12.18-29)

You have not come to something that can be touched, a blazing fire, and darkness, and gloom, and a tempest, and the sound of a trumpet, and a voice whose words made the hearers beg that not another word be spoken to them. (For they could not endure the order that was given, 'If even an animal touches the mountain, it shall be stoned to death.' Indeed, so terrifying was the sight that Moses said, 'I tremble with fear.') But you have come to Mount Zion and to the city of the living God, the heavenly Jerusalem, and to innumerable angels in festal gathering, and to the assembly of the firstborn who are enrolled in heaven, and to God the judge of all, and to the spirits of the righteous made perfect, and to Jesus, the mediator of a new covenant, and to the sprinkled blood that speaks a better word than the blood of Abel.

See that you do not refuse the one who is speaking; for if they did not escape when they refused the one who warned them on earth, how much less will we escape if we reject the one who warns from heaven! At that time his voice shook the earth; but now he has promised, 'Yet once more I will shake not only the earth but also the heaven.' This phrase 'Yet once more' indicates the removal of what is shaken – that is, created things – so that what cannot be shaken may remain. Therefore, since we are receiving a kingdom that cannot be shaken, let us give thanks, by which we offer to God an acceptable worship with reverence and awe; for indeed our God is a consuming fire.

Holy Week

Palm Sunday

Liturgy of the Palms: Mark 11.1-11 *or* John 12.12-16
                                            Ps 118. [1-2] 19-24 [25-29]

Liturgy of the Passion: Isaiah 50.4-9a
                                              Ps 31.9-16 [17-18]
                                            Philippians 2.5-11
                                            Mark 14.1 - 15.47 *or* 15.1-39 [40-47]

Liturgy of the Palms:

Hear the gospel of our Lord Jesus Christ according to Mark. (11.1-11)

When they were approaching Jerusalem, at Bethphage and Bethany, near the Mount of Olives, Jesus sent two of his disciples and said to them, 'Go into the village ahead of you, and immediately as you enter it, you will find tied there a colt that has never been ridden; untie it and bring it. If anyone says to you, "Why are you doing this?" just say this, "The Lord needs it and will send it back here immediately."' They went away and found a colt tied near a door, outside in the street. As they were untying it, some of the bystanders said to them, 'What are you doing, untying the colt?' They told them what Jesus had said; and they allowed them to take it. Then they brought the colt to Jesus and threw their cloaks on it; and he sat on it. Many people spread their cloaks on the road, and others spread leafy branches that they had cut in the fields. Then those who went ahead and those who followed were shouting,

    'Hosanna!
        Blessèd is the one who comes in the name of the Lord!
        Blessèd is the coming kingdom of our ancestor David!
    Hosanna in the highest heaven!'

Then he entered Jerusalem and went into the temple; and when he had looked around at everything, as it was already late, he went out to Bethany with the twelve.

This is the gospel of the Lord.

Or:

Hear the gospel of our Lord Jesus Christ according to John. (12.12-16)

The great crowd that had come to the festival heard that Jesus was coming to Jerusalem. So they took branches of palm trees and went out to meet him, shouting,

'Hosanna!

Blessèd is the one who comes in the name of the Lord –

the King of Israel!'

Jesus found a young donkey and sat on it; as it is written:

'Do not be afraid, daughter of Zion.

Look, your king is coming,

sitting on a donkey's colt!'

His disciples did not understand these things at first; but when Jesus was glorified, then they remembered that these things had been written of him and had been done to him.

This is the gospel of the Lord.

Liturgy of the Passion:

A reading from the prophecy of Isaiah. (50.4-9a)

The Lord God has given me

the tongue of a teacher,

that I may know how to sustain

the weary with a word.

Morning by morning he wakens –

wakens my ear to listen as those who are taught.

The Lord God has opened my ear, and I was not rebellious,

I did not turn backwards.

I gave my back to those who struck me,

and my cheeks to those who pulled out the beard;

I did not hide my face

from insult and spitting.

The Lord God helps me;

therefore I have not been disgraced;

therefore I have set my face like flint,

and I know that I shall not be put to shame;

he who vindicates me is near.

Who will contend with me?

Let us stand up together.

Who are my adversaries?

Let them confront me.

It is the Lord God who helps me;

who will declare me guilty?

This is the word of the Lord.

A reading from the Letter of Paul to the Philippians. (2.5-11)

Let the same mind be in you that was in Christ Jesus,
   who, though he was in the form of God,
      did not regard equality with God
      as something to be exploited,
   but emptied himself,
      taking the form of a slave,
      being born in human likeness.
   And being found in human form,
      he humbled himself
      and became obedient to the point of death –
      even death on a cross.
   Therefore God also highly exalted him
      and gave him the name
      that is above every name,
   so that at the name of Jesus
      every knee should bend,
      in heaven and on earth and under the earth,
   and every tongue should confess that Jesus Christ is Lord,
      to the glory of God the Father.

This is the word of the Lord.

Hear the passion of our Lord Jesus Christ according to Mark.
                     (Mark 14.1 - 15.47 or 15.1-39 [40-47])
[14.1 It was two days before the Passover and the festival of Unleavened Bread. The chief priests and the scribes were looking for a way to arrest Jesus by stealth and kill him; for they said, 'Not during the festival, or there may be a riot among the people.'

While he was at Bethany in the house of Simon the leper, as he sat at the table, a woman came with an alabaster jar of very costly ointment of nard, and she broke open the jar and poured the ointment on his head. But some were there who said to one another in anger, 'Why was the ointment wasted in this way? For this ointment could have been sold for more than three hundred denarii, and the money given to the poor.' And they scolded her. But Jesus said, 'Let her alone; why do you trouble her? She has performed a good service for me. For you always have the poor with you, and you can show kindness to them whenever you wish; but you will not always have me. She has done what she could; she has anointed my body beforehand for its burial. Truly I tell you, wherever the good news is proclaimed in the whole world, what she has done will be told in remembrance of her.'

Then Judas Iscariot, who was one of the twelve, went to the chief priests in order to betray him to them. When they heard it, they were greatly pleased, and promised to give him money. So he began to look for an opportunity to betray him.

On the first day of Unleavened Bread, when the Passover lamb is sacrificed, his disciples said to him, 'Where do you want us to go and make the preparations for you to eat the Passover?' So he sent two of his disciples, saying to them, 'Go into the city, and a man carrying a jar of water will meet you; follow him, and wherever he enters, say to the owner of the house, "The Teacher asks, Where is my guest room where I may eat the Passover with my disciples?" He will show you a large room upstairs, furnished and ready. Make preparations for us there.' So the disciples set out and went to the city, and found everything as he had told them; and they prepared the Passover meal.

When it was evening, he came with the twelve. And when they had taken their places and were eating, Jesus said, 'Truly I tell you, one of you will betray me, one who is eating with me.' They began to be distressed and to say to him one after another, 'Surely, not I?' He said to them, 'It is one of the twelve, one who is dipping bread into the bowl with me. For the Son of Man goes as it is written of him, but woe to that one by whom the Son of Man is betrayed! It would have been better for that one not to have been born.'

While they were eating, he took a loaf of bread, and after blessing it he broke it, gave it to them, and said, 'Take; this is my body.' Then he took a cup, and after giving thanks he gave it to them, and all of them drank from it. He said to them, 'This is my blood of the covenant, which is poured out for many. Truly I tell you, I will never again drink of the fruit of the vine until that day when I drink it new in the kingdom of God.'

When they had sung the hymn, they went out to the Mount of Olives. And Jesus said to them, 'You will all become deserters; for it is written,

"I will strike the shepherd,
    and the sheep will be scattered."

But after I am raised up, I will go before you to Galilee.' Peter said to him, 'Even though all become deserters, I will not.' Jesus said to him, 'Truly I tell you, this day, this very night, before the cock crows twice, you will deny me three times.' But he said vehemently, 'Even though I must die with you, I will not deny you.' And all of them said the same.

They went to a place called Gethsemane; and he said to his disciples,

'Sit here while I pray.' He took with him Peter and James and John, and began to be distressed and agitated. And he said to them, 'I am deeply grieved, even to death; remain here, and keep awake.' And going a little farther, he threw himself on the ground and prayed that, if it were possible, the hour might pass from him. He said, 'Abba, Father, for you all things are possible; remove this cup from me; yet, not what I want, but what you want.' He came and found them sleeping; and he said to Peter, 'Simon, are you asleep? Could you not keep awake one hour? Keep awake and pray that you may not come into the time of trial; the spirit indeed is willing, but the flesh is weak.' And again he went away and prayed, saying the same words. And once more he came and found them sleeping, for their eyes were very heavy; and they did not know what to say to him. He came a third time and said to them, 'Are you still sleeping and taking your rest? Enough! The hour has come; the Son of Man is betrayed into the hands of sinners. Get up, let us be going. See, my betrayer is at hand.'

Immediately, while he was still speaking, Judas, one of the twelve, arrived; and with him there was a crowd with swords and clubs, from the chief priests, the scribes, and the elders. Now the betrayer had given them a sign, saying, 'The one I will kiss is the man; arrest him and lead him away under guard.' So when he came, he went up to him at once and said, 'Rabbi!' and kissed him. Then they laid hands on him and arrested him. But one of those who stood near drew his sword and struck the slave of the high priest, cutting off his ear. Then Jesus said to them, 'Have you come out with swords and clubs to arrest me as though I were a bandit? Day after day I was with you in the temple teaching, and you did not arrest me. But let the scriptures be fulfilled.' All of them deserted him and fled.

A certain young man was following him, wearing nothing but a linen cloth. They caught hold of him, but he left the linen cloth and ran off naked.

They took Jesus to the high priest; and all the chief priests, the elders, and the scribes were assembled. Peter had followed him at a distance, right into the courtyard of the high priest; and he was sitting with the guards, warming himself at the fire. Now the chief priests and the whole council were looking for testimony against Jesus to put him to death; but they found none. For many gave false testimony against him, and their testimony did not agree. Some stood up and gave false testimony against him, saying, 'We heard him say, "I will destroy this temple that is made with hands, and in three days I will build another, not made with hands."' But even on this point their testimony did not agree. Then the high priest stood up before them and asked Jesus, 'Have you no answer? What is it that they testify against you?' But he was silent and did not answer. Again the high priest asked him, 'Are you the Messiah, the Son of the Blessèd One?' Jesus said, 'I am; and

"you will see the Son of Man

seated at the right hand of the Power",

and "coming with the clouds of heaven."'

Then the high priest tore his clothes and said, 'Why do we still need witnesses? You have heard his blasphemy! What is your decision?' All of them condemned him as deserving death. Some began to spit on him, to blindfold him, and to strike him, saying to him, 'Prophesy!' The guards also took him over and beat him.

While Peter was below in the courtyard, one of the servant-girls of the high priest came by. When she saw Peter warming himself, she stared at him and said, 'You also were with Jesus, the man from Nazareth.' But he denied it, saying, 'I do not know or understand what you are talking about.' And he went out into the forecourt. Then the cock crowed. And the servant-girl, on seeing him, began again to say to the bystanders, 'This man is one of them.' But again he denied it. Then after a little while the bystanders again said to Peter, 'Certainly you are one of them; for you are a Galilean.' But he began to curse, and he swore an oath, 'I do not know this man you are talking about.' At that moment the cock crowed for the second time. Then Peter remembered that Jesus had said to him, 'Before the cock crows twice, you will deny me three times.' And he broke down and wept.]

15.1 As soon as it was morning, the chief priests held a consultation with the elders and scribes and the whole council. They bound Jesus, led him away, and handed him over to Pilate. Pilate asked him, 'Are you the King of the Jews?' He answered him, 'You say so.' Then the chief priests accused him of many things. Pilate asked him again, 'Have you no answer? See how many charges they bring against you.' But Jesus made no further reply, so that Pilate was amazed.

Now at the festival he used to release a prisoner for them, anyone for whom they asked. Now a man called Barabbas was in prison with the rebels who had committed murder during the insurrection. So the crowd came and began to ask Pilate to do for them according to his custom. Then he answered them, 'Do you want me to release for you the King of the Jews?' For he realized that it was out of jealousy that the chief priests had handed him over. But the chief priests stirred up the crowd to have him release Barabbas for them instead.

Pilate spoke to them again, 'Then what do you wish me to do with the man you call the King of the Jews?' They shouted back, 'Crucify him!' Pilate asked them, 'Why, what evil has he done?' But they shouted all the more, 'Crucify him!' So Pilate, wishing to satisfy the crowd, released Barabbas for them; and after flogging Jesus, he handed him over to be crucified.

Then the soldiers led him into the courtyard of the palace (that is, the governor's headquarters); and they called together the whole cohort. And they clothed him in a purple cloak; and after twisting some thorns into a crown, they put it on him. And they began saluting him, 'Hail, King of the Jews!' They struck his head with a reed, spat upon him, and knelt down in homage to him. After mocking him, they stripped him of the purple cloak and put his own clothes on him. Then they led him out to crucify him.

They compelled a passer-by, who was coming in from the country, to carry his cross; it was Simon of Cyrene, the father of Alexander and Rufus. Then they brought Jesus to the place called Golgotha (which means the place of a skull). And they offered him wine mixed with myrrh; but he did not take it. And they crucified him, and divided his clothes among them, casting lots to decide what each should take.

It was nine o'clock in the morning when they crucified him. The inscription of the charge against him read, 'The King of the Jews.' And with him they crucified two bandits, one on his right and one on his left. Those who passed by derided him, shaking their heads and saying, 'Aha! You who would destroy the temple and build it in three days, save yourself, and come down from the cross!' In the same way the chief priests, along with the scribes, were also mocking him among themselves and saying, 'He saved others; he cannot save himself. Let the Messiah, the King of Israel, come down from the cross now, so that we may see and believe.' Those who were crucified with him also taunted him.

When it was noon, darkness came over the whole land until three in the afternoon. At three o'clock Jesus cried out with a loud voice, 'Eloi, Eloi, lema sabachthani?' which means, 'My God, my God, why have you forsaken me?' When some of the bystanders heard it, they said, 'Listen, he is calling for Elijah.' And someone ran, filled a sponge with sour wine, put it on a stick, and gave it to him to drink, saying, 'Wait, let us see whether Elijah will come to take him down.' Then Jesus gave a loud cry and breathed his last. And the curtain of the temple was torn in two, from top to bottom. Now when the centurion, who stood facing him, saw that in this way he breathed his

last, he said, 'Truly this man was God's Son!'
[⁴⁰ There were also women looking on from a distance; among them were Mary Magdalene, and Mary the mother of James the younger and of Joses, and Salome. These used to follow him and provided for him when he was in Galilee; and there were many other women who had come up with him to Jerusalem.

When evening had come, and since it was the day of Preparation, that is, the day before the sabbath, Joseph of Arimathea, a respected member of the council, who was also himself waiting expectantly for the kingdom of God, went boldly to Pilate and asked for the body of Jesus. Then Pilate wondered if he were already dead; and summoning the centurion, he asked him whether he had been dead for some time. When he learned from the centurion that he was dead, he granted the body to Joseph. Then Joseph bought a linen cloth, and taking down the body, wrapped it in the linen cloth, and laid it in a tomb that had been hewn out of the rock. He then rolled a stone against the door of the tomb. Mary Magdalene and Mary the mother of Joses saw where the body was laid.]

This is the passion of the Lord.

Second Service
Ps 69.1-18; Isaiah 5.1-7; Mark 12.1-12

A reading from the prophecy of Isaiah. (5.1-7)

Let me sing for my belovèd
　　my love-song concerning his vineyard:
My belovèd had a vineyard
　　on a very fertile hill.
He dug it and cleared it of stones,
　　and planted it with choice vines;
he built a watch-tower in the midst of it,
　　and hewed out a wine vat in it;
he expected it to yield grapes,
　　but it yielded wild grapes.

And now, inhabitants of Jerusalem
　　and people of Judah,
judge between me
　　and my vineyard.
What more was there to do for my vineyard
　　that I have not done in it?
When I expected it to yield grapes,
　　why did it yield wild grapes?

And now I will tell you
   what I will do to my vineyard.
I will remove its hedge,
   and it shall be devoured;
I will break down its wall,
   and it shall be trampled down.
I will make it a waste;
   it shall not be pruned or hoed,
   and it shall be overgrown with briers and thorns;
I will also command the clouds
   that they rain no rain upon it.

For the vineyard of the Lord of hosts
   is the house of Israel,
and the people of Judah
   are his pleasant planting;
he expected justice,
   but saw bloodshed;
righteousness,
   but heard a cry!

A reading from the gospel according to Mark. (12.1-12)

Jesus began to speak to them in parables. 'A man planted a vineyard,
put a fence around it, dug a pit for the wine press, and built a watch-
tower; then he leased it to tenants and went to another country.
When the season came, he sent a slave to the tenants to collect from
them his share of the produce of the vineyard. But they seized him,
and beat him, and sent him away empty-handed. And again he sent
another slave to them; this one they beat over the head and insulted.
Then he sent another, and that one they killed. And so it was with
many others; some they beat, and others they killed. He had still one
other, a beloved son. Finally he sent him to them, saying, "They will
respect my son." But those tenants said to one another, "This is the
heir; come, let us kill him, and the inheritance will be ours." So they
seized him, killed him, and threw him out of the vineyard. What
then will the owner of the vineyard do? He will come and destroy
the tenants and give the vineyard to others. Have you not read this
scripture:
   "The stone that the builders rejected
      has become the cornerstone;
   this was the Lord's doing,
      and it is amazing in our eyes"?'

When they realized that he had told this parable against them, they wanted to arrest him, but they feared the crowd. So they left him and went away.

Third Service
Pss 61,62; Zechariah 9.9-12; 1 Corinthians 2.1-12

A reading from the prophecy of Zechariah. (9.9-12)

Rejoice greatly, O daughter Zion!
    Shout aloud, O daughter Jerusalem!
Lo, your king comes to you;
    triumphant and victorious is he,
humble and riding on a donkey,
    on a colt, the foal of a donkey.
He will cut off the chariot from Ephraim
    and the warhorse from Jerusalem;
and the battle-bow shall be cut off,
    and he shall command peace to the nations;
his dominion shall be from sea to sea,
    and from the River to the ends of the earth.

As for you also,
    because of the blood of my covenant with you,
I will set your prisoners free
    from the waterless pit.
Return to your stronghold,
    O prisoners of hope;
today I declare that I will restore to you double.

A reading from the First Letter of Paul to the Corinthians. (2.1-12)

When I came to you, brothers and sisters, I did not come proclaiming the mystery of God to you in lofty words or wisdom. For I decided to know nothing among you except Jesus Christ, and him crucified. And I came to you in weakness and in fear and in much trembling. My speech and my proclamation were not with plausible words of wisdom, but with a demonstration of the Spirit and of power, so that your faith might rest not on human wisdom but on the power of God.

Yet among the mature we do speak wisdom, though it is not a wisdom of this age or of the rulers of this age, who are doomed to perish. But we speak God's wisdom, secret and hidden, which God decreed before the ages for our glory. None of the rulers of this age understood this; for if they had, they would not have crucified the

Lord of glory. But, as it is written,
  'What no eye has seen, nor ear heard,
    nor the human heart conceived,
  what God has prepared for those who love him' –
these things God has revealed to us through the Spirit; for the Spirit
searches everything, even the depths of God. For what human being
knows what is truly human except the human spirit that is within?
So also no one comprehends what is truly God's except the Spirit of
God. Now we have received not the spirit of the world, but the
Spirit that is from God, so that we may understand the gifts bestowed
on us by God.

Monday of Holy Week

Principal Service
Isaiah 42.1-9; Ps 36.5-11; Hebrews 9.11-15; John 12.1-11

A reading from the prophecy of Isaiah. (42.1-9)

Here is my servant, whom I uphold,
  my chosen, in whom my soul delights;
I have put my spirit upon him;
  he will bring forth justice to the nations.
He will not cry or lift up his voice,
  or make it heard in the street;
a bruised reed he will not break,
  and a dimly burning wick he will not quench;
  he will faithfully bring forth justice.
He will not grow faint or be crushed
  until he has established justice in the earth;
  and the coastlands wait for his teaching.

Thus says God, the Lord,
  who created the heavens and stretched them out,
  who spread out the earth and what comes from it,
  who gives breath to the people upon it
  and spirit to those who walk in it:
I am the Lord, I have called you in righteousness,
  I have taken you by the hand and kept you;
I have given you as a covenant to the people,
  a light to the nations,
to open the eyes that are blind,
  to bring out the prisoners from the dungeon,

from the prison those who sit in darkness.
I am the Lord, that is my name;
  my glory I give to no other, nor my praise to idols.
See, the former things have come to pass,
  and new things I now declare;
before they spring forth, I tell you of them.

This is the word of the Lord.

A reading from the Letter to the Hebrews. (9.11-15)

When Christ came as a high priest of the good things that have come,
then through the greater and perfect tent (not made with hands, that
is, not of this creation), he entered once for all into the Holy Place, not
with the blood of goats and calves, but with his own blood, thus
obtaining eternal redemption. For if the blood of goats and bulls,
with the sprinkling of the ashes of a heifer, sanctifies those who have
been defiled so that their flesh is purified, how much more will the
blood of Christ, who through the eternal Spirit offered himself without blemish to God, purify our conscience from dead works to worship the living God!

  For this reason he is the mediator of a new covenant, so that those
who are called may receive the promised eternal inheritance, because
a death has occurred that redeems them from the transgressions
under the first covenant.

This is the word of the Lord.

Hear the gospel of our Lord Jesus Christ according to John. (12.1-11)

Six days before the Passover Jesus came to Bethany, the home of
Lazarus, whom he had raised from the dead. There they gave a dinner for him. Martha served, and Lazarus was one of those at the table
with him. Mary took a pound of costly perfume made of pure nard,
anointed Jesus' feet, and wiped them with her hair. The house was
filled with the fragrance of the perfume. But Judas Iscariot, one of his
disciples (the one who was about to betray him), said, 'Why was this
perfume not sold for three hundred denarii and the money given to
the poor?' (He said this not because he cared about the poor, but
because he was a thief; he kept the common purse and used to steal
what was put into it.) Jesus said, 'Leave her alone. She bought it so
that she might keep it for the day of my burial. You always have the
poor with you, but you do not always have me.'

  When the great crowd of the Jews learned that he was there, they
came not only because of Jesus but also to see Lazarus, whom he had

raised from the dead. So the chief priests planned to put Lazarus to death as well, since it was on account of him that many of the Jews were deserting and were believing in Jesus.

This is the gospel of the Lord.

Second Service
Ps 41; Lamentations 1.1-12a; Luke 22.1-23

A reading from the Lamentations of Jeremiah. (1.1-12a)

How lonely sits the city
> that once was full of people!
How like a widow she has become,
> she that was great among the nations!
She that was a princess among the provinces
> has become a vassal.

She weeps bitterly in the night,
> with tears on her cheeks;
among all her lovers
> she has no one to comfort her;
all her friends have dealt treacherously with her,
> they have become her enemies.

Judah has gone into exile
> with suffering and hard servitude;
she lives now among the nations,
> and finds no resting-place;
her pursuers have all overtaken her
> in the midst of her distress.

The roads to Zion mourn,
> for no one comes to the festivals;
all her gates are desolate,
> her priests groan;
her young girls grieve,
> and her lot is bitter.

Her foes have become the masters,
> her enemies prosper,
because the Lord has made her suffer
> for the multitude of her transgressions;
her children have gone away,
> captives before the foe.

From daughter Zion has departed
> all her majesty.

Her princes have become like stags
    that find no pasture;
they fled without strength
    before the pursuer.

Jerusalem remembers,
    in the days of her affliction and wandering,
all the precious things
    that were hers in days of old.
When her people fell into the hand of the foe,
    and there was no one to help her,
the foe looked on mocking
    over her downfall.

Jerusalem sinned grievously,
    so she has become a mockery;
all who honoured her despise her,
    for they have seen her nakedness;
she herself groans,
    and turns her face away.

Her uncleanness was in her skirts;
    she took no thought of her future;
her downfall was appalling,
    with none to comfort her.
'O Lord, look at my affliction,
    for the enemy has triumphed!'

Enemies have stretched out their hands
    over all her precious things;
she has even seen the nations
    invade her sanctuary,
those whom you forbade
    to enter your congregation.

All her people groan
    as they search for bread;
they trade their treasures for food
    to revive their strength.
Look, O Lord, and see
    how worthless I have become.
Is it nothing to you,
    all you who pass by?
Look and see if there are any sorrows
    like my sorrow.

A reading from the gospel according to Luke. (22.1-23)

Now the festival of Unleavened Bread, which is called the Passover, was near. The chief priests and the scribes were looking for a way to put Jesus to death, for they were afraid of the people.

Then Satan entered into Judas called Iscariot, who was one of the twelve; he went away and conferred with the chief priests and officers of the temple police about how he might betray him to them. They were greatly pleased and agreed to give him money. So he consented and began to look for an opportunity to betray him to them when no crowd was present.

Then came the day of Unleavened Bread, on which the Passover lamb had to be sacrificed. So Jesus sent Peter and John, saying, 'Go and prepare the Passover meal for us that we may eat it.' They asked him, 'Where do you want us to make preparations for it?' 'Listen,' he said to them, 'when you have entered the city, a man carrying a jar of water will meet you; follow him into the house he enters and say to the owner of the house, "The teacher asks you, 'Where is the guest room, where I may eat the Passover with my disciples?'" He will show you a large room upstairs, already furnished. Make preparations for us there.' So they went and found everything as he had told them; and they prepared the Passover meal.

When the hour came, he took his place at the table, and the apostles with him. He said to them, 'I have eagerly desired to eat this Passover with you before I suffer; for I tell you, I will not eat it until it is fulfilled in the kingdom of God.' Then he took a cup, and after giving thanks he said, 'Take this and divide it among yourselves; for I tell you that from now on I will not drink of the fruit of the vine until the kingdom of God comes.' Then he took a loaf of bread, and when he had given thanks, he broke it and gave it to them, saying, 'This is my body, which is given for you. Do this in remembrance of me.' And he did the same with the cup after supper, saying, 'This cup that is poured out for you is the new covenant in my blood. But see, the one who betrays me is with me, and his hand is on the table. For the Son of Man is going as it has been determined, but woe to that one by whom he is betrayed!' Then they began to ask one another which one of them it could be who would do this.

Third Service

Ps 25; Lamentations 2.8-19; Colossians 1.18-23

A reading from the Lamentations of Jeremiah. (2.8-19)

The Lord determined to lay in ruins
    the wall of daughter Zion;
he stretched the line;
    he did not withhold his hand from destroying;
he caused rampart and wall to lament;
    they languish together.

Her gates have sunk into the ground;
    he has ruined and broken her bars;
her king and princes are among the nations;
    guidance is no more,
and her prophets obtain
    no vision from the Lord.

The elders of daughter Zion
    sit on the ground in silence;
they have thrown dust on their heads
    and put on sackcloth;
the young girls of Jerusalem
    have bowed their heads to the ground.

My eyes are spent with weeping;
    my stomach churns;
my bile is poured out on the ground
    because of the destruction of my people,
because infants and babes
    faint in the streets of the city.

They cry to their mothers,
    'Where is bread and wine?'
as they faint like the wounded
    in the streets of the city,
as their life is poured out
    on their mothers' bosom.

What can I say for you,
    to what compare you, O daughter Jerusalem?
To what can I liken you, that I may comfort you,
    O virgin daughter Zion?
For vast as the sea is your ruin;
    who can heal you?

Your prophets have seen for you
    false and deceptive visions;
they have not exposed your iniquity
    to restore your fortunes,
but have seen oracles for you
    that are false and misleading.

All who pass along the way
    clap their hands at you;
they hiss and wag their heads
    at daughter Jerusalem;
'Is this the city that was called
    the perfection of beauty,
    the joy of all the earth?'

All your enemies
    open their mouths against you;
they hiss, they gnash their teeth,
    they cry: 'We have devoured her!
Ah, this is the day we longed for;
    at last we have seen it!'

The Lord has done what he purposed,
    he has carried out his threat;
as he ordained long ago,
    he has demolished without pity;
he has made the enemy rejoice over you,
    and exalted the might of your foes.

Cry aloud to the Lord!
    O wall of daughter Zion!
Let tears stream down like a torrent
    day and night!
Give yourself no rest,
    your eyes no respite!

Arise, cry out in the night,
    at the beginning of the watches!
Pour out your heart like water
    before the presence of the Lord!
Lift your hands to him
    for the lives of your children,
who faint for hunger
    at the head of every street.

A reading from the Letter of Paul to the Colossians. (1.18-23)

Christ Jesus is the head of the body, the church; he is the beginning, the firstborn from the dead, so that he might come to have first place in everything. For in him all the fullness of God was pleased to dwell, and through him God was pleased to reconcile to himself all things, whether on earth or in heaven, by making peace through the blood of his cross.

And you who were once estranged and hostile in mind, doing evil deeds, he has now reconciled in his fleshly body through death, so as to present you holy and blameless and irreproachable before him – provided that you continue securely established and steadfast in the faith, without shifting from the hope promised by the gospel that you heard, which has been proclaimed to every creature under heaven. I, Paul, became a servant of this gospel.

Tuesday of Holy Week

Principal Service
Isaiah 49.1-7; Ps 71.1-8 [9-14]; 1 Corinthians 1.18-31; John 12.20-36

A reading from the prophecy of Isaiah. (49.1-7)

Listen to me, O coastlands,
    pay attention, you peoples from far away!
The Lord called me before I was born,
    while I was in my mother's womb he named me.
He made my mouth like a sharp sword,
    in the shadow of his hand he hid me;
he made me a polished arrow,
    in his quiver he hid me away.
And he said to me,
    'You are my servant, Israel, in whom I will be glorified.'
But I said, 'I have laboured in vain,
    I have spent my strength for nothing and vanity;
yet surely my cause is with the Lord,
    and my reward with my God.'

And now the Lord says,
    who formed me in the womb to be his servant,
to bring Jacob back to him,
    and that Israel might be gathered to him,
for I am honoured in the sight of the Lord,
    and my God has become my strength –

he says,
'It is too light a thing that you should be my servant
    to raise up the tribes of Jacob
    and to restore the survivors of Israel;
I will give you as a light to the nations,
    that my salvation may reach to the end of the earth.'
Thus says the Lord,
    the Redeemer of Israel and his Holy One,
to one deeply despised, abhorred by the nations,
    the slave of rulers,
'Kings shall see and stand up,
    princes, and they shall prostrate themselves,
because of the Lord, who is faithful,
    the Holy One of Israel, who has chosen you.'

This is the word of the Lord.

A reading from the First Letter of Paul to the Corinthians. (1.18-31)

The message about the cross is foolishness to those who are perishing, but to us who are being saved it is the power of God. For it is written,
'I will destroy the wisdom of the wise,
    and the discernment of the discerning I will thwart.'
Where is the one who is wise? Where is the scribe? Where is the debater of this age? Has not God made foolish the wisdom of the world? For since, in the wisdom of God, the world did not know God through wisdom, God decided, through the foolishness of our proclamation, to save those who believe. For Jews demand signs and Greeks desire wisdom, but we proclaim Christ crucified, a stumbling-block to Jews and foolishness to Gentiles, but to those who are the called, both Jews and Greeks, Christ the power of God and the wisdom of God. For God's foolishness is wiser than human wisdom, and God's weakness is stronger than human strength.

Consider your own call, brothers and sisters: not many of you were wise by human standards, not many were powerful, not many were of noble birth. But God chose what is foolish in the world to shame the wise; God chose what is weak in the world to shame the strong; God chose what is low and despised in the world, things that are not, to reduce to nothing things that are, so that no one might boast in the presence of God. He is the source of your life in Christ Jesus, who became for us wisdom from God, and righteousness and sanctification and redemption, in order that, as it is written, 'Let the one who boasts, boast in the Lord.'

This is the word of the Lord.

Hear the gospel of our Lord Jesus Christ according to John. (12.20-36)

Now among those who went up to worship at the festival were some Greeks. They came to Philip, who was from Bethsaida in Galilee, and said to him, 'Sir, we wish to see Jesus.' Philip went and told Andrew; then Andrew and Philip went and told Jesus. Jesus answered them, 'The hour has come for the Son of Man to be glorified. Very truly, I tell you, unless a grain of wheat falls into the earth and dies, it remains just a single grain; but if it dies, it bears much fruit. Those who love their life lose it, and those who hate their life in this world will keep it for eternal life. Whoever serves me must follow me, and where I am, there will my servant be also. Whoever serves me, the Father will honour.

'Now my soul is troubled. And what should I say – "Father, save me from this hour"? No, it is for this reason that I have come to this hour. Father, glorify your name.' Then a voice came from heaven, 'I have glorified it, and I will glorify it again.' The crowd standing there heard it and said that it was thunder. Others said, 'An angel has spoken to him.' Jesus answered, 'This voice has come for your sake, not for mine. Now is the judgement of this world; now the ruler of this world will be driven out. And I, when I am lifted up from the earth, will draw all people to myself.' He said this to indicate the kind of death he was to die. The crowd answered him, 'We have heard from the law that the Messiah remains for ever. How can you say that the Son of Man must be lifted up? Who is this Son of Man?' Jesus said to them, 'The light is with you for a little longer. Walk while you have the light, so that the darkness may not overtake you. If you walk in the darkness, you do not know where you are going. While you have the light, believe in the light, so that you may become children of light.' After Jesus had said this, he departed and hid from them.

This is the gospel of the Lord.

Second Service
Ps 27; Lamentations 3.1-18; Luke 22. [24-38] 39-53

A reading from the Lamentations of Jeremiah. (3.1-18)

I am one who has seen affliction
    under the rod of God's wrath;
he has driven and brought me into darkness
    without any light;
against me alone he turns his hand,
    again and again, all day long.

He has made my flesh and my skin waste away,
  and broken my bones;
he has besieged and enveloped me
  with bitterness and tribulation;
he has made me sit in darkness
  like the dead of long ago.

He has walled me about so that I cannot escape;
  he has put heavy chains on me;
though I call and cry for help,
  he shuts out my prayer;
he has blocked my ways with hewn stones,
  he has made my paths crooked.

He is a bear lying in wait for me,
  a lion in hiding;
he led me off my way and tore me to pieces;
  he has made me desolate;
he bent his bow
  and set me as a mark for his arrow.

He shot into my vitals
  the arrows of his quiver;
I have become the laughing-stock of all my people,
  the object of their taunt-songs all day long.
He has filled me with bitterness,
  he has glutted me with wormwood.

He has made my teeth grind on gravel,
  and made me cower in ashes;
my soul is bereft of peace;
  I have forgotten what happiness is;
so I say, 'Gone is my glory,
  and all that I had hoped for from the Lord.'

A reading from the gospel according to Luke. (22. [24-38] 39-53)

[A dispute also arose among the apostles as to which one of them was
to be regarded as the greatest. But Jesus said to them, 'The kings of
the Gentiles lord it over them; and those in authority over them are
called benefactors. But not so with you; rather the greatest among
you must become like the youngest, and the leader like one who
serves. For who is greater, the one who is at the table or the one who
serves? Is it not the one at the table? But I am among you as one who
serves.

  'You are those who have stood by me in my trials; and I confer on you, just as my Father has conferred on me, a kingdom, so that you may eat and drink at my table in my kingdom, and you will sit on thrones judging the twelve tribes of Israel.

'Simon, Simon, listen! Satan has demanded to sift all of you like wheat, but I have prayed for you that your own faith may not fail; and you, when once you have turned back, strengthen your brothers.' And he said to him, 'Lord, I am ready to go with you to prison and to death!' Jesus said, 'I tell you, Peter, the cock will not crow this day, until you have denied three times that you know me.'

He said to them, 'When I sent you out without a purse, bag, or sandals, did you lack anything?' They said, 'No, not a thing.' He said to them, 'But now, the one who has a purse must take it, and likewise a bag. And the one who has no sword must sell his cloak and buy one. For I tell you, this scripture must be fulfilled in me, "And he was counted among the lawless"; and indeed what is written about me is being fulfilled.' They said, 'Lord, look, here are two swords.' He replied, 'It is enough.']

[39] Jesus came out and went, as was his custom, to the Mount of Olives; and the disciples followed him. When he reached the place, he said to them, 'Pray that you may not come into the time of trial.' Then he withdrew from them about a stone's throw, knelt down, and prayed, 'Father, if you are willing, remove this cup from me; yet, not my will but yours be done.' Then an angel from heaven appeared to him and gave him strength. In his anguish he prayed more earnestly, and his sweat became like great drops of blood falling down on the ground. When he got up from prayer, he came to the disciples and found them sleeping because of grief, and he said to them, 'Why are you sleeping? Get up and pray that you may not come into the time of trial.'

While he was still speaking, suddenly a crowd came, and the one called Judas, one of the twelve, was leading them. He approached Jesus to kiss him; but Jesus said to him, 'Judas, is it with a kiss that you are betraying the Son of Man?' When those who were around him saw what was coming, they asked, 'Lord, should we strike with the sword?' Then one of them struck the slave of the high priest and cut off his right ear. But Jesus said, 'No more of this!' And he touched his ear and healed him. Then Jesus said to the chief priests, the officers of the temple police, and the elders who had come for him, 'Have you come out with swords and clubs as if I were a bandit? When I was with you day after day in the temple, you did not lay hands on me. But this is your hour, and the power of darkness!'

Third Service

Ps 55.12-22; Lamentations 3.40-51; Galatians 6.11-18

A reading from the Lamentations of Jeremiah. (3.40-51)

Let us test and examine our ways,
     and return to the Lord.
Let us lift up our hearts as well as our hands
     to God in heaven.
We have transgressed and rebelled,
     and you have not forgiven.

You have wrapped yourself with anger and pursued us,
     killing without pity;
you have wrapped yourself with a cloud
     so that no prayer can pass through.
You have made us filth and rubbish
     among the peoples.

All our enemies
     have opened their mouths against us;
panic and pitfall have come upon us,
     devastation and destruction.
My eyes flow with rivers of tears
     because of the destruction of my people.

My eyes will flow without ceasing,
     without respite,
until the Lord from heaven
     looks down and sees.
My eyes cause me grief
     at the fate of all the young women in my city.

A reading from the Letter of Paul to the Galatians. (6.11-18)

See what large letters I make when I am writing in my own hand! It is those who want to make a good showing in the flesh that try to compel you to be circumcised – only that they may not be persecuted for the cross of Christ. Even the circumcised do not themselves obey the law, but they want you to be circumcised so that they may boast about your flesh. May I never boast of anything except the cross of our Lord Jesus Christ, by which the world has been crucified to me, and I to the world. For neither circumcision nor uncircumcision is anything; but a new creation is everything! As for those who will follow this rule – peace be upon them, and mercy, and upon the Israel of God.

From now on, let no one make trouble for me; for I carry the marks of Jesus branded on my body.

May the grace of our Lord Jesus Christ be with your spirit, brothers and sisters. Amen.

Wednesday of Holy Week

Principal Service
Isaiah 50.4-9*a*; Ps 70; Hebrews 12.1-3; John 13.21-32

A reading from the prophecy of Isaiah. (50.4-9a)

> The Lord God has given me
>> the tongue of a teacher,
> that I may know how to sustain
>> the weary with a word.
> Morning by morning he wakens –
>> wakens my ear to listen as those who are taught.
> The Lord God has opened my ear,
>> and I was not rebellious,
>> I did not turn backwards.
> I gave my back to those who struck me,
>> and my cheeks to those who pulled out the beard;
> I did not hide my face
>> from insult and spitting.
>
> The Lord God helps me;
>> therefore I have not been disgraced;
> therefore I have set my face like flint,
>> and I know that I shall not be put to shame;
>> he who vindicates me is near.
> Who will contend with me?
>> Let us stand up together.
> Who are my adversaries?
>> Let them confront me.
> It is the Lord God who helps me;
>> who will declare me guilty?

This is the word of the Lord.

A reading from the Letter to the Hebrews. (12.1-3)

Since we are surrounded by so great a cloud of witnesses, let us also lay aside every weight and the sin that clings so closely, and let us run with perseverance the race that is set before us, looking to Jesus the pioneer and perfecter of our faith, who for the sake of the joy that was set before him endured the cross, disregarding its shame, and has taken his seat at the right hand of the throne of God.

Consider him who endured such hostility against himself from sinners, so that you may not grow weary or lose heart.

This is the word of the Lord.

Hear the gospel of our Lord Jesus Christ according to John. (13.21-32)

Jesus was troubled in spirit, and declared, 'Very truly, I tell you, one of you will betray me.' The disciples looked at one another, uncertain of whom he was speaking. One of his disciples – the one whom Jesus loved – was reclining next to him; Simon Peter therefore motioned to him to ask Jesus of whom he was speaking. So while reclining next to Jesus, he asked him, 'Lord, who is it?' Jesus answered, 'It is the one to whom I give this piece of bread when I have dipped it in the dish.' So when he had dipped the piece of bread, he gave it to Judas son of Simon Iscariot. After he received the piece of bread, Satan entered into him. Jesus said to him, 'Do quickly what you are going to do.' Now no one at the table knew why he said this to him. Some thought that, because Judas had the common purse, Jesus was telling him, 'Buy what we need for the festival'; or, that he should give something to the poor. So, after receiving the piece of bread, he immediately went out. And it was night.

When he had gone out, Jesus said, 'Now the Son of Man has been glorified, and God has been glorified in him. If God has been glorified in him, God will also glorify him in himself and will glorify him at once.'

This is the gospel of the Lord.

Second Service
Ps 102.1-17 [18-28];
Wisdom 1.16 - 2.1; 2.12-22 *or* Jeremiah 11.18-20;
Luke 22.54-71

A reading from the Wisdom of Solomon. (1.16 - 2.1; 2.12-22)

The ungodly by their words and deeds summoned death;
considering him a friend, they pined away
and made a covenant with him,
because they are fit to belong to his company.
For they reasoned unsoundly, saying to themselves,

'Short and sorrowful is our life,
and there is no remedy when a life comes to its end,
and no one has been known to return from Hades.

2.12 'Let us lie in wait for the righteous man,
because he is inconvenient to us and opposes our actions;
he reproaches us for sins against the law,
and accuses us of sins against our training.
He professes to have knowledge of God,
and calls himself a child of the Lord.
He became to us a reproof of our thoughts;
the very sight of him is a burden to us,
because his manner of life is unlike that of others,
and his ways are strange.
We are considered by him as something base,
and he avoids our ways as unclean;
he calls the last end of the righteous happy,
and boasts that God is his father.
Let us see if his words are true,
and let us test what will happen at the end of his life;
for if the righteous man is God's child, he will help him,
and will deliver him from the hand of his adversaries.
Let us test him with insult and torture,
so that we may find out how gentle he is,
and make trial of his forbearance.
Let us condemn him to a shameful death,
for, according to what he says, he will be protected.'

Thus they reasoned, but they were led astray,
for their wickedness blinded them,
and they did not know the secret purposes of God,
nor hoped for the wages of holiness,
nor discerned the prize for blameless souls.

Or:

A reading from the prophecy of Jeremiah. (11.18-20)

It was the Lord who made it known to me, and I knew;
  then you showed me their evil deeds.
But I was like a gentle lamb
  led to the slaughter.
And I did not know it was against me
  that they devised schemes, saying,
'Let us destroy the tree with its fruit,

let us cut him off from the land of the living,
    so that his name will no longer be remembered!'
But you, O Lord of hosts, who judge righteously,
    who try the heart and the mind,
let me see your retribution upon them,
    for to you I have committed my cause.

A reading from the gospel according to Luke. (22.54-71)

The chief priests, the officers of the temple police and the elders seized Jesus and led him away, bringing him into the high priest's house. But Peter was following at a distance. When they had kindled a fire in the middle of the courtyard and sat down together, Peter sat among them. Then a servant-girl, seeing him in the firelight, stared at him and said, 'This man also was with him.' But he denied it, saying, 'Woman, I do not know him.' A little later someone else, on seeing him, said, 'You also are one of them.' But Peter said, 'Man, I am not!' Then about an hour later yet another kept insisting, 'Surely this man also was with him; for he is a Galilean.' But Peter said, 'Man, I do not know what you are talking about!' At that moment, while he was still speaking, the cock crowed. The Lord turned and looked at Peter. Then Peter remembered the word of the Lord, how he had said to him, 'Before the cock crows today, you will deny me three times.' And he went out and wept bitterly.

Now the men who were holding Jesus began to mock him and beat him; they also blindfolded him and kept asking him, 'Prophesy! Who is it that struck you?' They kept heaping many other insults on him.

When day came, the assembly of the elders of the people, both chief priests and scribes, gathered together, and they brought him to their council. They said, 'If you are the Messiah, tell us.' He replied, 'If I tell you, you will not believe; and if I question you, you will not answer. But from now on the Son of Man will be seated at the right hand of the power of God.' All of them asked, 'Are you, then, the Son of God?' He said to them, 'You say that I am.' Then they said, 'What further testimony do we need? We have heard it ourselves from his own lips!'

Third Service
Ps 88; Isaiah 63.1-9; Revelation 14.18 - 15.4

A reading from the prophecy of Isaiah. (63.1-9)

'Who is this that comes from Edom,
    from Bozrah in garments stained crimson?
Who is this so splendidly robed,
    marching in his great might?'

'It is I, announcing vindication,
    mighty to save.'

'Why are your robes red,
    and your garments like theirs who tread the wine press?'

'I have trodden the wine press alone,
    and from the peoples no one was with me;
I trod them in my anger
    and trampled them in my wrath;
their juice spattered on my garments,
    and stained all my robes.
For the day of vengeance was in my heart,
    and the year for my redeeming work had come.
I looked, but there was no helper;
    I stared, but there was no one to sustain me;
so my own arm brought me victory,
    and my wrath sustained me.
I trampled down peoples in my anger,
    I crushed them in my wrath,
    and I poured out their lifeblood on the earth.'

I will recount the gracious deeds of the Lord,
    the praiseworthy acts of the Lord,
because of all that the Lord has done for us,
    and the great favour to the house of Israel
that he has shown them according to his mercy,
    according to the abundance of his steadfast love.
For he said, 'Surely they are my people,
    children who will not deal falsely';
    and he became their saviour in all their distress.
It was no messenger or angel
    but his presence that saved them;
in his love and in his pity he redeemed them;
    he lifted them up and carried them all the days of old.

A reading from the Revelation to John. (14.18 - 15.4)

Another angel came out from the altar, the angel who has authority over fire, and he called with a loud voice to him who had the sharp sickle, 'Use your sharp sickle and gather the clusters of the vine of the earth, for its grapes are ripe.' So the angel swung his sickle over the earth and gathered the vintage of the earth, and he threw it into the great wine press of the wrath of God. And the wine press was trodden outside the city, and blood flowed from the wine press, as high as a horse's bridle, for a distance of about two hundred miles.

Then I saw another portent in heaven, great and amazing: seven angels with seven plagues, which are the last, for with them the wrath of God is ended.

And I saw what appeared to be a sea of glass mixed with fire, and those who had conquered the beast and its image and the number of its name standing beside the sea of glass with harps of God in their hands. And they sing the song of Moses, the servant of God, and the song of the Lamb:

'Great and amazing are your deeds,
Lord God the Almighty!
Just and true are your ways,
King of the nations!
Lord, who will not fear
and glorify your name?
For you alone are holy.
All nations will come and worship before you,
for your judgements have been revealed.'

Maundy Thursday

Principal Service
Exodus 12.1-4 [5-10] 11-14; Ps 116.[1-2] 12-19;
1 Corinthians 11.23-26; John 13.1-17,31*b*-35

A reading from the Book of the Exodus. (12.1-4 [5-10] 11-14)

The Lord said to Moses and Aaron in the land of Egypt: This month shall mark for you the beginning of months; it shall be the first month of the year for you. Tell the whole congregation of Israel that on the tenth of this month they are to take a lamb for each family, a lamb for each household. If a household is too small for a whole lamb, it shall join its closest neighbour in obtaining one; the lamb shall be divided in proportion to the number of people who eat of it. [⁵ Your lamb shall be without blemish, a year-old male; you may take it from the sheep or from the goats. You shall keep it until the fourteenth day of this month; then the whole assembled congregation of Israel shall slaughter it at twilight. They shall take some of the blood and put it on the two doorposts and the lintel of the houses in which they eat it. They shall eat the lamb that same night; they shall eat it roasted over the fire with unleavened bread and bitter herbs. Do not eat any of it raw or boiled in water, but roasted over the fire, with its head, legs, and inner organs. You shall let none of it remain until the morning; anything that remains until the morning you shall burn.] [11] This is how you shall eat it: your loins girded, your sandals on your feet and your staff in your hand; and you shall eat it hurriedly. It is the passover of the Lord. For I will pass through the land of Egypt that night and I will strike down every first-born in the land of Egypt, both human beings and animals; on all the gods of Egypt I will execute judgements: I am the Lord. The blood shall be a sign for you on the houses where you live: when I see the blood, I will pass over you, and no plague will destroy you when I strike the land of Egypt.

This day shall be a day of remembrance for you. You shall celebrate it as a festival to the Lord; throughout your generations you shall observe it as a perpetual ordinance.

This is the word of the Lord.

A reading from the First Letter of Paul to the Corinthians. (11.23-26)

I received from the Lord what I also handed on to you, that the Lord Jesus on the night when he was betrayed took a loaf of bread, and when he had given thanks, he broke it and said, 'This is my body that is for you. Do this in remembrance of me.' In the same way he took the cup also, after supper, saying, 'This cup is the new covenant in my blood. Do this, as often as you drink it, in remembrance of me.' For as often as you eat this bread and drink the cup, you proclaim the Lord's death until he comes.

This is the word of the Lord.

Hear the gospel of our Lord Jesus Christ according to John.
(13.1-17, 31b-35)

Before the festival of the Passover, Jesus knew that his hour had come to depart from this world and go to the Father. Having loved his own who were in the world, he loved them to the end. The devil had already put it into the heart of Judas son of Simon Iscariot to betray him. And during supper Jesus, knowing that the Father had given all things into his hands, and that he had come from God and was going to God, got up from the table, took off his outer robe, and tied a towel around himself. Then he poured water into a basin and began to wash the disciples' feet and to wipe them with the towel that was tied around him. He came to Simon Peter, who said to him, 'Lord, are you going to wash my feet?' Jesus answered, 'You do not know now what I am doing, but later you will understand.' Peter said to him, 'You will never wash my feet.' Jesus answered, 'Unless I wash you, you have no share with me.' Simon Peter said to him, 'Lord, not my feet only but also my hands and my head!' Jesus said to him, 'One who has bathed does not need to wash, except for the feet, but is entirely clean. And you are clean, though not all of you.' For he knew who was to betray him; for this reason he said, 'Not all of you are clean.'

After he had washed their feet, had put on his robe, and had returned to the table, he said to them, 'Do you know what I have done to you? You call me Teacher and Lord – and you are right, for that is what I am. So if I, your Lord and Teacher, have washed your feet, you also ought to wash one another's feet. For I have set you an example, that you also should do as I have done to you. Very truly, I tell you, servants are not greater than their master, nor are messengers greater than the one who sent them. If you know these things, you are blessed if you do them.'

[31b] Then Jesus said, 'Now the Son of Man has been glorified, and God has been glorified in him. If God has been glorified in him, God will also glorify him in himself and will glorify him at once. Little children, I am with you only a little longer. You will look for me; and as I said to the Jews so now I say to you, "Where I am going, you cannot come." I give you a new commandment, that you love one another. Just as I have loved you, you also should love one another. By this everyone will know that you are my disciples, if you have love for one another.'

This is the gospel of the Lord.

Second Service
Ps 39; Leviticus 16.2-24; Luke 23.1-25

A reading from the book Leviticus. (16.2-24)

The Lord said to Moses:
Tell your brother Aaron not to come just at any time into the sanctuary inside the curtain before the mercy-seat that is upon the ark, or he will die; for I appear in the cloud upon the mercy-seat. Thus shall

Aaron come into the holy place: with a young bull for a sin-offering and a ram for a burnt-offering. He shall put on the holy linen tunic, and shall have the linen undergarments next to his body, fasten the linen sash, and wear the linen turban; these are the holy vestments. He shall bathe his body in water, and then put them on. He shall take from the congregation of the people of Israel two male goats for a sin offering, and one ram for a burnt offering.

Aaron shall offer the bull as a sin offering for himself, and shall make atonement for himself and for his house. He shall take the two goats and set them before the Lord at the entrance of the tent of meeting; and Aaron shall cast lots on the two goats, one lot for the Lord and the other lot for Azazel. Aaron shall present the goat on which the lot fell for the Lord, and offer it as a sin offering; but the goat on which the lot fell for Azazel shall be presented alive before the Lord to make atonement over it, that it may be sent away into the wilderness to Azazel.

Aaron shall present the bull as a sin offering for himself, and shall make atonement for himself and for his house; he shall slaughter the bull as a sin offering for himself. He shall take a censer full of coals of fire from the altar before the Lord, and two handfuls of crushed sweet incense, and he shall bring it inside the curtain and put the incense on the fire before the Lord, that the cloud of the incense may cover the mercy seat that is upon the covenant, or he will die. He shall take some of the blood of the bull, and sprinkle it with his finger on the front of the mercy seat, and before the mercy seat he shall sprinkle the blood with his finger seven times.

He shall slaughter the goat of the sin offering that is for the people and bring its blood inside the curtain, and do with its blood as he did with the blood of the bull, sprinkling it upon the mercy seat and before the mercy seat. Thus he shall make atonement for the sanctuary, because of the uncleannesses of the people of Israel, and because of their transgressions, all their sins; and so he shall do for the tent of meeting, which remains with them in the midst of their uncleannesses. No one shall be in the tent of meeting from the time he enters to make atonement in the sanctuary until he comes out and has made atonement for himself and for his house and for all the assembly of Israel. Then he shall go out to the altar that is before the Lord and make atonement on its behalf, and shall take some of the blood of the bull and of the blood of the goat, and put it on each of the horns of the altar. He shall sprinkle some of the blood on it with his finger seven times, and cleanse it and hallow it from the uncleannesses of the people of Israel.

When he has finished atoning for the holy place and the tent of meeting and the altar, he shall present the live goat. Then Aaron shall lay both his hands on the head of the live goat, and confess over it all the iniquities of the people of Israel, and all their transgressions, all their sins, putting them on the head of the goat, and sending it away into the wilderness by means of someone designated for the task. The goat shall bear on itself all their iniquities to a barren region; and the goat shall be set free in the wilderness.

Then Aaron shall enter the tent of meeting, and shall take off the linen vestments that he put on when he went into the holy place, and shall leave them there. He shall bathe his body in water in a holy place, and put on his vestments; then he shall come out and offer his burnt offering and the burnt offering of the people, making atonement for himself and for the people.

A reading from the gospel according to Luke. (23.1-25)

The assembly rose as a body and brought Jesus before Pilate. They began to accuse him, saying, 'We found this man perverting our nation, forbidding us to pay taxes to the emperor, and saying that he himself is the Messiah, a king.' Then Pilate asked him, 'Are you the king of the Jews?' He answered, 'You say so.' Then Pilate said to the chief priests and the crowds, 'I find no basis for an accusation against this man.' But they were insistent and said, 'He stirs up the people by teaching throughout all Judea, from Galilee where he began even to this place.'

When Pilate heard this, he asked whether the man was a Galilean. And when he learned that he was under Herod's jurisdiction, he sent him off to Herod, who was himself in Jerusalem at that time. When Herod saw Jesus, he was very glad, for he had been wanting to see him for a long time, because he had heard about him and was hoping to see him perform some sign. He questioned him at some length, but Jesus gave him no answer. The chief priests and the scribes stood by, vehemently accusing him. Even Herod with his soldiers treated him with contempt and mocked him; then he put an elegant robe on him, and sent him back to Pilate. That same day Herod and Pilate became friends with each other; before this they had been enemies.

Pilate then called together the chief priests, the leaders, and the people, and said to them, 'You brought me this man as one who was perverting the people; and here I have examined him in your presence and have not found this man guilty of any of your charges against him. Neither has Herod, for he sent him back to us. Indeed, he has done nothing to deserve death. I will therefore have him flogged and release him.'

Then they all shouted out together, 'Away with this fellow! Release Barabbas for us!' (This was a man who had been put in prison for an insurrection that had taken place in the city, and for murder.) Pilate, wanting to release Jesus, addressed them again; but they kept shouting, 'Crucify, crucify him!' A third time he said to them, 'Why, what evil has he done? I have found in him no ground for the sentence of death; I will therefore have him flogged and then release him.' But they kept urgently demanding with loud shouts that he should be crucified; and their voices prevailed. So Pilate gave his verdict that their demand should be granted. He released the man they asked for, the one who had been put in prison for insurrection and murder, and he handed Jesus over as they wished.

Third Service
Pss 42,43; Exodus 11; Ephesians 2.11-18

A reading from the Book of the Exodus. (Chapter 11)

The Lord said to Moses, 'I will bring one more plague upon Pharaoh and upon Egypt; afterwards he will let you go from here; indeed, when he lets you go, he will drive you away. Tell the people that every man is to ask his neighbour and every woman is to ask her neighbour for objects of silver and gold.' The Lord gave the people favour in the sight of the Egyptians. Moreover, Moses himself was a man of great importance in the land of Egypt, in the sight of Pharaoh's officials, and in the sight of the people.

Moses said, 'Thus says the Lord: About midnight I will go out through Egypt. Every firstborn in the land of Egypt shall die, from the firstborn of Pharaoh who sits on his throne to the firstborn of the female slave who is behind the handmill, and all the firstborn of the livestock. Then there will be a loud cry throughout the whole land of Egypt, such as has never been nor will ever be again. But not a dog shall growl at any of the Israelites – not at people, not at animals – so that you may know that the Lord makes a distinction between Egypt and Israel. Then all these officials of yours shall come down to me, and bow low to me, saying, "Leave us, you and all the people who follow you." After that I will leave.' And in hot anger he left Pharaoh.

The Lord said to Moses, 'Pharaoh will not listen to you, in order that my wonders may be multiplied in the land of Egypt.'

Moses and Aaron performed all these wonders before Pharaoh; but the Lord hardened Pharaoh's heart, and he did not let the people of Israel go out of his land.

A reading from the Letter of Paul to the Ephesians. (2.11-18)

Remember that at one time you Gentiles by birth, called 'the uncircumcision' by those who are called 'the circumcision' – a physical circumcision made in the flesh by human hands – remember that you were at that time without Christ, being aliens from the commonwealth of Israel, and strangers to the covenants of promise, having no hope and without God in the world. But now in Christ Jesus you who once were far off have been brought near by the blood of Christ. For he is our peace; in his flesh he has made both groups into one and has broken down the dividing wall, that is, the hostility between us. He has abolished the law with its commandments and ordinances, so that he might create in himself one new humanity in place of the two, thus making peace, and might reconcile both groups to God in one body through the cross, thus putting to death that hostility through it. So he came and proclaimed peace to you who were far off and peace to those who were near; for through him both of us have access in one Spirit to the Father.

Good Friday

Principal Service
Isaiah 52.13 - 53.12; Ps 22.1-11 [12-21]; Hebrews 10.15-25
or Hebrews 4.14-16; 5.7-9; John 18.1 - 19.42

A reading from the prophecy of Isaiah. (52.13 - 53.12)

See, my servant shall prosper;
he shall be exalted and lifted up, and shall be very high.
Just as there were many who were astonished at him –
so marred was his appearance, beyond human semblance,
and his form beyond that of mortals –
so he shall startle many nations;
kings shall shut their mouths because of him;
for that which had not been told them they shall see,
and that which they had not heard they shall contemplate.
Who has believed what we have heard?
And to whom has the arm of the Lord been revealed?
For he grew up before him like a young plant,
and like a root out of dry ground;

he had no form or majesty that we should look at him,
  nothing in his appearance that we should desire him.
He was despised and rejected by others;
  a man of suffering and acquainted with infirmity;
and as one from whom others hide their faces he was despised,
  and we held him of no account.

Surely he has borne our infirmities
  and carried our diseases;
yet we accounted him stricken,
  struck down by God, and afflicted.
But he was wounded for our transgressions,
  crushed for our iniquities;
upon him was the punishment that made us whole,
  and by his bruises we are healed.
All we like sheep have gone astray;
  we have all turned to our own way,
and the Lord has laid on him
  the iniquity of us all.

He was oppressed, and he was afflicted,
  yet he did not open his mouth;
like a lamb that is led to the slaughter,
  and like a sheep that before its shearers is silent,
  so he did not open his mouth.
By a perversion of justice he was taken away.
  Who could have imagined his future?
For he was cut off from the land of the living,
  stricken for the transgression of my people.
They made his grave with the wicked
  and his tomb with the rich,
although he had done no violence,
  and there was no deceit in his mouth.

Yet it was the will of the Lord to crush him with pain.
When you make his life an offering for sin,
  he shall see his offspring, and shall prolong his days;
through him the will of the Lord shall prosper.
  Out of his anguish he shall see light;
he shall find satisfaction through his knowledge.
  The righteous one, my servant, shall make many righteous,
  and he shall bear their iniquities.
Therefore I will allot him a portion with the great,
  and he shall divide the spoil with the strong;

because he poured out himself to death,
   and was numbered with the transgressors;
yet he bore the sin of many,
   and made intercession for the transgressors.

This is the word of the Lord.

A reading from the Letter to the Hebrews. (10.15-25)

The Holy Spirit also testifies to us, for after saying,
   'This is the covenant that I will make with them
      after those days, says the Lord:
   I will put my laws in their hearts,
      and I will write them on their minds',
he also adds,
   'I will remember their sins and their lawless deeds no more.'
Where there is forgiveness of these, there is no longer any offering for
sin.
   Therefore, my friends, since we have confidence to enter the sanctuary by the blood of Jesus, by the new and living way that he
opened for us through the curtain (that is, through his flesh), and
since we have a great priest over the house of God, let us approach
with a true heart in full assurance of faith, with our hearts sprinkled
clean from an evil conscience and our bodies washed with pure
water. Let us hold fast to the confession of our hope without wavering, for he who has promised is faithful. And let us consider how to
provoke one another to love and good deeds, not neglecting to meet
together, as is the habit of some, but encouraging one another, and all
the more as you see the Day approaching.

This is the word of the Lord.

Or:

A reading from the Letter to the Hebrews. (4.14-16; 5.7-9)

Since, then, we have a great high priest who has passed through the
heavens, Jesus, the Son of God, let us hold fast to our confession. For
we do not have a high priest who is unable to sympathize with our
weaknesses, but we have one who in every respect has been tested as
we are, yet without sin. Let us therefore approach the throne of grace
with boldness, so that we may receive mercy and find grace to help
in time of need.
5.7 In the days of his flesh, Jesus offered up prayers and supplications,
with loud cries and tears, to the one who was able to save him from
death, and he was heard because of his reverent submission.

Although he was a Son, he learned obedience through what he suffered; and having been made perfect, he became the source of eternal salvation for all who obey him.

This is the word of the Lord.

Hear the passion of our Lord Jesus Christ according to John.
(Chapters 18 & 19)

After Jesus had finished praying, he went out with his disciples across the Kidron valley to a place where there was a garden, which he and his disciples entered. Now Judas, who betrayed him, also knew the place, because Jesus often met there with his disciples. So Judas brought a detachment of soldiers together with police from the chief priests and the Pharisees, and they came there with lanterns and torches and weapons. Then Jesus, knowing all that was to happen to him, came forward and asked them, 'For whom are you looking?' They answered, 'Jesus of Nazareth.' Jesus replied, 'I am he.' Judas, who betrayed him, was standing with them. When Jesus said to them, 'I am he', they stepped back and fell to the ground. Again he asked them, 'For whom are you looking?' And they said, 'Jesus of Nazareth.' Jesus answered, 'I told you that I am he. So if you are looking for me, let these men go.' This was to fulfil the word that he had spoken, 'I did not lose a single one of those whom you gave me.' Then Simon Peter, who had a sword, drew it, struck the high priest's slave, and cut off his right ear. The slave's name was Malchus. Jesus said to Peter, 'Put your sword back into its sheath. Am I not to drink the cup that the Father has given me?'

So the soldiers, their officer, and the Jewish police arrested Jesus and bound him. First they took him to Annas, who was the father-in-law of Caiaphas, the high priest that year. Caiaphas was the one who had advised the Jews that it was better to have one person die for the people.

Simon Peter and another disciple followed Jesus. Since that disciple was known to the high priest, he went with Jesus into the courtyard of the high priest, but Peter was standing outside at the gate. So the other disciple, who was known to the high priest, went out, spoke to the woman who guarded the gate, and brought Peter in. The woman said to Peter, 'You are not also one of this man's disciples, are you?' He said, 'I am not.' Now the slaves and the police had made a charcoal fire because it was cold, and they were standing round it and warming themselves. Peter also was standing with them and warming himself.

Then the high priest questioned Jesus about his disciples and about his teaching. Jesus answered, 'I have spoken openly to the world; I have always taught in synagogues and in the temple, where all the Jews come together. I have said nothing in secret. Why do you ask me? Ask those who heard what I said to them; they know what I said.' When he had said this, one of the police standing nearby struck Jesus on the face, saying, 'Is that how you answer the high priest?' Jesus answered, 'If I have spoken wrongly, testify to the wrong. But if I have spoken rightly, why do you strike me?' Then Annas sent him bound to Caiaphas the high priest.

Now Simon Peter was standing and warming himself. They asked him, 'You are not also one of his disciples, are you?' He denied it and said, 'I am not.' One of the slaves of the high priest, a relative of the man whose ear Peter had cut off, asked, 'Did I not see you in the garden with him?' Again Peter denied it, and at that moment the cock crowed.

Then they took Jesus from Caiaphas to Pilate's headquarters. It was early in the morning. They themselves did not enter the headquarters, so as to avoid ritual defilement and to be able to eat the Passover. So Pilate went out to them and said, 'What accusation do you bring against this man?' They answered, 'If this man were not a criminal, we would not have handed him over to you.' Pilate said to them, 'Take him yourselves and judge him according to your law.' The Jews replied, 'We are not permitted to put anyone to death.' (This was to fulfil what Jesus had said when he indicated the kind of death he was to die.)

Then Pilate entered the headquarters again, summoned Jesus, and asked him, 'Are you the King of the Jews?' Jesus answered, 'Do you ask this on your own, or did others tell you about me?' Pilate replied, 'I am not a Jew, am I? Your own nation and the chief priests have handed you over to me. What have you done?' Jesus answered, 'My kingdom is not from this world. If my kingdom were from this world, my followers would be fighting to keep me from being handed over to the Jews. But as it is, my kingdom is not from here.' Pilate asked him, 'So you are a king?' Jesus answered, 'You say that I am a king. For this I was born, and for this I came into the world, to testify to the truth. Everyone who belongs to the truth listens to my voice.' Pilate asked him, 'What is truth?'

After he had said this, he went out to the Jews again and told them, 'I find no case against him. But you have a custom that I release someone for you at the Passover. Do you want me to release for you the King of the Jews?' They shouted in reply, 'Not this man, but Barabbas!' Now Barabbas was a bandit.

Then Pilate took Jesus and had him flogged. And the soldiers wove a crown of thorns and put it on his head, and they dressed him in a purple robe. They kept coming up to him, saying, 'Hail, King of the Jews!' and striking him on the face. Pilate went out again and said to them, 'Look, I am bringing him out to you to let you know that I find no case against him.' So Jesus came out, wearing the crown of thorns and the purple robe. Pilate said to them, 'Here is the man!' When the chief priests and the police saw him, they shouted, 'Crucify him! Crucify him!' Pilate said to them, 'Take him yourselves and crucify him; I find no case against him.' The Jews answered him, 'We have a law, and according to that law he ought to die because he has claimed to be the Son of God.'

Now when Pilate heard this, he was more afraid than ever. He entered his headquarters again and asked Jesus, 'Where are you from?' But Jesus gave him no answer. Pilate therefore said to him, 'Do you refuse to speak to me? Do you not know that I have power to release you, and power to crucify you?' Jesus answered him, 'You would have no power over me unless it had been given you from above; therefore the one who handed me over to you is guilty of a greater sin.' From then on Pilate tried to release him, but the Jews cried out, 'If you release this man, you are no friend of the emperor. Everyone who claims to be a king sets himself against the emperor.'

When Pilate heard these words, he brought Jesus outside and sat on the judge's bench at a place called The Stone Pavement, or in Hebrew Gabbatha. Now it was the day of Preparation for the Passover; and it was about noon. He said to the Jews, 'Here is your King!' They cried out, 'Away with him! Away with him! Crucify him!' Pilate asked them, 'Shall I crucify your King?' The chief priests answered, 'We have no king but the emperor.' Then he handed him over to them to be crucified.

So they took Jesus; and carrying the cross by himself, he went out to what is called The Place of the Skull, which in Hebrew is called Golgotha. There they crucified him, and with him two others, one on either side, with Jesus between them. Pilate also had an inscription written and put on the cross. It read, 'Jesus of Nazareth, the King of the Jews.' Many of the Jews read this inscription, because the place where Jesus was crucified was near the city; and it was written in Hebrew, in Latin, and in Greek. Then the chief priests of the Jews said to Pilate, 'Do not write, "The King of the Jews", but, "This man said, I am King of the Jews."' Pilate answered, 'What I have written I have written.' When the soldiers had crucified Jesus, they took his clothes and divided them into four parts, one for each soldier. They also took his tunic; now the tunic was seamless, woven in one piece from the top. So they said to one another, 'Let us not tear it, but cast lots for it to see who will get it.' This was to fulfil what the scripture says,

'They divided my clothes among themselves,
    and for my clothing they cast lots.'

And that is what the soldiers did.

Meanwhile, standing near the cross of Jesus were his mother, and his mother's sister, Mary the wife of Clopas, and Mary Magdalene. When Jesus saw his mother and the disciple whom he loved standing beside her, he said to his mother, 'Woman, here is your son.' Then he said to the disciple, 'Here is your mother.' And from that hour the disciple took her into his own home.

After this, when Jesus knew that all was now finished, he said (in order to fulfil the scripture), 'I am thirsty.' A jar full of sour wine was standing there. So they put a sponge full of the wine on a branch of hyssop and held it to his mouth. When Jesus had received the wine, he said, 'It is finished.' Then he bowed his head and gave up his spirit.

Since it was the day of Preparation, the Jews did not want the bodies left on the cross during the sabbath, especially because that sabbath was a day of great solemnity. So they asked Pilate to have the legs of the crucified men broken and the bodies removed. Then the soldiers came and broke the legs of the first and of the other who had been crucified with him. But when they came to Jesus and saw that he was already dead, they did not break his legs. Instead, one of the soldiers pierced his side with a spear, and at once blood and water came out. (He who saw this has testified so that you also may believe. His testimony is true, and he knows that he tells the truth.) These things occurred so that the scripture might be fulfilled, 'None of his bones shall be broken.' And again another passage of scripture says, 'They will look on the one whom they have pierced.'

After these things, Joseph of Arimathea, who was a disciple of Jesus, though a secret one because of his fear of the Jews, asked Pilate to let him take away the body of Jesus. Pilate gave him permission; so he came and removed his body. Nicodemus, who had at first come to Jesus by night, also came, bringing a mixture of myrrh and aloes, weighing about a hundred pounds. They took the body of Jesus and wrapped it with the spices in linen cloths, according to the burial custom of the Jews. Now there was a garden in the place where he was crucified, and in the garden there was a new tomb in which no one had ever been laid. And so, because it was the Jewish day of Preparation, and the tomb was nearby, they laid Jesus there.

This is the passion of the Lord.

Second Service

Pss 130,143; Genesis 22.1-18;
A part of John 18 & 19 *if not used at the Principal Service*
especially in the evening, John 19.38-42
or Colossians 1.18-23

A reading from the book Genesis. (22.1-18)

God tested Abraham. He said to him, 'Abraham!' And he said, 'Here I am.' He said, 'Take your son, your only son Isaac, whom you love, and go to the land of Moriah, and offer him there as a burnt-offering on one of the mountains that I shall show you.' So Abraham rose early in the morning, saddled his donkey, and took two of his young men with him, and his son Isaac; he cut the wood for the burnt-offering, and set out and went to the place in the distance that God had shown him. On the third day Abraham looked up and saw the place far away. Then Abraham said to his young men, 'Stay here with the donkey; the boy and I will go over there; we will worship, and then we will come back to you.' Abraham took the wood of the burnt-offering and laid it on his son Isaac, and he himself carried the fire and the knife. So the two of them walked on together. Isaac said to his father Abraham, 'Father!' And he said, 'Here I am, my son.' He said, 'The fire and the wood are here, but where is the lamb for a burnt-offering?' Abraham said, 'God himself will provide the lamb for a burnt-offering, my son.' So the two of them walked on together.

When they came to the place that God had shown him, Abraham built an altar there and laid the wood in order. He bound his son Isaac, and laid him on the altar, on top of the wood. Then Abraham reached out his hand and took the knife to kill his son. But the angel of the Lord called to him from heaven, and said, 'Abraham, Abraham!' And he said, 'Here I am.' He said, 'Do not lay your hand on the boy or do anything to him; for now I know that you fear God, since you have not withheld your son, your only son, from me.' And Abraham looked up and saw a ram, caught in a thicket by its horns. Abraham went and took the ram and offered it up as a burnt-offering instead of his son. So Abraham called that place 'The Lord will provide'; as it is said to this day, 'On the mount of the Lord it shall be provided.'

The angel of the Lord called to Abraham a second time from heaven, and said, 'By myself I have sworn, says the Lord: Because you have done this, and have not withheld your son, your only son, I will indeed bless you, and I will make your offspring as numerous as the stars of heaven and as the sand that is on the seashore. And your offspring shall possess the gate of their enemies, and by your offspring shall all the nations of the earth gain blessing for themselves, because you have obeyed my voice.'

A reading from the gospel according to John.
A part of John 18 & 19 if not used at the Principal Service (see page 182) especially in the evening, John 19.38-42.

Or:
A reading from the Letter of Paul to the Colossians. (1.18-23)

Christ Jesus is the head of the body, the church; he is the beginning, the firstborn from the dead, so that he might come to have first place in everything. For in him all the fullness of God was pleased to dwell, and through him God was pleased to reconcile to himself all things, whether on earth or in heaven, by making peace through the blood of his cross.

And you who were once estranged and hostile in mind, doing evil deeds, he has now reconciled in his fleshly body through death, so as to present you holy and blameless and irreproachable before him – provided that you continue securely established and steadfast in the faith, without shifting from the hope promised by the gospel that you heard, which has been proclaimed to every creature under heaven. I, Paul, became a servant of this gospel.

Third Service
Ps 69; Lamentations 5.15-22; *A part of* John 18 & 19 *if not read at the Principal Service (see page 182), or* Hebrews 10.1-10

A reading from the Lamentations of Jeremiah. (5.15-22)

The joy of our hearts has ceased;
    our dancing has been turned to mourning.
The crown has fallen from our head;
    woe to us, for we have sinned!
Because of this our hearts are sick,
    because of these things our eyes have grown dim:
because of Mount Zion,
    which lies desolate; jackals prowl over it.
But you, O Lord, reign for ever;
    your throne endures to all generations.
Why have you forgotten us completely?
    Why have you forsaken us these many days?
Restore us to yourself, O Lord,

that we may be restored;
renew our days as of old –
    unless you have utterly rejected us,
    and are angry with us beyond measure.

A reading from the gospel according to John.
A part of John, chapters 18 & 19, if not read at the Principal Service; see
page 182.

Or:

A reading from the Letter to the Hebrews. (10.1-10)

Since the law has only a shadow of the good things to come and not the true form of these realities, it can never, by the same sacrifices that are continually offered year after year, make perfect those who approach. Otherwise, would they not have ceased being offered, since the worshippers, cleansed once for all, would no longer have any consciousness of sin? But in these sacrifices there is a reminder of sin year after year. For it is impossible for the blood of bulls and goats to take away sins. Consequently, when Christ came into the world, he said,
    'Sacrifices and offerings you have not desired,
        but a body you have prepared for me;
    in burnt-offerings and sin-offerings
        you have taken no pleasure.
    Then I said, "See, God, I have come to do your will, O God"
        (in the scroll of the book it is written of me).'
When he said above, 'You have neither desired nor taken pleasure in sacrifices and offerings and burnt-offerings and sin-offerings' (these are offered according to the law), then he added, 'See, I have come to do your will.' He abolishes the first in order to establish the second. And it is by God's will that we have been sanctified through the offering of the body of Jesus Christ once for all.

Easter Eve

It is traditional not to celebrate the Eucharist on this day. Therefore, in those places where the Second Service and Third Service provision are normally used at Evening and Morning Prayer respectively, the Principal Service and Second Service provision should be so used. Where a special service is held, the Minister should choose appropriately. Where a Eucharist is celebrated, normative use is followed.

Principal Service
These readings are for use at services other than the Easter Vigil.
Job 14.1-14 *or* Lamentations 3.1-9,19-24; Ps 31.1-4 [5,15-16];
1 Peter 4.1-8; Matthew 27.57-66 *or* John 19.38-42

A reading from the Book of Job. (14.1-14)

'A mortal, born of woman,
    few of days and full of trouble,
comes up like a flower and withers,
    flees like a shadow and does not last.
Do you fix your eyes on such a one?
    Do you bring me into judgement with you?
Who can bring a clean thing out of an unclean?
    No one can.
Since their days are determined,
    and the number of their months is known to you,
    and you have appointed the bounds that they cannot pass,
look away from them, and desist,
    that they may enjoy, like labourers, their days.

'For there is hope for a tree, if it is cut down,
    that it will sprout again,
    and that its shoots will not cease.
Though its root grows old in the earth,
    and its stump dies in the ground,
yet at the scent of water it will bud
    and put forth branches like a young plant.
But mortals die, and are laid low;
    humans expire, and where are they?
As waters fail from a lake,
    and a river wastes away and dries up,
so mortals lie down and do not rise again;
    until the heavens are no more,
    they will not awake or be roused out of their sleep.

O that you would hide me in Sheol,
    that you would conceal me until your wrath is past,
    that you would appoint me a set time, and remember me!
If mortals die, will they live again?
    All the days of my service I would wait
    until my release should come.'

Or:

A reading from the Lamentations of Jeremiah. *(3.1-9,19-24)*

I am one who has seen affliction
    under the rod of God's wrath;
he has driven and brought me
    into darkness without any light;
against me alone he turns his hand,
    again and again, all day long.

He has made my flesh and my skin waste away,
    and broken my bones;
he has besieged and enveloped me
    with bitterness and tribulation;
he has made me sit in darkness
    like the dead of long ago.

He has walled me about so that I cannot escape;
    he has put heavy chains on me;
though I call and cry for help,
    he shuts out my prayer;
he has blocked my ways with hewn stones,
    he has made my paths crooked.

[19] The thought of my affliction and my homelessness
    is wormwood and gall!
My soul continually thinks of it
    and is bowed down within me.
But this I call to mind,
    and therefore I have hope:

The steadfast love of the Lord never ceases,
    his mercies never come to an end;
they are new every morning;
    great is your faithfulness.
'The Lord is my portion,' says my soul,
    'therefore I will hope in him.'

A reading from the First Letter of Peter. (4.1-8)

Since Christ suffered in the flesh, arm yourselves also with the same intention (for whoever has suffered in the flesh has finished with sin), so as to live for the rest of your earthly life no longer by human desires but by the will of God. You have already spent enough time in doing what the Gentiles like to do, living in licentiousness, passions, drunkenness, revels, carousing, and lawless idolatry. They are surprised that you no longer join them in the same excesses of dissipation, and so they blaspheme. But they will have to give an account to him who stands ready to judge the living and the dead. For this is the reason the gospel was proclaimed even to the dead, so that, though they had been judged in the flesh as everyone is judged, they might live in the spirit as God does.

The end of all things is near; therefore be serious and discipline yourselves for the sake of your prayers. Above all, maintain constant love for one another, for love covers a multitude of sins.

A reading from the gospel according to Matthew. (27.57-66)

When it was evening, there came a rich man from Arimathea, named Joseph, who was also a disciple of Jesus. He went to Pilate and asked for the body of Jesus; then Pilate ordered it to be given to him. So Joseph took the body and wrapped it in a clean linen cloth and laid it in his own new tomb, which he had hewn in the rock. He then rolled a great stone to the door of the tomb and went away. Mary Magdalene and the other Mary were there, sitting opposite the tomb.

The next day, that is, after the day of Preparation, the chief priests and the Pharisees gathered before Pilate and said, 'Sir, we remember what that impostor said while he was still alive, "After three days I will rise again." Therefore command that the tomb be made secure until the third day; otherwise his disciples may go and steal him away, and tell the people, "He has been raised from the dead", and the last deception would be worse than the first.' Pilate said to them, 'You have a guard of soldiers; go, make it as secure as you can.' So they went with the guard and made the tomb secure by sealing the stone.

Or:
A reading from the gospel according to John. (19.38-42)

Joseph of Arimathea, who was a disciple of Jesus, though a secret one because of his fear of the Jews, asked Pilate to let him take away the body of Jesus. Pilate gave him permission; so he came and removed his body. Nicodemus, who had at first come to Jesus by night, also came, bringing a mixture of myrrh and aloes, weighing about a hundred pounds. They took the body of Jesus and wrapped it with the spices in linen cloths, according to the burial custom of the Jews. Now there was a garden in the place where he was crucified, and in the garden there was a new tomb in which no one had ever been laid. And so, because it was the Jewish day of Preparation, and the tomb was nearby, they laid Jesus there.

Second Service
Ps 142; Hosea 6.1-6; John 2.18-22
Care should be taken that the Hosea reading is not also being used as a Canticle.

A reading from the prophecy of Hosea. (6.1-6)

'Come, let us return to the Lord;
    for it is he who has torn, and he will heal us;
    he has struck down, and he will bind us up.
After two days he will revive us;
    on the third day he will raise us up,
    that we may live before him.
Let us know, let us press on to know the Lord;
    his appearing is as sure as the dawn;
he will come to us like the showers,
    like the spring rains that water the earth.'
What shall I do with you, O Ephraim?
    What shall I do with you, O Judah?
Your love is like a morning cloud,
like the dew that goes away early.
Therefore I have hewn them by the prophets,
    I have killed them by the words of my mouth,
    and my judgement goes forth as the light.
For I desire steadfast love and not sacrifice,
    the knowledge of God rather than burnt-offerings.

A reading from the gospel according to John. (2.18-22)

The Jews said to Jesus, 'What sign can you show us for doing this?' Jesus answered them, 'Destroy this temple, and in three days I will raise it up.' The Jews then said, 'This temple has been under construction for forty-six years, and will you raise it up in three days?' But he was speaking of the temple of his body.

After he was raised from the dead, his disciples remembered that he had said this; and they believed the scripture and the word that Jesus had spoken.

Third Service
Ps 116; Job 19.21-27; 1 John 5.5-12

A reading from the Book of Job. (19.21-27)

Job said:
    'Have pity on me, have pity on me, O you my friends,
        for the hand of God has touched me!
    Why do you, like God, pursue me,
        never satisfied with my flesh?

    'O that my words were written down!
        O that they were inscribed in a book!
    O that with an iron pen and with lead
        they were engraved on a rock for ever!
    For I know that my Redeemer lives,
        and that at the last he will stand upon the earth;
    and after my skin has been thus destroyed,
        then in my flesh I shall see God,
    whom I shall see on my side,
        and my eyes shall behold, and not another.
    My heart faints within me!'

A reading from the First Letter of John. (5.5-12)

Who is it that conquers the world but the one who believes that Jesus is the Son of God?
  This is the one who came by water and blood, Jesus Christ, not with the water only but with the water and the blood. And the Spirit is the one that testifies, for the Spirit is the truth. There are three that testify: the Spirit and the water and the blood, and these three agree. If we receive human testimony, the testimony of God is greater; for this is the testimony of God that he has testified to his Son. Those who believe in the Son of God have the testimony in their hearts. Those who do not believe in God have made him a liar by not believing in the testimony that God has given concerning his Son. And this is the testimony: God gave us eternal life, and this life is in his Son. Whoever has the Son has life; whoever does not have the Son of God does not have life.

Easter

Easter Vigil

A minimum of three Old Testament readings should be chosen.
The reading from Exodus 14 should always be used.

Genesis 1.1 - 2.4a	Ps 136.1-9,23-26
Genesis 7.1-5,11-18; 8.6-18; 9.8-13	Ps 46
Genesis 22.1-18	Ps 16
Exodus 14.10-31; 15.20-21	*Cant:* Exodus 15.1b-13,17-18
Isaiah 55.1-11	*Canticle:* Isaiah 12.2-6
Baruch 3.9-15, 32-4.4	
or Proverbs 8.1-8,19-21; 9.4b-6	Ps 19
Ezekiel 36.24-28	Pss 42,43
Ezekiel 37.1-14	Ps 143
Zephaniah 3.14-20	Ps 98
Romans 6.3-11	Ps 114
Mark 16.1-8	

A reading from the book Genesis. (1.1 - 2.4a)

In the beginning when God created the heavens and the earth, the earth was a formless void and darkness covered the face of the deep, while a wind from God swept over the face of the waters. Then God said, 'Let there be light'; and there was light. And God saw that the light was good; and God separated the light from the darkness. God called the light Day, and the darkness he called Night. And there was evening and there was morning, the first day.

And God said, 'Let there be a dome in the midst of the waters, and let it separate the waters from the waters.' So God made the dome and separated the waters that were under the dome from the waters that were above the dome. And it was so. God called the dome Sky. And there was evening and there was morning, the second day.

And God said, 'Let the waters under the sky be gathered together into one place, and let the dry land appear.' And it was so. God called the dry land Earth, and the waters that were gathered together he called Seas. And God saw that it was good. Then God said, 'Let the earth put forth vegetation: plants yielding seed, and fruit trees of every kind on earth that bear fruit with the seed in it.' And it was so. The earth brought forth vegetation: plants yielding seed of every kind, and trees of every kind bearing fruit with the seed in it. And God saw that it was good. And there was evening and there was morning, the third day.

And God said, 'Let there be lights in the dome of the sky to separate the day from the night; and let them be for signs and for seasons and for days and years, and let them be lights in the dome of the sky to give light upon the earth.' And it was so. God made the two great lights – the greater light to rule the day and the lesser light to rule the night – and the stars. God set them in the dome of the sky to give light upon the earth, to rule over the day and over the night, and to separate the light from the darkness. And God saw that it was good. And there was evening and there was morning, the fourth day.

And God said, 'Let the waters bring forth swarms of living creatures, and let birds fly above the earth across the dome of the sky.' So God created the great sea monsters and every living creature that moves, of every kind, with which the waters swarm, and every winged bird of every kind. And God saw that it was good. God blessed them, saying, 'Be fruitful and multiply and fill the waters in the seas, and let birds multiply on the earth.' And there was evening and there was morning, the fifth day.

And God said, 'Let the earth bring forth living creatures of every kind: cattle and creeping things and wild animals of the earth of every kind.' And it was so. God made the wild animals of the earth of every kind, and the cattle of every kind, and everything that creeps upon the ground of every kind. And God saw that it was good.

Then God said, 'Let us make humankind in our image, according to our likeness; and let them have dominion over the fish of the sea, and over the birds of the air, and over the cattle, and over all the wild animals of the earth, and over every creeping thing that creeps upon the earth.'

So God created humankind in his image,
    in the image of God he created them;
    male and female he created them.

God blessed them, and God said to them, 'Be fruitful and multiply, and fill the earth and subdue it; and have dominion over the fish of the sea and over the birds of the air and over every living thing that moves upon the earth.' God said, 'See, I have given you every plant yielding seed that is upon the face of all the earth, and every tree with seed in its fruit; you shall have them for food. And to every beast of the earth, and to every bird of the air, and to everything that creeps on the earth, everything that has the breath of life, I have given every green plant for food.' And it was so. God saw everything that he had made, and indeed, it was very good. And there was evening and there was morning, the sixth day.

Thus the heavens and the earth were finished, and all their multitude. And on the seventh day God finished the work that he had done, and he rested on the seventh day from all the work that he had done. So God blessed the seventh day and hallowed it, because on it God rested from all the work that he had done in creation.

These are the generations of the heavens and the earth when they were created.

This is the word of the Lord.

A reading from the book Genesis. (7.1-5,11-18; 8.6-18; 9.8-13)

The Lord said to Noah, 'Go into the ark, you and all your household, for I have seen that you alone are righteous before me in this generation. Take with you seven pairs of all clean animals, the male and its mate; and a pair of the animals that are not clean, the male and its mate; and seven pairs of the birds of the air also, male and female, to keep their kind alive on the face of all the earth. For in seven days I will send rain on the earth for forty days and forty nights; and every living thing that I have made I will blot out from the face of the ground.' And Noah did all that the Lord had commanded him.

[11] In the six-hundredth year of Noah's life, in the second month, on the seventeenth day of the month, on that day all the fountains of the great deep burst forth, and the windows of the heavens were opened. The rain fell on the earth for forty days and forty nights. On the very same day Noah with his sons, Shem and Ham and Japheth, and Noah's wife and the three wives of his sons, entered the ark, they and every wild animal of every kind, and all domestic animals of every kind, and every creeping thing that creeps on the earth, and every bird of every kind – every bird, every winged creature. They went into the ark with Noah, two and two of all flesh in which there was the breath of life. And those that entered, male and female of all flesh, went in as God had commanded him; and the Lord shut him in.

The flood continued for forty days on the earth; and the waters increased, and bore up the ark, and it rose high above the earth. The waters swelled and increased greatly on the earth; and the ark floated on the face of the waters.

[8:6] At the end of forty days Noah opened the window of the ark that he had made and sent out the raven; and it went to and fro until the waters were dried up from the earth. Then he sent out the dove from him, to see if the waters had subsided from the face of the ground; but the dove found no place to set its foot, and it returned to him to the ark, for the waters were still on the face of the whole earth. So he put out his hand and took it and brought it into the ark with him. He waited another seven days, and again he sent out the dove from the ark; and the dove came back to him in the evening, and there in its beak was a freshly plucked olive leaf; so Noah knew that the waters had subsided from the earth. Then he waited another seven days, and sent out the dove; and it did not return to him any more.

In the six hundred and first year, in the first month, on the first day of the month, the waters were dried up from the earth; and Noah removed the covering of the ark, and looked, and saw that the face of the ground was drying. In the second month, on the twenty-seventh day of the month, the earth was dry. Then God said to Noah, 'Go out of the ark, you and your wife, and your sons and your sons' wives with you. Bring out with you every living thing that is with you of all flesh – birds and animals and every creeping thing that creeps on the earth – so that they may abound on the earth, and be fruitful and multiply on the earth.' So Noah went out with his sons and his wife and his sons' wives.

9.8 Then God said to Noah and to his sons with him, 'As for me, I am establishing my covenant with you and your descendants after you, and with every living creature that is with you, the birds, the domestic animals, and every animal of the earth with you, as many as came out of the ark. I establish my covenant with you, that never again shall all flesh be cut off by the waters of a flood, and never again shall there be a flood to destroy the earth.' God said, 'This is the sign of the covenant that I make between me and you and every living creature that is with you, for all future generations: I have set my bow in the clouds, and it shall be a sign of the covenant between me and the earth.'

This is the word of the Lord.

A reading from the book Genesis. (22.1-18)

God tested Abraham. He said to him, 'Abraham!' And he said, 'Here I am.' He said, 'Take your son, your only son Isaac, whom you love, and go to the land of Moriah, and offer him there as a burnt-offering on one of the mountains that I shall show you.' So Abraham rose early in the morning, saddled his donkey, and took two of his young men with him, and his son Isaac; he cut the wood for the burnt-offering, and set out and went to the place in the distance that God had shown him. On the third day Abraham looked up and saw the place far away. Then Abraham said to his young men, 'Stay here with the donkey; the boy and I will go over there; we will worship, and then we will come back to you.' Abraham took the wood of the burnt-offering and laid it on his son Isaac, and he himself carried the fire and the knife. So the two of them walked on together. Isaac said to his father Abraham, 'Father!' And he said, 'Here I am, my son.' He said, 'The fire and the wood are here, but where is the lamb for a burnt-offering?' Abraham said, 'God himself will provide the lamb for a burnt-offering, my son.' So the two of them walked on together.

When they came to the place that God had shown him, Abraham built an altar there and laid the wood in order. He bound his son Isaac, and laid him on the altar, on top of the wood. Then Abraham reached out his hand and took the knife to kill his son. But the angel of the Lord called to him from heaven, and said, 'Abraham, Abraham!' And he said, 'Here I am.' He said, 'Do not lay your hand on the boy or do anything to him; for now I know that you fear God, since you have not withheld your son, your only son, from me.' And Abraham looked up and saw a ram, caught in a thicket by its horns. Abraham went and took the ram and offered it up as a burnt-offering instead of his son. So Abraham called that place 'The Lord will provide'; as it is said to this day, 'On the mount of the Lord it shall be provided.'

The angel of the Lord called to Abraham a second time from heaven, and said, 'By myself I have sworn, says the Lord: Because you have done this, and have not withheld your son, your only son, I will indeed bless you, and I will make your offspring as numerous as the stars of heaven and as the sand that is on the seashore. And your offspring shall possess the gate of their enemies, and by your offspring shall all the nations of the earth gain blessing for themselves, because you have obeyed my voice.'

This is the word of the Lord.

A reading from the Book of the Exodus. (14.10-31; 15.20-21)

As Pharaoh drew near, the Israelites looked back, and there were the Egyptians advancing on them. In great fear the Israelites cried out to the Lord. They said to Moses, 'Was it because there were no graves in Egypt that you have taken us away to die in the wilderness? What have you done to us, bringing us out of Egypt? Is this not the very thing we told you in Egypt, "Let us alone and let us serve the Egyptians"? For it would have been better for us to serve the Egyptians than to die in the wilderness.' But Moses said to the people, 'Do not be afraid, stand firm, and see the deliverance that the Lord will accomplish for you today; for the Egyptians whom you see today you shall never see again. The Lord will fight for you, and you have only to keep still.'

Then the Lord said to Moses, 'Why do you cry out to me? Tell the

Israelites to go forward. But you lift up your staff, and stretch out your hand over the sea and divide it, that the Israelites may go into the sea on dry ground. Then I will harden the hearts of the Egyptians so that they will go in after them; and so I will gain glory for myself over Pharaoh and all his army, his chariots, and his chariot drivers. And the Egyptians shall know that I am the Lord, when I have gained glory for myself over Pharaoh, his chariots, and his chariot drivers.'

The angel of God who was going before the Israelite army moved and went behind them; and the pillar of cloud moved from in front of them and took its place behind them. It came between the army of Egypt and the army of Israel. And so the cloud was there with the darkness, and it lit up the night; one did not come near the other all night.

Then Moses stretched out his hand over the sea. The Lord drove the sea back by a strong east wind all night, and turned the sea into dry land; and the waters were divided. The Israelites went into the sea on dry ground, the waters forming a wall for them on their right and on their left. The Egyptians pursued, and went into the sea after them, all of Pharaoh's horses, chariots, and chariot drivers. At the morning watch the Lord in the pillar of fire and cloud looked down upon the Egyptian army, and threw the Egyptian army into panic. He clogged their chariot wheels so that they turned with difficulty. The Egyptians said, 'Let us flee from the Israelites, for the Lord is fighting for them against Egypt.'

Then the Lord said to Moses, 'Stretch out your hand over the sea, so that the water may come back upon the Egyptians, upon their chariots and chariot drivers.' So Moses stretched out his hand over the sea, and at dawn the sea returned to its normal depth. As the Egyptians fled before it, the Lord tossed the Egyptians into the sea. The waters returned and covered the chariots and the chariot drivers, the entire army of Pharaoh that had followed them into the sea; not one of them remained. But the Israelites walked on dry ground through the sea, the waters forming a wall for them on their right and on their left.

Thus the Lord saved Israel that day from the Egyptians; and Israel saw the Egyptians dead on the seashore. Israel saw the great work that the Lord did against the Egyptians. So the people feared the Lord and believed in the Lord and in his servant Moses.

15.20 Then the prophet Miriam, Aaron's sister, took a tambourine in her hand; and all the women went out after her with tambourines and with dancing. And Miriam sang to them: 'Sing to the Lord, for he has triumphed gloriously; horse and rider he has thrown into the sea.'

This reading is not announced as being ended and is followed immediately by the Canticle from Exodus.

A reading from the prophecy of Isaiah. (55.1-11)

Ho, everyone who thirsts,
    come to the waters;
and you that have no money,
    come, buy and eat!
Come, buy wine and milk
    without money and without price.
Why do you spend your money for that which is not bread,
    and your labour for that which does not satisfy?
Listen carefully to me, and eat what is good,
    and delight yourselves in rich food.
Incline your ear, and come to me;
    listen, so that you may live.
I will make with you an everlasting covenant,
    my steadfast, sure love for David.
See, I made him a witness to the peoples,
    a leader and commander for the peoples.
See, you shall call nations that you do not know,
    and nations that do not know you shall run to you,
because of the Lord your God, the Holy One of Israel,
    for he has glorified you.

Seek the Lord while he may be found,
    call upon him while he is near;
let the wicked forsake their way,
    and the unrighteous their thoughts;
let them return to the Lord,
    that he may have mercy on them,
and to our God,
    for he will abundantly pardon.
For my thoughts are not your thoughts,
    nor are your ways my ways, says the Lord.
For as the heavens are higher than the earth,
    so are my ways higher than your ways
    and my thoughts than your thoughts.

For as the rain and the snow come down from heaven,
    and do not return there until they have watered the earth,
making it bring forth and sprout,
    giving seed to the sower and bread to the eater,
so shall my word be that goes out from my mouth;
    it shall not return to me empty,
but it shall accomplish that which I purpose,
    and succeed in the thing for which I sent it.

This is the word of the Lord.

A reading from the Book of Baruch. (3.9-15, 32-4.4)

Hear the commandments of life, O Israel;
    give ear, and learn wisdom!
Why is it, O Israel,
    why is it that you are in the land of your enemies,
that you are growing old in a foreign country,
    that you are defiled with the dead,
    that you are counted among those in Hades?
You have forsaken the fountain of wisdom.
If you had walked in the way of God,
    you would be living in peace for ever.
Learn where there is wisdom,
    where there is strength,
    where there is understanding,
so that you may at the same time discern
    where there is length of days, and life,
    where there is light for the eyes, and peace.

Who has found her place?
    And who has entered her storehouses?
[32] But the one who knows all things knows her,
    he found her by his understanding.
The one who prepared the earth for all time
    filled it with four-footed creatures;
the one who sends forth the light, and it goes;
    he called it, and it obeyed him, trembling;
the stars shone in their watches, and were glad;
    he called them, and they said, 'Here we are!'
    They shone with gladness for him who made them.
This is our God;
    no other can be compared to him.
He found the whole way to knowledge,
    and gave her to his servant Jacob and to Israel,
    whom he loved.
Afterwards she appeared on earth
    and lived with humankind.

She is the book of the commandments of God,
    the law that endures for ever.
All who hold her fast will live,
    and those who forsake her will die.
Turn, O Jacob, and take her;
    walk towards the shining of her light.
Do not give your glory to another,

or your advantages to an alien people.
Happy are we, O Israel,
for we know what is pleasing to God.

This is the word of the Lord.

Or:

A reading from the book Proverbs. (8.1-8,19-21; 9.4b-6)

Does not wisdom call,
and does not understanding raise her voice?
On the heights, beside the way,
at the crossroads she takes her stand;
beside the gates in front of the town,
at the entrance of the portals she cries out:
'To you, O people, I call,
and my cry is to all that live.
O simple ones, learn prudence;
acquire intelligence, you who lack it.
Hear, for I will speak noble things,
and from my lips will come what is right;
for my mouth will utter truth;
wickedness is an abomination to my lips.
All the words of my mouth are righteous;
there is nothing twisted or crooked in them.
[19] My fruit is better than gold, even fine gold,
and my yield than choice silver.
I walk in the way of righteousness,
along the paths of justice,
endowing with wealth those who love me,
and filling their treasuries.
[9:4b] To those without sense she says,
'Come, eat of my bread
and drink of the wine I have mixed.
Lay aside immaturity, and live,
and walk in the way of insight.'

This is the word of the Lord.

A reading from the prophecy of Ezekiel. (36.24-28)

Thus says the Lord God: I will take you from the nations, and gather
you from all the countries, and bring you into your own land. I will
sprinkle clean water upon you, and you shall be clean from all your
uncleannesses, and from all your idols I will cleanse you. A new

heart I will give you, and a new spirit I will put within you; and I will remove from your body the heart of stone and give you a heart of flesh. I will put my spirit within you, and make you follow my statutes and be careful to observe my ordinances. Then you shall live in the land that I gave to your ancestors; and you shall be my people, and I will be your God.

This is the word of the Lord.

A reading from the prophecy of Ezekiel. (37.1-14)

The hand of the Lord came upon me, and he brought me out by the spirit of the Lord and set me down in the middle of a valley; it was full of bones. He led me all round them; there were very many lying in the valley, and they were very dry. He said to me, 'Mortal, can these bones live?' I answered, 'O Lord God, you know.' Then he said to me, 'Prophesy to these bones, and say to them: O dry bones, hear the word of the Lord. Thus says the Lord God to these bones: I will cause breath to enter you, and you shall live. I will lay sinews on you, and will cause flesh to come upon you, and cover you with skin, and put breath in you, and you shall live; and you shall know that I am the Lord.'

So I prophesied as I had been commanded; and as I prophesied, suddenly there was a noise, a rattling, and the bones came together, bone to its bone. I looked, and there were sinews on them, and flesh had come upon them, and skin had covered them; but there was no breath in them. Then he said to me, 'Prophesy to the breath, prophesy, mortal, and say to the breath: Thus says the Lord God: Come from the four winds, O breath, and breathe upon these slain, that they may live.' I prophesied as he commanded me, and the breath came into them, and they lived, and stood on their feet, a vast multitude.

Then he said to me, 'Mortal, these bones are the whole house of Israel. They say, "Our bones are dried up, and our hope is lost; we are cut off completely." Therefore prophesy, and say to them, Thus says the Lord God: I am going to open your graves, and bring you up from your graves, O my people; and I will bring you back to the land of Israel. And you shall know that I am the Lord, when I open your graves, and bring you up from your graves, O my people. I will put my spirit within you, and you shall live, and I will place you on your own soil; then you shall know that I, the Lord, have spoken and will act,' says the Lord.

This is the word of the Lord.

A reading from the prophecy of Zephaniah. (3.14-20)

Sing aloud, O daughter Zion;
  shout, O Israel!
Rejoice and exult with all your heart,
  O daughter Jerusalem!
The Lord has taken away the judgements against you,
  he has turned away your enemies.
The king of Israel, the Lord, is in your midst;
  you shall fear disaster no more.
On that day it shall be said to Jerusalem:
Do not fear, O Zion;
  do not let your hands grow weak.
The Lord, your God, is in your midst,
  a warrior who gives victory;
he will rejoice over you with gladness,
  he will renew you in his love;
he will exult over you with loud singing
  as on a day of festival.
I will remove disaster from you,
  so that you will not bear reproach for it.
I will deal with all your oppressors at that time.
And I will save the lame
  and gather the outcast,
and I will change their shame into praise
  and renown in all the earth.
At that time I will bring you home,
  at the time when I gather you;
for I will make you renowned and praised
  among all the peoples of the earth,
when I restore your fortunes
  before your eyes, says the Lord.

This is the word of the Lord.

A reading from the Letter of Paul to the Romans. (6.3-11)

Do you not know that all of us who have been baptized into Christ
Jesus were baptized into his death? Therefore we have been buried
with him by baptism into death, so that, just as Christ was raised
from the dead by the glory of the Father, so we too might walk in
newness of life.

For if we have been united with him in a death like his, we will certainly be united with him in a resurrection like his. We know that our
old self was crucified with him so that the body of sin might be

destroyed, and we might no longer be enslaved to sin. For whoever has died is freed from sin. But if we have died with Christ, we believe that we will also live with him. We know that Christ, being raised from the dead, will never die again; death no longer has dominion over him. The death he died, he died to sin, once for all; but the life he lives, he lives to God. So you also must consider yourselves dead to sin and alive to God in Christ Jesus.

This is the word of the Lord.

Hear the gospel of our Lord Jesus Christ according to Mark. (16.1-8)

When the sabbath was over, Mary Magdalene, and Mary the mother of James, and Salome bought spices, so that they might go and anoint him. And very early on the first day of the week, when the sun had risen, they went to the tomb. They had been saying to one another, 'Who will roll away the stone for us from the entrance to the tomb?' When they looked up, they saw that the stone, which was very large, had already been rolled back. As they entered the tomb, they saw a young man, dressed in a white robe, sitting on the right side; and they were alarmed. But he said to them, 'Do not be alarmed; you are looking for Jesus of Nazareth, who was crucified. He has been raised; he is not here. Look, there is the place they laid him. But go, tell his disciples and Peter that he is going ahead of you to Galilee; there you will see him, just as he told you.' So they went out and fled from the tomb, for terror and amazement had seized them; and they said nothing to anyone, for they were afraid.

This is the gospel of the Lord.

Easter Day

Principal Service
Acts 10.34-43 *or* Isaiah 25.6-9;
Ps 118. [1-2] 14-24;
1 Corinthians 15.1-11 *or* Acts 10.34-43;
The reading from Acts must be used as either the first or second reading.
John 20.1-18 *or* Mark 16.1-8

A reading from the prophecy of Isaiah. (25.6-9)

On this mountain
        the Lord of hosts will make for all peoples
    a feast of rich food, a feast of well-matured wines,
        of rich food filled with marrow,

of well-matured wines strained clear.
And he will destroy on this mountain
   the shroud that is cast over all peoples,
   the sheet that is spread over all nations;
he will swallow up death for ever.
Then the Lord God will wipe away the tears from all faces,
   and the disgrace of his people
      he will take away from all the earth,
   for the Lord has spoken.
It will be said on that day,
   Lo, this is our God; we have waited for him,
      so that he might save us.
This is the Lord for whom we have waited;
   let us be glad and rejoice in his salvation.

This is the word of the Lord.

A reading from the Acts of the Apostles. (10.34-43)

Peter began to speak to Cornelius and the assembled crowd in Caesarea: 'I truly understand that God shows no partiality, but in every nation anyone who fears him and does what is right is acceptable to him. You know the message he sent to the people of Israel, preaching peace by Jesus Christ – he is Lord of all. That message spread throughout Judea, beginning in Galilee after the baptism that John announced: how God anointed Jesus of Nazareth with the Holy Spirit and with power; how he went about doing good and healing all who were oppressed by the devil, for God was with him. We are witnesses to all that he did both in Judea and in Jerusalem. They put him to death by hanging him on a tree; but God raised him on the third day and allowed him to appear, not to all the people but to us who were chosen by God as witnesses, and who ate and drank with him after he rose from the dead. He commanded us to preach to the people and to testify that he is the one ordained by God as judge of the living and the dead. All the prophets testify about him that everyone who believes in him receives forgiveness of sins through his name.'

This is the word of the Lord.

A reading from the First Letter of Paul to the Corinthians. (15.1-11)

I should remind you, brothers and sisters, of the good news that I proclaimed to you, which you in turn received, in which also you stand, through which also you are being saved, if you hold firmly to the message that I proclaimed to you – unless you have come to believe in vain.

For I handed on to you as of first importance what I in turn had received: that Christ died for our sins in accordance with the scriptures, and that he was buried, and that he was raised on the third day in accordance with the scriptures, and that he appeared to Cephas, then to the twelve. Then he appeared to more than five hundred brothers and sisters at one time, most of whom are still alive, though some have died. Then he appeared to James, then to all the apostles. Last of all, as to someone untimely born, he appeared also to me. For I am the least of the apostles, unfit to be called an apostle, because I persecuted the church of God. But by the grace of God I am what I am, and his grace towards me has not been in vain. On the contrary, I worked harder than any of them – though it was not I, but the grace of God that is with me. Whether then it was I or they, so we proclaim and so you have come to believe.

This is the word of the Lord.

Hear the gospel of our Lord Jesus Christ according to John. (20.1-18)

Early on the first day of the week, while it was still dark, Mary Magdalene came to the tomb and saw that the stone had been removed from the tomb. So she ran and went to Simon Peter and the other disciple, the one whom Jesus loved, and said to them, 'They have taken the Lord out of the tomb, and we do not know where they have laid him.' Then Peter and the other disciple set out and went towards the tomb. The two were running together, but the other disciple outran Peter and reached the tomb first. He bent down to look in and saw the linen wrappings lying there, but he did not go in. Then Simon Peter came, following him, and went into the tomb. He saw the linen wrappings lying there, and the cloth that had been on Jesus' head, not lying with the linen wrappings but rolled up in a place by itself. Then the other disciple, who reached the tomb first, also went in, and he saw and believed; for as yet they did not understand the scripture, that he must rise from the dead. Then the disciples returned to their homes.

But Mary stood weeping outside the tomb. As she wept, she bent over to look into the tomb; and she saw two angels in white, sitting where the body of Jesus had been lying, one at the head and the other at the feet. They said to her, 'Woman, why are you weeping?' She said to them, 'They have taken away my Lord, and I do not know where they have laid him.' When she had said this, she turned round and saw Jesus standing there, but she did not know that it was Jesus.

Jesus said to her, 'Woman, why are you weeping? For whom are you looking?' Supposing him to be the gardener, she said to him, 'Sir, if you have carried him away, tell me where you have laid him, and I will take him away.' Jesus said to her, 'Mary!' She turned and said to him in Hebrew, 'Rabbouni!' (which means Teacher). Jesus said to her, 'Do not hold on to me, because I have not yet ascended to the Father. But go to my brothers and say to them, "I am ascending to my Father and your Father, to my God and your God."' Mary Magdalene went and announced to the disciples, 'I have seen the Lord'; and she told them that he had said these things to her.

This is the gospel of the Lord.

Or Mark 16.1-8 may be used, page 205, if not used at the Vigil.

Second Service
Pss 114,117; Ezekiel 37.1-14; Luke 24.13-35

A reading from the prophecy of Ezekiel. (37.1-14)

The hand of the Lord came upon me, and he brought me out by the spirit of the Lord and set me down in the middle of a valley; it was full of bones. He led me all round them; there were very many lying in the valley, and they were very dry. He said to me, 'Mortal, can these bones live?' I answered, 'O Lord God, you know.' Then he said to me, 'Prophesy to these bones, and say to them: O dry bones, hear the word of the Lord. Thus says the Lord God to these bones: I will cause breath to enter you, and you shall live. I will lay sinews on you, and will cause flesh to come upon you, and cover you with skin, and put breath in you, and you shall live; and you shall know that I am the Lord.'

So I prophesied as I had been commanded; and as I prophesied, suddenly there was a noise, a rattling, and the bones came together, bone to its bone. I looked, and there were sinews on them, and flesh had come upon them, and skin had covered them; but there was no breath in them. Then he said to me, 'Prophesy to the breath, prophesy, mortal, and say to the breath: Thus says the Lord God: Come from the four winds, O breath, and breathe upon these slain, that they may live.' I prophesied as he commanded me, and the breath came into them, and they lived, and stood on their feet, a vast multitude.

Then he said to me, 'Mortal, these bones are the whole house of Israel. They say, "Our bones are dried up, and our hope is lost; we are cut off completely." Therefore prophesy, and say to them, Thus says the Lord God: I am going to open your graves, and bring you up from your graves, O my people; and I will bring you back to the land of Israel. And you shall know that I am the Lord, when I open your graves, and bring you up from your graves, O my people. I will put my spirit within you, and you shall live, and I will place you on your own soil; then you shall know that I, the Lord, have spoken and will act, says the Lord.'

A reading from the gospel according to Luke. (24.13-35)

On the first day of the week, two of Jesus' disciples were going to a village called Emmaus, about seven miles from Jerusalem, and talking with each other about all these things that had happened. While they were talking and discussing, Jesus himself came near and went with them, but their eyes were kept from recognizing him. And he said to them, 'What are you discussing with each other while you walk along?' They stood still, looking sad. Then one of them, whose name was Cleopas, answered him, 'Are you the only stranger in Jerusalem who does not know the things that have taken place there in these days?' He asked them, 'What things?' They replied, 'The things about Jesus of Nazareth, who was a prophet mighty in deed and word before God and all the people, and how our chief priests and leaders handed him over to be condemned to death and crucified him. But we had hoped that he was the one to redeem Israel. Yes, and besides all this, it is now the third day since these things took place. Moreover, some women of our group astounded us. They were at the tomb early this morning, and when they did not find his body there, they came back and told us that they had indeed seen a vision of angels who said that he was alive. Some of those who were with us went to the tomb and found it just as the women had said; but they did not see him.' Then he said to them, 'Oh, how foolish you are, and how slow of heart to believe all that the prophets have declared! Was it not necessary that the Messiah should suffer these things and then enter into his glory?' Then beginning with Moses and all the prophets, he interpreted to them the things about himself in all the scriptures.

As they came near the village to which they were going, he walked ahead as if he were going on. But they urged him strongly, saying, 'Stay with us, because it is almost evening and the day is now nearly over.' So he went in to stay with them. When he was at the table with them, he took bread, blessed and broke it, and gave it to them. Then their eyes were opened, and they recognized him; and he vanished from their sight. They said to each other, 'Were not our hearts burning within us while he was talking to us on the road, while he was opening the scriptures to us?' That same hour they got up and returned to Jerusalem; and they found the eleven and their companions gathered together. They were saying, 'The Lord has risen indeed, and he has appeared to Simon!' Then they told what had happened on the road, and how he had been made known to them in the breaking of the bread.

Third Service

Ps 105 *or* Ps 66.1-12; Genesis 1.1-5,26-31; 2 Corinthians 5.14 - 6.2

A reading from the book Genesis. (1.1-5,26-31)

In the beginning when God created the heavens and the earth, the earth was a formless void and darkness covered the face of the deep, while a wind from God swept over the face of the waters. Then God said, 'Let there be light'; and there was light. And God saw that the light was good; and God separated the light from the darkness. God called the light Day, and the darkness he called Night. And there was evening and there was morning, the first day.

[26] Then God said, 'Let us make humankind in our image, according to our likeness; and let them have dominion over the fish of the sea, and over the birds of the air, and over the cattle, and over all the wild animals of the earth, and over every creeping thing that creeps upon the earth.'

So God created humankind in his image,
in the image of God he created them;
male and female he created them.

God blessed them, and God said to them, 'Be fruitful and multiply, and fill the earth and subdue it; and have dominion over the fish of the sea and over the birds of the air and over every living thing that moves upon the earth.' God said, 'See, I have given you every plant yielding seed that is upon the face of all the earth, and every tree with seed in its fruit; you shall have them for food. And to every beast of the earth, and to every bird of the air, and to everything that creeps on the earth, everything that has the breath of life, I have given every green plant for food.' And it was so. God saw everything that he had made, and indeed, it was very good. And there was evening and there was morning, the sixth day.

A reading from the Second Letter of Paul to the Corinthians. (5.14 - 6.2)

The love of Christ urges us on, because we are convinced that one has died for all; therefore all have died. And he died for all, so that those who live might live no longer for themselves, but for him who died and was raised for them.

From now on, therefore, we regard no one from a human point of view; even though we once knew Christ from a human point of view, we know him no longer in that way. So if anyone is in Christ, there is a new creation: everything old has passed away; see, everything has become new! All this is from God, who reconciled us to himself through Christ, and has given us the ministry of reconciliation; that is, in Christ God was reconciling the world to himself, not counting their trespasses against them, and entrusting the message of reconciliation to us. So we are ambassadors for Christ, since God is making his appeal through us; we entreat you on behalf of Christ, be reconciled to God. For our sake he made him to be sin who knew no sin, so that in him we might become the righteousness of God.

As we work together with him, we urge you also not to accept the grace of God in vain. For he says, 'At an acceptable time I have listened to you, and on a day of salvation I have helped you.' See, now is the acceptable time; see, now is the day of salvation!

Sundays of Eastertide

For those who require an Old Testament reading on the Sundays of Eastertide after Easter Day, provision is made. However, if used, the reading from Acts must be used as the second reading.

The Second Sunday of Easter

Principal Service
[Old Testament reading, where required: Exodus 14.10-31; 15.20-21, *see page 198];* Acts 4.32-35; Ps 133; 1 John 1.1 - 2.2; John 20.19-31

A reading from the Acts of the Apostles. (4.32-35)

The whole group of those who believed were of one heart and soul, and no one claimed private ownership of any possessions, but everything they owned was held in common. With great power the apostles gave their testimony to the resurrection of the Lord Jesus, and great grace was upon them all. There was not a needy person among them, for as many as owned lands or houses sold them and brought the proceeds of what was sold. They laid it at the apostles' feet, and it was distributed to each as any had need.

This is the word of the Lord.

A reading from the First Letter of John. (1.1 - 2.2)

We declare to you what was from the beginning, what we have heard, what we have seen with our eyes, what we have looked at and touched with our hands, concerning the word of life – this life was revealed, and we have seen it and testify to it, and declare to you the eternal life that was with the Father and was revealed to us – we declare to you what we have seen and heard so that you also may have fellowship with us; and truly our fellowship is with the Father and with his Son Jesus Christ. We are writing these things so that our joy may be complete.

This is the message we have heard from him and proclaim to you, that God is light and in him there is no darkness at all. If we say that we have fellowship with him while we are walking in darkness, we lie and do not do what is true; but if we walk in the light as he himself is in the light, we have fellowship with one another, and the blood of Jesus his Son cleanses us from all sin. If we say that we have no sin, we deceive ourselves, and the truth is not in us. If we confess our sins, he who is faithful and just will forgive us our sins and cleanse us from all unrighteousness. If we say that we have not sinned, we make him a liar, and his word is not in us.

My little children, I am writing these things to you so that you may not sin. But if anyone does sin, we have an advocate with the Father, Jesus Christ the righteous; and he is the atoning sacrifice for our sins, and not for ours only but also for the sins of the whole world.

This is the word of the Lord.

Hear the gospel of our Lord Jesus Christ according to John. (20.19-31)

When it was evening on that day, the first day of the week, and the doors of the house where the disciples had met were locked for fear of the Jews, Jesus came and stood among them and said, 'Peace be with you.' After he said this, he showed them his hands and his side. Then the disciples rejoiced when they saw the Lord. Jesus said to them again, 'Peace be with you. As the Father has sent me, so I send you.' When he had said this, he breathed on them and said to them, 'Receive the Holy Spirit. If you forgive the sins of any, they are forgiven them; if you retain the sins of any, they are retained.'

But Thomas (who was called the Twin), one of the twelve, was not with them when Jesus came. So the other disciples told him, 'We have seen the Lord.' But he said to them, 'Unless I see the mark of the nails in his hands, and put my finger in the mark of the nails and my hand in his side, I will not believe.'

A week later his disciples were again in the house, and Thomas was with them. Although the doors were shut, Jesus came and stood among them and said, 'Peace be with you.' Then he said to Thomas, 'Put your finger here and see my hands. Reach out your hand and put it in my side. Do not doubt but believe.' Thomas answered him, 'My Lord and my God!' Jesus said to him, 'Have you believed because you have seen me? Blessèd are those who have not seen and yet have come to believe.'

Now Jesus did many other signs in the presence of his disciples, which are not written in this book. But these are written so that you may come to believe that Jesus is the Messiah, the Son of God, and that through believing you may have life in his name.

This is the gospel of the Lord.

Second Service
Ps 143.1-11; Isaiah 26.1-9,19; Luke 24.1-12

A reading from the prophecy of Isaiah. (26.1-9)

This song will be sung in the land of Judah:
    We have a strong city;
        he sets up victory like walls and bulwarks.
    Open the gates,
        so that the righteous nation that keeps faith
        may enter in.
    Those of steadfast mind you keep in peace –
        in peace because they trust in you.
    Trust in the Lord for ever,
        for in the Lord God
        you have an everlasting rock.
    For he has brought low
        the inhabitants of the height;
        the lofty city he lays low.
    He lays it low to the ground,
        casts it to the dust.
    The foot tramples it,
        the feet of the poor,
        the steps of the needy.

    The way of the righteous is level;
        O Just One, you make smooth the path of the righteous.
    In the path of your judgements,
        O Lord, we wait for you;
    your name and your renown

are the soul's desire.
My soul yearns for you in the night,
　　my spirit within me earnestly seeks you.
For when your judgements are in the earth,
　　the inhabitants of the world learn righteousness.
¹⁹ Your dead shall live, your corpses shall rise.
　　O dwellers in the dust, awake and sing for joy!
For your dew is a radiant dew
　　and the earth will give birth to those long dead.

A reading from the gospel according to Luke. (24.1-12)

On the first day of the week, at early dawn, they came to the tomb, taking the spices that they had prepared. They found the stone rolled away from the tomb, but when they went in, they did not find the body. While they were perplexed about this, suddenly two men in dazzling clothes stood beside them. The women were terrified and bowed their faces to the ground, but the men said to them, 'Why do you look for the living among the dead? He is not here, but has risen. Remember how he told you, while he was still in Galilee, that the Son of Man must be handed over to sinners, and be crucified, and on the third day rise again.' Then they remembered his words, and returning from the tomb, they told all this to the eleven and to all the rest. Now it was Mary Magdalene, Joanna, Mary the mother of James, and the other women with them who told this to the apostles. But these words seemed to them an idle tale, and they did not believe them. But Peter got up and ran to the tomb; stooping and looking in, he saw the linen cloths by themselves; then he went home, amazed at what had happened.

Third Service
Ps 22.20-31; Isaiah 53.6-12; Romans 4.13-25

A reading from the prophecy of Isaiah. (53.6-12)

All we like sheep have gone astray;
　　we have all turned to our own way,
and the Lord has laid on him
　　the iniquity of us all.

He was oppressed, and he was afflicted,
　　yet he did not open his mouth;
like a lamb that is led to the slaughter,
　　and like a sheep that before its shearers is silent,
　　so he did not open his mouth.

By a perversion of justice he was taken away.
    Who could have imagined his future?
For he was cut off from the land of the living,
    stricken for the transgression of my people.
They made his grave with the wicked
    and his tomb with the rich,
although he had done no violence,
    and there was no deceit in his mouth.

Yet it was the will of the Lord to crush him with pain.
When you make his life an offering for sin,
    he shall see his offspring, and shall prolong his days;
through him the will of the Lord shall prosper.
    Out of his anguish he shall see light;
he shall find satisfaction through his knowledge.
    The righteous one, my servant,
        shall make many righteous,
    and he shall bear their iniquities.
Therefore I will allot him a portion with the great,
    and he shall divide the spoil with the strong;
because he poured out himself to death,
    and was numbered with the transgressors;
yet he bore the sin of many,
    and made intercession for the transgressors.

A reading from the Letter of Paul to the Romans. (4.13-25)

The promise that he would inherit the world did not come to Abraham or to his descendants through the law but through the righteousness of faith. If it is the adherents of the law who are to be the heirs, faith is null and the promise is void. For the law brings wrath; but where there is no law, neither is there violation.

For this reason it depends on faith, in order that the promise may rest on grace and be guaranteed to all his descendants, not only to the adherents of the law but also to those who share the faith of Abraham (for he is the father of all of us, as it is written, 'I have made you the father of many nations') – in the presence of the God in whom he believed, who gives life to the dead and calls into existence the things that do not exist. Hoping against hope, he believed that he would become 'the father of many nations', according to what was said, 'So numerous shall your descendants be.' He did not weaken in faith when he considered his own body, which was already as good as dead (for he was about a hundred years old), or when he considered the barrenness of Sarah's womb. No distrust made him waver concerning the promise of God, but he grew strong in his faith as he gave glory to God, being fully convinced that God was able to do what he had promised. Therefore his faith 'was reckoned to him as righteousness.' Now the words, 'it was reckoned to him', were written not for his sake alone, but for ours also. It will be reckoned to us who believe in him who raised Jesus our Lord from the dead, who was handed over to death for our trespasses and was raised for our justification.

The Third Sunday of Easter

Principal Service
[Old Testament reading, where required: Zephaniah 3.14-20, *see page 204]*
Acts 3.12-19; Ps 4; 1 John 3.1-7; Luke 24.36b-48

A reading from the Acts of the Apostles. (3.12-19)

When Peter saw the lame man walk, he addressed the people, 'You Israelites, why do you wonder at this, or why do you stare at us, as though by our own power or piety we had made him walk? The God of Abraham, the God of Isaac, and the God of Jacob, the God of our ancestors has glorified his servant Jesus, whom you handed over and rejected in the presence of Pilate, though he had decided to release him. But you rejected the Holy and Righteous One and asked to have a murderer given to you, and you killed the Author of life, whom God raised from the dead. To this we are witnesses. And by faith in his name, his name itself has made this man strong, whom you see and know; and the faith that is through Jesus has given him this perfect health in the presence of all of you.

'And now, friends, I know that you acted in ignorance, as did also your rulers. In this way God fulfilled what he had foretold through all the prophets, that his Messiah would suffer. Repent therefore, and turn to God so that your sins may be wiped out.'

This is the word of the Lord.

A reading from the First Letter of John. (3.1-7)

See what love the Father has given us, that we should be called children of God; and that is what we are. The reason the world does not know us is that it did not know him. Belovèd, we are God's children now; what we will be has not yet been revealed. What we do know is this: when he is revealed, we will be like him, for we will see him as he is. And all who have this hope in him purify themselves, just as he is pure.

Everyone who commits sin is guilty of lawlessness; sin is lawlessness. You know that he was revealed to take away sins, and in him there is no sin. No one who abides in him sins; no one who sins has either seen him or known him. Little children, let no one deceive you. Everyone who does what is right is righteous, just as he is righteous.

This is the word of the Lord.

Hear the gospel of our Lord Jesus Christ according to Luke. (24.36b-48)

Jesus himself stood among the eleven and their companions and said to them, 'Peace be with you.' They were startled and terrified, and thought that they were seeing a ghost. He said to them, 'Why are you frightened, and why do doubts arise in your hearts? Look at my hands and my feet; see that it is I myself. Touch me and see; for a ghost does not have flesh and bones as you see that I have.' And when he had said this, he showed them his hands and his feet. While in their joy they were disbelieving and still wondering, he said to them, 'Have you anything here to eat?' They gave him a piece of broiled fish, and he took it and ate in their presence.

Then he said to them, 'These are my words that I spoke to you while I was still with you – that everything written about me in the law of Moses, the prophets, and the psalms must be fulfilled.' Then he opened their minds to understand the scriptures, and he said to them, 'Thus it is written, that the Messiah is to suffer and to rise from the dead on the third day, and that repentance and forgiveness of sins is to be proclaimed in his name to all nations, beginning from Jerusalem. You are witnesses of these things.'

This is the gospel of the Lord.

Second Service
Ps 142; Deuteronomy 7.7-13; Revelation 2.1-11;
if a Eucharist: Luke 16.19-31

A reading from the book Deuteronomy. (7.7-13)

Moses said to all Israel: It was not because you were more numerous than any other people that the Lord set his heart on you and chose you – for you were the fewest of all peoples. It was because the Lord loved you and kept the oath that he swore to your ancestors, that the Lord has brought you out with a mighty hand, and redeemed you from the house of slavery, from the hand of Pharaoh king of Egypt. Know therefore that the Lord your God is God, the faithful God who maintains covenant loyalty with those who love him and keep his commandments, to a thousand generations, and who repays in their own person those who reject him. He does not delay but repays in their own person those who reject him. Therefore, observe diligently the commandment – the statutes and the ordinances – that I am commanding you today.

If you heed these ordinances, by diligently observing them, the Lord your God will maintain with you the covenant loyalty that he swore to your ancestors; he will love you, bless you, and multiply you; he will bless the fruit of your womb and the fruit of your ground, your grain and your wine and your oil, the increase of your cattle and the issue of your flock, in the land that he swore to your ancestors to give you.

A reading from the Revelation to John. (2.1-11)

'To the angel of the church in Ephesus write: These are the words of him who holds the seven stars in his right hand, who walks among the seven golden lampstands:

'I know your works, your toil and your patient endurance. I know that you cannot tolerate evildoers; you have tested those who claim to be apostles but are not, and have found them to be false. I also know that you are enduring patiently and bearing up for the sake of my name, and that you have not grown weary. But I have this against you, that you have abandoned the love you had at first. Remember then from what you have fallen; repent, and do the works you did at first. If not, I will come to you and remove your lampstand from its place, unless you repent. Yet this is to your credit: you hate the works of the Nicolaitans, which I also hate. Let anyone who has an ear listen to what the Spirit is saying to the churches. To everyone who conquers, I will give permission to eat from the tree of life that is in the paradise of God.

'And to the angel of the church in Smyrna write: These are the words of the first and the last, who was dead and came to life:

'I know your affliction and your poverty, even though you are rich. I know the slander on the part of those who say that they are Jews and are not, but are a synagogue of Satan. Do not fear what you are about to suffer. Beware, the devil is about to throw some of you into prison so that you may be tested, and for ten days you will have affliction. Be faithful until death, and I will give you the crown of life. Let anyone who has an ear listen to what the Spirit is saying to the churches. Whoever conquers will not be harmed by the second death.'

If a Eucharist:
Hear the gospel of our Lord Jesus Christ according to Luke. *(16.19-31)*

Jesus said to the disciples, 'There was a rich man who was dressed in purple and fine linen and who feasted sumptuously every day. And at his gate lay a poor man named Lazarus, covered with sores, who longed to satisfy his hunger with what fell from the rich man's table; even the dogs would come and lick his sores. The poor man died and was carried away by the angels to be with Abraham. The rich man also died and was buried. In Hades, where he was being tormented, he looked up and saw Abraham far away with Lazarus by his side. He called out, "Father Abraham, have mercy on me, and send Lazarus to dip the tip of his finger in water and cool my tongue; for I am in agony in these flames." But Abraham said, "Child, remember that during your lifetime you received your good things, and Lazarus in like manner evil things; but now he is comforted here, and you are in agony. Besides all this, between you and us a great chasm has been fixed, so that those who might want to pass from here to you cannot do so, and no one can cross from there to us." He said, "Then, father, I beg you to send him to my father's house – for I have five brothers – that he may warn them, so that they will not also come into this place of torment." Abraham replied, "They have Moses and the prophets; they should listen to them." He said, "No, father Abraham; but if someone goes to them from the dead, they will repent." He said to him, "If they do not listen to Moses and the prophets, neither will they be convinced even if someone rises from the dead."'

This is the gospel of the Lord.

Third Service
Ps 77.11-20; Isaiah 63.7-15; 1 Corinthians 10.1-13

A reading from the prophecy of Isaiah. *(63.7-15)*

I will recount the gracious deeds of the Lord,
    the praiseworthy acts of the Lord,
because of all that the Lord has done for us,
    and the great favour to the house of Israel
that he has shown them according to his mercy,
    according to the abundance of his steadfast love.
For he said, 'Surely they are my people,
    children who will not deal falsely';
and he became their saviour
    in all their distress.

It was no messenger or angel
  but his presence that saved them;
in his love and in his pity he redeemed them;
  he lifted them up and carried them all the days of old.
But they rebelled
  and grieved his holy spirit;
therefore he became their enemy;
  he himself fought against them.
Then they remembered the days of old,
  of Moses his servant.
Where is the one who brought them up out of the sea
  with the shepherds of his flock?
Where is the one who put within them
  his holy spirit,
who caused his glorious arm
  to march at the right hand of Moses,
who divided the waters before them
  to make for himself an everlasting name,
  who led them through the depths?
Like a horse in the desert,
  they did not stumble.
Like cattle that go down into the valley,
  the spirit of the Lord gave them rest.
Thus you led your people,
  to make for yourself a glorious name.
Look down from heaven and see,
  from your holy and glorious habitation.
Where are your zeal and your might?
The yearning of your heart and your compassion?
They are withheld from me.

A reading from the First Letter of Paul to the Corinthians. (10.1-13)

I do not want you to be unaware, brothers and sisters, that our ancestors were all under the cloud, and all passed through the sea, and all
were baptized into Moses in the cloud and in the sea, and all ate the
same spiritual food, and all drank the same spiritual drink. For they
drank from the spiritual rock that followed them, and the rock was
Christ. Nevertheless, God was not pleased with most of them, and
they were struck down in the wilderness.

  Now these things occurred as examples for us, so that we might not
desire evil as they did. Do not become idolaters as some of them did;
as it is written, 'The people sat down to eat and drink, and they rose

up to play.' We must not indulge in sexual immorality as some of them did, and twenty-three thousand fell in a single day. We must not put Christ to the test, as some of them did, and were destroyed by serpents. And do not complain as some of them did, and were destroyed by the destroyer. These things happened to them to serve as an example, and they were written down to instruct us, on whom the ends of the ages have come. So if you think you are standing, watch out that you do not fall. No testing has overtaken you that is not common to everyone. God is faithful, and he will not let you be tested beyond your strength, but with the testing he will also provide the way out so that you may be able to endure it.

The Fourth Sunday of Easter

Principal Service
[Old Testament reading, where required:
Genesis 7.1-5,11-18; 8.6-18; 9.8-13, *see page 196]*
Acts 4.5-12; Ps 23; 1 John 3.16-24; John 10.11-18

A reading from the Acts of the Apostles. (4.5-12)

The rulers, elders, and scribes assembled in Jerusalem, with Annas the high priest, Caiaphas, John, and Alexander, and all who were of the high-priestly family. When they had made the prisoners, Peter and John, stand in their midst, they inquired, 'By what power or by what name did you do this?' Then Peter, filled with the Holy Spirit, said to them, 'Rulers of the people and elders, if we are questioned today because of a good deed done to someone who was sick and are asked how this man has been healed, let it be known to all of you, and to all the people of Israel, that this man is standing before you in good health by the name of Jesus Christ of Nazareth, whom you cru-cified, whom God raised from the dead. This Jesus is
"the stone that was rejected by you,
     the builders; it has become the cornerstone."
There is salvation in no one else, for there is no other name under heaven given among mortals by which we must be saved.'

This is the word of the Lord.

A reading from the First Letter of John. (3.16-24)

We know love by this, that Christ Jesus laid down his life for us – and we ought to lay down our lives for one another. How does God's love abide in anyone who has the world's goods and sees a brother or sister in need and yet refuses help?

Little children, let us love, not in word or speech, but in truth and action. And by this we will know that we are from the truth and will reassure our hearts before him whenever our hearts condemn us; for God is greater than our hearts, and he knows everything. Belovèd, if our hearts do not condemn us, we have boldness before God; and we receive from him whatever we ask, because we obey his commandments and do what pleases him.

And this is his commandment, that we should believe in the name of his Son Jesus Christ and love one another, just as he has commanded us. All who obey his commandments abide in him, and he abides in them. And by this we know that he abides in us, by the Spirit that he has given us.

This is the word of the Lord.

Hear the gospel of our Lord Jesus Christ according to John. (10.11-18)

Jesus said to the Pharisees, 'I am the good shepherd. The good shepherd lays down his life for the sheep. The hired hand, who is not the shepherd and does not own the sheep, sees the wolf coming and leaves the sheep and runs away – and the wolf snatches them and scatters them. The hired hand runs away because a hired hand does not care for the sheep. I am the good shepherd. I know my own and my own know me, just as the Father knows me and I know the Father. And I lay down my life for the sheep. I have other sheep that do not belong to this fold. I must bring them also, and they will listen to my voice. So there will be one flock, one shepherd. For this reason the Father loves me, because I lay down my life in order to take it up again. No one takes it from me, but I lay it down of my own accord. I have power to lay it down, and I have power to take it up again. I have received this command from my Father.'

This is the gospel of the Lord.

Second Service
Ps 81.8-16; Exodus 16.4-15; Revelation 2.12-17;
if a Eucharist: John 6.30-40

A reading from the Book of the Exodus. (16.4-15)

The Lord said to Moses, 'I am going to rain bread from heaven for you, and each day the people shall go out and gather enough for that day. In that way I will test them, whether they will follow my instruction or not. On the sixth day, when they prepare what they bring in, it will be twice as much as they gather on other days.' So

Moses and Aaron said to all the Israelites, 'In the evening you shall know that it was the Lord who brought you out of the land of Egypt, and in the morning you shall see the glory of the Lord, because he has heard your complaining against the Lord. For what are we, that you complain against us?' And Moses said, 'When the Lord gives you meat to eat in the evening and your fill of bread in the morning, because the Lord has heard the complaining that you utter against him – what are we? Your complaining is not against us but against the Lord.'

Then Moses said to Aaron, 'Say to the whole congregation of the Israelites, "Draw near to the Lord, for he has heard your complaining."' And as Aaron spoke to the whole congregation of the Israelites, they looked towards the wilderness, and the glory of the Lord appeared in the cloud. The Lord spoke to Moses and said, 'I have heard the complaining of the Israelites; say to them, "At twilight you shall eat meat, and in the morning you shall have your fill of bread; then you shall know that I am the Lord your God."'

In the evening quails came up and covered the camp; and in the morning there was a layer of dew around the camp. When the layer of dew lifted, there on the surface of the wilderness was a fine flaky substance, as fine as frost on the ground. When the Israelites saw it, they said to one another, 'What is it?' For they did not know what it was. Moses said to them, 'It is the bread that the Lord has given you to eat.'

A reading from the Revelation to John. (2.12-17)

'To the angel of the church in Pergamum write: These are the words of him who has the sharp two-edged sword:

'I know where you are living, where Satan's throne is. Yet you are holding fast to my name, and you did not deny your faith in me even in the days of Antipas my witness, my faithful one, who was killed among you, where Satan lives. But I have a few things against you: you have some there who hold to the teaching of Balaam, who taught Balak to put a stumbling-block before the people of Israel, so that they would eat food sacrificed to idols and practise fornication. So you also have some who hold to the teaching of the Nicolaitans. Repent then. If not, I will come to you soon and make war against them with the sword of my mouth. Let anyone who has an ear listen to what the Spirit is saying to the churches. To everyone who conquers I will give some of the hidden manna, and I will give a white stone, and on the white stone is written a new name that no one knows except the one who receives it.'

If a Eucharist:
Hear the gospel of our Lord Jesus Christ according to John. *(6.30-40)*

The crowd said to Jesus, 'What sign are you going to give us , so that we may see it and believe you? What work are you performing? Our ancestors ate the manna in the wilderness; as it is written, "He gave them bread from heaven to eat."' Then Jesus said to them, 'Very truly, I tell you, it was not Moses who gave you the bread from heaven, but it is my Father who gives you the true bread from heaven. For the bread of God is that which comes down from heaven and gives life to the world.' They said to him, 'Sir, give us this bread always.'

Jesus said to them, 'I am the bread of life. Whoever comes to me will never be hungry, and whoever believes in me will never be thirsty. But I said to you that you have seen me and yet do not believe. Everything that the Father gives me will come to me, and anyone who comes to me I will never drive away; for I have come down from heaven, not to do my own will, but the will of him who sent me. And this is the will of him who sent me, that I should lose nothing of all that he has given me, but raise it up on the last day. This is indeed the will of my Father, that all who see the Son and believe in him may have eternal life; and I will raise them up on the last day.'

This is the gospel of the Lord.

Third Service
Ps 119.89-96; Nehemiah 7.73*b* - 8.12; Luke 24.25-32

A reading from the Book of Nehemiah. *(7.73b - 8.1-12)*

When the seventh month came – the people of Israel being settled in their towns – all the people gathered together into the square before the Water Gate. They told the scribe Ezra to bring the book of the law of Moses, which the Lord had given to Israel. Accordingly, the priest Ezra brought the law before the assembly, both men and women and all who could hear with understanding. This was on the first day of the seventh month. He read from it facing the square before the Water Gate from early morning until midday, in the presence of the men and the women and those who could understand; and the ears of all the people were attentive to the book of the law. The scribe Ezra stood on a wooden platform that had been made for the purpose; and beside him stood Mattithiah, Shema, Anaiah, Uriah, Hilkiah, and Maaseiah on his right hand; and Pedaiah, Mishael, Malchijah, Hashum, Hash-baddanah, Zechariah, and Meshullam on his left hand. And Ezra opened the book in the sight of all the people, for he was standing above all the people; and when he opened it, all the people stood up. Then Ezra blessed the Lord, the great God, and all the people answered, 'Amen, Amen', lifting up their hands. Then they bowed their heads and worshipped the Lord with their faces to the ground. Also Jeshua, Bani, Sherebiah, Jamin, Akkub, Shabbethai, Hodiah, Maaseiah, Kelita, Azariah, Jozabad, Hanan, Pelaiah, the Levites, helped the people to understand the law, while the people remained in their places. So they read from the book, from the law of God, with interpretation. They gave the sense, so that the people understood the reading.

And Nehemiah, who was the governor, and Ezra the priest and scribe, and the Levites who taught the people said to all the people, 'This day is holy to the Lord your God; do not mourn or weep.' For all the people wept when they heard the words of the law. Then he said to them, 'Go your way, eat the fat and drink sweet wine and send portions of them to those for whom nothing is prepared, for this day is holy to our Lord; and do not be grieved, for the joy of the Lord is your strength.' So the Levites stilled all the people, saying, 'Be quiet, for this day is holy; do not be grieved.' And all the people went their way to eat and drink and to send portions and to make great rejoicing, because they had understood the words that were declared to them.

A reading from the gospel according to Luke. (24.25-32)

Jesus said to the two disciples on the way to Emmaus, 'Oh, how foolish you are, and how slow of heart to believe all that the prophets have declared! Was it not necessary that the Messiah should suffer these things and then enter into his glory?' Then beginning with Moses and all the prophets, he interpreted to them the things about himself in all the scriptures.

As they came near the village to which they were going, he walked ahead as if he were going on. But they urged him strongly, saying, 'Stay with us, because it is almost evening and the day is now nearly over.' So he went in to stay with them. When he was at the table with them, he took bread, blessed and broke it, and gave it to them. Then their eyes were opened, and they recognized him; and he vanished from their sight. They said to each other, 'Were not our hearts burning within us while he was talking to us on the road, while he was opening the scriptures to us?'

The Fifth Sunday of Easter

Principal Service

[Old Testament reading, where required: Baruch 3.9-15,32-4.4, *see page 201, or* Genesis 22.1-18, *see page 197]*
Acts 8.26-40; Ps 22.25-31; 1 John 4.7-21; John 15.1-8

A reading from the Acts of the Apostles. (8.26-40)

An angel of the Lord said to Philip, 'Get up and go towards the south to the road that goes down from Jerusalem to Gaza.' (This is a wilderness road.) So he got up and went. Now there was an Ethiopian eunuch, a court official of the Candace, queen of the Ethiopians, in charge of her entire treasury. He had come to Jerusalem to worship and was returning home; seated in his chariot, he was reading the prophet Isaiah. Then the Spirit said to Philip, 'Go over to this chariot and join it.' So Philip ran up to it and heard him reading the prophet Isaiah. He asked, 'Do you understand what you are reading?' He replied, 'How can I, unless someone guides me?' And he invited Philip to get in and sit beside him. Now the passage of the scripture that he was reading was this:
      'Like a sheep he was led to the slaughter,
            and like a lamb silent before its shearer,
                  so he does not open his mouth.
      In his humiliation justice was denied him.
            Who can describe his generation?
                  For his life is taken away from the earth.'
The eunuch asked Philip, 'About whom, may I ask you, does the prophet say this, about himself or about someone else?' Then Philip began to speak, and starting with this scripture, he proclaimed to him the good news about Jesus. As they were going along the road, they came to some water; and the eunuch said, 'Look, here is water! What is to prevent me from being baptized?' He commanded the chariot to stop, and both of them, Philip and the eunuch, went down into the water, and Philip baptized him. When they came up out of the water, the Spirit of the Lord snatched Philip away; the eunuch saw him no more, and went on his way rejoicing. But Philip found himself at Azotus, and as he was passing through the region, he proclaimed the good news to all the towns until he came to Caesarea.

This is the word of the Lord.

A reading from the First Letter of John. (4.7-21)

Belovèd, let us love one another, because love is from God; everyone who loves is born of God and knows God. Whoever does not love does not know God, for God is love. God's love was revealed among us in this way: God sent his only Son into the world so that we might live through him. In this is love, not that we loved God but that he loved us and sent his Son to be the atoning sacrifice for our sins. Belovèd, since God loved us so much, we also ought to love one another. No one has ever seen God; if we love one another, God lives in us, and his love is perfected in us.

By this we know that we abide in him and he in us, because he has given us of his Spirit. And we have seen and do testify that the Father has sent his Son as the Saviour of the world. God abides in those who confess that Jesus is the Son of God, and they abide in God. So we have known and believe the love that God has for us.

God is love, and those who abide in love abide in God, and God abides in them. Love has been perfected among us in this: that we may have boldness on the day of judgement, because as he is, so are we in this world. There is no fear in love, but perfect love casts out fear; for fear has to do with punishment, and whoever fears has not reached perfection in love. We love because he first loved us. Those who say, 'I love God', and hate their brothers or sisters, are liars; for those who do not love a brother or sister whom they have seen, cannot love God whom they have not seen. The commandment we have from him is this: those who love God must love their brothers and sisters also.

This is the word of the Lord.

Hear the gospel of our Lord Jesus Christ according to John. (15.1-8)

Jesus said to the eleven, 'I am the true vine, and my Father is the vine-grower. He removes every branch in me that bears no fruit. Every branch that bears fruit he prunes to make it bear more fruit. You have already been cleansed by the word that I have spoken to you. Abide in me as I abide in you. Just as the branch cannot bear fruit by itself unless it abides in the vine, neither can you unless you abide in me. I am the vine, you are the branches. Those who abide in me and I in them bear much fruit, because apart from me you can do nothing. Whoever does not abide in me is thrown away like a branch and withers; such branches are gathered, thrown into the fire, and burned. If you abide in me, and my words abide in you, ask for whatever you wish, and it will be done for you. My Father is glorified by this, that you bear much fruit and become my disciples.'

This is the gospel of the Lord.

Second Service

Ps 96; Isaiah 60.1-14; Revelation 3.1-13;
if a Eucharist: Mark 16.9-16

A reading from the prophecy of Isaiah. (60.1-14)

Arise, shine; for your light has come,
    and the glory of the Lord has risen upon you.
For darkness shall cover the earth,
    and thick darkness the peoples;
but the Lord will arise upon you,
    and his glory will appear over you.
Nations shall come to your light,
    and kings to the brightness of your dawn.

Lift up your eyes and look around;
    they all gather together, they come to you;
your sons shall come from far away,
    and your daughters shall be carried on their nurses' arms.
Then you shall see and be radiant;
    your heart shall thrill and rejoice,
because the abundance of the sea shall be brought to you,
    the wealth of the nations shall come to you.
A multitude of camels shall cover you,
    the young camels of Midian and Ephah;
    all those from Sheba shall come.
They shall bring gold and frankincense,
    and shall proclaim the praise of the Lord.
All the flocks of Kedar shall be gathered to you,
    the rams of Nebaioth shall minister to you;
they shall be acceptable on my altar,
    and I will glorify my glorious house.

Who are these that fly like a cloud,
    and like doves to their windows?
For the coastlands shall wait for me,
    the ships of Tarshish first,
to bring your children from far away,
    their silver and gold with them,
for the name of the Lord your God,
    and for the Holy One of Israel,
    because he has glorified you.
Foreigners shall build up your walls,
    and their kings shall minister to you;
for in my wrath I struck you down,

but in my favour I have had mercy on you.
Your gates shall always be open;
    day and night they shall not be shut,
so that nations shall bring you their wealth,
    with their kings led in procession.
For the nation and kingdom
    that will not serve you shall perish;
    those nations shall be utterly laid waste.
The glory of Lebanon shall come to you,
    the cypress, the plane, and the pine,
to beautify the place of my sanctuary;
    and I will glorify where my feet rest.
The descendants of those who oppressed you
    shall come bending low to you,
and all who despised you
    shall bow down at your feet;
they shall call you the City of the Lord,
    the Zion of the Holy One of Israel.

A reading from the Revelation to John. (3.1-13)

'To the angel of the church in Sardis write: These are the words of him who has the seven spirits of God and the seven stars:

'I know your works; you have a name for being alive, but you are dead. Wake up, and strengthen what remains and is at the point of death, for I have not found your works perfect in the sight of my God. Remember then what you received and heard; obey it, and repent. If you do not wake up, I will come like a thief, and you will not know at what hour I will come to you. Yet you have still a few people in Sardis who have not soiled their clothes; they will walk with me, dressed in white, for they are worthy. If you conquer, you will be clothed like them in white robes, and I will not blot your name out of the book of life; I will confess your name before my Father and before his angels. Let anyone who has an ear listen to what the Spirit is saying to the churches.

'And to the angel of the church in Philadelphia write:
    These are the words of the holy one, the true one,
        who has the key of David,
        who opens and no one will shut,
            who shuts and no one opens:

'I know your works. Look, I have set before you an open door, which no one is able to shut. I know that you have but little power, and yet you have kept my word and have not denied my name. I will make those of the synagogue of Satan who say that they are Jews and are not, but are lying – I will make them come and bow down before your feet, and they will learn that I have loved you. Because you have kept my word of patient endurance, I will keep you from the hour of trial that is coming on the whole world to test the inhabitants of the earth. I am coming soon; hold fast to what you have, so that no one may seize your crown. If you conquer, I will make you a pillar in the temple of my God; you will never go out of it. I will write on you the name of my God, and the name of the city of my God, the new Jerusalem that comes down from my God out of heaven, and my own new name. Let anyone who has an ear listen to what the Spirit is saying to the churches.'

If a Eucharist:
Hear the gospel of our Lord Jesus Christ according to Mark. *(16.9-16)*

After Jesus rose early on the first day of the week, he appeared first to Mary Magdalene, from whom he had cast out seven demons. She went out and told those who had been with him, while they were mourning and weeping. But when they heard that he was alive and had been seen by her, they would not believe it.

After this he appeared in another form to two of them, as they were walking into the country. And they went back and told the rest, but they did not believe them.

Later he appeared to the eleven themselves as they were sitting at the table; and he upbraided them for their lack of faith and stubbornness, because they had not believed those who saw him after he had risen. And he said to them, 'Go into all the world and proclaim the good news to the whole creation. The one who believes and is baptized will be saved; but the one who does not believe will be condemned.'

This is the gospel of the Lord.

Third Service
Ps 44.15-26; 2 Maccabees 7.7-14 or Daniel 3.16-28;
Hebrews 11.32 - 12.2

A reading from the Second Book of the Maccabees. (7.7-14)

After the first of the seven brothers had been put to death, they brought forward the second for their sport. They tore off the skin of his head with the hair, and asked him, 'Will you eat the swine's flesh rather than have your body punished limb by limb?' He replied in the language of his ancestors and said to them, 'No.' Therefore he in turn underwent tortures as the first brother had done. And when he was at his last breath, he said, 'You accursed wretch, you dismiss us from this present life, but the King of the universe will raise us up to an everlasting renewal of life, because we have died for his laws.'

After him, the third was the victim of their sport. When it was demanded, he quickly put out his tongue and courageously stretched forth his hands, and said nobly, 'I got these from Heaven, and because of his laws I disdain them, and from him I hope to get them back again.' As a result the king himself and those with him were astonished at the young man's spirit, for he regarded his sufferings as nothing.

After he too had died, they maltreated and tortured the fourth in the same way. When he was near death, he said, 'One cannot but choose to die at the hands of mortals and to cherish the hope God gives of being raised again by him. But for you there will be no resurrection to life!'

Or:

A reading from the Book of Daniel. *(3.16-28)*

Shadrach, Meshach, and Abednego answered the king,
'O Nebuchadnezzar, we have no need to present a defence to you in this matter. If our God whom we serve is able to deliver us from the furnace of blazing fire and out of your hand, O king, let him deliver us. But if not, be it known to you, O king, that we will not serve your gods and we will not worship the golden statue that you have set up.'

Then Nebuchadnezzar was so filled with rage against Shadrach, Meshach, and Abednego that his face was distorted. He ordered the furnace to be heated up seven times more than was customary, and ordered some of the strongest guards in his army to bind Shadrach, Meshach, and Abednego and to throw them into the furnace of blazing fire. So the men were bound, still wearing their tunics, their trousers, their hats, and their other garments, and they were thrown into the furnace of blazing fire. Because the king's command was urgent and the furnace was so overheated, the raging flames killed the men who lifted Shadrach, Meshach, and Abednego. But the three men, Shadrach, Meshach, and Abednego, fell down, bound, into the furnace of blazing fire.

Then King Nebuchadnezzar was astonished and rose up quickly. He said to his counsellors, 'Was it not three men that we threw bound into the fire?' They answered the king, 'True, O king.' He replied, 'But I see four men unbound, walking in the middle of the fire, and they are not hurt; and the fourth has the appearance of a god.' Nebuchadnezzar then approached the door of the furnace of blazing fire and said, 'Shadrach, Meshach, and Abednego, servants of the Most High God, come out! Come here!' So Shadrach, Meshach, and Abednego came out from the fire. And the satraps, the prefects, the governors, and the king's counsellors gathered together and saw that the fire had not had any power over the bodies of those men; the hair of their heads was not singed, their tunics were not harmed, and not even the smell of fire came from them. Nebuchadnezzar said, 'Blessèd be the God of Shadrach, Meshach, and Abednego, who has sent his angel and delivered his servants who trusted in him. They disobeyed the king's command and yielded up their bodies rather than serve and worship any god except their own God.

A reading from the Letter to the Hebrews. (11.32 - 12.2)

What more should I say? For time would fail me to tell of Gideon, Barak, Samson, Jephthah, of David and Samuel and the prophets – who through faith conquered kingdoms, administered justice, obtained promises, shut the mouths of lions, quenched raging fire, escaped the edge of the sword, won strength out of weakness, became mighty in war, put foreign armies to flight. Women received their dead by resurrection. Others were tortured, refusing to accept release, in order to obtain a better resurrection. Others suffered mocking and flogging, and even chains and imprisonment. They were stoned to death, they were sawn in two, they were killed by the sword; they went about in skins of sheep and goats, destitute, persecuted, tormented – of whom the world was not worthy. They wandered in deserts and mountains, and in caves and holes in the ground.

Yet all these, though they were commended for their faith, did not receive what was promised, since God had provided something better so that they would not, without us, be made perfect.

Therefore, since we are surrounded by so great a cloud of witnesses, let us also lay aside every weight and the sin that clings so closely, and let us run with perseverance the race that is set before us, looking to Jesus the pioneer and perfecter of our faith, who for the sake of the joy that was set before him endured the cross, disregarding its shame, and has taken his seat at the right hand of the throne of God.

The Sixth Sunday of Easter

Principal Service

[*Old Testament reading, where required:* Isaiah 55.1-11, *see page 200*]
Acts 10.44-48; Ps 98; 1 John 5.1-6; John 15.9-17

A reading from the Acts of the Apostles. (10.44-48)

While Peter was still speaking, the Holy Spirit fell upon all who heard the word. The circumcised believers who had come with Peter were astounded that the gift of the Holy Spirit had been poured out even on the Gentiles, for they heard them speaking in tongues and extolling God. Then Peter said, 'Can anyone withhold the water for baptizing these people who have received the Holy Spirit just as we have?' So he ordered them to be baptized in the name of Jesus Christ. Then they invited him to stay for several days.

This is the word of the Lord.

A reading from the First Letter of John. (5.1-6)

Everyone who believes that Jesus is the Christ has been born of God, and everyone who loves the parent loves the child. By this we know that we love the children of God, when we love God and obey his commandments. For the love of God is this, that we obey his commandments. And his commandments are not burdensome, for whatever is born of God conquers the world. And this is the victory that conquers the world, our faith. Who is it that conquers the world but the one who believes that Jesus is the Son of God?
  This is the one who came by water and blood, Jesus Christ, not with the water only but with the water and the blood. And the Spirit is the one that testifies, for the Spirit is the truth.

This is the word of the Lord.

Hear the gospel of our Lord Jesus Christ according to John. (15.9-17)

Jesus said to the eleven, 'As the Father has loved me, so I have loved you; abide in my love. If you keep my commandments, you will abide in my love, just as I have kept my Father's commandments and abide in his love. I have said these things to you so that my joy may be in you, and that your joy may be complete.
  'This is my commandment, that you love one another as I have loved you. No one has greater love than this, to lay down one's life for one's friends. You are my friends if you do what I command you. I do not call you servants any longer, because the servant does not

know what the master is doing; but I have called you friends, because I have made known to you everything that I have heard from my Father. You did not choose me but I chose you. And I appointed you to go and bear fruit, fruit that will last, so that the Father will give you whatever you ask him in my name. I am giving you these commands so that you may love one another.'

This is the gospel of the Lord.

Second Service
Ps 45; Song of Solomon 4.16 - 5.2; 8.6-7; Revelation 3.14-22; *if a Eucharist:* Luke 22.24-30

A reading from the Song of Solomon. (4.16 - 5.2 & 8.6-7)

> Awake, O north wind,
> > and come, O south wind!
> Blow upon my garden
> > that its fragrance may be wafted abroad.
> Let my belovèd come to his garden,
> > and eat its choicest fruits.
>
> I come to my garden, my sister, my bride;
> > I gather my myrrh with my spice,
> I eat my honeycomb with my honey,
> > I drink my wine with my milk.
> Eat, friends, drink,
> > and be drunk with love.
>
> I slept, but my heart was awake.
> Listen! my belovèd is knocking.
> 'Open to me, my sister, my love,
> > my dove, my perfect one;
> for my head is wet with dew,
> > my locks with the drops of the night.'

8.6   Set me as a seal upon your heart,
> > as a seal upon your arm;
> for love is strong as death,
> > passion fierce as the grave.
> Its flashes are flashes of fire,
> > a raging flame.
> Many waters cannot quench love,
> > neither can floods drown it.
> If one offered for love all the wealth of one's house,
> > it would be utterly scorned.

A reading from the Revelation to John. (3.14-22)

'To the angel of the church in Laodicea write: The words of the Amen, the faithful and true witness, the origin of God's creation:

'I know your works; you are neither cold nor hot. I wish that you were either cold or hot. So, because you are lukewarm, and neither cold nor hot, I am about to spit you out of my mouth. For you say, "I am rich, I have prospered, and I need nothing." You do not realize that you are wretched, pitiable, poor, blind, and naked. Therefore I counsel you to buy from me gold refined by fire so that you may be rich; and white robes to clothe you and to keep the shame of your nakedness from being seen; and salve to anoint your eyes so that you may see. I reprove and discipline those whom I love. Be earnest, therefore, and repent. Listen! I am standing at the door, knocking; if you hear my voice and open the door, I will come in to you and eat with you, and you with me. To the one who conquers I will give a place with me on my throne, just as I myself conquered and sat down with my Father on his throne. Let anyone who has an ear listen to what the Spirit is saying to the churches.'

If a Eucharist:
Hear the gospel of our Lord Jesus Christ according to Luke. *(22.24-30)*

A dispute arose among the apostles as to which one of them was to be regarded as the greatest. But Jesus said to them, 'The kings of the Gentiles lord it over them; and those in authority over them are called benefactors. But not so with you; rather the greatest among you must become like the youngest, and the leader like one who serves. For who is greater, the one who is at the table or the one who serves? Is it not the one at the table? But I am among you as one who serves.

'You are those who have stood by me in my trials; and I confer on you, just as my Father has conferred on me, a kingdom, so that you may eat and drink at my table in my kingdom, and you will sit on thrones judging the twelve tribes of Israel.'

This is the gospel of the Lord.

Third Service
Ps 104.26-32; Ezekiel 47.1-12; John 21.1-19

A reading from the prophecy of Ezekiel. (47.1-12)

The Lord brought me back to the entrance of the temple; there, water was flowing from below the threshold of the temple towards the east (for the temple faced east); and the water was flowing down from below the south end of the threshold of the temple, south of the altar. Then he brought me out by way of the north gate, and led me round on the outside to the outer gate that faces towards the east; and the water was coming out on the south side.

Going on eastwards with a cord in his hand, the man measured one thousand cubits, and then led me through the water; and it was ankle-deep. Again he measured one thousand, and led me through the water; and it was knee-deep. Again he measured one thousand, and led me through the water; and it was up to the waist. Again he measured one thousand, and it was a river that I could not cross, for the water had risen; it was deep enough to swim in, a river that could not be crossed. He said to me, 'Mortal, have you seen this?'

Then he led me back along the bank of the river. As I came back, I saw on the bank of the river a great many trees on one side and on the other. He said to me, 'This water flows towards the eastern region and goes down into the Arabah; and when it enters the sea, the sea of stagnant waters, the water will become fresh. Wherever the river goes, every living creature that swarms will live, and there will be very many fish, once these waters reach there. It will become fresh; and everything will live where the river goes. People will stand fishing beside the sea from En-gedi to En-eglaim; it will be a place for the spreading of nets; its fish will be of a great many kinds, like the fish of the Great Sea. But its swamps and marshes will not become fresh; they are to be left for salt. On the banks, on both sides of the river, there will grow all kinds of trees for food. Their leaves will not wither nor their fruit fail, but they will bear fresh fruit every month, because the water for them flows from the sanctuary. Their fruit will be for food, and their leaves for healing.'

A reading from the gospel according to John. (21.1-19)

Jesus showed himself again to the disciples by the Sea of Tiberias; and he showed himself in this way. Gathered there together were Simon Peter, Thomas called the Twin, Nathanael of Cana in Galilee, the sons of Zebedee, and two others of his disciples. Simon Peter said to them, 'I am going fishing.' They said to him, 'We will go with you.' They went out and got into the boat, but that night they caught nothing.

Just after daybreak, Jesus stood on the beach; but the disciples did not know that it was Jesus. Jesus said to them, 'Children, you have no fish, have you?' They answered him, 'No.' He said to them, 'Cast the net to the right side of the boat, and you will find some.' So they cast it, and now they were not able to haul it in because there were so many fish. That disciple whom Jesus loved said to Peter, 'It is the Lord!' When Simon Peter heard that it was the Lord, he put on some clothes, for he was naked, and jumped into the lake. But the other disciples came in the boat, dragging the net full of fish, for they were not far from the land, only about a hundred yards off.

When they had gone ashore, they saw a charcoal fire there, with fish on it, and bread. Jesus said to them, 'Bring some of the fish that you have just caught.' So Simon Peter went aboard and hauled the net ashore, full of large fish, a hundred and fifty-three of them; and though there were so many, the net was not torn. Jesus said to them, 'Come and have breakfast.' Now none of the disciples dared to ask him, 'Who are you?' because they knew it was the Lord. Jesus came and took the bread and gave it to them, and did the same with the fish. This was now the third time that Jesus appeared to the disciples after he was raised from the dead.

When they had finished breakfast, Jesus said to Simon Peter, 'Simon son of John, do you love me more than these?' He said to him, 'Yes, Lord; you know that I love you.' Jesus said to him, 'Feed my lambs.' A second time he said to him, 'Simon son of John, do you love me?' He said to him, 'Yes, Lord; you know that I love you.' Jesus said to him, 'Tend my sheep.' He said to him the third time, 'Simon son of John, do you love me?' Peter felt hurt because he said to him the third time, 'Do you love me?' And he said to him, 'Lord, you know everything; you know that I love you.' Jesus said to him, 'Feed my sheep. Very truly, I tell you, when you were younger, you used to fasten your own belt and to go wherever you wished. But when you grow old, you will stretch out your hands, and someone else will fasten a belt around you and take you where you do not wish to go.' (He said this to indicate the kind of death by which he would glorify God.) After this he said to him, 'Follow me.'

Ascension Day

Evening Prayer on the Eve
Pss 15,24; 2 Samuel 23.1-5; Colossians 2.20 - 3.4

A reading from the Second Book of Samuel. (23.1-5)

These are the last words of David: The oracle of David, son of Jesse, the oracle of the man whom God exalted, the anointed of the God of Jacob, the favourite of the Strong One of Israel:

The spirit of the Lord speaks through me, his word is upon my tongue. The God of Israel has spoken, the Rock of Israel has said to me: One who rules over people justly, ruling in the fear of God, is like the light of morning, like the sun rising on a cloudless morning, gleaming from the rain on the grassy land.

Is not my house like this with God? For he has made with me an everlasting covenant, ordered in all things and secure. Will he not cause to prosper all my help and my desire?

A reading from the Letter of Paul to the Colossians. (2.20 - 3.4)

If with Christ you died to the elemental spirits of the universe, why do you live as if you still belonged to the world? Why do you submit to regulations, 'Do not handle, Do not taste, Do not touch'? All these regulations refer to things that perish with use; they are simply human commands and teachings. These have indeed an appearance of wisdom in promoting self-imposed piety, humility, and severe treatment of the body, but they are of no value in checking self-indulgence.

So if you have been raised with Christ, seek the things that are above, where Christ is, seated at the right hand of God. Set your minds on things that are above, not on things that are on earth, for you have died, and your life is hidden with Christ in God. When Christ who is your life is revealed, then you also will be revealed with him in glory.

Principal Service
Acts 1.1-11 *or* Daniel 7.9-14;
Ps 47 *or* Ps 93;
Ephesians 1.15-23 *or* Acts 1.1-11;
The reading from Acts must be used as either the first or second reading.
Luke 24.44-53

A reading from the Book of Daniel. (7.9-14)

As I watched, thrones were set in place, and an Ancient One took his throne; his clothing was white as snow, and the hair of his head like pure wool; his throne was fiery flames, and its wheels were burning fire. A stream of fire issued and flowed out from his presence. A thousand thousand served him, and ten thousand times ten thousand stood attending him. The court sat in judgement, and the books were opened.

I watched then because of the noise of the arrogant words that the horn was speaking. And as I watched, the beast was put to death, and its body destroyed and given over to be burned with fire. As for the rest of the beasts, their dominion was taken away, but their lives were prolonged for a season and a time.

As I watched in the night visions, I saw one like a human being coming with the clouds of heaven. And he came to the Ancient One and was presented before him.

To him was given dominion and glory and kingship, that all peoples, nations, and languages should serve him. His dominion is an everlasting dominion that shall not pass away, and his kingship is one that shall never be destroyed.

This is the word of the Lord.

A reading from the Acts of the Apostles. (1.1-11)

In the first book, Theophilus, I wrote about all that Jesus did and taught from the beginning until the day when he was taken up to heaven, after giving instructions through the Holy Spirit to the apostles whom he had chosen. After his suffering he presented himself alive to them by many convincing proofs, appearing to them over the course of forty days and speaking about the kingdom of God. While staying with them, he ordered them not to leave Jerusalem, but to wait there for the promise of the Father. 'This', he said, 'is what you have heard from me; for John baptized with water, but you will be baptized with the Holy Spirit not many days from now.'

So when they had come together, they asked him, 'Lord, is this the time when you will restore the kingdom to Israel?' He replied, 'It is not for you to know the times or periods that the Father has set by his own authority. But you will receive power when the Holy Spirit has come upon you; and you will be my witnesses in Jerusalem, in all Judea and Samaria, and to the ends of the earth.' When he had said this, as they were watching, he was lifted up, and a cloud took him out of their sight. While he was going and they were gazing up towards heaven, suddenly two men in white robes stood by them. They said, 'Men of Galilee, why do you stand looking up towards heaven? This Jesus, who has been taken up from you into heaven, will come in the same way as you saw him go into heaven.'

This is the word of the Lord.

A reading from the Letter of Paul to the Ephesians. (1.15-23)

I have heard of your faith in the Lord Jesus and your love towards all the saints, and for this reason I do not cease to give thanks for you as I remember you in my prayers. I pray that the God of our Lord Jesus

Christ, the Father of glory, may give you a spirit of wisdom and revelation as you come to know him, so that, with the eyes of your heart enlightened, you may know what is the hope to which he has called you, what are the riches of his glorious inheritance among the saints, and what is the immeasurable greatness of his power for us who believe, according to the working of his great power. God put this power to work in Christ when he raised him from the dead and seated him at his right hand in the heavenly places, far above all rule and authority and power and dominion, and above every name that is named, not only in this age but also in the age to come. And he has put all things under his feet and has made him the head over all things for the church, which is his body, the fullness of him who fills all in all.

This is the word of the Lord.

Hear the gospel of our Lord Jesus Christ according to Luke. (24.44-53)

Jesus said to his disciples, 'These are my words that I spoke to you while I was still with you – that everything written about me in the law of Moses, the prophets, and the psalms must be fulfilled.' Then he opened their minds to understand the scriptures, and he said to them, 'Thus it is written, that the Messiah is to suffer and to rise from the dead on the third day, and that repentance and forgiveness of sins is to be proclaimed in his name to all nations, beginning from Jerusalem. You are witnesses of these things. And see, I am sending upon you what my Father promised; so stay here in the city until you have been clothed with power from on high.'

   Then he led them out as far as Bethany, and, lifting up his hands, he blessed them. While he was blessing them, he withdrew from them and was carried up into heaven. And they worshipped him, and returned to Jerusalem with great joy; and they were continually in the temple blessing God.

This is the gospel of the Lord.

Second Service
Ps 8; The Prayer of Azariah 29-37 *or* 2 Kings 2.1-15; Revelation 5; *if a Eucharist:* Matthew 28.16-20

The Song of the Three, from The Prayer of Azariah. (29-37)

'Blessèd are you, O Lord, God of our ancestors,
   and to be praised and highly exalted for ever;
And blessèd is your glorious, holy name,

and to be highly praised and highly exalted for ever.
Blessèd are you in the temple of your holy glory,
   and to be extolled and highly glorified for ever.
Blessèd are you who look into the depths
 from your throne on the cherubim,
   and to be praised and highly exalted for ever.
Blessèd are you on the throne of your kingdom,
   and to be extolled and highly exalted for ever.
Blessèd are you in the firmament of heaven,
   and to be sung and glorified for ever.

'Bless the Lord, all you works of the Lord;
   sing praise to him and highly exalt him for ever.
Bless the Lord, you heavens;
   sing praise to him and highly exalt him for ever.
Bless the Lord, you angels of the Lord;
   sing praise to him and highly exalt him for ever.'

Or:

A reading from the Second Book of the Kings. (2.1-15)

When the Lord was about to take Elijah up to heaven by a whirlwind, Elijah and Elisha were on their way from Gilgal. Elijah said to Elisha, 'Stay here; for the Lord has sent me as far as Bethel.' But Elisha said, 'As the Lord lives, and as you yourself live, I will not leave you.' So they went down to Bethel. The company of prophets who were in Bethel came out to Elisha, and said to him, 'Do you know that today the Lord will take your master away from you?' And he said, 'Yes, I know; keep silent.'

Elijah said to him, 'Elisha, stay here; for the Lord has sent me to Jericho.' But he said, 'As the Lord lives, and as you yourself live, I will not leave you.' So they came to Jericho. The company of prophets who were at Jericho drew near to Elisha, and said to him, 'Do you know that today the Lord will take your master away from you?' And he answered, 'Yes, I know; be silent.'

Then Elijah said to him, 'Stay here; for the Lord has sent me to the Jordan.' But he said, 'As the Lord lives, and as you yourself live, I will not leave you.' So the two of them went on. Fifty men of the company of prophets also went, and stood at some distance from them, as they both were standing by the Jordan. Then Elijah took his mantle and rolled it up, and struck the water; the water was parted to the one side and to the other, until the two of them crossed on dry ground.

When they had crossed, Elijah said to Elisha, 'Tell me what I may do for you, before I am taken from you.' Elisha said, 'Please let me inherit a double share of your spirit.' He responded, 'You have asked a hard thing; yet, if you see me as I am being taken from you, it will be granted you; if not, it will not.' As they continued walking and talking, a chariot of fire and horses of fire separated the two of them, and Elijah ascended in a whirlwind into heaven. Elisha kept watching and crying out, 'Father, father! The chariots of Israel and its horsemen!' But when he could no longer see him, he grasped his own clothes and tore them in two pieces.

He picked up the mantle of Elijah that had fallen from him, and went back and stood on the bank of the Jordan. He took the mantle of Elijah that had fallen from him, and struck the water, saying, 'Where is the Lord, the God of Elijah?' When he had struck the water, the water was parted to the one side and to the other, and Elisha went over.

When the company of prophets who were at Jericho saw him at a distance, they declared, 'The spirit of Elijah rests on Elisha.' They came to meet him and bowed to the ground before him.

A reading from the Revelation to John. (Chapter 5)

I saw in the right hand of the one seated on the throne a scroll written on the inside and on the back, sealed with seven seals; and I saw a mighty angel proclaiming with a loud voice, 'Who is worthy to open the scroll and break its seals?' And no one in heaven or on earth or under the earth was able to open the scroll or to look into it. And I began to weep bitterly because no one was found worthy to open the scroll or to look into it. Then one of the elders said to me, 'Do not weep. See, the Lion of the tribe of Judah, the Root of David, has conquered, so that he can open the scroll and its seven seals.'

Then I saw between the throne and the four living creatures and among the elders a Lamb standing as if it had been slaughtered, having seven horns and seven eyes, which are the seven spirits of God sent out into all the earth. He went and took the scroll from the right hand of the one who was seated on the throne. When he had taken the scroll, the four living creatures and the twenty-four elders fell before the Lamb, each holding a harp and golden bowls full of incense, which are the prayers of the saints.

They sing a new song:

'You are worthy to take the scroll and to open its seals,
for you were slaughtered and by your blood
you ransomed for God saints from every tribe
and language and people and nation;

you have made them to be a kingdom and priests
serving our God,
and they will reign on earth.'
Then I looked, and I heard the voice of many angels surrounding the throne and the living creatures and the elders; they numbered myriads of myriads and thousands of thousands, singing with full voice,
'Worthy is the Lamb that was slaughtered
to receive power and wealth and wisdom and might
and honour and glory and blessing!'
Then I heard every creature in heaven and on earth and under the earth and in the sea, and all that is in them, singing,
'To the one seated on the throne and to the Lamb
be blessing and honour and glory and might
for ever and ever!'
And the four living creatures said, 'Amen!' And the elders fell down and worshipped.

If a Eucharist:
Hear the gospel of our Lord Jesus Christ according to Matthew.

(28.16-20)
The eleven disciples went to Galilee, to the mountain to which Jesus had directed them. When they saw him, they worshipped him; but some doubted. And Jesus came and said to them, 'All authority in heaven and on earth has been given to me. Go therefore and make disciples of all nations, baptizing them in the name of the Father and of the Son and of the Holy Spirit, and teaching them to obey everything that I have commanded you. And remember, I am with you always, to the end of the age.'

This is the gospel of the Lord.

Third Service
Ps 110; Isaiah 52.7-15; Hebrews 7. [11-25] 26-28

A reading from the prophecy of Isaiah. (52.7-15)

How beautiful upon the mountains
are the feet of the messenger who announces peace,
who brings good news,
who announces salvation,
who says to Zion, 'Your God reigns.'
Listen! Your sentinels lift up their voices,
together they sing for joy;
for in plain sight they see the return of the Lord to Zion.

Break forth together into singing, you ruins of Jerusalem;
for the Lord has comforted his people,
    he has redeemed Jerusalem.
The Lord has bared his holy arm
    before the eyes of all the nations;
and all the ends of the earth shall see the salvation of our God.

Depart, depart, go out from there!
    Touch no unclean thing;
go out from the midst of it, purify yourselves,
    you who carry the vessels of the Lord.
For you shall not go out in haste,
    and you shall not go in flight;
for the Lord will go before you,
    and the God of Israel will be your rearguard.
See, my servant shall prosper;
    he shall be exalted and lifted up, and shall be very high.
Just as there were many who were astonished at him
    – so marred was his appearance,
        beyond human semblance,
        and his form beyond that of mortals –
so he shall startle many nations;
    kings shall shut their mouths because of him;
for that which had not been told them they shall see,
    and that which they had not heard they shall contemplate.

A reading from the Letter to the Hebrews. (7. [11-25] 26-28)

[11 If perfection had been attainable through the levitical priesthood – for the people received the law under this priesthood – what further need would there have been to speak of another priest arising according to the order of Melchizedek, rather than one according to the order of Aaron? For when there is a change in the priesthood, there is necessarily a change in the law as well. Now the one of whom these things are spoken belonged to another tribe, from which no one has ever served at the altar. For it is evident that our Lord was descended from Judah, and in connection with that tribe Moses said nothing about priests.

It is even more obvious when another priest arises, resembling Melchizedek, one who has become a priest, not through a legal requirement concerning physical descent, but through the power of an indestructible life. For it is attested of him,

'You are a priest for ever, according to the order of Melchizedek.'

There is, on the one hand, the abrogation of an earlier commandment because it was weak and ineffectual (for the law made nothing perfect); there is, on the other hand, the introduction of a better hope, through which we approach God.

This was confirmed with an oath; for others who became priests took their office without an oath, but this one became a priest with an oath, because of the one who said to him,

'The Lord has sworn
    and will not change his mind,
"You are a priest for ever"' –

accordingly Jesus has also become the guarantee of a better covenant.

Furthermore, the former priests were many in number, because they were prevented by death from continuing in office; but he holds his priesthood permanently, because he continues for ever. Consequently he is able for all time to save those who approach God through him, since he always lives to make intercession for them.

For] 26 It was fitting that we should have such a high priest, holy, blameless, undefiled, separated from sinners, and exalted above the heavens. Unlike the other high priests, he has no need to offer sacrifices day after day, first for his own sins, and then for those of the people; this he did once for all when he offered himself. For the law appoints as high priests those who are subject to weakness, but the word of the oath, which came later than the law, appoints a Son who has been made perfect for ever.

The Seventh Sunday of Easter

Principal Service

[*Old Testament reading, where required:* Ezekiel 36.24-28, *see page 202*]
Acts 1.15-17,21-26; Ps 1; 1 John 5.9-13; John 17.6-19

A reading from the Acts of the Apostles. (1.15-17,21-26)

Peter stood up among the believers (together the crowd numbered about one hundred and twenty people) and said, 'Friends, the scripture had to be fulfilled, which the Holy Spirit through David foretold concerning Judas, who became a guide for those who arrested Jesus – for he was numbered among us and was allotted his share in this ministry.'
21 So one of the men who have accompanied us throughout the time that the Lord Jesus went in and out among us, beginning from the baptism of John until the day when he was taken up from us – one of these must become a witness with us to his resurrection.' So they

proposed two, Joseph called Barsabbas, who was also known as Justus, and Matthias. Then they prayed and said, 'Lord, you know everyone's heart. Show us which one of these two you have chosen to take the place in this ministry and apostleship from which Judas turned aside to go to his own place.' And they cast lots for them, and the lot fell on Matthias; and he was added to the eleven apostles.

This is the word of the Lord.

A reading from the First Letter of John. (5.9-13)

If we receive human testimony, the testimony of God is greater; for this is the testimony of God that he has testified to his Son. Those who believe in the Son of God have the testimony in their hearts. Those who do not believe in God have made him a liar by not believing in the testimony that God has given concerning his Son. And this is the testimony: God gave us eternal life, and this life is in his Son. Whoever has the Son has life; whoever does not have the Son of God does not have life.

I write these things to you who believe in the name of the Son of God, so that you may know that you have eternal life.

This is the word of the Lord.

Hear the gospel of our Lord Jesus Christ according to John. (17.6-19)

Jesus looked up to heaven and said, 'Father, I have made your name known to those whom you gave me from the world. They were yours, and you gave them to me, and they have kept your word. Now they know that everything you have given me is from you; for the words that you gave to me I have given to them, and they have received them and know in truth that I came from you; and they have believed that you sent me. I am asking on their behalf; I am not asking on behalf of the world, but on behalf of those whom you gave me, because they are yours. All mine are yours, and yours are mine; and I have been glorified in them. And now I am no longer in the world, but they are in the world, and I am coming to you. Holy Father, protect them in your name that you have given me, so that they may be one, as we are one. While I was with them, I protected them in your name that you have given me. I guarded them, and not one of them was lost except the one destined to be lost, so that the scripture might be fulfilled. But now I am coming to you, and I speak these things in the world so that they may have my joy made complete in themselves. I have given them your word, and the world has hated them because they do not belong to the world, just as I do not belong to the world. I am not asking you to take them out of the world, but I ask you to protect them from the evil one. They do not belong to the world, just as I do not belong to the world. Sanctify them in the truth; your word is truth. As you have sent me into the world, so I have sent them into the world. And for their sakes I sanctify myself, so that they also may be sanctified in truth.'

This is the gospel of the Lord.

Second Service
Ps 147.1-11; Isaiah 61; Luke 4.14-21

A reading from the prophecy of Isaiah. (Chapter 61)

The spirit of the Lord God is upon me,
> because the Lord has anointed me;
he has sent me to bring good news to the oppressed,
> to bind up the broken-hearted,
to proclaim liberty to the captives,
> and release to the prisoners;
to proclaim the year of the Lord's favour,
> and the day of vengeance of our God;
> to comfort all who mourn;
to provide for those who mourn in Zion –
> to give them a garland instead of ashes,
the oil of gladness instead of mourning,
> the mantle of praise instead of a faint spirit.
They will be called oaks of righteousness,
> the planting of the Lord, to display his glory.
They shall build up the ancient ruins,
> they shall raise up the former devastations;
they shall repair the ruined cities,
> the devastations of many generations.

Strangers shall stand and feed your flocks,
> foreigners shall till your land and dress your vines;
but you shall be called priests of the Lord,
> you shall be named ministers of our God;
you shall enjoy the wealth of the nations,
> and in their riches you shall glory.
Because their shame was double,
> and dishonour was proclaimed as their lot,
therefore they shall possess a double portion;
> everlasting joy shall be theirs.
For I the Lord love justice,

I hate robbery and wrongdoing;
I will faithfully give them their recompense,
    and I will make an everlasting covenant with them.
Their descendants shall be known among the nations,
    and their offspring among the peoples;
all who see them shall acknowledge
    that they are a people whom the Lord has blessed.
I will greatly rejoice in the Lord,
    my whole being shall exult in my God;
for he has clothed me with the garments of salvation,
    he has covered me with the robe of righteousness,
as a bridegroom decks himself with a garland,
    and as a bride adorns herself with her jewels.

For as the earth brings forth its shoots,
    and as a garden causes what is sown in it to spring up,
so the Lord God will cause righteousness and praise
    to spring up before all the nations.

A reading from the gospel according to Luke. (4.14-21)

Jesus, filled with the power of the Spirit, returned to Galilee, and a report about him spread through all the surrounding country. He began to teach in their synagogues and was praised by everyone.

When he came to Nazareth, where he had been brought up, he went to the synagogue on the sabbath day, as was his custom. He stood up to read, and the scroll of the prophet Isaiah was given to him. He unrolled the scroll and found the place where it was written:
'The Spirit of the Lord is upon me,
    because he has anointed me
        to bring good news to the poor.
He has sent me to proclaim release to the captives
    and recovery of sight to the blind,
        to let the oppressed go free,
    to proclaim the year of the Lord's favour.'
And he rolled up the scroll, gave it back to the attendant, and sat down. The eyes of all in the synagogue were fixed on him. Then he began to say to them, 'Today this scripture has been fulfilled in your hearing.'

Third Service
Ps 76; Isaiah 14.3-15; Revelation 14.1-13

A reading from the prophecy of Isaiah. (14.3-15)

When the Lord has given you rest from your pain and turmoil and
the hard service with which you were made to serve, you will take
up this taunt against the king of Babylon:
How the oppressor has ceased!
How his insolence has ceased!
The Lord has broken the staff of the wicked,
the sceptre of rulers,
that struck down the peoples in wrath
with unceasing blows,
that ruled the nations in anger
with unrelenting persecution.
The whole earth is at rest and quiet;
they break forth into singing.
The cypresses exult over you,
the cedars of Lebanon, saying,
'Since you were laid low,
no one comes to cut us down.'
Sheol beneath is stirred up
to meet you when you come;
it rouses the shades to greet you,
all who were leaders of the earth;
it raises from their thrones
all who were kings of the nations.
All of them will speak
and say to you:
'You too have become as weak as we are!
You have become like us!'
Your pomp is brought down to Sheol,
and the sound of your harps;
maggots are the bed beneath you,
and worms are your covering.

How you are fallen from heaven,
O Day Star, son of Dawn!
How you are cut down to the ground,
you who laid the nations low!
You said in your heart,
'I will ascend to heaven;
I will raise my throne
above the stars of God;
I will sit on the mount of assembly

on the heights of Zaphon;
I will ascend to the tops of the clouds,
    I will make myself like the Most High.'
But you are brought down to Sheol,
    to the depths of the Pit.

A reading from the Revelation to John. *(14.1-13)*

I looked, and there was the Lamb, standing on Mount Zion! And with him were one hundred and forty-four thousand who had his name and his Father's name written on their foreheads. And I heard a voice from heaven like the sound of many waters and like the sound of loud thunder; the voice I heard was like the sound of harpists playing on their harps, and they sing a new song before the throne and before the four living creatures and before the elders. No one could learn that song except the one hundred and forty-four thousand who have been redeemed from the earth. It is these who have not defiled themselves with women, for they are virgins; these follow the Lamb wherever he goes. They have been redeemed from humankind as first fruits for God and the Lamb, and in their mouth no lie was found; they are blameless.

Then I saw another angel flying in mid-heaven, with an eternal gospel to proclaim to those who live on the earth – to every nation and tribe and language and people. He said in a loud voice, 'Fear God and give him glory, for the hour of his judgement has come; and worship him who made heaven and earth, the sea and the springs of water.'

Then another angel, a second, followed, saying, 'Fallen, fallen is Babylon the great! She has made all nations drink of the wine of the wrath of her fornication.'

Then another angel, a third, followed them, crying with a loud voice, 'Those who worship the beast and its image, and receive a mark on their foreheads or on their hands, they will also drink the wine of God's wrath, poured unmixed into the cup of his anger, and they will be tormented with fire and sulphur in the presence of the holy angels and in the presence of the Lamb. And the smoke of their torment goes up for ever and ever. There is no rest day or night for those who worship the beast and its image and for anyone who receives the mark of its name.'

Here is a call for the endurance of the saints, those who keep the commandments of God and hold fast to the faith of Jesus.

And I heard a voice from heaven saying, 'Write this: Blessèd are the dead who from now on die in the Lord.' 'Yes,' says the Spirit, 'they will rest from their labours, for their deeds follow them.'

Pentecost (Whit Sunday)

Evening Prayer on the Eve
Ps 48; Deuteronomy 16.9-15; John 7.37-39

A reading from the book Deuteronomy. (16.9-15)

The Lord said to Moses: You shall count seven weeks; begin to count the seven weeks from the time the sickle is first put to the standing grain. Then you shall keep the festival of weeks to the Lord your God, contributing a freewill-offering in proportion to the blessing that you have received from the Lord your God. Rejoice before the Lord your God – you and your sons and your daughters, your male and female slaves, the Levites resident in your towns, as well as the strangers, the orphans, and the widows who are among you – at the place that the Lord your God will choose as a dwelling for his name. Remember that you were a slave in Egypt, and diligently observe these statutes.

You shall keep the festival of booths for seven days, when you have gathered in the produce from your threshing-floor and your wine press. Rejoice during your festival, you and your sons and your daughters, your male and female slaves, as well as the Levites, the strangers, the orphans, and the widows resident in your towns. For seven days you shall keep the festival to the Lord your God at the place that the Lord will choose; for the Lord your God will bless you in all your produce and in all your undertakings, and you shall surely celebrate.

A reading from the gospel according to John. (7.37-39)

On the last day of the festival, the great day, while Jesus was standing there, he cried out, 'Let anyone who is thirsty come to me, and let the one who believes in me drink. As the scripture has said, "Out of the believer's heart shall flow rivers of living water."' Now he said this about the Spirit, which believers in him were to receive; for as yet there was no Spirit, because Jesus was not yet glorified.

Principal Service
The reading from Acts must be used as either the first or second reading.
Acts 2.1-21 *or* Ezekiel 37.1-14; Ps 104.24-36 *or* Ps 24-34,35*b*;
Romans 8.22-27 *or* Acts 2.1-21; John 15.26-27; 16.4*b*-15

A reading from the prophecy of Ezekiel. (37.1-14)

The hand of the Lord came upon me, and he brought me out by the spirit of the Lord and set me down in the middle of a valley; it was full of bones. He led me all round them; there were very many lying in the valley, and they were very dry. He said to me, 'Mortal, can these bones live?' I answered, 'O Lord God, you know.' Then he said to me, 'Prophesy to these bones, and say to them: O dry bones, hear the word of the Lord. Thus says the Lord God to these bones: I will cause breath to enter you, and you shall live. I will lay sinews on you, and will cause flesh to come upon you, and cover you with skin, and put breath in you, and you shall live; and you shall know that I am the Lord.'

So I prophesied as I had been commanded; and as I prophesied, suddenly there was a noise, a rattling, and the bones came together, bone to its bone. I looked, and there were sinews on them, and flesh had come upon them, and skin had covered them; but there was no breath in them. Then he said to me, 'Prophesy to the breath, prophesy, mortal, and say to the breath: Thus says the Lord God: Come from the four winds, O breath, and breathe upon these slain, that they may live.' I prophesied as he commanded me, and the breath came into them, and they lived, and stood on their feet, a vast multitude.

Then he said to me, 'Mortal, these bones are the whole house of Israel. They say, "Our bones are dried up, and our hope is lost; we are cut off completely." Therefore prophesy, and say to them, Thus says the Lord God: I am going to open your graves, and bring you up from your graves, O my people; and I will bring you back to the land of Israel. And you shall know that I am the Lord, when I open your graves, and bring you up from your graves, O my people. I will put my spirit within you, and you shall live, and I will place you on your own soil; then you shall know that I, the Lord, have spoken and will act, says the Lord.'

This is the word of the Lord.

A reading from the Acts of the Apostles. (2.1-21)

When the day of Pentecost had come, the disciples were all together in one place. And suddenly from heaven there came a sound like the rush of a violent wind, and it filled the entire house where they were sitting. Divided tongues, as of fire, appeared among them, and a tongue rested on each of them. All of them were filled with the Holy Spirit and began to speak in other languages, as the Spirit gave them ability.

Now there were devout Jews from every nation under heaven living in Jerusalem. And at this sound the crowd gathered and was bewildered, because each one heard them speaking in the native language of each. Amazed and astonished, they asked, 'Are not all these who are speaking Galileans? And how is it that we hear, each of us, in our own native language? Parthians, Medes, Elamites, and residents of Mesopotamia, Judea and Cappadocia, Pontus and Asia, Phrygia and Pamphylia, Egypt and the parts of Libya belonging to Cyrene, and visitors from Rome, both Jews and proselytes, Cretans and Arabs – in our own languages we hear them speaking about God's deeds of power.' All were amazed and perplexed, saying to one another, 'What does this mean?' But others sneered and said, 'They are filled with new wine.'

But Peter, standing with the eleven, raised his voice and addressed them: 'Men of Judea and all who live in Jerusalem, let this be known to you, and listen to what I say. Indeed, these are not drunk, as you suppose, for it is only nine o'clock in the morning. No, this is what was spoken through the prophet Joel:

"In the last days it will be, God declares,
that I will pour out my Spirit upon all flesh,
>and your sons and your daughters shall prophesy,
>and your young men shall see visions,
>and your old men shall dream dreams.
Even upon my slaves, both men and women,
>in those days I will pour out my Spirit;
>and they shall prophesy.
And I will show portents in the heaven above
>and signs on the earth below,
>blood, and fire, and smoky mist.
The sun shall be turned to darkness
>and the moon to blood,
>before the coming of the Lord's great and glorious day.
Then everyone who calls on the name of the Lord
>shall be saved."

This is the word of the Lord.

A reading from the Letter of Paul to the Romans. (8.22-27)

We know that the whole creation has been groaning in labour pains until now; and not only the creation, but we ourselves, who have the first fruits of the Spirit, groan inwardly while we wait for adoption, the redemption of our bodies. For in hope we were saved. Now hope that is seen is not hope. For who hopes for what is seen? But if we hope for what we do not see, we wait for it with patience. Likewise the Spirit helps us in our weakness; for we do not know how to pray as we ought, but that very Spirit intercedes with sighs too deep for words. And God, who searches the heart, knows what is the mind of the Spirit, because the Spirit intercedes for the saints according to the will of God.

This is the word of the Lord.

Hear the gospel of our Lord Jesus Christ according to John.
(15.26-27 & 16.4b-15)

Jesus said to the eleven, 'When the Advocate comes, whom I will send to you from the Father, the Spirit of truth who comes from the Father, he will testify on my behalf. You also are to testify because you have been with me from the beginning.

[16.4b] 'I did not say these things to you from the beginning, because I was with you. But now I am going to him who sent me; yet none of you asks me, "Where are you going?" But because I have said these things to you, sorrow has filled your hearts. Nevertheless, I tell you the truth: it is to your advantage that I go away, for if I do not go away, the Advocate will not come to you; but if I go, I will send him to you. And when he comes, he will prove the world wrong about sin and righteousness and judgement: about sin, because they do not believe in me; about righteousness, because I am going to the Father and you will see me no longer; about judgement, because the ruler of this world has been condemned.

'I still have many things to say to you, but you cannot bear them now. When the Spirit of truth comes, he will guide you into all the truth; for he will not speak on his own, but will speak whatever he hears, and he will declare to you the things that are to come. He will glorify me, because he will take what is mine and declare it to you. All that the Father has is mine. For this reason I said that he will take what is mine and declare it to you.'

This is the gospel of the Lord.

Second Service
Ps 139.1-12 [13-18,23-24]; Ezekiel 36.22-28; Acts 2.22-38;
if a Eucharist: John 20.19-23

A reading from the prophecy of Ezekiel. (36.22-28)

The word of the Lord came to me: Say to the house of Israel, Thus says the Lord God: It is not for your sake, O house of Israel, that I am about to act, but for the sake of my holy name, which you have profaned among the nations to which you came. I will sanctify my great name, which has been profaned among the nations, and which you have profaned among them; and the nations shall know that I am the

Lord, says the Lord God, when through you I display my holiness before their eyes. I will take you from the nations, and gather you from all the countries, and bring you into your own land. I will sprinkle clean water upon you, and you shall be clean from all your uncleannesses, and from all your idols I will cleanse you. A new heart I will give you, and a new spirit I will put within you; and I will remove from your body the heart of stone and give you a heart of flesh. I will put my spirit within you, and make you follow my statutes and be careful to observe my ordinances. Then you shall live in the land that I gave to your ancestors; and you shall be my people, and I will be your God.

A reading from the Acts of the Apostles. (2.22-38)

Peter, standing with the eleven, raised his voice and addressed them: 'You that are Israelites, listen to what I have to say: Jesus of Nazareth, a man attested to you by God with deeds of power, wonders, and signs that God did through him among you, as you yourselves know – this man, handed over to you according to the definite plan and foreknowledge of God, you crucified and killed by the hands of those outside the law. But God raised him up, having freed him from death, because it was impossible for him to be held in its power. For David says concerning him,
"I saw the Lord always before me,
for he is at my right hand so that I will not be shaken;
therefore my heart was glad, and my tongue rejoiced;
moreover, my flesh will live in hope.
For you will not abandon my soul to Hades,
or let your Holy One experience corruption.
You have made known to me the ways of life;
you will make me full of gladness with your presence."
'Fellow Israelites, I may say to you confidently of our ancestor David that he both died and was buried, and his tomb is with us to this day. Since he was a prophet, he knew that God had sworn with an oath to him that he would put one of his descendants on his throne. Foreseeing this, David spoke of the resurrection of the Messiah, saying,
"He was not abandoned to Hades,
nor did his flesh experience corruption."
This Jesus God raised up, and of that all of us are witnesses. Being therefore exalted at the right hand of God, and having received from the Father the promise of the Holy Spirit, he has poured out this that you both see and hear. For David did not ascend into the heavens, but he himself says,

"The Lord said to my Lord,
 'Sit at my right hand,
   until I make your enemies your footstool.'"
Therefore let the entire house of Israel know with certainty that God
has made him both Lord and Messiah, this Jesus whom you crucified.'

  Now when they heard this, they were cut to the heart and said to
Peter and to the other apostles, 'Brothers, what should we do?' Peter
said to them, 'Repent, and be baptized every one of you in the name
of Jesus Christ so that your sins may be forgiven; and you will receive
the gift of the Holy Spirit.'

If a Eucharist:
Hear the gospel of our Lord Jesus Christ according to John. *(20.19-23)*

When it was evening on that day, the first day of the week, and the
doors of the house where the disciples had met were locked for fear
of the Jews, Jesus came and stood among his disciples and said,
'Peace be with you.' After he said this, he showed them his hands
and his side. Then the disciples rejoiced when they saw the Lord.
Jesus said to them again, 'Peace be with you. As the Father has sent
me, so I send you.' When he had said this, he breathed on them and
said to them, 'Receive the Holy Spirit. If you forgive the sins of any,
they are forgiven them; if you retain the sins of any, they are
retained.'

This is the gospel of the Lord.

Third Service
Ps 145; Isaiah 11.1-9 *or* Wisdom 7.15-23 [24-27]; 1 Corinthians 12.4-13

A reading from the prophecy of Isaiah. *(11.1-9)*

A shoot shall come out from the stock of Jesse,
    and a branch shall grow out of his roots.
The spirit of the Lord shall rest on him,
    the spirit of wisdom and understanding,
    the spirit of counsel and might,
    the spirit of knowledge and the fear of the Lord.
His delight shall be in the fear of the Lord.

He shall not judge by what his eyes see,
    or decide by what his ears hear;
but with righteousness he shall judge the poor,
    and decide with equity for the meek of the earth;
he shall strike the earth with the rod of his mouth,

and with the breath of his lips he shall kill the wicked.
Righteousness shall be the belt around his waist,
    and faithfulness the belt around his loins.
The wolf shall live with the lamb,
    the leopard shall lie down with the kid,
the calf and the lion and the fatling together,
    and a little child shall lead them.
The cow and the bear shall graze,
    their young shall lie down together;
    and the lion shall eat straw like the ox.
The nursing child shall play over the hole of the asp,
    and the weaned child shall put its hand on the adder's den.
They will not hurt or destroy
    on all my holy mountain;
for the earth will be full of the knowledge of the Lord
    as the waters cover the sea.

A reading from the First Letter of Paul to the Corinthians. (12.4-13)

There are varieties of gifts, but the same Spirit; and there are varieties of services, but the same Lord; and there are varieties of activities, but it is the same God who activates all of them in everyone. To each is given the manifestation of the Spirit for the common good. To one is given through the Spirit the utterance of wisdom, and to another the utterance of knowledge according to the same Spirit, to another faith by the same Spirit, to another gifts of healing by the one Spirit, to another the working of miracles, to another prophecy, to another the discernment of spirits, to another various kinds of tongues, to another the interpretation of tongues. All these are activated by one and the same Spirit, who allots to each one individually just as the Spirit chooses.

For just as the body is one and has many members, and all the members of the body, though many, are one body, so it is with Christ. For in the one Spirit we were all baptized into one body – Jews or Greeks, slaves or free – and we were all made to drink of one Spirit.

Ordinary Time -
Summer & Autumn

Trinity Sunday

Evening Prayer on the Eve
Pss 97,98; Isaiah 40.12-31; Mark 1.1-13

A reading from the prophecy of Isaiah. (40.12-31)

Who has measured the waters in the hollow of his hand
    and marked off the heavens with a span,
enclosed the dust of the earth in a measure,
    and weighed the mountains in scales
    and the hills in a balance?
Who has directed the spirit of the Lord,
    or as his counsellor has instructed him?
Whom did he consult for his enlightenment,
    and who taught him the path of justice?
Who taught him knowledge,
    and showed him the way of understanding?
Even the nations are like a drop from a bucket,
    and are accounted as dust on the scales;
    see, he takes up the isles like fine dust.
Lebanon would not provide fuel enough,
    nor are its animals enough for a burnt-offering.
All the nations are as nothing before him;
    they are accounted by him
    as less than nothing and emptiness.

To whom then will you liken God,
    or what likeness compare with him?
An idol? – A workman casts it,
    and a goldsmith overlays it with gold,
    and casts for it silver chains.
As a gift one chooses mulberry wood
    – wood that will not rot –
    then seeks out a skilled artisan
    to set up an image that will not topple.

Have you not known? Have you not heard?
    Has it not been told you from the beginning?

Have you not understood from the foundations of the earth?
It is he who sits above the circle of the earth,
    and its inhabitants are like grasshoppers;
who stretches out the heavens like a curtain,
    and spreads them like a tent to live in;
who brings princes to naught,
    and makes the rulers of the earth as nothing.

Scarcely are they planted, scarcely sown,
    scarcely has their stem taken root in the earth,
when he blows upon them, and they wither,
    and the tempest carries them off like stubble.

To whom then will you compare me,
    or who is my equal? says the Holy One.
Lift up your eyes on high and see:
    Who created these?
He who brings out their host and numbers them,
    calling them all by name;
because he is great in strength,
    mighty in power,
    not one is missing.

Why do you say, O Jacob,
    and speak, O Israel,
'My way is hidden from the Lord,
    and my right is disregarded by my God'?
Have you not known? Have you not heard?
The Lord is the everlasting God,
    the Creator of the ends of the earth.
He does not faint or grow weary;
    his understanding is unsearchable.
He gives power to the faint,
    and strengthens the powerless.
Even youths will faint and be weary,
    and the young will fall exhausted;
but those who wait for the Lord shall renew their strength,
    they shall mount up with wings like eagles,
they shall run and not be weary,
    they shall walk and not faint.

A reading from the gospel according to Mark. (1.1-13)

The beginning of the good news of Jesus Christ, the Son of God.
As it is written in the prophet Isaiah,
'See, I am sending my messenger ahead of you,
who will prepare your way;
the voice of one crying out in the wilderness:
"Prepare the way of the Lord, make his paths straight".'
John the baptizer appeared in the wilderness, proclaiming a baptism
of repentance for the forgiveness of sins. And people from the whole
Judean countryside and all the people of Jerusalem were going out to
him, and were baptized by him in the river Jordan, confessing their
sins. Now John was clothed with camel's hair, with a leather belt
around his waist, and he ate locusts and wild honey. He proclaimed,
'The one who is more powerful than I is coming after me; I am not
worthy to stoop down and untie the thong of his sandals. I have baptized you with water; but he will baptize you with the Holy Spirit.'
  In those days Jesus came from Nazareth of Galilee and was baptized
by John in the Jordan. And just as he was coming up out of the water,
he saw the heavens torn apart and the Spirit descending like a dove
on him. And a voice came from heaven, 'You are my Son, the
Belovèd; with you I am well pleased.' And the Spirit immediately
drove him out into the wilderness. He was in the wilderness for forty
days, tempted by Satan; and he was with the wild beasts; and the
angels waited on him.

Principal Service
Isaiah 6.1-8; Ps 29; Romans 8.12-17; John 3.1-17

A reading from the prophecy of Isaiah. (6.1-8)

In the year that King Uzziah died, I saw the Lord sitting on a throne,
high and lofty; and the hem of his robe filled the temple. Seraphs
were in attendance above him; each had six wings: with two they
covered their faces, and with two they covered their feet, and with
two they flew. And one called to another and said:
'Holy, holy, holy is the Lord of hosts;
the whole earth is full of his glory.'
The pivots on the thresholds shook at the voices of those who called,
and the house filled with smoke. And I said: 'Woe is me! I am lost,
for I am a man of unclean lips, and I live among a people of unclean
lips; yet my eyes have seen the King, the Lord of hosts!'
  Then one of the seraphs flew to me, holding a live coal that had been
taken from the altar with a pair of tongs. The seraph touched my

mouth with it and said: 'Now that this has touched your lips, your guilt has departed and your sin is blotted out.' Then I heard the voice of the Lord saying, 'Whom shall I send, and who will go for us?' And I said, 'Here am I; send me!'

This is the word of the Lord.

A reading from the Letter of Paul to the Romans. (8.12-17)

Brothers and sisters, we are debtors, not to the flesh, to live according to the flesh – for if you live according to the flesh, you will die; but if by the Spirit you put to death the deeds of the body, you will live. For all who are led by the Spirit of God are children of God. For you did not receive a spirit of slavery to fall back into fear, but you have received a spirit of adoption. When we cry, 'Abba! Father!' it is that very Spirit bearing witness with our spirit that we are children of God, and if children, then heirs, heirs of God and joint heirs with Christ – if, in fact, we suffer with him so that we may also be glorified with him.

This is the word of the Lord.

Hear the gospel of our Lord Jesus Christ according to John. (3.1-17)

There was a Pharisee named Nicodemus, a leader of the Jews. He came to Jesus by night and said to him, 'Rabbi, we know that you are a teacher who has come from God; for no one can do these signs that you do apart from the presence of God.' Jesus answered him, 'Very truly, I tell you, no one can see the kingdom of God without being born from above.' Nicodemus said to him, 'How can anyone be born after having grown old? Can one enter a second time into the mother's womb and be born?' Jesus answered, 'Very truly, I tell you, no one can enter the kingdom of God without being born of water and Spirit. What is born of the flesh is flesh, and what is born of the Spirit is spirit. Do not be astonished that I said to you, "You must be born from above." The wind blows where it chooses, and you hear the sound of it, but you do not know where it comes from or where it goes. So it is with everyone who is born of the Spirit.' Nicodemus said to him, 'How can these things be?' Jesus answered him, 'Are you a teacher of Israel, and yet you do not understand these things? 'Very truly, I tell you, we speak of what we know and testify to what we have seen; yet you do not receive our testimony. If I have told you about earthly things and you do not believe, how can you believe if I tell you about heavenly things? No one has ascended into heaven except the one who descended from heaven, the Son of Man. And just as Moses lifted up the serpent in the wilderness, so must the Son of Man be lifted up, that whoever believes in him may have eternal life.

'For God so loved the world that he gave his only Son, so that everyone who believes in him may not perish but may have eternal life.

'Indeed, God did not send the Son into the world to condemn the world, but in order that the world might be saved through him.'

This is the gospel of the Lord.

Second Service
Ps 104.1-9; Ezekiel 1.4-10,22-28a;
Revelation 4; *if a Eucharist:* Mark 1.1-13

A reading from the prophecy of Ezekiel. (1.4-10,22-28a)

As I looked, a stormy wind came out of the north: a great cloud with brightness around it and fire flashing forth continually, and in the middle of the fire, something like gleaming amber. In the middle of it was something like four living creatures. This was their appearance: they were of human form. Each had four faces, and each of them had four wings. Their legs were straight, and the soles of their feet were like the sole of a calf's foot; and they sparkled like burnished bronze. Under their wings on their four sides they had human hands. And the four had their faces and their wings thus: their wings touched one another; each of them moved straight ahead, without turning as they moved. As for the appearance of their faces: the four had the face of a human being, the face of a lion on the right side, the face of an ox on the left side, and the face of an eagle.
22 Over the heads of the living creatures there was something like a dome, shining like crystal, spread out above their heads. Under the dome their wings were stretched out straight, one towards another; and each of the creatures had two wings covering its body. When they moved, I heard the sound of their wings like the sound of mighty waters, like the thunder of the Almighty, a sound of tumult like the sound of an army; when they stopped, they let down their wings. And there came a voice from above the dome over their heads; when they stopped, they let down their wings.

And above the dome over their heads there was something like a throne, in appearance like sapphire; and seated above the likeness of a throne was something that seemed like a human form. Upwards from what appeared like the loins I saw something like gleaming amber, something that looked like fire enclosed all round; and downwards from what looked like the loins I saw something that looked like fire, and there was a splendour all round. Like the bow in a cloud on a rainy day, such was the appearance of the splendour all round. This was the appearance of the likeness of the glory of the Lord.

A reading from the Revelation to John. (Chapter 4)

I looked, and there in heaven a door stood open! And the first voice, which I had heard speaking to me like a trumpet, said, 'Come up here, and I will show you what must take place after this.' At once I was in the spirit, and there in heaven stood a throne, with one seated on the throne! And the one seated there looks like jasper and cornelian, and around the throne is a rainbow that looks like an emerald. Around the throne are twenty-four thrones, and seated on the thrones are twenty-four elders, dressed in white robes, with golden crowns on their heads. Coming from the throne are flashes of lightning, and rumblings and peals of thunder, and in front of the throne burn seven flaming torches, which are the seven spirits of God; and in front of the throne there is something like a sea of glass, like crystal. Around the throne, and on each side of the throne, are four living creatures, full of eyes in front and behind: the first living creature like a lion, the second living creature like an ox, the third living creature with a face like a human face, and the fourth living creature like a flying eagle. And the four living creatures, each of them with six wings, are full of eyes all around and inside. Day and night without ceasing they sing,

'Holy, holy, holy,
the Lord God the Almighty,
who was and is and is to come.'

And whenever the living creatures give glory and honour and thanks to the one who is seated on the throne, who lives for ever and ever, the twenty-four elders fall before the one who is seated on the throne and worship the one who lives for ever and ever; they cast their crowns before the throne, singing,

'You are worthy, our Lord and God,
to receive glory and honour and power,
for you created all things,
and by your will they existed and were created.'

If a Eucharist:
Hear the gospel of our Lord Jesus Christ according to Mark. *(1.1-13)*

The beginning of the good news of Jesus Christ, the Son of God.
As it is written in the prophet Isaiah,
'See, I am sending my messenger ahead of you,
who will prepare your way;
the voice of one crying out in the wilderness:
"Prepare the way of the Lord,
make his paths straight"',
John the baptizer appeared in the wilderness, proclaiming a baptism
of repentance for the forgiveness of sins. And people from the whole
Judean countryside and all the people of Jerusalem were going out to
him, and were baptized by him in the river Jordan, confessing their
sins. Now John was clothed with camel's hair, with a leather belt
around his waist, and he ate locusts and wild honey. He proclaimed,
'The one who is more powerful than I is coming after me; I am not
worthy to stoop down and untie the thong of his sandals. I have baptized you with water; but he will baptize you with the Holy Spirit.'

In those days Jesus came from Nazareth of Galilee and was baptized
by John in the Jordan. And just as he was coming up out of the water,
he saw the heavens torn apart and the Spirit descending like a dove
on him. And a voice came from heaven, 'You are my Son, the
Belovèd; with you I am well pleased.'

And the Spirit immediately drove him out into the wilderness. He
was in the wilderness for forty days, tempted by Satan; and he was
with the wild beasts; and the angels waited on him.

This is the gospel of the Lord.

Third Service
Ps 33.1-12; Proverbs 8.1-4,22-31; 2 Corinthians 13.[5-10] 11-13

A reading from the book Proverbs. (8.1-4)

Does not wisdom call,
and does not understanding raise her voice?
On the heights, beside the way,
at the crossroads she takes her stand;
beside the gates in front of the town,
at the entrance of the portals she cries out:
'To you, O people, I call,
and my cry is to all that live.
22 The Lord created me at the beginning of his work,

the first of his acts of long ago.
Ages ago I was set up, at the first,
    before the beginning of the earth.
When there were no depths I was brought forth,
    when there were no springs abounding with water.
Before the mountains had been shaped, before the hills,
    I was brought forth –
when he had not yet made earth and fields,
    or the world's first bits of soil.
When he established the heavens, I was there,
    when he drew a circle on the face of the deep,
when he made firm the skies above,
    when he established the fountains of the deep,
when he assigned to the sea its limit,
    so that the waters might not transgress his command,
when he marked out the foundations of the earth,
    then I was beside him, like a master worker;
and I was daily his delight,
    rejoicing before him always,
rejoicing in his inhabited world
    and delighting in the human race.

A reading from the Second Letter of Paul to the Corinthians.
(13.[5-10] 11-13)

[⁵ Examine yourselves to see whether you are living in the faith. Test yourselves. Do you not realize that Jesus Christ is in you? – unless, indeed, you fail to pass the test! I hope you will find out that we have not failed. But we pray to God that you may not do anything wrong – not that we may appear to have passed the test, but that you may do what is right, though we may seem to have failed. For we cannot do anything against the truth, but only for the truth. For we rejoice when we are weak and you are strong. This is what we pray for, that you may become perfect. So I write these things while I am away from you, so that when I come, I may not have to be severe in using the authority that the Lord has given me for building up and not for tearing down.]

¹¹ Finally, brothers and sisters, farewell. Put things in order, listen to my appeal, agree with one another, live in peace; and the God of love and peace will be with you. Greet one another with a holy kiss. All the saints greet you.

The grace of the Lord Jesus Christ, the love of God, and the communion of the Holy Spirit be with all of you.

Day of Thanksgiving for Holy Communion
Corpus Christi (Thursday after Trinity Sunday)

Evening Prayer on the Eve (*if required*)
Pss 110,111; Exodus 16.2-15; John 6.22-35

A reading from the Book of the Exodus. (16.2-15)

The whole congregation of the Israelites complained against Moses and Aaron in the wilderness. The Israelites said to them, 'If only we had died by the hand of the Lord in the land of Egypt, when we sat by the fleshpots and ate our fill of bread; for you have brought us out into this wilderness to kill this whole assembly with hunger.'

Then the Lord said to Moses, 'I am going to rain bread from heaven for you, and each day the people shall go out and gather enough for that day. In that way I will test them, whether they will follow my instruction or not. On the sixth day, when they prepare what they bring in, it will be twice as much as they gather on other days.' So Moses and Aaron said to all the Israelites, 'In the evening you shall know that it was the Lord who brought you out of the land of Egypt, and in the morning you shall see the glory of the Lord, because he has heard your complaining against the Lord. For what are we, that you complain against us?' And Moses said, 'When the Lord gives you meat to eat in the evening and your fill of bread in the morning, because the Lord has heard the complaining that you utter against him – what are we? Your complaining is not against us but against the Lord.'

Then Moses said to Aaron, 'Say to the whole congregation of the Israelites, "Draw near to the Lord, for he has heard your complaining."' And as Aaron spoke to the whole congregation of the Israelites, they looked towards the wilderness, and the glory of the Lord appeared in the cloud. The Lord spoke to Moses and said, 'I have heard the complaining of the Israelites; say to them, "At twilight you shall eat meat, and in the morning you shall have your fill of bread; then you shall know that I am the Lord your God."'

In the evening quails came up and covered the camp; and in the morning there was a layer of dew around the camp. When the layer of dew lifted, there on the surface of the wilderness was a fine flaky substance, as fine as frost on the ground. When the Israelites saw it, they said to one another, 'What is it?' For they did not know what it was. Moses said to them, 'It is the bread that the Lord has given you to eat.'

A reading from the gospel according to John. (6.22-35)

The next day the crowd that had stayed on the other side of the lake saw that there had been only one boat there. They also saw that Jesus had not got into the boat with his disciples, but that his disciples had gone away alone. Then some boats from Tiberias came near the place where they had eaten the bread after the Lord had given thanks. So when the crowd saw that neither Jesus nor his disciples were there, they themselves got into the boats and went to Capernaum looking for Jesus.

When they found him on the other side of the lake, they said to him, 'Rabbi, when did you come here?' Jesus answered them, 'Very truly, I tell you, you are looking for me, not because you saw signs, but because you ate your fill of the loaves. Do not work for the food that perishes, but for the food that endures for eternal life, which the Son of Man will give you. For it is on him that God the Father has set his seal.' Then they said to him, 'What must we do to perform the works of God?' Jesus answered them, 'This is the work of God, that you believe in him whom he has sent.' So they said to him, 'What sign are you going to give us then, so that we may see it and believe you? What work are you performing? Our ancestors ate the manna in the wilderness; as it is written, "He gave them bread from heaven to eat."' Then Jesus said to them, 'Very truly, I tell you, it was not Moses who gave you the bread from heaven, but it is my Father who gives you the true bread from heaven. For the bread of God is that which comes down from heaven and gives life to the world.' They said to him, 'Sir, give us this bread always.'

Jesus said to them, 'I am the bread of life. Whoever comes to me will never be hungry, and whoever believes in me will never be thirsty.'

Eucharist

Genesis 14.18-20; Ps 116.12-19; 1 Corinthians 11.23-26; John 6.51-58

A reading from the book Genesis. (14.18-20)

King Melchizedek of Salem brought out bread and wine; he was priest of God Most High. He blessed Abram and said,
    'Blessèd be Abram by God Most High,
        maker of heaven and earth;
    and blessèd be God Most High,
    who has delivered your enemies into your hand!'
And Abram gave him one-tenth of everything.

This is the word of the Lord.

A reading from the First Letter of Paul to the Corinthians. (11.23-26)

I received from the Lord what I also handed on to you, that the Lord Jesus on the night when he was betrayed took a loaf of bread, and when he had given thanks, he broke it and said, 'This is my body that is for you. Do this in remembrance of me.' In the same way he took the cup also, after supper, saying, 'This cup is the new covenant in my blood. Do this, as often as you drink it, in remembrance of me.' For as often as you eat this bread and drink the cup, you proclaim the Lord's death until he comes.

This is the word of the Lord.

Hear the gospel of our Lord Jesus Christ according to John. (6.51-58)

Jesus said to the Jews, 'I am the living bread that came down from heaven. Whoever eats of this bread will live for ever; and the bread that I will give for the life of the world is my flesh.'

The Jews then disputed among themselves, saying, 'How can this man give us his flesh to eat?' So Jesus said to them, 'Very truly, I tell you, unless you eat the flesh of the Son of Man and drink his blood, you have no life in you. Those who eat my flesh and drink my blood have eternal life, and I will raise them up on the last day; for my flesh is true food and my blood is true drink. Those who eat my flesh and drink my blood abide in me, and I in them. Just as the living Father sent me, and I live because of the Father, so whoever eats me will live because of me. This is the bread that came down from heaven, not like that which your ancestors ate, and they died. But the one who eats this bread will live for ever.'

This is the gospel of the Lord.

Morning Prayer
Ps 147; Deuteronomy 8.2-16; 1 Corinthians 10.1-17

A reading from the book Deuteronomy. (8.2-16)

Moses said to all Israel: Remember the long way that the Lord your God has led you these forty years in the wilderness, in order to humble you, testing you to know what was in your heart, whether or not you would keep his commandments. He humbled you by letting you hunger, then by feeding you with manna, with which neither you nor your ancestors were acquainted, in order to make you understand that one does not live by bread alone, but by every word that comes from the mouth of the Lord. The clothes on your back did not wear out and your feet did not swell these forty years. Know then in your heart that as a parent disciplines a child so the Lord your God disciplines you. Therefore keep the commandments of the Lord your God, by walking in his ways and by fearing him. For the Lord your God is bringing you into a good land, a land with flowing streams, with springs and underground waters welling up in valleys and hills, a land of wheat and barley, of vines and fig trees and pomegranates, a land of olive trees and honey, a land where you may eat bread without scarcity, where you will lack nothing, a land whose stones are iron and from whose hills you may mine copper. You shall eat your fill and bless the Lord your God for the good land that he has given you.

Take care that you do not forget the Lord your God, by failing to keep his commandments, his ordinances, and his statutes, which I am commanding you today. When you have eaten your fill and have built fine houses and live in them, and when your herds and flocks have multiplied, and your silver and gold is multiplied, and all that you have is multiplied, then do not exalt yourself, forgetting the Lord your God, who brought you out of the land of Egypt, out of the house of slavery, who led you through the great and terrible wilderness, an arid waste-land with poisonous snakes and scorpions. He made water flow for you from flint rock, and fed you in the wilderness with manna that your ancestors did not know, to humble you and to test you, and in the end to do you good.

A reading from the First Letter of Paul to the Corinthians. (10.1-17)

I do not want you to be unaware, brothers and sisters, that our ancestors were all under the cloud, and all passed through the sea, and all were baptized into Moses in the cloud and in the sea, and all ate the same spiritual food, and all drank the same spiritual drink. For they drank from the spiritual rock that followed them, and the rock was Christ. Nevertheless, God was not pleased with most of them, and they were struck down in the wilderness.

Now these things occurred as examples for us, so that we might not desire evil as they did. Do not become idolaters as some of them did; as it is written, 'The people sat down to eat and drink, and they rose up to play.' We must not indulge in sexual immorality as some of them did, and twenty-three thousand fell in a single day. We must not put Christ to the test, as some of them did, and were destroyed by serpents. And do not complain as some of them did, and were destroyed by the destroyer. These things happened to them to serve as an example, and they were written down to instruct us, on whom the ends of the ages have come. So if you think you are standing, watch out that you do not fall. No testing has overtaken you that is not common to everyone. God is faithful, and he will not let you be tested beyond your strength, but with the testing he will also provide the way out so that you may be able to endure it.

Therefore, my dear friends, flee from the worship of idols. I speak as to sensible people; judge for yourselves what I say. The cup of blessing that we bless, is it not a sharing in the blood of Christ? The bread that we break, is it not a sharing in the body of Christ? Because there is one bread, we who are many are one body, for we all partake of the one bread.

Evening Prayer
Pss 23,42,43; Proverbs 9.1-5; Luke 9.11-17

A reading from the book Proverbs. (9.1-5)

Wisdom has built her house,
    she has hewn her seven pillars.
She has slaughtered her animals, she has mixed her wine,
    she has also set her table.
She has sent out her servant-girls,
    she calls from the highest places in the town,
'You that are simple, turn in here!'
To those without sense she says,
'Come, eat of my bread and drink of the wine I have mixed.'

A reading from the gospel according to Luke. (9.11-17)

When the crowds found out that Jesus and his disciples had gone to Bethsaida, they followed him; and he welcomed them, and spoke to them about the kingdom of God, and healed those who needed to be cured.

The day was drawing to a close, and the twelve came to him and said, 'Send the crowd away, so that they may go into the surrounding villages and countryside, to lodge and get provisions; for we are here in a deserted place.' But he said to them, 'You give them something to eat.' They said, 'We have no more than five loaves and two fish – unless we are to go and buy food for all these people.' For there were about five thousand men. And he said to his disciples, 'Make them sit down in groups of about fifty each.' They did so and made them all sit down. And taking the five loaves and the two fish, he looked up to heaven, and blessed and broke them, and gave them to the disciples to set before the crowd. And all ate and were filled. What was left over was gathered up, twelve baskets of broken pieces.

The First Sunday after Trinity

If the Sunday between 24 & 28 May inclusive follows Trinity Sunday, Proper 3 (page 91) is used.

Proper 4

Sunday between 29 May & 4 June inclusive (if after Trinity Sunday)

Principal Service

Continuous	Related
1 Samuel 3.1-10[11-20]	Deuteronomy 5.12-15
Ps 139.1-6,13-18	Ps 81.1-10
	2 Corinthians 4.5-12
	Mark 2.23 - 3.6

A reading from the First Book of Samuel. (3.1-10 [11-20])

The boy Samuel was ministering to the Lord under Eli. The word of the Lord was rare in those days; visions were not widespread.

At that time Eli, whose eyesight had begun to grow dim so that he could not see, was lying down in his room; the lamp of God had not yet gone out, and Samuel was lying down in the temple of the Lord, where the ark of God was. Then the Lord called, 'Samuel! Samuel!' and he said, 'Here I am!' and ran to Eli, and said, 'Here I am, for you called me.' But he said, 'I did not call; lie down again.' So he went and lay down. The Lord called again, 'Samuel!' Samuel got up and went to Eli, and said, 'Here I am, for you called me.' But he said, 'I did not call, my son; lie down again.' Now Samuel did not yet know the Lord, and the word of the Lord had not yet been revealed to him. The Lord called Samuel again, a third time. And he got up and went to Eli, and said, 'Here I am, for you called me.' Then Eli perceived that the Lord was calling the boy. Therefore Eli said to Samuel, 'Go, lie down; and if he calls you, you shall say, "Speak, Lord, for your servant is listening."' So Samuel went and lay down in his place.

Now the Lord came and stood there, calling as before, 'Samuel! Samuel!' And Samuel said, 'Speak, for your servant is listening.' [11 Then the Lord said to Samuel, 'See, I am about to do something in Israel that will make both ears of anyone who hears of it tingle. On that day I will fulfil against Eli all that I have spoken concerning his house, from beginning to end. For I have told him that I am about to punish his house for ever, for the iniquity that he knew, because his sons were blaspheming God, and he did not restrain them. Therefore I swear to the house of Eli that the iniquity of Eli's house shall not be expiated by sacrifice or offering for ever.'

Samuel lay there until morning; then he opened the doors of the house of the Lord. Samuel was afraid to tell the vision to Eli. But Eli called Samuel and said, 'Samuel, my son.' He said, 'Here I am.' Eli said, 'What was it that he told you? Do not hide it from me. May God do so to you and more also, if you hide anything from me of all that he told you.' So Samuel told him everything and hid nothing from him. Then he said, 'It is the Lord; let him do what seems good to him.'

As Samuel grew up, the Lord was with him and let none of his words fall to the ground. And all Israel from Dan to Beer-sheba knew that Samuel was a trustworthy prophet of the Lord.]

This is the word of the Lord.

Or:

A reading from the book Deuteronomy. (5.12-15)

Observe the sabbath day and keep it holy, as the Lord your God commanded you. For six days you shall labour and do all your work. But the seventh day is a sabbath to the Lord your God; you shall not do any work – you, or your son or your daughter, or your male or female slave, or your ox or your donkey, or any of your livestock, or the resident alien in your towns, so that your male and female slave may rest as well as you. Remember that you were a slave in the land of Egypt, and the Lord your God brought you out from there with a mighty hand and an outstretched arm; therefore the Lord your God commanded you to keep the sabbath day.

This is the word of the Lord.

A reading from the Second Letter of Paul to the Corinthians. (4.5-12)

We do not proclaim ourselves; we proclaim Jesus Christ as Lord and ourselves as your slaves for Jesus' sake. For it is the God who said, 'Let light shine out of darkness', who has shone in our hearts to give the light of the knowledge of the glory of God in the face of Jesus Christ.

But we have this treasure in clay jars, so that it may be made clear that this extraordinary power belongs to God and does not come from us. We are afflicted in every way, but not crushed; perplexed, but not driven to despair; persecuted, but not forsaken; struck down, but not destroyed; always carrying in the body the death of Jesus, so that the life of Jesus may also be made visible in our bodies. For while we live, we are always being given up to death for Jesus' sake, so that the life of Jesus may be made visible in our mortal flesh. So death is at work in us, but life in you.

This is the word of the Lord.

Hear the gospel of our Lord Jesus Christ according to Mark. (2.23 - 3.6)

One sabbath Jesus was going through the cornfields; and as they made their way his disciples began to pluck heads of grain. The Pharisees said to him, 'Look, why are they doing what is not lawful on the sabbath?' And he said to them, 'Have you never read what David did when he and his companions were hungry and in need of food? He entered the use of God, when Abiathar was high priest, and ate the bread of the Presence, which it is not lawful for any but the priests to eat, and he gave some to his companions.' Then he said to them, 'The sabbath was made for humankind, and not humankind for the sabbath; so the Son of Man is lord even of the sabbath.'

Again he entered the synagogue, and a man was there who had a withered hand. They watched him to see whether he would cure him on the sabbath, so that they might accuse him. And he said to the man who had the withered hand, 'Come forward.' Then he said to them, 'Is it lawful to do good or to do harm on the sabbath, to save life or to kill?' But they were silent. He looked around at them with anger; he was grieved at their hardness of heart and said to the man, 'Stretch out your hand.' He stretched it out, and his hand was restored. The Pharisees went out and immediately conspired with the Herodians against him, how to destroy him.

This is the gospel of the Lord.

Second Service
Ps 35 *or* 35.1-10; Jeremiah 5.1-19;
Romans 7.7-25; *if a Eucharist:* Luke 7.1-10

A reading from the prophecy of Jeremiah. (5.1-19)

Run to and fro through the streets of Jerusalem,
    look around and take note!
Search its squares and see
    if you can find one person
who acts justly
    and seeks truth –
so that I may pardon Jerusalem.
Although they say, 'As the Lord lives',
    yet they swear falsely.
O Lord, do your eyes not look for truth?
You have struck them,
    but they felt no anguish;
you have consumed them,

but they refused to take correction.
They have made their faces harder than rock;
 they have refused to turn back.

Then I said, 'These are only the poor,
 they have no sense;
for they do not know the way of the Lord,
 the law of their God.
Let me go to the rich
 and speak to them;
surely they know the way of the Lord,
 the law of their God.'
But they all alike had broken the yoke,
 they had burst the bonds.

Therefore a lion from the forest shall kill them,
 a wolf from the desert shall destroy them.
A leopard is watching against their cities;
 everyone who goes out of them shall be torn in pieces –
because their transgressions are many,
 their apostasies are great.

How can I pardon you?
 Your children have forsaken me,
 and have sworn by those who are no gods.
When I fed them to the full,
 they committed adultery
 and trooped to the houses of prostitutes.
They were well-fed lusty stallions,
 each neighing for his neighbour's wife.
Shall I not punish them for these things?
        says the Lord;
 and shall I not bring retribution
 on a nation such as this?

Go up through her vine-rows and destroy,
 but do not make a full end;
strip away her branches,
 for they are not the Lord's.
For the house of Israel and the house of Judah
 have been utterly faithless to me,
        says the Lord.
They have spoken falsely of the Lord,
 and have said, 'He will do nothing.
No evil will come upon us,

and we shall not see sword or famine.'
The prophets are nothing but wind,
     for the word is not in them.
Thus shall it be done to them!

Therefore thus says the Lord, the God of hosts:
Because they have spoken this word,
I am now making my words in your mouth a fire,
     and this people wood, and the fire shall devour them.
I am going to bring upon you
     a nation from far away, O house of Israel,
                                        says the Lord.

It is an enduring nation,
     it is an ancient nation,
a nation whose language you do not know,
     nor can you understand what they say.
Their quiver is like an open tomb;
     all of them are mighty warriors.
They shall eat up your harvest and your food;
     they shall eat up your sons and your daughters;
they shall eat up your flocks and your herds;
     they shall eat up your vines and your fig trees;
they shall destroy with the sword
     your fortified cities in which you trust.

But even in those days, says the Lord, I will not make a full end of
you. And when your people say, 'Why has the Lord our God done
all these things to us?' you shall say to them, 'As you have forsaken
me and served foreign gods in your land, so you shall serve strangers
in a land that is not yours.'

A reading from the Letter of Paul to the Romans. (7.7-25)

What then should we say? That the law is sin? By no means! Yet, if
it had not been for the law, I would not have known sin. I would not
have known what it is to covet if the law had not said, 'You shall not
covet.' But sin, seizing an opportunity in the commandment, produced in me all kinds of covetousness. Apart from the law sin lies
dead. I was once alive apart from the law, but when the commandment came, sin revived and I died, and the very commandment that
promised life proved to be death to me. For sin, seizing an opportunity in the commandment, deceived me and through it killed me. So
the law is holy, and the commandment is holy and just and good.
  Did what is good, then, bring death to me? By no means! It was sin,

working death in me through what is good, in order that sin might be shown to be sin, and through the commandment might become sinful beyond measure.

For we know that the law is spiritual; but I am of the flesh, sold into slavery under sin. I do not understand my own actions. For I do not do what I want, but I do the very thing I hate. Now if I do what I do not want, I agree that the law is good. But in fact it is no longer I that do it, but sin that dwells within me. For I know that nothing good dwells within me, that is, in my flesh. I can will what is right, but I cannot do it. For I do not do the good I want, but the evil I do not want is what I do. Now if I do what I do not want, it is no longer I that do it, but sin that dwells within me.

So I find it to be a law that when I want to do what is good, evil lies close at hand. For I delight in the law of God in my inmost self, but I see in my members another law at war with the law of my mind, making me captive to the law of sin that dwells in my members. Wretched man that I am! Who will rescue me from this body of death? Thanks be to God through Jesus Christ our Lord!

So then, with my mind I am a slave to the law of God, but with my flesh I am a slave to the law of sin.

If a Eucharist:
Hear the gospel of our Lord Jesus Christ according to Luke. *(7.1-10)*

After Jesus had finished all his sayings in the hearing of the people, he entered Capernaum. A centurion there had a slave whom he valued highly, and who was ill and close to death. When he heard about Jesus, he sent some Jewish elders to him, asking him to come and heal his slave. When they came to Jesus, they appealed to him earnestly, saying, 'He is worthy of having you do this for him, for he loves our people, and it is he who built our synagogue for us.' And Jesus went with them, but when he was not far from the house, the centurion sent friends to say to him, 'Lord, do not trouble yourself, for I am not worthy to have you come under my roof; therefore I did not presume to come to you. But only speak the word, and let my servant be healed. For I also am a man set under authority, with soldiers under me; and I say to one, "Go", and he goes, and to another, "Come", and he comes, and to my slave, "Do this", and the slave does it.' When Jesus heard this he was amazed at him, and turning to the crowd that followed him, he said, 'I tell you, not even in Israel have I found such faith.' When those who had been sent returned to the house, they found the slave in good health.

This is the gospel of the Lord.

Proper 4 – Second Service

Third Service

A reading from the book Deuteronomy. (5.1-21)

Moses convened all Israel, and said to them: Hear, O Israel, the statutes and ordinances that I am addressing to you today; you shall learn them and observe them diligently. The Lord our God made a covenant with us at Horeb. Not with our ancestors did the Lord make this covenant, but with us, who are all of us here alive today. The Lord spoke with you face to face at the mountain, out of the fire. (At that time I was standing between the Lord and you to declare to you the words of the Lord; for you were afraid because of the fire and did not go up the mountain.) And he said:

I am the Lord your God, who brought you out of the land of Egypt, out of the house of slavery; you shall have no other gods before me.

You shall not make for yourself an idol, whether in the form of anything that is in heaven above, or that is on the earth beneath, or that is in the water under the earth. You shall not bow down to them or worship them; for I the Lord your God am a jealous God, punishing children for the iniquity of parents, to the third and fourth generation of those who reject me, but showing steadfast love to the thousandth generation of those who love me and keep my commandments.

You shall not make wrongful use of the name of the Lord your God, for the Lord will not acquit anyone who misuses his name.

Observe the sabbath day and keep it holy, as the Lord your God commanded you. For six days you shall labour and do all your work. But the seventh day is a sabbath to the Lord your God; you shall not do any work – you, or your son or your daughter, or your male or female slave, or your ox or your donkey, or any of your livestock, or the resident alien in your towns, so that your male and female slave may rest as well as you. Remember that you were a slave in the land of Egypt, and the Lord your God brought you out from there with a mighty hand and an outstretched arm; therefore the Lord your God commanded you to keep the sabbath day.

Honour your father and your mother, as the Lord your God commanded you, so that your days may be long and that it may go well with you in the land that the Lord your God is giving you.

You shall not murder.

Neither shall you commit adultery.

Neither shall you steal.

Neither shall you bear false witness against your neighbour.

Neither shall you covet your neighbour's wife.

Neither shall you desire your neighbour's house, or field, or male or female slave, or ox, or donkey, or anything that belongs to your neighbour.

A reading from the Acts of the Apostles. (21.17-39a)

When we arrived in Jerusalem, the brothers welcomed us warmly. The next day Paul went with us to visit James; and all the elders were present. After greeting them, he related one by one the things that God had done among the Gentiles through his ministry. When they heard it, they praised God. Then they said to him, 'You see, brother, how many thousands of believers there are among the Jews, and they are all zealous for the law. They have been told about you that you teach all the Jews living among the Gentiles to forsake Moses, and that you tell them not to circumcise their children or observe the customs. What then is to be done? They will certainly hear that you have come. So do what we tell you. We have four men who are under a vow. Join these men, go through the rite of purification with them, and pay for the shaving of their heads. Thus all will know that there is nothing in what they have been told about you, but that you yourself observe and guard the law. But as for the Gentiles who have become believers, we have sent a letter with our judgement that they should abstain from what has been sacrificed to idols and from blood and from what is strangled and from fornication.' Then Paul took the men, and the next day, having purified himself, he entered the temple with them, making public the completion of the days of purification when the sacrifice would be made for each of them.

When the seven days were almost completed, the Jews from Asia, who had seen him in the temple, stirred up the whole crowd. They seized him, shouting, 'Fellow-Israelites, help! This is the man who is teaching everyone everywhere against our people, our law, and this place; more than that, he has actually brought Greeks into the temple and has defiled this holy place.' For they had previously seen Trophimus the Ephesian with him in the city, and they supposed that Paul had brought him into the temple. Then all the city was aroused, and the people rushed together. They seized Paul and dragged him out of the temple, and immediately the doors were shut. While they were trying to kill him, word came to the tribune of the cohort that all Jerusalem was in an uproar. Immediately he took soldiers and centurions and ran down to them. When they saw the tribune and the soldiers, they stopped beating Paul. Then the tribune came, arrested him, and ordered him to be bound with two chains; he inquired who he was and what he had done. Some in the crowd shouted one thing, some another; and as he could not learn the facts because of the uproar, he ordered him to be brought into the barracks. When Paul came to the steps, the violence of the mob was so great that he had to be carried by the soldiers. The crowd that followed kept shouting, 'Away with him!'

Just as Paul was about to be brought into the barracks, he said to the tribune, 'May I say something to you?' The tribune replied, 'Do you know Greek? Then you are not the Egyptian who recently stirred up a revolt and led the four thousand assassins out into the wilderness?' Paul replied, 'I am a Jew, from Tarsus in Cilicia, a citizen of an important city.'

Proper 5

Sunday between 5 & 11 June inclusive (if after Trinity Sunday)

Principal Service

Continuous	*Related*
1 Samuel 8.4-11[12-15]16-20 [11.14-15]	Genesis 3.8-15
Ps 138	Ps 130

2 Corinthians 4.13 - 5.1
Mark 3.20-35

A reading from the First Book of Samuel. (8.4-11[12-15]16-20 [11.14-15])

All the elders of Israel gathered together and came to Samuel at Ramah, and said to him, 'You are old and your sons do not follow in your ways; appoint for us, then, a king to govern us, like other nations.' But the thing displeased Samuel when they said, 'Give us a king to govern us.' Samuel prayed to the Lord, and the Lord said to Samuel, 'Listen to the voice of the people in all that they say to you; for they have not rejected you, but they have rejected me from being king over them. Just as they have done to me, from the day I brought them up out of Egypt to this day, forsaking me and serving other gods, so also they are doing to you. Now then, listen to their voice; only – you shall solemnly warn them, and show them the ways of the king who shall reign over them.'

So Samuel reported all the words of the Lord to the people who were asking him for a king. He said, 'These will be the ways of the king who will reign over you: he will take your sons and appoint them to his chariots and to be his horsemen, and to run before his chariots; [12 and he will appoint for himself commanders of thousands and commanders of fifties, and some to plough his ground and to reap his harvest, and to make his implements of war and the equipment of his chariots. He will take your daughters to be perfumers and cooks and bakers. He will take the best of your fields and vineyards and olive orchards and give them to his courtiers. He will take one-tenth of your grain and of your vineyards and give it to his officers and his courtiers.] [16] He will take your male and female slaves, and the best of your cattle and donkeys, and put them to his work. He will take one-tenth of your flocks, and you shall be his slaves. And in that day you will cry out because of your king, whom you have chosen for yourselves; but the Lord will not answer you in that day.'

But the people refused to listen to the voice of Samuel; they said, 'No! but we are determined to have a king over us, so that we also may be like other nations, and that our king may govern us and go out before us and fight our battles.'

[[11.14] Samuel said to the people, 'Come, let us go to Gilgal and there renew the kingship.' So all the people went to Gilgal, and there they made Saul king before the Lord in Gilgal. There they sacrificed offerings of well-being before the Lord, and there Saul and all the Israelites rejoiced greatly.]

This is the word of the Lord.

Or:
A reading from the book Genesis. (3.8-15)

The man and the woman heard the sound of the Lord God walking in the garden at the time of the evening breeze, and the man and his wife hid themselves from the presence of the Lord God among the trees of the garden. But the Lord God called to the man, and said to him, 'Where are you?' He said, 'I heard the sound of you in the garden, and I was afraid, because I was naked; and I hid myself.' He said, 'Who told you that you were naked? Have you eaten from the tree of which I commanded you not to eat?' The man said, 'The woman whom you gave to be with me, she gave me fruit from the tree, and I ate.' Then the Lord God said to the woman, 'What is this that you have done?' The woman said, 'The serpent tricked me, and I ate.' The Lord God said to the serpent,
      'Because you have done this,
            cursed are you among all animals
            and among all wild creatures;
      upon your belly you shall go,
            and dust you shall eat
            all the days of your life.

Proper 5 – Principal Service

I will put enmity between you and the woman,
  and between your offspring and hers;
he will strike your head,
  and you will strike his heel.'

This is the word of the Lord.

A reading from the Second Letter of Paul to the Corinthians. (4.13 - 5.1)

Just as we have the same spirit of faith that is in accordance with scripture – 'I believed, and so I spoke' – we also believe, and so we speak, because we know that the one who raised the Lord Jesus will raise us also with Jesus, and will bring us with you into his presence. Yes, everything is for your sake, so that grace, as it extends to more and more people, may increase thanksgiving, to the glory of God.

So we do not lose heart. Even though our outer nature is wasting away, our inner nature is being renewed day by day. For this slight momentary affliction is preparing us for an eternal weight of glory beyond all measure, because we look not at what can be seen but at what cannot be seen; for what can be seen is temporary, but what cannot be seen is eternal.

For we know that if the earthly tent we live in is destroyed, we have a building from God, a house not made with hands, eternal in the heavens.

This is the word of the Lord.

Hear the gospel of our Lord Jesus Christ according to Mark. (3.20-35)

The crowd came together again, so that Jesus and his apostles could not even eat. When his family heard it, they went out to restrain him, for people were saying, 'He has gone out of his mind.' And the scribes who came down from Jerusalem said, 'He has Beelzebul, and by the ruler of the demons he casts out demons.' And he called them to him, and spoke to them in parables, 'How can Satan cast out Satan? If a kingdom is divided against itself, that kingdom cannot stand. And if a house is divided against itself, that house will not be able to stand. And if Satan has risen up against himself and is divided, he cannot stand, but his end has come. But no one can enter a strong man's house and plunder his property without first tying up the strong man; then indeed the house can be plundered.

'Truly I tell you, people will be forgiven for their sins and whatever blasphemies they utter; but whoever blasphemes against the Holy Spirit can never have forgiveness, but is guilty of an eternal sin' – for they had said, 'He has an unclean spirit.'

Then his mother and his brothers came; and standing outside, they sent to him and called him. A crowd was sitting around him; and they said to him, 'Your mother and your brothers and sisters are outside, asking for you.' And he replied, 'Who are my mother and my brothers?' And looking at those who sat around him, he said, 'Here are my mother and my brothers! Whoever does the will of God is my brother and sister and mother.'

This is the gospel of the Lord.

Second Service
Ps 37.1-11[12-14]; Jeremiah 6.16-21;
Romans 9.1-13; *if a Eucharist:* Luke 7.11-17

A reading from the prophecy of Jeremiah. (6.16-21)

Thus says the Lord:
Stand at the crossroads, and look,
    and ask for the ancient paths,
where the good way lies; and walk in it,
    and find rest for your souls.
But they said, 'We will not walk in it.'
Also I raised up sentinels for you:
    'Give heed to the sound of the trumpet!'
But they said, 'We will not give heed.'
Therefore hear, O nations,
    and know, O congregation, what will happen to them.
Hear, O earth; I am going to bring disaster on this people,
    the fruit of their schemes,
because they have not given heed to my words;
    and as for my teaching, they have rejected it.
Of what use to me is frankincense that comes from Sheba,
    or sweet cane from a distant land?
Your burnt-offerings are not acceptable,
    nor are your sacrifices pleasing to me.
Therefore thus says the Lord:
See, I am laying before this people
    stumbling-blocks against which they shall stumble;
parents and children together,
    neighbour and friend shall perish.

A reading from the Letter of Paul to the Romans. (9.1-13)

I am speaking the truth in Christ – I am not lying; my conscience confirms it by the Holy Spirit – I have great sorrow and unceasing anguish in my heart. For I could wish that I myself were accursed and cut off from Christ for the sake of my own people, my kindred according to the flesh. They are Israelites, and to them belong the adoption, the glory, the covenants, the giving of the law, the worship, and the promises; to them belong the patriarchs, and from them, according to the flesh, comes the Messiah, who is over all, God blessèd for ever. Amen.

It is not as though the word of God had failed. For not all Israelites truly belong to Israel, and not all of Abraham's children are his true descendants; but 'It is through Isaac that descendants shall be named after you.' This means that it is not the children of the flesh who are the children of God, but the children of the promise are counted as descendants. For this is what the promise said, 'About this time I will return and Sarah shall have a son.' Nor is that all; something similar happened to Rebecca when she had conceived children by one husband, our ancestor Isaac. Even before they had been born or had done anything good or bad (so that God's purpose of election might continue, not by works but by his call) she was told, 'The elder shall serve the younger.' As it is written,

'I have loved Jacob,
but I have hated Esau.'

If a Eucharist:
Hear the gospel of our Lord Jesus Christ according to Luke. (7.11-17)

Jesus went to a town called Nain, and his disciples and a large crowd went with him. As he approached the gate of the town, a man who had died was being carried out. He was his mother's only son, and she was a widow; and with her was a large crowd from the town. When the Lord saw her, he had compassion for her and said to her, 'Do not weep.' Then he came forward and touched the bier, and the bearers stood still. And he said, 'Young man, I say to you, rise!' The dead man sat up and began to speak, and Jesus gave him to his mother. Fear seized all of them; and they glorified God, saying, 'A great prophet has risen among us!' and 'God has looked favourably on his people!' This word about him spread throughout Judea and all the surrounding country.

This is the gospel of the Lord.

Third Service
Ps 36; Deuteronomy 6.10-25; Acts 22.22 - 23.11

A reading from the book Deuteronomy. (6.10-25)

Moses said to all Israel: When the Lord your God has brought you into the land that he swore to your ancestors, to Abraham, to Isaac, and to Jacob, to give you – a land with fine, large cities that you did not build, houses filled with all sorts of goods that you did not fill, hewn cisterns that you did not hew, vineyards and olive groves that you did not plant – and when you have eaten your fill, take care that you do not forget the Lord, who brought you out of the land of Egypt, out of the house of slavery. The Lord your God you shall fear; him you shall serve, and by his name alone you shall swear. Do not follow other gods, any of the gods of the peoples who are all around you, because the Lord your God, who is present with you, is a jealous God. The anger of the Lord your God would be kindled against you and he would destroy you from the face of the earth.

Do not put the Lord your God to the test, as you tested him at Massah. You must diligently keep the commandments of the Lord your God, and his decrees, and his statutes that he has commanded you. Do what is right and good in the sight of the Lord, so that it may go well with you, and so that you may go in and occupy the good land that the Lord swore to your ancestors to give you, thrusting out all your enemies from before you, as the Lord has promised.

When your children ask you in time to come, 'What is the meaning of the decrees and the statutes and the ordinances that the Lord our God has commanded you?' then you shall say to your children, 'We were Pharaoh's slaves in Egypt, but the Lord brought us out of Egypt with a mighty hand. The Lord displayed before our eyes great and awesome signs and wonders against Egypt, against Pharaoh and all his household. He brought us out from there in order to bring us in, to give us the land that he promised on oath to our ancestors. Then the Lord commanded us to observe all these statutes, to fear the Lord our God, for our lasting good, so as to keep us alive, as is now the case. If we diligently observe this entire commandment before the Lord our God, as he has commanded us, we will be in the right.'

A reading from the Acts of the Apostles. (22.22 - 23.11)

Up to this point the people listened to Paul, but then they shouted, 'Away with such a fellow from the earth! For he should not be allowed to live.' And while they were shouting, throwing off their cloaks, and tossing dust into the air, the tribune directed that he was to be brought into the barracks, and ordered him to be examined by flogging, to find out the reason for this outcry against him. But when they had tied him up with thongs, Paul said to the centurion who was standing by, 'Is it legal for you to flog a Roman citizen who is uncondemned?' When the centurion heard that, he went to the tribune and said to him, 'What are you about to do? This man is a Roman citizen.' The tribune came and asked Paul, 'Tell me, are you a Roman citizen?' And he said, 'Yes.' The tribune answered, 'It cost me a large sum of money to get my citizenship.' Paul said, 'But I was born a citizen.' Immediately those who were about to examine him drew back from him; and the tribune also was afraid, for he realized that Paul was a Roman citizen and that he had bound him.

Since he wanted to find out what Paul was being accused of by the Jews, the next day he released him and ordered the chief priests and the entire council to meet. He brought Paul down and had him stand before them.

While Paul was looking intently at the council he said, 'Brothers, up to this day I have lived my life with a clear conscience before God.' Then the high priest Ananias ordered those standing near him to strike him on the mouth. At this Paul said to him, 'God will strike you, you whitewashed wall! Are you sitting there to judge me according to the law, and yet in violation of the law you order me to be struck?' Those standing nearby said, 'Do you dare to insult God's high priest?' And Paul said, 'I did not realize, brothers, that he was high priest; for it is written, "You shall not speak evil of a leader of your people."'

When Paul noticed that some were Sadducees and others were Pharisees, he called out in the council, 'Brothers, I am a Pharisee, a son of Pharisees. I am on trial concerning the hope of the resurrection of the dead.' When he said this, a dissension began between the Pharisees and the Sadducees, and the assembly was divided. (The Sadducees say that there is no resurrection, or angel, or spirit; but the Pharisees acknowledge all three.) Then a great clamour arose, and certain scribes of the Pharisees' group stood up and contended, 'We find nothing wrong with this man. What if a spirit or an angel has spoken to him?' When the dissension became violent, the tribune, fearing that they would tear Paul to pieces, ordered the soldiers to go down, take him by force, and bring him into the barracks.

That night the Lord stood near him and said, 'Keep up your courage! For just as you have testified for me in Jerusalem, so you must bear witness also in Rome.'

Proper 6

Sunday between 12 & 18 June inclusive (if after Trinity Sunday)

Principal Service

Continuous	*Related*
1 Samuel 15.34 - 16.13	Ezekiel 17.22-24
Ps 20	Ps 92.1-4,12-15 *or* 92.1-8

2 Corinthians 5.6-10[11-13]14-17
Mark 4.26-34

A reading from the First Book of Samuel. (15.34 - 16.13)

Samuel went to Ramah; and Saul went up to his house in Gibeah of Saul. Samuel did not see Saul again until the day of his death, but Samuel grieved over Saul. And the Lord was sorry that he had made Saul king over Israel.

The Lord said to Samuel, 'How long will you grieve over Saul? I have rejected him from being king over Israel. Fill your horn with oil and set out; I will send you to Jesse the Bethlehemite, for I have provided for myself a king among his sons.' Samuel said, 'How can I go? If Saul hears of it, he will kill me.' And the Lord said, 'Take a heifer with you, and say, "I have come to sacrifice to the Lord." Invite Jesse to the sacrifice, and I will show you what you shall do; and you shall anoint for me the one whom I name to you.' Samuel did what the Lord commanded, and came to Bethlehem. The elders of the city came to meet him trembling, and said, 'Do you come peaceably?' He said, 'Peaceably; I have come to sacrifice to the Lord; sanctify yourselves and come with me to the sacrifice.' And he sanctified Jesse and his sons and invited them to the sacrifice.

When they came, he looked on Eliab and thought, 'Surely the Lord's anointed is now before the Lord.' But the Lord said to Samuel, 'Do not look on his appearance or on the height of his stature, because I have rejected him; for the Lord does not see as mortals see; they look on the outward appearance, but the Lord looks on the heart.' Then Jesse called Abinadab, and made him pass before Samuel. He said, 'Neither has the Lord chosen this one.' Then Jesse made Shammah pass by. And he said, 'Neither has the Lord chosen this one.' Jesse made seven of his sons pass before Samuel, and Samuel said to Jesse, 'The Lord has not chosen any of these.' Samuel said to Jesse, 'Are all your sons here?' And he said, 'There remains yet the youngest, but he is keeping the sheep.' And Samuel said to Jesse, 'Send and bring him; for we will not sit down until he comes here.' He sent and brought him in. Now he was ruddy, and had beautiful eyes, and was

handsome. The Lord said, 'Rise and anoint him; for this is the one.'
 Then Samuel took the horn of oil, and anointed him in the presence
of his brothers; and the spirit of the Lord came mightily upon David
from that day forward. Samuel then set out and went to Ramah.

This is the word of the Lord.

Or:

A reading from the prophecy of Ezekiel. *(17.22-24)*

Thus says the Lord God:
> I myself will take a sprig
>> from the lofty top of a cedar;
>> I will set it out.
> I will break off a tender one
>> from the topmost of its young twigs;
> I myself will plant it
>> on a high and lofty mountain.
> On the mountain height of Israel
>> I will plant it,
> in order that it may produce boughs and bear fruit,
>> and become a noble cedar.
> Under it every kind of bird will live;
>> in the shade of its branches will nest
>> winged creatures of every kind.
> All the trees of the field shall know
>> that I am the Lord.
> I bring low the high tree,
>> I make high the low tree;
> I dry up the green tree
>> and make the dry tree flourish.
> I the Lord have spoken;
>> I will accomplish it.

This is the word of the Lord.

A reading from the Second Letter of Paul to the Corinthians.
(5.6-10 [11-13] 14-17)
We are always confident; even though we know that while we are at
home in the body we are away from the Lord – for we walk by faith,
not by sight. Yes, we do have confidence, and we would rather be
away from the body and at home with the Lord. So whether we are
at home or away, we make it our aim to please him. For all of us
must appear before the judgement seat of Christ, so that each may

receive recompense for what has been done in the body, whether good or evil.

[11 Therefore, knowing the fear of the Lord, we try to persuade others; but we ourselves are well known to God, and I hope that we are also well known to your consciences. We are not commending ourselves to you again, but giving you an opportunity to boast about us, so that you may be able to answer those who boast in outward appearance and not in the heart. For if we are beside ourselves, it is for God; if we are in our right mind, it is for you.]

14 For the love of Christ urges us on, because we are convinced that one has died for all; therefore all have died. And he died for all, so that those who live might live no longer for themselves, but for him who died and was raised for them.

From now on, therefore, we regard no one from a human point of view; even though we once knew Christ from a human point of view, we know him no longer in that way. So if anyone is in Christ, there is a new creation: everything old has passed away; see, everything has become new!

This is the word of the Lord.

Hear the gospel of our Lord Jesus Christ according to Mark. (4.26-34)

Jesus said to the crowd, 'The kingdom of God is as if someone would scatter seed on the ground, and would sleep and rise night and day, and the seed would sprout and grow, he does not know how. The earth produces of itself, first the stalk, then the head, then the full grain in the head. But when the grain is ripe, at once he goes in with his sickle, because the harvest has come.'

He also said, 'With what can we compare the kingdom of God, or what parable will we use for it? It is like a mustard seed, which, when sown upon the ground, is the smallest of all the seeds on earth; yet when it is sown it grows up and becomes the greatest of all shrubs, and puts forth large branches, so that the birds of the air can make nests in its shade.'

With many such parables he spoke the word to them, as they were able to hear it; he did not speak to them except in parables, but he explained everything in private to his disciples.

This is the gospel of the Lord.

Second Service

Ps 39; Jeremiah 7.1-16; Romans 9.14-26; *if a Eucharist:* Luke 7.36 - 8.3

A reading from the prophecy of Jeremiah. *(7.1-16)*

The word that came to Jeremiah from the Lord: Stand in the gate of the Lord's house, and proclaim there this word, and say, Hear the word of the Lord, all you people of Judah, you that enter these gates to worship the Lord. Thus says the Lord of hosts, the God of Israel: Amend your ways and your doings, and let me dwell with you in this place. Do not trust in these deceptive words: 'This is the temple of the Lord, the temple of the Lord, the temple of the Lord.'

For if you truly amend your ways and your doings, if you truly act justly one with another, if you do not oppress the alien, the orphan, and the widow, or shed innocent blood in this place, and if you do not go after other gods to your own hurt, then I will dwell with you in this place, in the land that I gave of old to your ancestors for ever and ever.

Here you are, trusting in deceptive words to no avail. Will you steal, murder, commit adultery, swear falsely, make offerings to Baal, and go after other gods that you have not known, and then come and stand before me in this house, which is called by my name, and say, 'We are safe!' – only to go on doing all these abominations? Has this house, which is called by my name, become a den of robbers in your sight? You know, I too am watching, says the Lord. Go now to my place that was in Shiloh, where I made my name dwell at first, and see what I did to it for the wickedness of my people Israel. And now, because you have done all these things, says the Lord, and when I spoke to you persistently, you did not listen, and when I called you, you did not answer, therefore I will do to the house that is called by my name, in which you trust, and to the place that I gave to you and to your ancestors, just what I did to Shiloh. And I will cast you out of my sight, just as I cast out all your kinsfolk, all the offspring of Ephraim.

As for you, do not pray for this people, do not raise a cry or prayer on their behalf, and do not intercede with me, for I will not hear you.

A reading from the Letter of Paul to the Romans. *(9.14-26)*

What then are we to say? Is there injustice on God's part? By no means! For he says to Moses,

    'I will have mercy on whom I have mercy,

        and I will have compassion on whom I have compassion.'

So it depends not on human will or exertion, but on God who shows mercy. For the scripture says to Pharaoh, 'I have raised you up for the very purpose of showing my power in you, so that my name may be proclaimed in all the earth.' So then he has mercy on whomsoever he chooses, and he hardens the heart of whomsoever he chooses.

You will say to me then, 'Why then does he still find fault? For who can resist his will?' But who indeed are you, a human being, to argue with God? Will what is moulded say to the one who moulds it, 'Why have you made me like this?' Has the potter no right over the clay, to make out of the same lump one object for special use and another for ordinary use? What if God, desiring to show his wrath and to make known his power, has endured with much patience the objects of wrath that are made for destruction; and what if he has done so in order to make known the riches of his glory for the objects of mercy, which he has prepared beforehand for glory – including us whom he has called, not from the Jews only but also from the Gentiles? As indeed he says in Hosea,

'Those who were not my people I will call "my people",
and her who was not beloved I will call "beloved".'
'And in the very place where it was said to them,
    "You are not my people",
there they shall be called children of the living God.'

If a Eucharist:
Hear the gospel of our Lord Jesus Christ according to Luke. *(7.36 - 8.3)*

One of the Pharisees asked Jesus to eat with him, and he went into the Pharisee's house and took his place at the table. And a woman in the city, who was a sinner, having learned that he was eating in the Pharisee's house, brought an alabaster jar of ointment. She stood behind him at his feet, weeping, and began to bathe his feet with her tears and to dry them with her hair. Then she continued kissing his feet and anointing them with the ointment. Now when the Pharisee who had invited him saw it, he said to himself, 'If this man were a prophet, he would have known who and what kind of woman this is who is touching him – that she is a sinner.' Jesus spoke up and said to him, 'Simon, I have something to say to you.' 'Teacher,' he replied, 'speak.' 'A certain creditor had two debtors; one owed five hundred denarii, and the other fifty. When they could not pay, he cancelled the debts for both of them. Now which of them will love him more?' Simon answered, 'I suppose the one for whom he cancelled the greater debt.' And Jesus said to him, 'You have judged rightly.' Then turning towards the woman, he said to Simon, 'Do you see this woman? I entered your house; you gave me no water for my feet, but she has bathed my feet with her tears and dried them with her hair. You gave me no kiss, but from the time I came in she has not stopped kissing my feet. You did not anoint my head with oil, but she has anointed my feet with ointment. Therefore, I tell you, her sins, which were many, have been forgiven; hence she has shown great love. But the one to whom little is forgiven, loves little.' Then he said to her, 'Your sins are forgiven.' But those who were at the table with him began to say among themselves, 'Who is this who even forgives sins?' And he said to the woman, 'Your faith has saved you; go in peace.'

Soon afterwards he went on through cities and villages, proclaiming and bringing the good news of the kingdom of God. The twelve were with him, as well as some women who had been cured of evil spirits and infirmities: Mary, called Magdalene, from whom seven demons had gone out, and Joanna, the wife of Herod's steward Chuza, and Susanna, and many others, who provided for them out of their resources.

This is the gospel of the Lord.

Third Service
Pss 42,43; Deuteronomy 10.12 - 11.1; Acts 23.12-35

A reading from the book Deuteronomy. (10.12 - 11.1)

Moses said to all Israel: So now, O Israel, what does the Lord your God require of you? Only to fear the Lord your God, to walk in all his ways, to love him, to serve the Lord your God with all your heart and with all your soul, and to keep the commandments of the Lord your God and his decrees that I am commanding you today, for your own well-being. Although heaven and the heaven of heavens belong to the Lord your God, the earth with all that is in it, yet the Lord set his heart in love on your ancestors alone and chose you, their descendants after them, out of all the peoples, as it is today. Circumcise, then, the foreskin of your heart, and do not be stubborn any longer. For the Lord your God is God of gods and Lord of lords, the great God, mighty and awesome, who is not partial and takes no bribe, who executes justice for the orphan and the widow, and who loves the strangers, providing them with food and clothing. You shall also love the stranger, for you were strangers in the land of Egypt. You shall fear the Lord your God; him alone you shall worship; to him you shall hold fast, and by his name you shall swear. He is your praise; he is your God, who has done for you these great and awesome things that your own eyes have seen. Your ancestors went down to Egypt seventy persons; and now the Lord your God has made you as numerous as the stars in heaven.

You shall love the Lord your God, therefore, and keep his charge, his decrees, his ordinances, and his commandments always.

A reading from the Acts of the Apostles. (23.12-35)

The Jews joined in a conspiracy and bound themselves by an oath neither to eat nor drink until they had killed Paul. There were more than forty who joined in this conspiracy. They went to the chief priests and elders and said, 'We have strictly bound ourselves by an oath to taste no food until we have killed Paul. Now then, you and the council must notify the tribune to bring him down to you, on the pretext that you want to make a more thorough examination of his case. And we are ready to do away with him before he arrives.'

Now the son of Paul's sister heard about the ambush; so he went and gained entrance to the barracks and told Paul. Paul called one of the centurions and said, 'Take this young man to the tribune, for he has something to report to him.' So he took him, brought him to the tribune, and said, 'The prisoner Paul called me and asked me to bring this young man to you; he has something to tell you.' The tribune took him by the hand, drew him aside privately, and asked, 'What is it that you have to report to me?' He answered, 'The Jews have agreed to ask you to bring Paul down to the council tomorrow, as though they were going to inquire more thoroughly into his case. But do not be persuaded by them, for more than forty of their men are lying in ambush for him. They have bound themselves by an oath neither to eat nor drink until they kill him. They are ready now and are waiting for your consent.' So the tribune dismissed the young man, ordering him, 'Tell no one that you have informed me of this.'

Then he summoned two of the centurions and said, 'Get ready to leave by nine o'clock tonight for Caesarea with two hundred soldiers, seventy horsemen, and two hundred spearmen. Also provide mounts for Paul to ride, and take him safely to Felix the governor.' He wrote a letter to this effect:

'Claudius Lysias to his Excellency the governor Felix, greetings. This man was seized by the Jews and was about to be killed by them, but when I had learned that he was a Roman citizen, I came with the guard and rescued him. Since I wanted to know the charge for which they accused him, I had him brought to their council. I found that he was accused concerning questions of their law, but was charged with nothing deserving death or imprisonment. When I was informed that there would be a plot against the man, I sent him to you at once, ordering his accusers also to state before you what they have against him.'

So the soldiers, according to their instructions, took Paul and brought him during the night to Antipatris. The next day they let the horsemen go on with him, while they returned to the barracks. When they came to Caesarea and delivered the letter to the governor, they presented Paul also before him. On reading the letter, he asked what province he belonged to, and when he learned that he was from Cilicia, he said, 'I will give you a hearing when your accusers arrive.' Then he ordered that he be kept under guard in Herod's head-quarters.

Proper 7

Sunday between 19 & 25 June inclusive (if after Trinity Sunday)

Principal Service

Continuous	*Related*
1 Samuel 17.[1a,4-11,19-23] 32-49	Job 38.1-11
Ps 9.9-20	Ps 107.[1-3] 23-32
Or:	
1 Samuel 17.57 - 18.5,10-16	
Ps 133	

2 Corinthians 6.1-13
Mark 4.35-41

A reading from the First Book of Samuel. *(17.[1a,4-11,19-23] 32-49)*

[The Philistines gathered their armies for battle; [4] and there came out from the camp of the Philistines a champion named Goliath, of Gath, whose height was six cubits and a span. He had a helmet of bronze on his head, and he was armoured with a coat of mail; the weight of the coat was five thousand shekels of bronze. He had greaves of bronze on his legs and a javelin of bronze slung between his shoulders. The shaft of his spear was like a weaver's beam, and his spear's head weighed six hundred shekels of iron; and his shield-bearer went before him. He stood and shouted to the ranks of Israel, 'Why have you come out to draw up for battle? Am I not a Philistine, and are you not servants of Saul? Choose a man for yourselves, and let him come down to me. If he is able to fight with me and kill me, then we will be your servants; but if I prevail against him and kill him, then you shall be our servants and serve us.' And the Philistine said,

'Today I defy the ranks of Israel! Give me a man, that we may fight together.' When Saul and all Israel heard these words of the Philistine, they were dismayed and greatly afraid.

[19] Now Saul, and they, and all the men of Israel, were in the valley of Elah, fighting with the Philistines. David rose early in the morning, left someone in charge of the sheep, took the provisions, and went as Jesse had commanded him. He came to the encampment as the army was going forth to the battle line, shouting the war cry. Israel and the Philistines drew up for battle, army against army. David left the things in charge of the keeper of the baggage, ran to the ranks, and went and greeted his brothers. As he talked with them, the champion, the Philistine of Gath, Goliath by name, came up out of the ranks of the Philistines, and spoke the same words as before. And David heard him.]

[32] David said to Saul, 'Let no one's heart fail because of him; your servant will go and fight with this Philistine.' Saul said to David, 'You are not able to go against this Philistine to fight with him; for you are just a boy, and he has been a warrior from his youth.' But David said to Saul, 'Your servant used to keep sheep for his father; and whenever a lion or a bear came, and took a lamb from the flock, I went after it and struck it down, rescuing the lamb from its mouth; and if it turned against me, I would catch it by the jaw, strike it down, and kill it. Your servant has killed both lions and bears; and this uncircumcised Philistine shall be like one of them, since he has defied the armies of the living God.' David said, 'The Lord, who saved me from the paw of the lion and from the paw of the bear, will save me from the hand of this Philistine.' So Saul said to David, 'Go, and may the Lord be with you!'

Saul clothed David with his armour; he put a bronze helmet on his head and clothed him with a coat of mail. David strapped Saul's sword over the armour, and he tried in vain to walk, for he was not used to them. Then David said to Saul, 'I cannot walk with these; for I am not used to them.' So David removed them. Then he took his staff in his hand, and chose five smooth stones from the wadi, and put them in his shepherd's bag, in the pouch; his sling was in his hand, and he drew near to the Philistine.

The Philistine came on and drew near to David, with his shield-bearer in front of him. When the Philistine looked and saw David, he disdained him, for he was only a youth, ruddy and handsome in appearance. The Philistine said to David, 'Am I a dog, that you come to me with sticks?' And the Philistine cursed David by his gods. The Philistine said to David, 'Come to me, and I will give your flesh to the birds of the air and to the wild animals of the field.' But David said to the Philistine, 'You come to me with sword and spear and javelin; but I come to you in the name of the Lord of hosts, the God of the armies of Israel, whom you have defied. This very day the Lord will deliver you into my hand, and I will strike you down and cut off your head; and I will give the dead bodies of the Philistine army this very day to the birds of the air and to the wild animals of the earth, so that all the earth may know that there is a God in Israel, and that all this assembly may know that the Lord does not save by sword and spear; for the battle is the Lord's and he will give you into our hand.'

When the Philistine drew nearer to meet David, David ran quickly towards the battle line to meet the Philistine. David put his hand in his bag, took out a stone, slung it, and struck the Philistine on his forehead; the stone sank into his forehead, and he fell face down on the ground.

This is the word of the Lord.

Or:

A reading from the First Book of Samuel. (17.57 - 18.5,10-16)

On David's return from killing the Philistine, Abner took him and brought him before Saul, with the head of the Philistine in his hand. Saul said to him, 'Whose son are you, young man?' And David answered, 'I am the son of your servant Jesse the Bethlehemite.'

When David had finished speaking to Saul, the soul of Jonathan was bound to the soul of David, and Jonathan loved him as his own soul. Saul took him that day and would not let him return to his father's house. Then Jonathan made a covenant with David, because he loved him as his own soul. Jonathan stripped himself of the robe that he was wearing, and gave it to David, and his armour, and even his sword and his bow and his belt. David went out and was successful wherever Saul sent him; as a result, Saul set him over the army. And all the people, even the servants of Saul, approved.
¹⁰ The next day an evil spirit from God rushed upon Saul, and he raved within his house, while David was playing the lyre, as he did day by day.

Saul had his spear in his hand; and Saul threw the spear, for he thought, 'I will pin David to the wall.' But David eluded him twice. Saul was afraid of David, because the Lord was with him but had departed from Saul. So Saul removed him from his presence, and made him a commander of a thousand; and David marched out and came in, leading the army. David had success in all his undertakings; for the Lord was with him. When Saul saw that he had great success, he stood in awe of him. But all Israel and Judah loved David; for it was he who marched out and came in leading them.

This is the word of the Lord.

Or:

A reading from the Book of Job. (38.1-11)

The Lord answered Job out of the whirlwind:
> 'Who is this that darkens counsel by words without knowledge?
> Gird up your loins like a man,
>> I will question you, and you shall declare to me.
> 'Where were you when I laid the foundation of the earth?
>> Tell me, if you have understanding.
> Who determined its measurements – surely you know!
>> Or who stretched the line upon it?
> On what were its bases sunk,
>> or who laid its cornerstone
> when the morning stars sang together
>> and all the heavenly beings shouted for joy?

> 'Or who shut in the sea with doors
>> when it burst out from the womb? –
> when I made the clouds its garment,
>> and thick darkness its swaddling band,
> and prescribed bounds for it,
>> and set bars and doors,
> and said, "Thus far shall you come, and no farther,
>> and here shall your proud waves be stopped"?'

This is the word of the Lord.

A reading from the Second Letter of Paul to the Corinthians. (6.1-13)

As we work together with him, we urge you also not to accept the grace of God in vain. For he says,
> 'At an acceptable time I have listened to you,
>> and on a day of salvation I have helped you.'

See, now is the acceptable time; see, now is the day of salvation! We are putting no obstacle in anyone's way, so that no fault may be found with our ministry, but as servants of God we have commended ourselves in every way: through great endurance, in afflictions, hardships, calamities, beatings, imprisonments, riots, labours, sleepless nights, hunger; by purity, knowledge, patience, kindness, holiness of spirit, genuine love, truthful speech, and the power of God; with the weapons of righteousness for the right hand and for the left;

in honour and dishonour, in ill repute and good repute. We are treated as impostors, and yet are true; as unknown, and yet are well known; as dying, and see – we are alive; as punished, and yet not killed; as sorrowful, yet always rejoicing; as poor, yet making many rich; as having nothing, and yet possessing everything.

We have spoken frankly to you Corinthians; our heart is wide open to you. There is no restriction in our affections, but only in yours. In return – I speak as to children – open wide your hearts also.

This is the word of the Lord.

Hear the gospel of our Lord Jesus Christ according to Mark. (4.35-41)

When evening had come, Jesus said to the disciples, 'Let us go across to the other side.' And leaving the crowd behind, they took him with them in the boat, just as he was. Other boats were with him. A great gale arose, and the waves beat into the boat, so that the boat was already being swamped. But he was in the stern, asleep on the cushion; and they woke him up and said to him, 'Teacher, do you not care that we are perishing?' He woke up and rebuked the wind, and said to the sea, 'Peace! Be still!' Then the wind ceased, and there was a dead calm. He said to them, 'Why are you afraid? Have you still no faith?' And they were filled with great awe and said to one another, 'Who then is this, that even the wind and the sea obey him?'

This is the gospel of the Lord.

Second Service
Ps 49; Jeremiah 10.1-16; Romans 11.25-36; *if a Eucharist:* Luke 8.26-39

A reading from the prophecy of Jeremiah. (10.1-16)

Hear the word that the Lord speaks to you, O house of Israel. Thus says the Lord:
> Do not learn the way of the nations,
>> or be dismayed at the signs of the heavens;
>> for the nations are dismayed at them.
> For the customs of the peoples are false:
> a tree from the forest is cut down,
>> and worked with an axe by the hands of an artisan;
> people deck it with silver and gold;
>> they fasten it with hammer and nails
>> so that it cannot move.
> Their idols are like scarecrows in a cucumber field,
>> and they cannot speak;

they have to be carried,
      for they cannot walk.
Do not be afraid of them,
      for they cannot do evil,
      nor is it in them to do good.

There is none like you, O Lord;
      you are great, and your name is great in might.
Who would not fear you, O King of the nations?
      For that is your due;
among all the wise ones of the nations
      and in all their kingdoms
      there is no one like you.
They are both stupid and foolish;
      the instruction given by idols
      is no better than wood!
Beaten silver is brought from Tarshish,
      and gold from Uphaz.
They are the work of the artisan
            and of the hands of the goldsmith;
      their clothing is blue and purple;
      they are all the product of skilled workers.
But the Lord is the true God;
      he is the living God and the everlasting King.
At his wrath the earth quakes,
      and the nations cannot endure his indignation.

   Thus shall you say to them: The gods who did not make the heavens and the earth shall perish from the earth and from under the heavens.

   It is he who made the earth by his power,
      who established the world by his wisdom,
      and by his understanding stretched out the heavens.
When he utters his voice,
      there is a tumult of waters in the heavens,
      and he makes the mist rise from the ends of the earth.
He makes lightnings for the rain,
      and he brings out the wind from his storehouses.
Everyone is stupid and without knowledge;
      goldsmiths are all put to shame by their idols;
for their images are false,
      and there is no breath in them.
They are worthless, a work of delusion;
      at the time of their punishment they shall perish.

Not like these is the Lord, the portion of Jacob,
    for he is the one who formed all things,
    and Israel is the tribe of his inheritance;
    the Lord of hosts is his name.

A reading from the Letter of Paul to the Romans. *(11.25-36)*

So that you may not claim to be wiser than you are, brothers and sisters, I want you to understand this mystery: a hardening has come upon part of Israel, until the full number of the Gentiles has come in. And so all Israel will be saved; as it is written,
    'Out of Zion will come the Deliverer;
        he will banish ungodliness from Jacob.'
    'And this is my covenant with them,
        when I take away their sins.'
As regards the gospel they are enemies of God for your sake; but as regards election they are beloved, for the sake of their ancestors; for the gifts and the calling of God are irrevocable. Just as you were once disobedient to God but have now received mercy because of their disobedience, so they have now been disobedient in order that, by the mercy shown to you, they too may now receive mercy. For God has imprisoned all in disobedience so that he may be merciful to all.
  O the depth of the riches and wisdom and knowledge of God! How unsearchable are his judgements and how inscrutable his ways!
    'For who has known the mind of the Lord?
        Or who has been his counsellor?'
    'Or who has given a gift to him,
        to receive a gift in return?'
For from him and through him and to him are all things. To him be the glory for ever. Amen.

If a Eucharist:
Hear the gospel of our Lord Jesus Christ according to Luke. *(8.26-39)*

Jesus and his disciples arrived at the country of the Gerasenes, which is opposite Galilee. As he stepped out on land, a man of the city who had demons met him. For a long time he had worn no clothes, and he did not live in a house but in the tombs. When he saw Jesus, he fell down before him and shouted at the top of his voice, 'What have you to do with me, Jesus, Son of the Most High God? I beg you, do not torment me' – for Jesus had commanded the unclean spirit to come out of the man. (For many times it had seized him; he was kept under guard and bound with chains and shackles, but he would break the bonds and be driven by the demon into the wilds.) Jesus then asked him, 'What is your name?' He said, 'Legion'; for many demons had entered him. They begged him not to order them to go back into the abyss.

Now there on the hillside a large herd of swine was feeding; and the demons begged Jesus to let them enter these. So he gave them permission. Then the demons came out of the man and entered the swine, and the herd rushed down the steep bank into the lake and was drowned.

When the swineherds saw what had happened, they ran off and told it in the city and in the country. Then people came out to see what had happened, and when they came to Jesus, they found the man from whom the demons had gone sitting at the feet of Jesus, clothed and in his right mind. And they were afraid. Those who had seen it told them how the one who had been possessed by demons had been healed. Then all the people of the surrounding country of the Gerasenes asked Jesus to leave them; for they were seized with great fear. So he got into the boat and returned. The man from whom the demons had gone begged that he might be with him; but Jesus sent him away, saying, 'Return to your home, and declare how much God has done for you.' So he went away, proclaiming throughout the city how much Jesus had done for him.

This is the gospel of the Lord.

Third Service
Ps 48; Deuteronomy 11.1-15; Acts 27.1-12

A reading from the book Deuteronomy. (11.1-15)

Moses said to all Israel: You shall love the Lord your God, therefore, and keep his charge, his decrees, his ordinances, and his commandments always. Remember today that it was not your children (who have not known or seen the discipline of the Lord your God), but it is you who must acknowledge his greatness, his mighty hand and his outstretched arm, his signs and his deeds that he did in Egypt to Pharaoh, the king of Egypt, and to all his land; what he did to the Egyptian army, to their horses and chariots, how he made the water of the Red Sea flow over them as they pursued you, so that the Lord has destroyed them to this day; what he did to you in the wilderness, until you came to this place; and what he did to Dathan and Abiram, sons of Eliab son of Reuben, how in the midst of all Israel the earth opened its mouth and swallowed them up, along with their households, their tents, and every living being in their company; for it is your own eyes that have seen every great deed that the Lord did.

Keep, then, this entire commandment that I am commanding you today, so that you may have strength to go in and occupy the land that you are crossing over to occupy, and so that you may live long in the land that the Lord swore to your ancestors to give to them and their descendants, a land flowing with milk and honey. For the land that you are about to enter to occupy is not like the land of Egypt, from which you have come, where you sow your seed and irrigate by foot like a vegetable garden. But the land that you are crossing over to occupy is a land of hills and valleys, watered by rain from the sky, a land that the Lord your God looks after. The eyes of the Lord your God are always on it, from the beginning of the year to the end of the year.

If you will only heed his every commandment that I am commanding you today – loving the Lord your God, and serving him with all your heart and with all your soul – then he will give the rain for your land in its season, the early rain and the later rain, and you will gather in your grain, your wine, and your oil; and he will give grass in your fields for your livestock, and you will eat your fill.

A reading from the Acts of the Apostles. (27.1-12)

When it was decided that we were to sail for Italy, they transferred Paul and some other prisoners to a centurion of the Augustan Cohort, named Julius. Embarking on a ship of Adramyttium that was about to set sail to the ports along the coast of Asia, we put to sea, accompanied by Aristarchus, a Macedonian from Thessalonica. The next day we put in at Sidon; and Julius treated Paul kindly, and allowed him to go to his friends to be cared for. Putting out to sea from there, we sailed under the lee of Cyprus, because the winds were against us. After we had sailed across the sea that is off Cilicia and Pamphylia, we came to Myra in Lycia. There the centurion found an Alexandrian ship bound for Italy and put us on board. We sailed slowly for a number of days and arrived with difficulty off Cnidus, and as the wind was against us, we sailed under the lee of Crete off Salmone. Sailing past it with difficulty, we came to a place called Fair Havens, near the city of Lasea.

Since much time had been lost and sailing was now dangerous, because even the Fast had already gone by, Paul advised them, saying, 'Sirs, I can see that the voyage will be with danger and much heavy loss, not only of the cargo and the ship, but also of our lives.' But the centurion paid more attention to the pilot and to the owner of the ship than to what Paul said. Since the harbour was not suitable for spending the winter, the majority was in favour of putting to sea from there, on the chance that somehow they could reach Phoenix, where they could spend the winter. It was a harbour of Crete, facing south-west and north-west.

Proper 8

Sunday between 26 June & 2 July inclusive

Principal Service

Continuous   *Related*
2 Samuel 1.1,17-27   Wisdom of Solomon 1.13-15 & 2.23-24
Ps 130   *Canticle:* Lamentations 3.23-33
                      or Ps 30
           2 Corinthians 8.7-15
           Mark 5.21-43

A reading from the Second Book of Samuel. *(1.1,17-27)*

After the death of Saul, when David had returned from defeating the Amalekites, David remained two days in Ziklag.
[17] David intoned this lamentation over Saul and his son Jonathan. (He ordered that The Song of the Bow be taught to the people of Judah; it is written in the Book of Jashar.) He said:
    Your glory, O Israel, lies slain upon your high places!
       How the mighty have fallen!
    Tell it not in Gath,
       proclaim it not in the streets of Ashkelon;
    or the daughters of the Philistines will rejoice,
       the daughters of the uncircumcised will exult.

    You mountains of Gilboa,
       let there be no dew or rain upon you,
       nor bounteous fields!
    For there the shield of the mighty was defiled,
       the shield of Saul, anointed with oil no more.

    From the blood of the slain,
       from the fat of the mighty,
    the bow of Jonathan did not turn back,
       nor the sword of Saul return empty.

    Saul and Jonathan, belovèd and lovely!
       In life and in death they were not divided;
    they were swifter than eagles,
       they were stronger than lions.
    O daughters of Israel, weep over Saul,

who clothed you with crimson, in luxury,
who put ornaments of gold on your apparel.

How the mighty have fallen
in the midst of the battle!
Jonathan lies slain upon your high places.
I am distressed for you, my brother Jonathan;
greatly beloved were you to me;
your love to me was wonderful,
passing the love of women.

How the mighty have fallen,
and the weapons of war perished!

This is the word of the Lord.

Or:

A reading from the Wisdom of Solomon. *(1.13-15 & 2.23-24)*

God did not make death,
and he does not delight in the death of the living.
For he created all things so that they might exist;
the generative forces of the world are wholesome,
and there is no destructive poison in them,
and the dominion of Hades is not on earth.
For righteousness is immortal.

2.23 For God created us for incorruption,
and made us in the image of his own eternity,
but through the devil's envy death entered the world,
and those who belong to his company experience it.

This is the word of the Lord.

The Canticle from Lamentations may be read as the first reading in place of the reading from The Wisdom of Solomon:
A reading from the Lamentations of Jeremiah. *(3.23-33)*

The mercies of the Lord are new every morning;
great is your faithfulness.
'The Lord is my portion,' says my soul,
'therefore I will hope in him.'

The Lord is good to those who wait for him,
to the soul that seeks him.
It is good that one should wait quietly
for the salvation of the Lord.
It is good for one to bear

the yoke in youth,
to sit alone in silence
    when the Lord has imposed it,
to put one's mouth to the dust
    (there may yet be hope),
to give one's cheek to the smiter,
    and be filled with insults.

For the Lord will not reject for ever.
Although he causes grief, he will have compassion
    according to the abundance of his steadfast love;
for he does not willingly afflict or grieve anyone.

This is the word of the Lord.

A reading from the Second Letter of Paul to the Corinthians. *(8.7-15)*

As you excel in everything – in faith, in speech, in knowledge, in utmost eagerness, and in our love for you – so we want you to excel also in this generous undertaking.

I do not say this as a command, but I am testing the genuineness of your love against the earnestness of others. For you know the generous act of our Lord Jesus Christ, that though he was rich, yet for your sakes he became poor, so that by his poverty you might become rich. And in this matter I am giving my advice: it is appropriate for you who began last year not only to do something but even to desire to do something – now finish doing it, so that your eagerness may be matched by completing it according to your means. For if the eagerness is there, the gift is acceptable according to what one has – not according to what one does not have. I do not mean that there should be relief for others and pressure on you, but it is a question of a fair balance between your present abundance and their need, so that their abundance may be for your need, in order that there may be a fair balance. As it is written,
    'The one who had much did not have too much,
        and the one who had little did not have too little.'

This is the word of the Lord.

Hear the gospel of our Lord Jesus Christ according to Mark. *(5.21-43)*

When Jesus had crossed again in the boat to the other side, a great crowd gathered round him; and he was by the lake. Then one of the leaders of the synagogue named Jairus came and, when he saw him, fell at his feet and begged him repeatedly, 'My little daughter is at the point of death. Come and lay your hands on her, so that she may be made well, and live.' So he went with him.

And a large crowd followed him and pressed in on him. Now there was a woman who had been suffering from haemorrhages for twelve years. She had endured much under many physicians, and had spent all that she had; and she was no better, but rather grew worse. She had heard about Jesus, and came up behind him in the crowd and touched his cloak, for she said, 'If I but touch his clothes, I will be made well.' Immediately her haemorrhage stopped; and she felt in her body that she was healed of her disease. Immediately aware that power had gone forth from him, Jesus turned about in the crowd and said, 'Who touched my clothes?' And his disciples said to him, 'You see the crowd pressing in on you; how can you say, "Who touched me?"' He looked all round to see who had done it. But the woman, knowing what had happened to her, came in fear and trembling, fell down before him, and told him the whole truth. He said to her, 'Daughter, your faith has made you well; go in peace, and be healed of your disease.'

While he was still speaking, some people came from the leader's house to say, 'Your daughter is dead. Why trouble the teacher any further?' But overhearing what they said, Jesus said to the leader of the synagogue, 'Do not fear, only believe.' He allowed no one to follow him except Peter, James, and John, the brother of James. When they came to the house of the leader of the synagogue, he saw a commotion, people weeping and wailing loudly. When he had entered, he said to them, 'Why do you make a commotion and weep? The child is not dead but sleeping.' And they laughed at him. Then he put them all outside, and took the child's father and mother and those who were with him, and went in where the child was. He took her by the hand and said to her, 'Talitha cum', which means, 'Little girl, get up!' And immediately the girl got up and began to walk about (she was twelve years of age). At this they were overcome with amazement. He strictly ordered them that no one should know this, and told them to give her something to eat.

This is the gospel of the Lord.

Second Service
Pss [52] 53; Jeremiah 11.1-14;
Romans 13.1-10; *if a Eucharist:* Luke 9.51-62

A reading from the prophecy of Jeremiah. (11.1-14)

The word that came to Jeremiah from the Lord: Hear the words of this covenant, and speak to the people of Judah and the inhabitants of Jerusalem. You shall say to them, Thus says the Lord, the God of Israel: Cursed be anyone who does not heed the words of this covenant, which I commanded your ancestors when I brought them out of the land of Egypt, from the iron-smelter, saying, Listen to my voice, and do all that I command you. So shall you be my people, and I will be your God, that I may perform the oath that I swore to your ancestors, to give them a land flowing with milk and honey, as at this day. Then I answered, 'So be it, Lord.'

And the Lord said to me: Proclaim all these words in the cities of Judah, and in the streets of Jerusalem: Hear the words of this covenant and do them. For I solemnly warned your ancestors when I brought them up out of the land of Egypt, warning them persistently, even to this day, saying, Obey my voice. Yet they did not obey or incline their ear, but everyone walked in the stubbornness of an evil will. So I brought upon them all the words of this covenant, which I commanded them to do, but they did not.

And the Lord said to me: Conspiracy exists among the people of Judah and the inhabitants of Jerusalem. They have turned back to the iniquities of their ancestors of old, who refused to heed my words; they have gone after other gods to serve them; the house of Israel and the house of Judah have broken the covenant that I made with their ancestors. Therefore, thus says the Lord, assuredly I am going to bring disaster upon them that they cannot escape; though they cry out to me, I will not listen to them. Then the cities of Judah and the inhabitants of Jerusalem will go and cry out to the gods to whom they make offerings, but they will never save them in the time of their trouble. For your gods have become as many as your towns, O Judah; and as many as the streets of Jerusalem are the altars to shame that you have set up, altars to make offerings to Baal.

As for you, do not pray for this people, or lift up a cry or prayer on their behalf, for I will not listen when they call to me in the time of their trouble.

A reading from the Letter of Paul to the Romans. (13.1-10)

Let every person be subject to the governing authorities; for there is no authority except from God, and those authorities that exist have been instituted by God. Therefore whoever resists authority resists what God has appointed, and those who resist will incur judgement. For rulers are not a terror to good conduct, but to bad. Do you wish to have no fear of the authority? Then do what is good, and you will receive its approval; for it is God's servant for your good. But if you do what is wrong, you should be afraid, for the authority does not bear the sword in vain! It is the servant of God to execute wrath on the wrongdoer. Therefore one must be subject, not only because of wrath but also because of conscience. For the same reason you also pay taxes, for the authorities are God's servants, busy with this very thing. Pay to all what is due to them – taxes to whom taxes are due, revenue to whom revenue is due, respect to whom respect is due, honour to whom honour is due.

Owe no one anything, except to love one another; for the one who loves another has fulfilled the law. The commandments, 'You shall not commit adultery; You shall not murder; You shall not steal; You shall not covet'; and any other commandment, are summed up in this word, 'Love your neighbour as yourself.' Love does no wrong to a neighbour; therefore, love is the fulfilling of the law.

If a Eucharist:
Hear the gospel of our Lord Jesus Christ according to Luke. (9.51-62)

When the days drew near for Jesus to be taken up, he set his face to go to Jerusalem. And he sent messengers ahead of him. On their way they entered a village of the Samaritans to make ready for him; but they did not receive him, because his face was set towards Jerusalem. When his disciples James and John saw it, they said, 'Lord, do you want us to command fire to come down from heaven and consume them?' But he turned and rebuked them. Then they went on to another village.

As they were going along the road, someone said to him, 'I will follow you wherever you go.' And Jesus said to him, 'Foxes have holes, and birds of the air have nests; but the Son of Man has nowhere to lay his head.' To another he said, 'Follow me.' But he said, 'Lord, first let me go and bury my father.' But Jesus said to him, 'Let the dead bury their own dead; but as for you, go and proclaim the kingdom of God.' Another said, 'I will follow you, Lord; but let me first say farewell to those at my home.' Jesus said to him, 'No one who puts a hand to the plough and looks back is fit for the kingdom of God.'

This is the gospel of the Lord.

Third Service
Ps 56; Deuteronomy 15.1-11; Acts 27.[13-32] 33-44

A reading from the book Deuteronomy. *(15.1-11)*

Moses said to all Israel: Every seventh year you shall grant a remission of debts.   And this is the manner of the remission: every creditor shall remit the claim that is held against a neighbour, not exacting it from a neighbour who is a member of the community, because the Lord's remission has been proclaimed.   From a foreigner you may exact it, but you must remit your claim on whatever any member of your community owes you.   There will, however, be no one in need among you, because the Lord is sure to bless you in the land that the Lord your God is giving you as a possession to occupy, if only you will obey the Lord your God by diligently observing this entire commandment that I command you today.   When the Lord your God has blessed you, as he promised you, you will lend to many nations, but you will not borrow; you will rule over many nations, but they will not rule over you.

If there is among you anyone in need, a member of your community in any of your towns within the land that the Lord your God is giving you, do not be hard-hearted or tight-fisted towards your needy neighbour.   You should rather open your hand, willingly lending enough to meet the need, whatever it may be.   Be careful that you do not entertain a mean thought, thinking, 'The seventh year, the year of remission, is near', and therefore view your needy neighbour with hostility and give nothing; your neighbour might cry to the Lord against you, and you would incur guilt.   Give liberally and be ungrudging when you do so, for on this account the Lord your God will bless you in all your work and in all that you undertake.   Since there will never cease to be some in need on the earth, I therefore command you, 'Open your hand to the poor and needy neighbour in your land.'

A reading from the Acts of the Apostles. *(27.[13-32] 33-44)*

[Paul's captors hoped to sail for Pheonix in Crete, and when a moderate south wind began to blow, they thought they could achieve their purpose; so they weighed anchor and began to sail past Crete, close to the shore.   But soon a violent wind, called the northeaster, rushed down from Crete.   Since the ship was caught and could not be turned with its head to the wind, we gave way to it and were driven.   By running under the lee of a small island called Cauda we were scarcely able to get the ship's boat under control.   After hoisting it up they took measures to undergird the ship; then, fearing that they would run on the Syrtis, they lowered the sea-anchor and so were driven. We were being pounded by the storm so violently that on the next day they began to throw the cargo overboard, and on the third day with their own hands they threw the ship's tackle overboard. When neither sun nor stars appeared for many days, and no small tempest raged, all hope of our being saved was at last abandoned.

Since they had been without food for a long time, Paul then stood up among them and said, 'Men, you should have listened to me and not have set sail from Crete and thereby avoided this damage and loss. I urge you now to keep up your courage, for there will be no loss of life among you, but only of the ship. For last night there stood by me an angel of the God to whom I belong and whom I worship, and he said, "Do not be afraid, Paul; you must stand before the emperor; and indeed, God has granted safety to all those who are sailing with you." So keep up your courage, men, for I have faith in God that it will be exactly as I have been told. But we will have to run aground on some island.'

When the fourteenth night had come, as we were drifting across the sea of Adria, about midnight the sailors suspected that they were nearing land. So they took soundings and found twenty fathoms; a little farther on they took soundings again and found fifteen fathoms. Fearing that we might run on the rocks, they let down four anchors from the stern and prayed for day to come. But when the sailors tried to escape from the ship and had lowered the boat into the sea, on the pretext of putting out anchors from the bow, Paul said to the centurion and the soldiers, 'Unless these men stay in the ship, you cannot be saved.' Then the soldiers cut away the ropes of the boat and set it adrift.]

[33] Just before daybreak, Paul urged all of them to take some food, saying, 'Today is the fourteenth day that you have been in suspense and remaining without food, having eaten nothing. Therefore I urge you to take some food, for it will help you survive; for none of you will lose a hair from your heads.' After he had said this, he took bread; and giving thanks to God in the presence of all, he broke it and began to eat. Then all of them were encouraged and took food for themselves (we were in all two hundred and seventy-six persons in the ship). After they had satisfied their hunger, they lightened the ship by throwing the wheat into the sea.

In the morning they did not recognize the land, but they noticed a bay with a beach, on which they planned to run the ship ashore, if they could. So they cast off the anchors and left them in the sea. At the same time they loosened the ropes that tied the steering-oars; then hoisting the foresail to the wind, they made for the beach. But striking a reef, they ran the ship aground; the bow stuck and remained immovable, but the stern was being broken up by the force of the waves. The soldiers' plan was to kill the prisoners, so that none might swim away and escape; but the centurion, wishing to save Paul, kept them from carrying out their plan. He ordered those who could swim to jump overboard first and make for the land, and the rest to follow, some on planks and others on pieces of the ship. And so it was that all were brought safely to land.

Proper 9

Sunday between 3 & 9 July inclusive

Principal Service

Continuous	*Related*
2 Samuel 5.1-5,9-10	Ezekiel 2.1-5
Ps 48	Ps 123

2 Corinthians 12.2-10
Mark 6.1-13

A reading from the Second Book of Samuel. *(5.1-5,9-10)*

All the tribes of Israel came to David at Hebron, and said, 'Look, we are your bone and flesh. For some time, while Saul was king over us, it was you who led out Israel and brought it in. The Lord said to you: It is you who shall be shepherd of my people Israel, you who shall be ruler over Israel.' So all the elders of Israel came to the king at Hebron; and King David made a covenant with them at Hebron before the Lord, and they anointed David king over Israel. David was thirty years old when he began to reign, and he reigned for forty years. At Hebron he reigned over Judah for seven years and six months; and at Jerusalem he reigned over all Israel and Judah for thirty-three years.
⁹ David occupied the stronghold, and named it the city of David. David built the city all around from the Millo inwards. And David became greater and greater, for the Lord, the God of hosts, was with him.

This is the word of the Lord.

Or:
A reading from the prophecy of Ezekiel. *(2.1-5)*

He said to me: O mortal, stand up on your feet, and I will speak with you. And when he spoke to me, a spirit entered into me and set me on my feet; and I heard him speaking to me. He said to me, Mortal, I am sending you to the people of Israel, to a nation of rebels who have rebelled against me; they and their ancestors have transgressed against me to this very day. The descendants are impudent and stubborn. I am sending you to them, and you shall say to them, 'Thus says the Lord God.' Whether they hear or refuse to hear (for they are a rebellious house), they shall know that there has been a prophet among them.

This is the word of the Lord.

A reading from the Second Letter of Paul to the Corinthians. *(12.2-10)*

I know a person in Christ who fourteen years ago was caught up to the third heaven – whether in the body or out of the body I do not know; God knows. And I know that such a person – whether in the body or out of the body I do not know; God knows – was caught up into Paradise and heard things that are not to be told, that no mortal is permitted to repeat. On behalf of such a one I will boast, but on my own behalf I will not boast, except of my weaknesses. But if I wish to boast, I will not be a fool, for I will be speaking the truth. But I refrain from it, so that no one may think better of me than what is seen in me or heard from me, even considering the exceptional character of the revelations. Therefore, to keep me from being too elated, a thorn was given to me in the flesh, a messenger of Satan to torment me, to keep me from being too elated. Three times I appealed to the Lord about this, that it would leave me, but he said to me, 'My grace is sufficient for you, for power is made perfect in weakness.' So, I will boast all the more gladly of my weaknesses, so that the power of Christ may dwell in me. Therefore I am content with weaknesses, insults, hardships, persecutions, and calamities for the sake of Christ; for whenever I am weak, then I am strong.

This is the word of the Lord.

Hear the gospel of our Lord Jesus Christ according to Mark. *(6.1-13)*

Jesus came to his home town, and his disciples followed him. On the sabbath he began to teach in the synagogue, and many who heard him were astounded. They said, 'Where did this man get all this? What is this wisdom that has been given to him? What deeds of power are being done by his hands! Is not this the carpenter, the son of Mary and brother of James and Joses and Judas and Simon, and are not his sisters here with us?' And they took offence at him. Then Jesus said to them, 'Prophets are not without honour, except in their home town, and among their own kin, and in their own house.' And he could do no deed of power there, except that he laid his hands on a few sick people and cured them. And he was amazed at their unbelief.

Then he went about among the villages teaching. He called the twelve and began to send them out two by two, and gave them authority over the unclean spirits. He ordered them to take nothing for their journey except a staff; no bread, no bag, no money in their belts; but to wear sandals and not to put on two tunics. He said to them, 'Wherever you enter a house, stay there until you leave the place. If any place will not welcome you and they refuse to hear you, as you leave, shake off the dust that is on your feet as a testimony against them.' So they went out and proclaimed that all should repent. They cast out many demons, and anointed with oil many who were sick and cured them.

This is the gospel of the Lord.

Second Service
Pss [63] 64; Jeremiah 20.1-11a;
Romans 14.1-17; *if a Eucharist:* Luke 10.1-11,16-20

A reading from the prophecy of Jeremiah. (20.1-11a)

The priest Pashhur son of Immer, who was chief officer in the house of the Lord, heard Jeremiah prophesying in the court of the Lord's house in Topheth that the Lord of hosts would bring disaster upon the city, and Pashhur struck the prophet Jeremiah, and put him in the stocks that were in the upper Benjamin Gate of the house of the Lord. The next morning when Pashhur released Jeremiah from the stocks, Jeremiah said to him, The Lord has named you not Pashhur but 'Terror-all-around.' For thus says the Lord: I am making you a terror to yourself and to all your friends; and they shall fall by the sword of their enemies while you look on. And I will give all Judah into the hand of the king of Babylon; he shall carry them captive to Babylon, and shall kill them with the sword. I will give all the wealth of this city, all its gains, all its prized belongings, and all the treasures of the kings of Judah into the hand of their enemies, who shall plunder them, and seize them, and carry them to Babylon. And you, Pashhur, and all who live in your house, shall go into captivity, and to

Babylon you shall go; there you shall die, and there you shall be buried, you and all your friends, to whom you have prophesied falsely.

O Lord, you have enticed me,
and I was enticed;
you have overpowered me,
and you have prevailed.
I have become a laughing-stock all day long;
everyone mocks me.
For whenever I speak, I must cry out,
I must shout, 'Violence and destruction!'
For the word of the Lord has become for me
a reproach and derision all day long.
If I say, 'I will not mention him,
or speak any more in his name',
then within me there is something like a burning fire
shut up in my bones;
I am weary with holding it in,
and I cannot.
For I hear many whispering:
'Terror is all around!
Denounce him! Let us denounce him!'
All my close friends are watching for me to stumble.
'Perhaps he can be enticed,
and we can prevail against him,
and take our revenge on him.'
But the Lord is with me like a dread warrior;
therefore my persecutors will stumble,
and they will not prevail.

A reading from the Letter of Paul to the Romans. (14.1-17)

Welcome those who are weak in faith, but not for the purpose of quarrelling over opinions. Some believe in eating anything, while the weak eat only vegetables. Those who eat must not despise those who abstain, and those who abstain must not pass judgement on those who eat; for God has welcomed them. Who are you to pass judgement on servants of another? It is before their own lord that they stand or fall. And they will be upheld, for the Lord is able to make them stand.

Some judge one day to be better than another, while others judge all days to be alike. Let all be fully convinced in their own minds. Those who observe the day, observe it in honour of the Lord. Also those who eat, eat in honour of the Lord, since they give thanks to God; while those who abstain, abstain in honour of the Lord and give thanks to God.

We do not live to ourselves, and we do not die to ourselves. If we live, we live to the Lord, and if we die, we die to the Lord; so then, whether we live or whether we die, we are the Lord's. For to this end Christ died and lived again, so that he might be Lord of both the dead and the living.

Why do you pass judgement on your brother or sister? Or you, why do you despise your brother or sister? For we will all stand before the judgement seat of God. For it is written,

'As I live, says the Lord, every knee shall bow to me,

and every tongue shall give praise to God.'

So then, each of us will be accountable to God.

Let us therefore no longer pass judgement on one another, but resolve instead never to put a stumbling-block or hindrance in the way of another. I know and am persuaded in the Lord Jesus that nothing is unclean in itself; but it is unclean for anyone who thinks it unclean. If your brother or sister is being injured by what you eat, you are no longer walking in love. Do not let what you eat cause the ruin of one for whom Christ died. So do not let your good be spoken of as evil. For the kingdom of God is not food and drink but righteousness and peace and joy in the Holy Spirit.

If a Eucharist:

Hear the gospel of our Lord Jesus Christ according to Luke.

(10.1-11, 16-20)

The Lord Jesus appointed seventy others and sent them on ahead of him in pairs to every town and place where he himself intended to go. He said to them, 'The harvest is plentiful, but the labourers are few; therefore ask the Lord of the harvest to send out labourers into his harvest. Go on your way. See, I am sending you out like lambs into the midst of wolves. Carry no purse, no bag, no sandals; and greet no one on the road. Whatever house you enter, first say, "Peace to this house!" And if anyone is there who shares in peace, your peace will rest on that person; but if not, it will return to you. Remain in the same house, eating and drinking whatever they provide, for the labourer deserves to be paid. Do not move about from house to house. Whenever you enter a town and its people welcome you, eat what is set before you; cure the sick who are there, and say to them, "The kingdom of God has come near to you." But whenever you enter a town and they do not welcome you, go out into its streets and say, "Even the dust of your town that clings to our feet, we wipe off in protest against you. Yet know this: the kingdom of God has come near."

[16] 'Whoever listens to you listens to me, and whoever rejects you rejects me, and whoever rejects me rejects the one who sent me.'

The seventy returned with joy, saying, 'Lord, in your name even the demons submit to us!' He said to them, 'I watched Satan fall from heaven like a flash of lightning. See, I have given you authority to tread on snakes and scorpions, and over all the power of the enemy; and nothing will hurt you. Nevertheless, do not rejoice at this, that the spirits submit to you, but rejoice that your names are written in heaven.'

This is the gospel of the Lord.

Third Service
Ps 57; Deuteronomy 24.10-22; Acts 28.1-16

A reading from the book Deuteronomy. (24.10-22)

Moses continued to speak to all Israel: When you make your neighbour a loan of any kind, you shall not go into the house to take the pledge. You shall wait outside, while the person to whom you are making the loan brings the pledge out to you. If the person is poor, you shall not sleep in the garment given you as the pledge. You shall give the pledge back by sunset, so that your neighbour may sleep in the cloak and bless you; and it will be to your credit before the Lord your God.

You shall not withhold the wages of poor and needy labourers, whether other Israelites or aliens who reside in your land in one of your towns. You shall pay them their wages daily before sunset, because they are poor and their livelihood depends on them; otherwise they might cry to the Lord against you, and you would incur guilt.

Parents shall not be put to death for their children, nor shall children be put to death for their parents; only for their own crimes may persons be put to death.

You shall not deprive a resident alien or an orphan of justice; you shall not take a widow's garment in pledge. Remember that you were a slave in Egypt and the Lord your God redeemed you from there; therefore I command you to do this.

When you reap your harvest in your field and forget a sheaf in the field, you shall not go back to get it; it shall be left for the alien, the orphan, and the widow, so that the Lord your God may bless you in all your undertakings. When you beat your olive trees, do not strip what is left; it shall be for the alien, the orphan, and the widow.

When you gather the grapes of your vineyard, do not glean what is left; it shall be for the alien, the orphan, and the widow. Remember that you were a slave in the land of Egypt; therefore I am commanding you to do this.

A reading from the Acts of the Apostles. (28.1-16)

After we had reached safety, we then learned that the island was called Malta. The natives showed us unusual kindness. Since it had begun to rain and was cold, they kindled a fire and welcomed all of us round it. Paul had gathered a bundle of brushwood and was putting it on the fire, when a viper, driven out by the heat, fastened itself on his hand. When the natives saw the creature hanging from his hand, they said to one another, 'This man must be a murderer; though he has escaped from the sea, justice has not allowed him to live.' He, however, shook off the creature into the fire and suffered no harm. They were expecting him to swell up or drop dead, but after they had waited a long time and saw that nothing unusual had happened to him, they changed their minds and began to say that he was a god.

Now in the neighbourhood of that place were lands belonging to the leading man of the island, named Publius, who received us and entertained us hospitably for three days. It so happened that the father of Publius lay sick in bed with fever and dysentery. Paul visited him and cured him by praying and putting his hands on him. After this happened, the rest of the people on the island who had diseases also came and were cured. They bestowed many honours on us, and when we were about to sail, they put on board all the provisions we needed.

Three months later we set sail on a ship that had wintered at the island, an Alexandrian ship with the Twin Brothers as its figurehead. We put in at Syracuse and stayed there for three days; then we weighed anchor and came to Rhegium. After one day there a south wind sprang up, and on the second day we came to Puteoli. There we found believers and were invited to stay with them for seven days. And so we came to Rome. The believers from there, when they heard of us, came as far as the Forum of Appius and Three Taverns to meet us. On seeing them, Paul thanked God and took courage.

When we came into Rome, Paul was allowed to live by himself, with the soldier who was guarding him.

Proper 10

Sunday between 10 & 16 July inclusive

Principal Service

Continuous	*Related*
2 Samuel 6.1-5,12*b*-19	Amos 7.7-15
Ps 24	Ps 85.8-13
	Ephesians 1.3-14
	Mark 6.14-29

A reading from the Second Book of Samuel. (6.1-5,12b-19)

David again gathered all the chosen men of Israel, thirty thousand. David and all the people with him set out and went from Baale-judah, to bring up from there the ark of God, which is called by the name of the Lord of hosts who is enthroned on the cherubim. They carried the ark of God on a new cart, and brought it out of the house of Abinadab, which was on the hill. Uzzah and Ahio, the sons of Abinadab, were driving the new cart with the ark of God; and Ahio went in front of the ark. David and all the house of Israel were dancing before the Lord with all their might, with songs and lyres and harps and tambourines and castanets and cymbals.
¹²ᵇ David went and brought up the ark of God from the house of Obed-edom to the city of David with rejoicing; and when those who bore the ark of the Lord had gone six paces, he sacrificed an ox and a fatling. David danced before the Lord with all his might; David was girded with a linen ephod. So David and all the house of Israel brought up the ark of the Lord with shouting, and with the sound of the trumpet.

As the ark of the Lord came into the city of David, Michal daughter of Saul looked out of the window, and saw King David leaping and dancing before the Lord; and she despised him in her heart.

They brought in the ark of the Lord, and set it in its place, inside the tent that David had pitched for it; and David offered burnt-offerings and offerings of well-being before the Lord. When David had finished offering the burnt-offerings and the offerings of well-being, he blessed the people in the name of the Lord of hosts, and distributed food among all the people, the whole multitude of Israel, both men and women, to each a cake of bread, a portion of meat, and a cake of raisins. Then all the people went back to their homes.

This is the word of the Lord.

Or:

A reading from the prophecy of Amos. (7.7-15)

This is what the Lord showed me: the Lord was standing beside a wall built with a plumb-line, with a plumb-line in his hand. And the Lord said to me, 'Amos, what do you see?' And I said, 'A plumb-line.' Then the Lord said,

'See, I am setting a plumb-line
    in the midst of my people Israel;
    I will never again pass them by;
the high places of Isaac shall be made desolate,
    and the sanctuaries of Israel shall be laid waste,
    and I will rise against the house of Jeroboam with the sword.'

Then Amaziah, the priest of Bethel, sent to King Jeroboam of Israel, saying, 'Amos has conspired against you in the very centre of the house of Israel; the land is not able to bear all his words. For thus Amos has said,

"Jeroboam shall die by the sword,
    and Israel must go into exile
    away from his land."'

And Amaziah said to Amos, 'O seer, go, flee away to the land of Judah, earn your bread there, and prophesy there; but never again prophesy at Bethel, for it is the king's sanctuary, and it is a temple of the kingdom.'

Then Amos answered Amaziah, 'I am no prophet, nor a prophet's son; but I am a herdsman, and a dresser of sycomore trees, and the Lord took me from following the flock, and the Lord said to me, "Go, prophesy to my people Israel."'

This is the word of the Lord.

A reading from the Letter of Paul to the Ephesians. (1.3-14)

Blessèd be the God and Father of our Lord Jesus Christ, who has blessed us in Christ with every spiritual blessing in the heavenly places, just as he chose us in Christ before the foundation of the world to be holy and blameless before him in love. He destined us for adoption as his children through Jesus Christ, according to the good pleasure of his will, to the praise of his glorious grace that he freely bestowed on us in the Belovèd. In him we have redemption through his blood, the forgiveness of our trespasses, according to the riches of his grace that he lavished on us. With all wisdom and insight he has made known to us the mystery of his will, according to his good pleasure that he set forth in Christ, as a plan for the fullness of time, to gather up all things in him, things in heaven and things on earth. In Christ we have also obtained an inheritance, having been destined according to the purpose of him who accomplishes all things according to his counsel and will, so that we, who were the first to set our hope on Christ, might live for the praise of his glory. In him you also, when you had heard the word of truth, the gospel of your salvation, and had believed in him, were marked with the seal of the promised Holy Spirit; this is the pledge of our inheritance towards redemption as God's own people, to the praise of his glory.

This is the word of the Lord.

Hear the gospel of our Lord Jesus Christ according to Mark. (6.14-29)

King Herod heard of Jesus' disciples casting out demons and anointing with oil many who were sick and curing them, for Jesus' name had become known. Some were saying, 'John the baptizer has been raised from the dead; and for this reason these powers are at work in him.' But others said, 'It is Elijah.' And others said, 'It is a prophet, like one of the prophets of old.' But when Herod heard of it, he said, 'John, whom I beheaded, has been raised.'

For Herod himself had sent men who arrested John, bound him, and put him in prison on account of Herodias, his brother Philip's wife, because Herod had married her. For John had been telling Herod, 'It is not lawful for you to have your brother's wife.' And Herodias had a grudge against him, and wanted to kill him. But she could not, for Herod feared John, knowing that he was a righteous and holy man, and he protected him. When he heard him, he was greatly perplexed; and yet he liked to listen to him. But an opportunity came when Herod on his birthday gave a banquet for his courtiers and officers and for the leaders of Galilee. When his daughter Herodias came in and danced, she pleased Herod and his guests; and the king said to the girl, 'Ask me for whatever you wish, and I will give it.' And he solemnly swore to her, 'Whatever you ask me, I will give you, even half of my kingdom.' She went out and said to her mother, 'What should I ask for?' She replied, 'The head of John the baptizer.' Immediately she rushed back to the king and requested, 'I want you to give me at once the head of John the Baptist on a platter.' The king was deeply grieved; yet out of regard for his oaths and for the guests, he did not want to refuse her. Immediately the king sent a soldier of the guard with orders to bring John's head. He went and beheaded him in the prison, brought his head on a platter, and gave it to the girl. Then the girl gave it to her mother. When his disciples heard about it, they came and took his body, and laid it in a tomb.

This is the gospel of the Lord.

Second Service

Ps 66 *or* 66.1-9; Job 4.1; 5.6-27 *or* Ecclesiasticus 4.11-31;
Romans 15.14-29; *if a Eucharist:* Luke 10.25-37

A reading from the Book of Job. *(4.1 & 5.6-27)*

Eliphaz the Temanite then answered Job, who had cursed the day of his birth:

5.6 'Misery does not come from the earth,
    nor does trouble sprout from the ground;
but human beings are born to trouble
    just as sparks fly upward.

'As for me, I would seek God,
    and to God I would commit my cause.
He does great things and unsearchable,
    marvellous things without number.
He gives rain on the earth
    and sends waters on the fields;
he sets on high those who are lowly,
    and those who mourn are lifted to safety.
He frustrates the devices of the crafty,
    so that their hands achieve no success.
He takes the wise in their own craftiness;
    and the schemes of the wily are brought to a quick end.
They meet with darkness in the daytime,
    and grope at noonday as in the night.
But he saves the needy from the sword of their mouth,
    from the hand of the mighty.
So the poor have hope,
    and injustice shuts its mouth.

'How happy is the one whom God reproves;
    therefore do not despise the discipline of the Almighty.
For he wounds, but he binds up;
    he strikes, but his hands heal.
He will deliver you from six troubles;
    in seven no harm shall touch you.
In famine he will redeem you from death,
    and in war from the power of the sword.
You shall be hidden from the scourge of the tongue,
    and shall not fear destruction when it comes.
At destruction and famine you shall laugh,
    and shall not fear the wild animals of the earth.
For you shall be in league with the stones of the field,

and the wild animals shall be at peace with you.
You shall know that your tent is safe,
　　you shall inspect your fold and miss nothing.
You shall know that your descendants will be many,
　　and your offspring like the grass of the earth.
You shall come to your grave in ripe old age,
　　as a shock of grain comes up to the threshing-floor
　　　　in its season.
See, we have searched this out; it is true.
　　Hear, and know it for yourself.'

Or:

A reading from the book Ecclesiasticus. (4.11-31)

Wisdom teaches her children
　　and gives help to those who seek her.
Whoever loves her loves life,
　　and those who seek her from early morning are filled with joy.
Whoever holds her fast inherits glory,
　　and the Lord blesses the place she enters.
Those who serve her minister to the Holy One;
　　the Lord loves those who love her.
Those who obey her will judge the nations,
　　and all who listen to her will live secure.
If they remain faithful, they will inherit her;
　　their descendants will also obtain her.
For at first she will walk with them on tortuous paths;
　　she will bring fear and dread upon them,
and will torment them by her discipline
　　until she trusts them,
and she will test them with her ordinances.
Then she will come straight back to them again
　　　　and gladden them,
　　and will reveal her secrets to them.
If they go astray she will forsake them,
　　and hand them over to their ruin.

Watch for the opportune time, and beware of evil,
　　and do not be ashamed to be yourself.
For there is a shame that leads to sin,
　　and there is a shame that is glory and favour.
Do not show partiality, to your own harm,
　　or deference, to your downfall.
Do not refrain from speaking at the proper moment,

and do not hide your wisdom.
For wisdom becomes known through speech,
    and education through the words of the tongue.
Never speak against the truth,
    but be ashamed of your ignorance.
Do not be ashamed to confess your sins,
    and do not try to stop the current of a river.
Do not subject yourself to a fool,
    or show partiality to a ruler.
Fight to the death for truth,
    and the Lord God will fight for you.

Do not be reckless in your speech,
    or sluggish and remiss in your deeds.
Do not be like a lion in your home,
    or suspicious of your servants.
Do not let your hand be stretched out to receive
    and closed when it is time to give.

A reading from the Letter of Paul to the Romans. (15.14-29)

I myself feel confident about you, my brothers and sisters, that you yourselves are full of goodness, filled with all knowledge, and able to instruct one another. Nevertheless, on some points I have written to you rather boldly by way of reminder, because of the grace given me by God to be a minister of Christ Jesus to the Gentiles in the priestly service of the gospel of God, so that the offering of the Gentiles may be acceptable, sanctified by the Holy Spirit. In Christ Jesus, then, I have reason to boast of my work for God. For I will not venture to speak of anything except what Christ has accomplished through me to win obedience from the Gentiles, by word and deed, by the power of signs and wonders, by the power of the Spirit of God, so that from Jerusalem and as far around as Illyricum I have fully proclaimed the good news of Christ. Thus I make it my ambition to proclaim the good news, not where Christ has already been named, so that I do not build on someone else's foundation, but as it is written,
    'Those who have never been told of him shall see,
    and those who have never heard of him shall understand.'

This is the reason that I have so often been hindered from coming to you. But now, with no further place for me in these regions, I desire, as I have for many years, to come to you when I go to Spain. For I do hope to see you on my journey and to be sent on by you, once I have enjoyed your company for a little while. At present, however, I am going to Jerusalem in a ministry to the saints; for Macedonia and

Achaia have been pleased to share their resources with the poor among the saints at Jerusalem. They were pleased to do this, and indeed they owe it to them; for if the Gentiles have come to share in their spiritual blessings, they ought also to be of service to them in material things. So, when I have completed this, and have delivered to them what has been collected, I will set out by way of you to Spain; and I know that when I come to you, I will come in the fullness of the blessing of Christ.

If a Eucharist:
Hear the gospel of our Lord Jesus Christ according to Luke. *(10.25-37)*

A lawyer stood up to test Jesus. 'Teacher,' he said, 'what must I do to inherit eternal life?' He said to him, 'What is written in the law? What do you read there?' He answered, 'You shall love the Lord your God with all your heart, and with all your soul, and with all your strength, and with all your mind; and your neighbour as yourself.' And he said to him, 'You have given the right answer; do this, and you will live.'

But wanting to justify himself, he asked Jesus, 'And who is my neighbour?' Jesus replied, 'A man was going down from Jerusalem to Jericho, and fell into the hands of robbers, who stripped him, beat him, and went away, leaving him half dead. Now by chance a priest was going down that road; and when he saw him, he passed by on the other side. So likewise a Levite, when he came to the place and saw him, passed by on the other side. But a Samaritan while travelling came near him; and when he saw him, he was moved with pity. He went to him and bandaged his wounds, having poured oil and wine on them. Then he put him on his own animal, brought him to an inn, and took care of him. The next day he took out two denarii, gave them to the innkeeper, and said, "Take care of him; and when I come back, I will repay you whatever more you spend." Which of these three, do you think, was a neighbour to the man who fell into the hands of the robbers?' He said, 'The one who showed him mercy.' Jesus said to him, 'Go and do likewise.'

This is the gospel of the Lord.

Third Service
Ps 65; Deuteronomy 28.1-14; Acts 28.17-30

A reading from the book Deuteronomy. *(28.1-14)*

Moses continued to speak to all Israel: If you will only obey the Lord your God, by diligently observing all his commandments that I am commanding you today, the Lord your God will set you high above all the nations of the earth; all these blessings shall come upon you and overtake you, if you obey the Lord your God:
   Blessèd shall you be in the city,
      and blessèd shall you be in the field.
   Blessèd shall be the fruit of your womb, the fruit of your ground,
      and the fruit of your livestock,
         both the increase of your cattle and the issue of your flock.
   Blessèd shall be your basket and your kneading-bowl.
   Blessèd shall you be when you come in,
      and blessèd shall you be when you go out.
The Lord will cause your enemies who rise against you to be defeated before you; they shall come out against you one way, and flee before you seven ways. The Lord will command the blessing upon you in your barns, and in all that you undertake; he will bless you in the land that the Lord your God is giving you. The Lord will establish you as his holy people, as he has sworn to you, if you keep the commandments of the Lord your God and walk in his ways. All the peoples of the earth shall see that you are called by the name of the Lord, and they shall be afraid of you. The Lord will make you abound in prosperity, in the fruit of your womb, in the fruit of your livestock, and in the fruit of your ground in the land that the Lord swore to your ancestors to give you. The Lord will open for you his rich storehouse, the heavens, to give the rain of your land in its season and to bless all your undertakings. You will lend to many nations, but you will not borrow. The Lord will make you the head, and not the tail; you shall be only at the top, and not at the bottom – if you obey the commandments of the Lord your God, which I am commanding you today, by diligently observing them, and if you do not turn aside from any of the words that I am commanding you today, either to the right or to the left, following other gods to serve them.

A reading from the Acts of the Apostles. *(28.17-31)*

Paul called together the local leaders of the Jews in Rome. When they had assembled, he said to them, 'Brothers, though I had done nothing against our people or the customs of our ancestors, yet I was arrested in Jerusalem and handed over to the Romans. When they had examined me, the Romans wanted to release me, because there was no reason for the death penalty in my case. But when the Jews objected, I was compelled to appeal to the emperor – even though I had no charge to bring against my nation. For this reason therefore I have asked to see you and speak with you, since it is for the sake of the hope of Israel that I am bound with this chain.' They replied, 'We have received no letters from Judea about you, and none of the brothers coming here has reported or spoken anything evil about you. But we would like to hear from you what you think, for with regard to this sect we know that everywhere it is spoken against.'

After they had fixed a day to meet him, they came to him at his lodgings in great numbers. From morning until evening he explained the matter to them, testifying to the kingdom of God and trying to convince them about Jesus both from the law of Moses and from the prophets. Some were convinced by what he had said, while others refused to believe. So they disagreed with each other; and as they were leaving, Paul made one further statement: 'The Holy Spirit was right in saying to your ancestors through the prophet Isaiah,

"Go to this people and say,
You will indeed listen, but never understand,
    and you will indeed look, but never perceive.
For this people's heart has grown dull,
    and their ears are hard of hearing,
    and they have shut their eyes;
so that they might not look with their eyes,
    and listen with their ears,
    and understand with their heart and turn –
    and I would heal them."

Let it be known to you then that this salvation of God has been sent to the Gentiles; they will listen.'

Paul lived there for two whole years at his own expense and welcomed all who came to him.

Proper 11

Sunday between 17 & 23 July inclusive

Principal Service

Continuous	*Related*
2 Samuel 7.1-14*a*	Jeremiah 23.1-6
Ps 89.20-37	Ps 23

Ephesians 2.11-22
Mark 6.30-34,53-56

A reading from the Second Book of Samuel. *(7.1-14a)*

When King David was settled in his house, and the Lord had given him rest from all his enemies around him, he said to the prophet Nathan, 'See now, I am living in a house of cedar, but the ark of God stays in a tent.' Nathan said to the king, 'Go, do all that you have in mind; for the Lord is with you.'

But that same night the word of the Lord came to Nathan: Go and tell my servant David: Thus says the Lord: Are you the one to build me a house to live in? I have not lived in a house since the day I brought up the people of Israel from Egypt to this day, but I have been moving about in a tent and a tabernacle. Wherever I have moved about among all the people of Israel, did I ever speak a word with any of the tribal leaders of Israel, whom I commanded to shepherd my people Israel, saying, 'Why have you not built me a house of cedar?' Now therefore thus you shall say to my servant David: Thus says the Lord of hosts: I took you from the pasture, from following the sheep to be prince over my people Israel; and I have been with you wherever you went, and have cut off all your enemies from before you; and I will make for you a great name, like the name of the great ones of the earth. And I will appoint a place for my people Israel and will plant them, so that they may live in their own place, and be disturbed no more; and evildoers shall afflict them no more, as formerly, from the time that I appointed judges over my people Israel; and I will give you rest from all your enemies. Moreover, the Lord declares to you that the Lord will make you a house. When your days are fulfilled and you lie down with your ancestors, I will raise up your offspring after you, who shall come forth from your body, and I will establish his kingdom. He shall build a house for my name, and I will establish the throne of his kingdom for ever. I will be a father to him, and he shall be a son to me.

This is the word of the Lord.

Or:

A reading from the prophecy of Jeremiah. *(23.1-6)*

Woe to the shepherds who destroy and scatter the sheep of my pasture! says the Lord. Therefore, thus says the Lord, the God of Israel, concerning the shepherds who shepherd my people: It is you who have scattered my flock, and have driven them away, and you have not attended to them. So I will attend to you for your evil doings, says the Lord. Then I myself will gather the remnant of my flock out of all the lands where I have driven them, and I will bring them back to their fold, and they shall be fruitful and multiply. I will raise up shepherds over them who will shepherd them, and they shall not fear any longer, or be dismayed, nor shall any be missing, says the Lord.

The days are surely coming, says the Lord, when I will raise up for David a righteous Branch, and he shall reign as king and deal wisely, and shall execute justice and righteousness in the land. In his days Judah will be saved and Israel will live in safety. And this is the name by which he will be called: 'The Lord is our righteousness.'

This is the word of the Lord.

A reading from the Letter of Paul to the Ephesians. *(2.11-22)*

Remember that at one time you Gentiles by birth, called 'the uncircumcision' by those who are called 'the circumcision' – a physical circumcision made in the flesh by human hands – remember that you were at that time without Christ, being aliens from the commonwealth of Israel, and strangers to the covenants of promise, having no hope and without God in the world. But now in Christ Jesus you who once were far off have been brought near by the blood of Christ. For he is our peace; in his flesh he has made both groups into one and has broken down the dividing wall, that is, the hostility between us. He has abolished the law with its commandments and ordinances, so that he might create in himself one new humanity in place of the two, thus making peace, and might reconcile both groups to God in one body through the cross, thus putting to death that hostility through it. So he came and proclaimed peace to you who were far off and peace to those who were near; for through him both of us have access in one Spirit to the Father. So then you are no longer strangers and aliens, but you are citizens with the saints and also members of the household of God, built upon the foundation of the apostles and prophets, with Christ Jesus himself as the cornerstone. In him the whole structure is joined together and grows into a holy temple in the Lord; in whom you also are built together spiritually into a dwelling-place for God.

This is the word of the Lord.

Hear the gospel of our Lord Jesus Christ according to Mark.
(6.30-34,53-56)

The apostles gathered around Jesus, and told him all that they had done and taught. He said to them, 'Come away to a deserted place all by yourselves and rest a while.' For many were coming and going, and they had no leisure even to eat. And they went away in the boat to a deserted place by themselves. Now many saw them going and recognized them, and they hurried there on foot from all the towns and arrived ahead of them. As he went ashore, he saw a great crowd; and he had compassion for them, because they were like sheep without a shepherd; and he began to teach them many things. ⁵³ When they had crossed over, they came to land at Gennesaret and moored the boat. When they got out of the boat, people at once recognized him, and rushed about that whole region and began to bring the sick on mats to wherever they heard he was. And wherever he went, into villages or cities or farms, they laid the sick in the market-places, and begged him that they might touch even the fringe of his cloak; and all who touched it were healed.

This is the gospel of the Lord.

Second Service
Ps 73 *or* 73.21-28; Job 13.13 - 14.6 *or* Ecclesiasticus 18.1-14; Hebrews 2.5-18; *if a Eucharist:* Luke 10.38-42

A reading from the Book of Job. *(13.13 - 14.6)*

Job said,
   'Let me have silence, and I will speak,
      and let come on me what may.
   I will take my flesh in my teeth,
      and put my life in my hand.
   See, he will kill me; I have no hope;
      but I will defend my ways to his face.
   This will be my salvation,
      that the godless shall not come before him.
   Listen carefully to my words,
      and let my declaration be in your ears.
   I have indeed prepared my case;
      I know that I shall be vindicated.
   Who is there that will contend with me?
      For then I would be silent and die.
   Only grant two things to me,
      then I will not hide myself from your face:

withdraw your hand far from me,
 and do not let dread of you terrify me.
Then call, and I will answer;
 or let me speak, and you reply to me.
How many are my iniquities and my sins?
 Make me know my transgression and my sin.
Why do you hide your face,
 and count me as your enemy?
Will you frighten a windblown leaf
 and pursue dry chaff?
For you write bitter things against me,
 and make me reap the iniquities of my youth.
You put my feet in the stocks,
 and watch all my paths;
 you set a bound to the soles of my feet.
One wastes away like a rotten thing,
 like a garment that is moth-eaten.

'A mortal, born of woman, few of days and full of trouble,
 comes up like a flower and withers,
 flees like a shadow and does not last.
Do you fix your eyes on such a one?
 Do you bring me into judgement with you?
Who can bring a clean thing out of an unclean?
 No one can.
Since their days are determined,
 and the number of their months is known to you,
 and you have appointed the bounds that they cannot pass,
look away from them, and desist,
 that they may enjoy, like labourers, their days. '

Or:

A reading from the book Ecclesiasticus. (18.1-14)

He who lives for ever created the whole universe;
 the Lord alone is just.
To none has he given power to proclaim his works;
 and who can search out his mighty deeds?
Who can measure his majestic power?
 And who can fully recount his mercies?
It is not possible to diminish or increase them,
 nor is it possible to fathom the wonders of the Lord.
When human beings have finished,
 they are just beginning,

and when they stop,
    they are still perplexed.
What are human beings, and of what use are they?
    What is good in them, and what is evil?
The number of days in their life is great
    if they reach one hundred years.
Like a drop of water from the sea and a grain of sand,
    so are a few years among the days of eternity.
That is why the Lord is patient with them
    and pours out his mercy upon them.
He sees and recognizes that their end is miserable;
    therefore he grants them forgiveness all the more.
The compassion of human beings is for their neighbours,
    but the compassion of the Lord is for every living thing.
He rebukes and trains and teaches them,
    and turns them back, as a shepherd his flock.
He has compassion on those who accept his discipline
    and who are eager for his precepts.

A reading from the Letter to the Hebrews. (2.5-18)

God did not subject the coming world, about which we are speaking, to angels. But someone has testified somewhere,
    'What are human beings that you are mindful of them,
        or mortals, that you care for them?
    You have made them for a little while lower than the angels;
        you have crowned them with glory and honour,
        subjecting all things under their feet.'
Now in subjecting all things to them, God left nothing outside their control. As it is, we do not yet see everything in subjection to them, but we do see Jesus, who for a little while was made lower than the angels, now crowned with glory and honour because of the suffering of death, so that by the grace of God he might taste death for everyone.

It was fitting that God, for whom and through whom all things exist, in bringing many children to glory, should make the pioneer of their salvation perfect through sufferings. For the one who sanctifies and those who are sanctified all have one Father. For this reason Jesus is not ashamed to call them brothers and sisters, saying,
    'I will proclaim your name to my brothers and sisters,
        in the midst of the congregation I will praise you.'
And again,
    'I will put my trust in him.'

And again,

'Here am I and the children whom God has given me.'

Since, therefore, the children share flesh and blood, he himself like-wise shared the same things, so that through death he might destroy the one who has the power of death, that is, the devil, and free those who all their lives were held in slavery by the fear of death. For it is clear that he did not come to help angels, but the descendants of Abraham. Therefore he had to become like his brothers and sisters in every respect, so that he might be a merciful and faithful high priest in the service of God, to make a sacrifice of atonement for the sins of the people. Because he himself was tested by what he suffered, he is able to help those who are being tested.

If a Eucharist:
***Hear the gospel of our Lord Jesus Christ according to Luke.** (10.38-42)*

Jesus entered a certain village, where a woman named Martha wel-comed him into her home. She had a sister named Mary, who sat at the Lord's feet and listened to what he was saying. But Martha was distracted by her many tasks; so she came to him and asked, 'Lord, do you not care that my sister has left me to do all the work by myself? Tell her then to help me.' But the Lord answered her, 'Martha, Martha, you are worried and distracted by many things; there is need of only one thing. Mary has chosen the better part, which will not be taken away from her.'

This is the gospel of the Lord.

Third Service
Pss 67, 70; Deuteronomy 30.1-10; 1 Peter 3.8-18

A reading from the book Deuteronomy. (30.1-10)

Moses continued to address all Israel: When all these things have happened to you, the blessings and the curses that I have set before you, if you call them to mind among all the nations where the Lord your God has driven you, and return to the Lord your God, and you and your children obey him with all your heart and with all your soul, just as I am commanding you today, then the Lord your God will restore your fortunes and have compassion on you, gathering you again from all the peoples among whom the Lord your God has scattered you. Even if you are exiled to the ends of the world, from there the Lord your God will gather you, and from there he will bring you back. The Lord your God will bring you into the land that your ancestors possessed, and you will possess it; he will make you more prosperous and numerous than your ancestors.

Moreover, the Lord your God will circumcise your heart and the heart of your descendants, so that you will love the Lord your God with all your heart and with all your soul, in order that you may live. The Lord your God will put all these curses on your enemies and on the adversaries who took advantage of you. Then you shall again obey the Lord, observing all his commandments that I am commanding you today, and the Lord your God will make you abundantly prosperous in all your undertakings, in the fruit of your body, in the fruit of your livestock, and in the fruit of your soil. For the Lord will again take delight in prospering you, just as he delighted in prospering your ancestors, when you obey the Lord your God by observing his commandments and decrees that are written in this book of the law, because you turn to the Lord your God with all your heart and with all your soul.

A reading from the First Letter of Peter. (3.8-18)

Finally, all of you, have unity of spirit, sympathy, love for one another, a tender heart, and a humble mind. Do not repay evil for evil or abuse for abuse; but, on the contrary, repay with a blessing. It is for this that you were called – that you might inherit a blessing. For

'Those who desire life
    and desire to see good days,
let them keep their tongues from evil
    and their lips from speaking deceit;
let them turn away from evil and do good;
    let them seek peace and pursue it.
For the eyes of the Lord are on the righteous,
    and his ears are open to their prayer.
But the face of the Lord is against those who do evil.'

Now who will harm you if you are eager to do what is good? But even if you do suffer for doing what is right, you are blessed. Do not fear what they fear, and do not be intimidated, but in your hearts sanctify Christ as Lord. Always be ready to make your defence to anyone who demands from you an account of the hope that is in you; yet do it with gentleness and reverence. Keep your conscience clear, so that, when you are maligned, those who abuse you for your good conduct in Christ may be put to shame. For it is better to suffer for doing good, if suffering should be God's will, than to suffer for doing evil. For Christ also suffered for sins once for all, the righteous for the unrighteous, in order to bring you to God. He was put to death in the flesh, but made alive in the spirit.

Proper 12

Sunday between 24 & 30 July inclusive

Principal Service

Continuous	*Related*
2 Samuel 11.1-15	2 Kings 4.42-44
Ps 14	Ps 145.10-18

Ephesians 3.14-21

John 6.1-21

A reading from the Second Book of Samuel. (11.1-15)

In the spring of the year, the time when kings go out to battle, David sent Joab with his officers and all Israel with him; they ravaged the Ammonites, and besieged Rabbah. But David remained at Jerusalem.

It happened, late one afternoon, when David rose from his couch and was walking about on the roof of the king's house, that he saw from the roof a woman bathing; the woman was very beautiful. David sent someone to inquire about the woman. It was reported, 'This is Bathsheba daughter of Eliam, the wife of Uriah the Hittite.' So David sent messengers to fetch her, and she came to him, and he lay with her (now she was purifying herself after her period). Then she returned to her house. The woman conceived; and she sent and told David, 'I am pregnant.'

So David sent word to Joab, 'Send me Uriah the Hittite.' And Joab sent Uriah to David. When Uriah came to him, David asked how Joab and the people fared, and how the war was going. Then David said to Uriah, 'Go down to your house, and wash your feet.' Uriah went out of the king's house, and there followed him a present from the king. But Uriah slept at the entrance of the king's house with all the servants of his lord, and did not go down to his house. When they told David, 'Uriah did not go down to his house', David said to Uriah, 'You have just come from a journey. Why did you not go down to your house?' Uriah said to David, 'The ark and Israel and Judah remain in booths; and my lord Joab and the servants of my lord are camping in the open field; shall I then go to my house, to eat and to drink, and to lie with my wife? As you live, and as your soul lives, I will not do such a thing.' Then David said to Uriah, 'Remain here today also, and tomorrow I will send you back.' So Uriah remained in Jerusalem that day. On the next day, David invited him to eat and drink in his presence and made him drunk; and in the evening he went out to lie on his couch with the servants of his lord, but he did not go down to his house.

In the morning David wrote a letter to Joab, and sent it by the hand of Uriah. In the letter he wrote, 'Set Uriah in the forefront of the hardest fighting, and then draw back from him, so that he may be struck down and die.'

This is the word of the Lord.

Or:
A reading from the Second Book of the Kings. (4.42-44)

A man came from Baal-shalishah, bringing food from the first fruits to Elisha, the man of God: twenty loaves of barley and fresh ears of grain in his sack. Elisha said, 'Give it to the people and let them eat.' But his servant said, 'How can I set this before a hundred people?' So he repeated, 'Give it to the people and let them eat, for thus says the Lord, "They shall eat and have some left."' He set it before them, they ate, and had some left, according to the word of the Lord.

This is the word of the Lord.

A reading from the Letter of Paul to the Ephesians. (3.14-21)

I bow my knees before the Father, from whom every family in heaven and on earth takes its name. I pray that, according to the riches of his glory, he may grant that you may be strengthened in your inner being with power through his Spirit, and that Christ may dwell in your hearts through faith, as you are being rooted and grounded in love. I pray that you may have the power to comprehend, with all the saints, what is the breadth and length and height and depth, and to know the love of Christ that surpasses knowledge, so that you may be filled with all the fullness of God.

Now to him who by the power at work within us is able to accomplish abundantly far more than all we can ask or imagine, to him be glory in the church and in Christ Jesus to all generations, for ever and ever. Amen.

This is the word of the Lord.

Hear the gospel of our Lord Jesus Christ according to John. (6.1-21)

Jesus went to the other side of the Sea of Galilee, also called the Sea of Tiberias. A large crowd kept following him, because they saw the signs that he was doing for the sick. Jesus went up the mountain and sat down there with his disciples. Now the Passover, the festival of the Jews, was near. When he looked up and saw a large crowd coming towards him, Jesus said to Philip, 'Where are we to buy bread for these people to eat?' He said this to test him, for he himself knew what he was going to do. Philip answered him, 'Six months' wages would not buy enough bread for each of them to get a little.' One of his disciples, Andrew, Simon Peter's brother, said to him, 'There is a boy here who has five barley loaves and two fish. But what are they among so many people?' Jesus said, 'Make the people sit down.' Now there was a great deal of grass in the place; so they sat down, about five thousand in all. Then Jesus took the loaves, and when he had given thanks, he distributed them to those who were seated; so also the fish, as much as they wanted. When they were satisfied, he told his disciples, 'Gather up the fragments left over, so that nothing may be lost.' So they gathered them up, and from the fragments of the five barley loaves, left by those who had eaten, they filled twelve baskets. When the people saw the sign that he had done, they began to say, 'This is indeed the prophet who is to come into the world.'

When Jesus realized that they were about to come and take him by force to make him king, he withdrew again to the mountain by himself.

When evening came, his disciples went down to the lake, got into a boat, and started across the lake to Capernaum. It was now dark, and Jesus had not yet come to them. The lake became rough because a strong wind was blowing. When they had rowed about three or four miles, they saw Jesus walking on the lake and coming near the boat, and they were terrified. But he said to them, 'It is I; do not be afraid.' Then they wanted to take him into the boat, and immediately the boat reached the land towards which they were going.

This is the gospel of the Lord.

Second Service
Ps 74 *or* 74.12-17; Job 19.1-27a *or* Ecclesiasticus 38.24-34; Hebrews 8; *if a Eucharist:* Luke 11.1-13

A reading from the Book of Job. *(19.1-27a)*

Job said:
  'How long will you torment me,
    and break me in pieces with words?
  These ten times you have cast reproach upon me;
    are you not ashamed to wrong me?
  And even if it is true that I have erred,
    my error remains with me.
  If indeed you magnify yourselves against me,
    and make my humiliation an argument against me,
  know then that God has put me in the wrong,

and closed his net around me.
Even when I cry out, "Violence!" I am not answered;
    I call aloud, but there is no justice.
He has walled up my way so that I cannot pass,
    and he has set darkness upon my paths.
He has stripped my glory from me,
    and taken the crown from my head.
He breaks me down on every side, and I am gone,
    he has uprooted my hope like a tree.
He has kindled his wrath against me,
    and counts me as his adversary.
His troops come on together;
    they have thrown up siege-works against me,
    and encamp around my tent.

'He has put my family far from me,
    and my acquaintances are wholly estranged from me.
My relatives and my close friends have failed me;
    the guests in my house have forgotten me;
my serving-girls count me as a stranger;
    I have become an alien in their eyes.
I call to my servant, but he gives me no answer;
    I must myself plead with him.
My breath is repulsive to my wife;
    I am loathsome to my own family.
Even young children despise me;
    when I rise, they talk against me.
All my intimate friends abhor me,
    and those whom I loved have turned against me.
My bones cling to my skin and to my flesh,
    and I have escaped by the skin of my teeth.
Have pity on me, have pity on me, O you my friends,
    for the hand of God has touched me!
Why do you, like God, pursue me,
    never satisfied with my flesh?

'O that my words were written down!
    O that they were inscribed in a book!
O that with an iron pen and with lead
    they were engraved on a rock for ever!
For I know that my Redeemer lives,
    and that at the last he will stand upon the earth;
and after my skin has been thus destroyed,
    then in my flesh I shall see God,

whom I shall see on my side,
    and my eyes shall behold, and not another.'

Or:

A reading from the book Ecclesiasticus. (38.24-34)

The wisdom of the scribe depends on the opportunity of leisure;
    only the one who has little business can become wise.
How can one become wise who handles the plough,
    and who glories in the shaft of a goad,
who drives oxen and is occupied with their work,
    and whose talk is about bulls?
He sets his heart on ploughing furrows,
    and he is careful about fodder for the heifers.
So it is with every artisan and master artisan
    who labours by night as well as by day;
those who cut the signets of seals,
    each is diligent in making a great variety;
they set their heart on painting a lifelike image,
    and they are careful to finish their work.
So it is with the smith, sitting by the anvil,
    intent on his ironwork;
the breath of the fire melts his flesh,
    and he struggles with the heat of the furnace;
the sound of the hammer deafens his ears,
    and his eyes are on the pattern of the object.
He sets his heart on finishing his handiwork,
    and he is careful to complete its decoration.
So it is with is the potter sitting at his work
    and turning the wheel with his feet;
he is always deeply concerned over his products,
    and he produces them in quantity.
He moulds the clay with his arm
    and makes it pliable with his feet;
he sets his heart on finishing the glazing,
    and he takes care in firing the kiln.

All these rely on their hands,
    and all are skilful in their own work.
Without them no city can be inhabited,
    and wherever they live, they will not go hungry.
Yet they are not sought out for the council of the people,
    nor do they attain eminence in the public assembly.
They do not sit in the judge's seat,

nor do they understand the decisions of the courts;
they cannot expound discipline or judgement,
and they are not found among the rulers.
But they maintain the fabric of the world,
and their concern is for the exercise of their trade.
How different the one who devotes himself
to the study of the law of the Most High!

A reading from the Letter to the Hebrews. *(Chapter 8)*

The main point in what we are saying is this: we have such a high priest, one who is seated at the right hand of the throne of the Majesty in the heavens, a minister in the sanctuary and the true tent that the Lord, and not any mortal, has set up. For every high priest is appointed to offer gifts and sacrifices; hence it is necessary for this priest also to have something to offer. Now if he were on earth, he would not be a priest at all, since there are priests who offer gifts according to the law. They offer worship in a sanctuary that is a sketch and shadow of the heavenly one; for Moses, when he was about to erect the tent, was warned, 'See that you make everything according to the pattern that was shown you on the mountain.' But Jesus has now obtained a more excellent ministry, and to that degree he is the mediator of a better covenant, which has been enacted through better promises. For if that first covenant had been faultless, there would have been no need to look for a second one.
God finds fault with them when he says:
'The days are surely coming, says the Lord,
when I will establish a new covenant
with the house of Israel
and with the house of Judah;
not like the covenant that I made with their ancestors,
on the day when I took them by the hand to lead them
out of the land of Egypt;
for they did not continue in my covenant,
and so I had no concern for them,
says the Lord.
This is the covenant that I will make with the house of Israel
after those days, says the Lord:
I will put my laws in their minds,
and write them on their hearts,
and I will be their God,
and they shall be my people.
And they shall not teach one another

or say to each other, "Know the Lord",
for they shall all know me,
from the least of them to the greatest.
For I will be merciful towards their iniquities,
and I will remember their sins no more.'
In speaking of 'a new covenant', he has made the first one obsolete.
And what is obsolete and growing old will soon disappear.

If a Eucharist:
Hear the gospel of our Lord Jesus Christ according to Luke. *(11.1-13)*

Jesus was praying in a certain place, and after he had finished, one of his disciples said to him, 'Lord, teach us to pray, as John taught his disciples.' He said to them, 'When you pray, say:
Father, hallowed be your name.
Your kingdom come.
Give us each day our daily bread.
And forgive us our sins,
for we ourselves forgive everyone indebted to us.
And do not bring us to the time of trial.'
And he said to them, 'Suppose one of you has a friend, and you go to him at midnight and say to him, "Friend, lend me three loaves of bread; for a friend of mine has arrived, and I have nothing to set before him." And he answers from within, "Do not bother me; the door has already been locked, and my children are with me in bed; I cannot get up and give you anything." I tell you, even though he will not get up and give him anything because he is his friend, at least because of his persistence he will get up and give him whatever he needs.
'So I say to you, Ask, and it will be given to you; search, and you will find; knock, and the door will be opened for you. For everyone who asks receives, and everyone who searches finds, and for everyone who knocks, the door will be opened. Is there anyone among you who, if your child asks for a fish, will give a snake instead of a fish? Or if the child asks for an egg, will give a scorpion? If you then, who are evil, know how to give good gifts to your children, how much more will the heavenly Father give the Holy Spirit to those who ask him!'

This is the gospel of the Lord.

Third Service

Ps 75; Song of Solomon 2 *or* 1 Maccabees 2.[1-14] 15-22; 1 Peter 4.7-14

A reading from the Song of Solomon. (Chapter 2)

> I am a rose of Sharon,
>> a lily of the valleys.
> As a lily among brambles,
>> so is my love among maidens.
>
> As an apple tree among the trees of the wood,
>> so is my belovèd among young men.
> With great delight I sat in his shadow,
>> and his fruit was sweet to my taste.
> He brought me to the banqueting house,
>> and his intention towards me was love.
> Sustain me with raisins, refresh me with apples;
>> for I am faint with love.
> O that his left hand were under my head,
>> and that his right hand embraced me!
> I adjure you, O daughters of Jerusalem,
>> by the gazelles or the wild does:
> do not stir up or awaken love
>> until it is ready!
>
> The voice of my belovèd!
>> Look, he comes,
> leaping upon the mountains,
>> bounding over the hills.
> My belovèd is like a gazelle
>> or a young stag.
> Look, there he stands behind our wall,
>> gazing in at the windows, looking through the lattice.
> My belovèd speaks and says to me:
> 'Arise, my love, my fair one,
>> and come away;
> for now the winter is past,
>> the rain is over and gone.
> The flowers appear on the earth;
>> the time of singing has come,
> and the voice of the turtle-dove
>> is heard in our land.
> The fig tree puts forth its figs,
>> and the vines are in blossom;
>> they give forth fragrance.

Arise, my love, my fair one,
    and come away.
O my dove, in the clefts of the rock,
    in the covert of the cliff,
let me see your face,
    let me hear your voice;
for your voice is sweet,
    and your face is lovely.
Catch us the foxes,
    the little foxes,
that ruin the vineyards –
    for our vineyards are in blossom.'

My belovèd is mine and I am his;
    he pastures his flock among the lilies.
Until the day breathes
    and the shadows flee,
turn, my belovèd, be like a gazelle
    or a young stag on the cleft mountains.

Or:

A reading from the First Book of the Maccabees. *(2.[1-14] 15-22)*

[In those days Mattathias son of John son of Simeon, a priest of the family of Joarib, moved from Jerusalem and settled in Modein. He had five sons, John surnamed Gaddi, Simon called Thassi, Judas called Maccabeus, Eleazar called Avaran, and Jonathan called Apphus. He saw the blasphemies being committed in Judah and Jerusalem, and said,

'Alas! Why was I born to see this,
    the ruin of my people, the ruin of the holy city,
and to live there when it was given over to the enemy,
the sanctuary given over to aliens?
Her temple has become like a person without honour;
    her glorious vessels have been carried into exile.
Her infants have been killed in her streets,
    her youths by the sword of the foe.
What nation has not inherited her palaces
    and has not seized her spoils?
All her adornment has been taken away;
    no longer free, she has become a slave.
And see, our holy place, our beauty,
    and our glory have been laid waste;
    the Gentiles have profaned them.

Why should we live any longer?'
Then Mattathias and his sons tore their clothes, put on sackcloth, and mourned greatly.]

[15] The king's officers who were enforcing the apostasy came to the town of Modein to make them offer sacrifice. Many from Israel came to them; and Mattathias and his sons were assembled. Then the king's officers spoke to Mattathias as follows: 'You are a leader, honoured and great in this town, and supported by sons and brothers. Now be the first to come and do what the king commands, as all the Gentiles and the people of Judah and those that are left in Jerusalem have done. Then you and your sons will be numbered among the Friends of the king, and you and your sons will be honoured with silver and gold and many gifts.'

But Mattathias answered and said in a loud voice: 'Even if all the nations that live under the rule of the king obey him, and have chosen to obey his commandments, everyone of them abandoning the religion of their ancestors, I and my sons and my brothers will continue to live by the covenant of our ancestors. Far be it from us to desert the law and the ordinances. We will not obey the king's words by turning aside from our religion to the right hand or to the left.'

A reading from the First Letter of Peter. (4.7-14)

The end of all things is near; therefore be serious and discipline yourselves for the sake of your prayers. Above all, maintain constant love for one another, for love covers a multitude of sins. Be hospitable to one another without complaining. Like good stewards of the manifold grace of God, serve one another with whatever gift each of you has received. Whoever speaks must do so as one speaking the very words of God; whoever serves must do so with the strength that God supplies, so that God may be glorified in all things through Jesus Christ. To him belong the glory and the power for ever and ever. Amen.

Belovèd, do not be surprised at the fiery ordeal that is taking place among you to test you, as though something strange were happening to you. But rejoice in so far as you are sharing Christ's sufferings, so that you may also be glad and shout for joy when his glory is revealed. If you are reviled for the name of Christ, you are blessed, because the spirit of glory, which is the Spirit of God, is resting on you.

Proper 13

Sunday between 31 July & 6 August inclusive

Principal Service

Continuous
2 Samuel 11.26 - 12.13*a*
Ps 51.1-12

Related
Exodus 16.2-4,9-15
Ps 78.23-29

Ephesians 4.1-16
John 6.24-35

A reading from the Second Book of Samuel. *(11.26 - 12.13a)*

When the wife of Uriah heard that her husband was dead, she made lamentation for him. When the mourning was over, David sent and brought her to his house, and she became his wife, and bore him a son.

But the thing that David had done displeased the Lord, and the Lord sent Nathan to David. He came to him, and said to him, 'There were two men in a certain city, one rich and the other poor. The rich man had very many flocks and herds; but the poor man had nothing but one little ewe lamb, which he had bought. He brought it up, and it grew up with him and with his children; it used to eat of his meagre fare, and drink from his cup, and lie in his bosom, and it was like a daughter to him. Now there came a traveller to the rich man, and he was loath to take one of his own flock or herd to prepare for the wayfarer who had come to him, but he took the poor man's lamb, and prepared that for the guest who had come to him.' Then David's anger was greatly kindled against the man. He said to Nathan, 'As the Lord lives, the man who has done this deserves to die; he shall restore the lamb fourfold, because he did this thing, and because he had no pity.'

Nathan said to David, 'You are the man! Thus says the Lord, the God of Israel: I anointed you king over Israel, and I rescued you from the hand of Saul; I gave you your master's house, and your master's wives into your bosom, and gave you the house of Israel and of Judah; and if that had been too little, I would have added as much more. Why have you despised the word of the Lord, to do what is evil in his sight? You have struck down Uriah the Hittite with the sword, and have taken his wife to be your wife, and have killed him with the sword of the Ammonites. Now therefore the sword shall never depart from your house, for you have despised me, and have taken the wife of Uriah the Hittite to be your wife. Thus says the Lord: I will raise up trouble against you from within your own house;

and I will take your wives before your eyes, and give them to your neighbour, and he shall lie with your wives in the sight of this very sun. For you did it secretly; but I will do this thing before all Israel, and before the sun.' David said to Nathan, 'I have sinned against the Lord.'

This is the word of the Lord.

Or:

A reading from the Book of the Exodus. *(16.2-4,9-15)*

The whole congregation of the Israelites complained against Moses and Aaron in the wilderness. The Israelites said to them, 'If only we had died by the hand of the Lord in the land of Egypt, when we sat by the fleshpots and ate our fill of bread; for you have brought us out into this wilderness to kill this whole assembly with hunger.'

Then the Lord said to Moses, 'I am going to rain bread from heaven for you, and each day the people shall go out and gather enough for that day. In that way I will test them, whether they will follow my instruction or not.

⁹ Then Moses said to Aaron, 'Say to the whole congregation of the Israelites, "Draw near to the Lord, for he has heard your complaining."' And as Aaron spoke to the whole congregation of the Israelites, they looked towards the wilderness, and the glory of the Lord appeared in the cloud. The Lord spoke to Moses and said, 'I have heard the complaining of the Israelites; say to them, "At twilight you shall eat meat, and in the morning you shall have your fill of bread; then you shall know that I am the Lord your God."'

In the evening quails came up and covered the camp; and in the morning there was a layer of dew around the camp. When the layer of dew lifted, there on the surface of the wilderness was a fine flaky substance, as fine as frost on the ground. When the Israelites saw it, they said to one another, 'What is it?' For they did not know what it was. Moses said to them, 'It is the bread that the Lord has given you to eat.'

This is the word of the Lord.

A reading from the Letter of Paul to the Ephesians. *(4.1-16)*

I, the prisoner in the Lord, beg you to lead a life worthy of the calling to which you have been called, with all humility and gentleness, with patience, bearing with one another in love, making every effort to maintain the unity of the Spirit in the bond of peace. There is one body and one Spirit, just as you were called to the one hope of your calling, one Lord, one faith, one baptism, one God and Father of all,

Proper 13 – Principal Service

who is above all and through all and in all.

But each of us was given grace according to the measure of Christ's gift. Therefore it is said,

'When he ascended on high he made captivity itself a captive;
he gave gifts to his people.'

(When it says, 'He ascended', what does it mean but that he had also descended into the lower parts of the earth? He who descended is the same one who ascended far above all the heavens, so that he might fill all things.) The gifts he gave were that some would be apostles, some prophets, some evangelists, some pastors and teachers, to equip the saints for the work of ministry, for building up the body of Christ, until all of us come to the unity of the faith and of the knowledge of the Son of God, to maturity, to the measure of the full stature of Christ. We must no longer be children, tossed to and fro and blown about by every wind of doctrine, by people's trickery, by their craftiness in deceitful scheming. But speaking the truth in love, we must grow up in every way into him who is the head, into Christ, from whom the whole body, joined and knitted together by every ligament with which it is equipped, as each part is working properly, promotes the body's growth in building itself up in love.

This is the word of the Lord.

Hear the gospel of our Lord Jesus Christ according to John. (6.24-35)

When the crowd saw that neither Jesus nor his disciples were at the place where they had eaten the bread after the Lord had given thanks, they themselves got into the boats and went to Capernaum looking for Jesus.

When they found him on the other side of the lake, they said to him, 'Rabbi, when did you come here?' Jesus answered them, 'Very truly, I tell you, you are looking for me, not because you saw signs, but because you ate your fill of the loaves. Do not work for the food that perishes, but for the food that endures for eternal life, which the Son of Man will give you. For it is on him that God the Father has set his seal.' Then they said to him, 'What must we do to perform the works of God?' Jesus answered them, 'This is the work of God, that you believe in him whom he has sent.' So they said to him, 'What sign are you going to give us then, so that we may see it and believe you? What work are you performing? Our ancestors ate the manna in the wilderness; as it is written, "He gave them bread from heaven to eat."' Then Jesus said to them, 'Very truly, I tell you, it was not Moses who gave you the bread from heaven, but it is my Father who gives you the true bread from heaven. For the bread of God is that

which comes down from heaven and gives life to the world.' They
said to him, 'Sir, give us this bread always.'

  Jesus said to them, 'I am the bread of life. Whoever comes to me will
never be hungry, and whoever believes in me will never be thirsty.'

This is the gospel of the Lord.

Second Service
Ps 88 *or* 88.1-9; Job 28 *or* Ecclesiasticus 42.15-25;
Hebrews 11.17-31; *if a Eucharist:* Luke 12.13-21

A reading from the Book of Job. *(Chapter 28)*

Job said:
> 'Surely there is a mine for silver,
>>   and a place for gold to be refined.
> Iron is taken out of the earth,
>>   and copper is smelted from ore.
> Miners put an end to darkness,
>>   and search out to the farthest bound
>>   the ore in gloom and deep darkness.
> They open shafts in a valley away from human habitation;
>>   they are forgotten by travellers,
>>   they sway suspended, remote from people.
> As for the earth, out of it comes bread;
>>   but underneath it is turned up as by fire.
> Its stones are the place of sapphires,
>>   and its dust contains gold.

> 'That path no bird of prey knows,
>>   and the falcon's eye has not seen it.
> The proud wild animals have not trodden it;
>>   the lion has not passed over it.

> 'They put their hand to the flinty rock,
>>   and overturn mountains by the roots.
> They cut out channels in the rocks,
>>   and their eyes see every precious thing.
> The sources of the rivers they probe;
>>   hidden things they bring to light.

> 'But where shall wisdom be found?
>>   And where is the place of understanding?
> Mortals do not know the way to it,
>>   and it is not found in the land of the living.
> The deep says, "It is not in me",

and the sea says, "It is not with me."
It cannot be bought for gold,
    and silver cannot be weighed out as its price.
It cannot be valued in the gold of Ophir,
    in precious onyx or sapphire.
Gold and glass cannot equal it,
    nor can it be exchanged for jewels of fine gold.
No mention shall be made of coral or of crystal;
    the price of wisdom is above pearls.
The chrysolite of Ethiopia cannot compare with it,
    nor can it be valued in pure gold.

'Where then does wisdom come from?
    And where is the place of understanding?
It is hidden from the eyes of all living,
    and concealed from the birds of the air.
Abaddon and Death say,
    "We have heard a rumour of it with our ears."

'God understands the way to it,
    and he knows its place.
For he looks to the ends of the earth,
    and sees everything under the heavens.
When he gave to the wind its weight,
    and apportioned out the waters by measure;
when he made a decree for the rain,
    and a way for the thunderbolt;
then he saw it and declared it;
    he established it, and searched it out.
And he said to humankind,
"Truly, the fear of the Lord, that is wisdom;
    and to depart from evil is understanding."'

Or:

A reading from the book Ecclesiasticus. (42.15-25)

I will now call to mind the works of the Lord,
    and will declare what I have seen.
By the word of the Lord his works are made;
    and all his creatures do his will.
The sun looks down on everything with its light,
    and the work of the Lord is full of his glory.
The Lord has not empowered even his holy ones
    to recount all his marvellous works,

which the Lord the Almighty has established
    so that the universe may stand firm in his glory.
He searches out the abyss and the human heart;
    he understands their innermost secrets.
For the Most High knows all that may be known;
    he sees from of old the things that are to come.
He discloses what has been and what is to be,
    and he reveals the traces of hidden things.
No thought escapes him,
    and nothing is hidden from him.
He has set in order the splendours of his wisdom;
    he is from all eternity one and the same.
Nothing can be added or taken away,
    and he needs no one to be his counsellor.
How desirable are all his works,
    and how sparkling they are to see!
All these things live and remain for ever;
    each creature is preserved to meet a particular need.
All things come in pairs, one opposite to the other,
    and he has made nothing incomplete.
Each supplements the virtues of the other.
    Who could ever tire of seeing his glory?

A reading from the Letter to the Hebrews. (11.17-31)

By faith Abraham, when put to the test, offered up Isaac. He who had received the promises was ready to offer up his only son, of whom he had been told, 'It is through Isaac that descendants shall be named after you.' He considered the fact that God is able even to raise someone from the dead – and figuratively speaking, he did receive him back. By faith Isaac invoked blessings for the future on Jacob and Esau. By faith Jacob, when dying, blessed each of the sons of Joseph, 'bowing in worship over the top of his staff.' By faith Joseph, at the end of his life, made mention of the exodus of the Israelites and gave instructions about his burial.

By faith Moses was hidden by his parents for three months after his birth, because they saw that the child was beautiful; and they were not afraid of the king's edict. By faith Moses, when he was grown up, refused to be called a son of Pharaoh's daughter, choosing rather to share ill-treatment with the people of God than to enjoy the fleeting pleasures of sin. He considered abuse suffered for the Christ to be greater wealth than the treasures of Egypt, for he was looking ahead to the reward. By faith he left Egypt, unafraid of the king's anger; for he persevered as though he saw him who is invisible. By faith he kept the Passover and the sprinkling of blood, so that the destroyer of the firstborn would not touch the firstborn of Israel.

By faith the people passed through the Red Sea as if it were dry land, but when the Egyptians attempted to do so they were drowned. By faith the walls of Jericho fell after they had been encircled for seven days. By faith Rahab the prostitute did not perish with those who were disobedient, because she had received the spies in peace.

If a Eucharist:
Hear the gospel of our Lord Jesus Christ according to Luke. *(12.13-21)*

Someone in the crowd said to Jesus, 'Teacher, tell my brother to divide the family inheritance with me.' But he said to him, 'Friend, who set me to be a judge or arbitrator over you?' And he said to them, 'Take care! Be on your guard against all kinds of greed; for one's life does not consist in the abundance of possessions.' Then he told them a parable: 'The land of a rich man produced abundantly. And he thought to himself, "What should I do, for I have no place to store my crops?" Then he said, "I will do this: I will pull down my barns and build larger ones, and there I will store all my grain and my goods. And I will say to my soul, Soul, you have ample goods laid up for many years; relax, eat, drink, be merry." But God said to him, "You fool! This very night your life is being demanded of you. And the things you have prepared, whose will they be?" So it is with those who store up treasures for themselves but are not rich towards God.'

This is the gospel of the Lord.

Third Service
Ps 86; Song of Solomon 5.2-16 *or* 1 Maccabees 3.1-12; 2 Peter 1.1-15

A reading from the Song of Solomon. *(5.2-16)*

I slept, but my heart was awake.
    Listen! my belovèd is knocking.
'Open to me, my sister, my love, my dove, my perfect one;
    for my head is wet with dew,
    my locks with the drops of the night.'
I had put off my garment;
    how could I put it on again?
I had bathed my feet;
    how could I soil them?
My belovèd thrust his hand into the opening,

and my inmost being yearned for him.
I arose to open to my belovèd,
      and my hands dripped with myrrh,
my fingers with liquid myrrh,
      upon the handles of the bolt.
I opened to my belovèd,
      but my belovèd had turned and was gone.
My soul failed me when he spoke.
I sought him, but did not find him;
      I called him, but he gave no answer.
Making their rounds in the city
      the sentinels found me;
they beat me, they wounded me,
      they took away my mantle, those sentinels of the walls.
I adjure you, O daughters of Jerusalem,
      if you find my belovèd, tell him this: I am faint with love.

What is your belovèd more than another belovèd,
      O fairest among women?
What is your belovèd more than another belovèd,
      that you thus adjure us?

My belovèd is all radiant and ruddy,
      distinguished among ten thousand.
His head is the finest gold;
      his locks are wavy, black as a raven.
His eyes are like doves beside springs of water,
      bathed in milk, fitly set.
His cheeks are like beds of spices,
      yielding fragrance.
His lips are lilies,
      distilling liquid myrrh.
His arms are rounded gold,
      set with jewels.
His body is ivory work,
      encrusted with sapphires.
His legs are alabaster columns,
      set upon bases of gold.
His appearance is like Lebanon,
      choice as the cedars.
His speech is most sweet,
      and he is altogether desirable.
This is my belovèd and this is my friend,
      O daughters of Jerusalem.

Or:

A reading from the First Book of the Maccabees. *(3.1-12)*

Mattathias's son Judas, who was called Maccabeus, took command in his place. All his brothers and all who had joined his father helped him; they gladly fought for Israel. He extended the glory of his people. Like a giant he put on his breastplate; he bound on his armour of war and waged battles, protecting the camp by his sword. He was like a lion in his deeds, like a lion's cub roaring for prey. He searched out and pursued those who broke the law; he burned those who troubled his people. Lawbreakers shrank back for fear of him; all the evildoers were confounded; and deliverance prospered by his hand. He embittered many kings, but he made Jacob glad by his deeds, and his memory is blessed for ever. He went through the cities of Judah; he destroyed the ungodly out of the land; thus he turned away wrath from Israel. He was renowned to the ends of the earth; he gathered in those who were perishing.

Apollonius now gathered together Gentiles and a large force from Samaria to fight against Israel. When Judas learned of it, he went out to meet him, and he defeated and killed him. Many were wounded and fell, and the rest fled. Then they seized their spoils; and Judas took the sword of Apollonius, and used it in battle for the rest of his life.

A reading from the Second Letter of Peter. *(1.1-15)*

Simeon Peter, a servant and apostle of Jesus Christ, To those who have received a faith as precious as ours through the righteousness of our God and Saviour Jesus Christ:

May grace and peace be yours in abundance in the knowledge of God and of Jesus our Lord.

His divine power has given us everything needed for life and godliness, through the knowledge of him who called us by his own glory and goodness. Thus he has given us, through these things, his precious and very great promises, so that through them you may escape from the corruption that is in the world because of lust, and may become participants in the divine nature. For this very reason, you must make every effort to support your faith with goodness, and goodness with knowledge, and knowledge with self-control, and self-control with endurance, and endurance with godliness, and godliness with mutual affection, and mutual affection with love. For if these things are yours and are increasing among you, they keep you from being ineffective and unfruitful in the knowledge of our Lord Jesus Christ. For anyone who lacks these things is nearsighted and blind, and is forgetful of the cleansing of past sins. Therefore, brothers and sisters, be all the more eager to confirm your call and election, for if you do this, you will never stumble. For in this way, entry into the eternal kingdom of our Lord and Saviour Jesus Christ will be richly provided for you.

Therefore I intend to keep on reminding you of these things, though you know them already and are established in the truth that has come to you. I think it right, as long as I am in this body, to refresh your memory, since I know that my death will come soon, as indeed our Lord Jesus Christ has made clear to me. And I will make every effort so that after my departure you may be able at any time to recall these things.

Proper 14

Sunday between 7 & 13 August inclusive

Principal Service

Continuous	*Related*
2 Samuel 18.5-9,15,31-33	1 Kings 19.4-8
Ps 130	Ps 34.1-8

Ephesians 4.25 – 5.2
John 6.35,41-51

A reading from the Second Book of Samuel. (18.5-9,15,31-33)

King David gave orders to Joab and Abishai and Ittai, saying, 'Deal gently for my sake with the young man Absalom.' And all the people heard when the king gave orders to all the commanders concerning Absalom.

So the army went out into the field against Israel; and the battle was fought in the forest of Ephraim. The men of Israel were defeated there by the servants of David, and the slaughter there was great on that day, twenty thousand men. The battle spread over the face of all the country; and the forest claimed more victims that day than the sword.

Absalom happened to meet the servants of David. Absalom was riding on his mule, and the mule went under the thick branches of a great oak. His head caught fast in the oak, and he was left hanging between heaven and earth, while the mule that was under him went on.

[15] And ten young men, Joab's armour-bearers, surrounded Absalom and struck him, and killed him.

[31] Then the Cushite came to tke king; and the Cushite said, 'Good

tidings for my lord the king! For the Lord has vindicated you this day, delivering you from the power of all who rose up against you.' The king said to the Cushite, 'Is it well with the young man Absalom?' The Cushite answered, 'May the enemies of my lord the king, and all who rise up to do you harm, be like that young man.'

The king was deeply moved, and went up to the chamber over the gate, and wept; and as he went, he said, 'O my son Absalom, my son, my son Absalom! Would that I had died instead of you, O Absalom, my son, my son!'

This is the word of the Lord.

Or:

A reading from the First Book of the Kings. (19.4-8)

Elijah went a day's journey into the wilderness, and came and sat down under a solitary broom tree. He asked that he might die: 'It is enough; now, O Lord, take away my life, for I am no better than my ancestors.' Then he lay down under the broom tree and fell asleep. Suddenly an angel touched him and said to him, 'Get up and eat.' He looked, and there at his head was a cake baked on hot stones, and a jar of water. He ate and drank, and lay down again. The angel of the Lord came a second time, touched him, and said, 'Get up and eat, otherwise the journey will be too much for you.' He got up, and ate and drank; then he went in the strength of that food for forty days and forty nights to Horeb the mount of God.

This is the word of the Lord.

A reading from the Letter of Paul to the Ephesians. (4.25 - 5.2)

Putting away falsehood, let all of us speak the truth to our neighbours, for we are members of one another. Be angry but do not sin; do not let the sun go down on your anger, and do not make room for the devil. Thieves must give up stealing; rather let them labour and work honestly with their own hands, so as to have something to share with the needy. Let no evil talk come out of your mouths, but only what is useful for building up, as there is need, so that your words may give grace to those who hear. And do not grieve the Holy Spirit of God, with which you were marked with a seal for the day of redemption. Put away from you all bitterness and wrath and anger and wrangling and slander, together with all malice, and be kind to one another, tender-hearted, forgiving one another, as God in Christ has forgiven you. Therefore be imitators of God, as belovèd children, and live in love, as Christ loved us and gave himself up for us, a fragrant offering and sacrifice to God.

This is the word of the Lord.

Hear the gospel of our Lord Jesus Christ according to John. (6.35,41-51)

Jesus said to the crowd, 'I am the bread of life. Whoever comes to me will never be hungry, and whoever believes in me will never be thirsty.'
⁴¹ Then the Jews began to complain about him because he said, 'I am the bread that came down from heaven.' They were saying, 'Is not this Jesus, the son of Joseph, whose father and mother we know? How can he now say, "I have come down from heaven"?' Jesus answered them, 'Do not complain among yourselves. No one can come to me unless drawn by the Father who sent me; and I will raise that person up on the last day. It is written in the prophets, "And they shall all be taught by God." Everyone who has heard and learned from the Father comes to me. Not that anyone has seen the Father except the one who is from God; he has seen the Father. Very truly, I tell you, whoever believes has eternal life. I am the bread of life. Your ancestors ate the manna in the wilderness, and they died. This is the bread that comes down from heaven, so that one may eat of it and not die. I am the living bread that came down from heaven. Whoever eats of this bread will live for ever; and the bread that I will give for the life of the world is my flesh.'

This is the gospel of the Lord.

Second Service
Ps 91 *or* 91.1-12; Job 39.1 - 40.4 *or* Ecclesiasticus 43.13-33; Hebrews 12.1-17; *if a Eucharist:* Luke 12.32-40

A reading from the Book of Job. (39.1 - 40.4)

'Do you know when the mountain goats give birth?
　　Do you observe the calving of the deer?
Can you number the months that they fulfil,
　　and do you know the time when they give birth,
when they crouch to give birth to their offspring,
　　and are delivered of their young?
Their young ones become strong, they grow up in the open;
　　they go forth, and do not return to them.

'Who has let the wild ass go free?
　　Who has loosed the bonds of the swift ass,
to which I have given the steppe for its home,
　　the salt land for its dwelling-place?
It scorns the tumult of the city;
　　it does not hear the shouts of the driver.

It ranges the mountains as its pasture,
    and it searches after every green thing.

'Is the wild ox willing to serve you?
    Will it spend the night at your crib?
Can you tie it in the furrow with ropes,
    or will it harrow the valleys after you?
Will you depend on it because its strength is great,
and will you hand over your labour to it?
Do you have faith in it that it will return,
    and bring your grain to your threshing-floor?

'The ostrich's wings flap wildly,
    though its pinions lack plumage.
For it leaves its eggs to the earth,
    and lets them be warmed on the ground,
forgetting that a foot may crush them,
    and that a wild animal may trample them.
It deals cruelly with its young, as if they were not its own;
    though its labour should be in vain, yet it has no fear;
because God has made it forget wisdom,
    and given it no share in understanding.
When it spreads its plumes aloft,
    it laughs at the horse and its rider.

'Do you give the horse its might?
    Do you clothe its neck with mane?
Do you make it leap like the locust?
    Its majestic snorting is terrible.
It paws violently, exults mightily;
    it goes out to meet the weapons.
It laughs at fear, and is not dismayed;
    it does not turn back from the sword.
Upon it rattle the quiver,
    the flashing spear, and the javelin.
fierceness and rage it swallows the ground;
    it cannot stand still at the sound of the trumpet.
When the trumpet sounds, it says "Aha!"
    From a distance it smells the battle,
    the thunder of the captains, and the shouting.

'Is it by your wisdom that the hawk soars,
    and spreads its wings towards the south?
Is it at your command that the eagle mounts up
    and makes its nest on high?

It lives on the rock and makes its home
in the fastness of the rocky crag.
From there it spies the prey;
its eyes see it from far away.
Its young ones suck up blood;
and where the slain are, there it is.'

And the Lord said to Job:
'Shall a fault-finder contend with the Almighty?
Anyone who argues with God must respond.'

Then Job answered the Lord:
'See, I am of small account; what shall I answer you?
I lay my hand on my mouth.'

Or:

A reading from the book Ecclesiasticus. *(43.13-33)*

By the command of the Most High, he sends the driving snow
and speeds the lightnings of his judgement.
Therefore the storehouses are opened,
and the clouds fly out like birds.
In his majesty he gives the clouds their strength,
and the hailstones are broken in pieces.
The voice of his thunder rebukes the earth;
when he appears, the mountains shake.
At his will the south wind blows;
so do the storm from the north and the whirlwind.
He scatters the snow like birds flying down,
and its descent is like locusts alighting.
The eye is dazzled by the beauty of its whiteness,
and the mind is amazed as it falls.
He pours frost over the earth like salt,
and icicles form like pointed thorns.
The cold north wind blows,
and ice freezes on the water;
it settles on every pool of water,
and the water puts it on like a breastplate.
He consumes the mountains and burns up the wilderness,
and withers the tender grass like fire.
A mist quickly heals all things;
the falling dew gives refreshment from the heat.
By his plan he stilled the deep
and planted islands in it.

Those who sail the sea tell of its dangers,
　　and we marvel at what we hear.
In it are strange and marvellous creatures,
　　all kinds of living things, and huge sea-monsters.
Because of him each of his messengers succeeds,
　　and by his word all things hold together.

We could say more but could never say enough;
　　let the final word be: 'He is the all.'
Where can we find the strength to praise him?
　　For he is greater than all his works.
Awesome is the Lord and very great,
　　and marvellous is his power.
Glorify the Lord and exalt him as much as you can,
　　for he surpasses even that.
When you exalt him, summon all your strength,
　　and do not grow weary, for you cannot praise him enough.
Who has seen him and can describe him?
　　Or who can extol him as he is?
Many things greater than these lie hidden,
　　for I have seen but few of his works.
For the Lord has made all things,
　　and to the godly he has given wisdom.

A reading from the Letter to the Hebrews. (12.1-17)

Since we are surrounded by so great a cloud of witnesses, let us also lay aside every weight and the sin that clings so closely, and let us run with perseverance the race that is set before us, looking to Jesus the pioneer and perfecter of our faith, who for the sake of the joy that was set before him endured the cross, disregarding its shame, and has taken his seat at the right hand of the throne of God.

Consider him who endured such hostility against himself from sinners, so that you may not grow weary or lose heart. In your struggle against sin you have not yet resisted to the point of shedding your blood. And you have forgotten the exhortation that addresses you as children –

'My child, do not regard lightly the discipline of the Lord,
　　or lose heart when you are punished by him;
for the Lord disciplines those whom he loves,
　　and chastises every child whom he accepts.'

Endure trials for the sake of discipline. God is treating you as children; for what child is there whom a parent does not discipline? If you do not have that discipline in which all children share, then you are illegitimate and not his children. Moreover, we had human parents to discipline us, and we respected them. Should we not be even more willing to be subject to the Father of spirits and live? For they disciplined us for a short time as seemed best to them, but he disciplines us for our good, in order that we may share his holiness. Now, discipline always seems painful rather than pleasant at the time, but later it yields the peaceful fruit of righteousness to those who have been trained by it.

Therefore lift your drooping hands and strengthen your weak knees, and make straight paths for your feet, so that what is lame may not be put out of joint, but rather be healed.

Pursue peace with everyone, and the holiness without which no one will see the Lord. See to it that no one fails to obtain the grace of God; that no root of bitterness springs up and causes trouble, and through it many become defiled. See to it that no one becomes like Esau, an immoral and godless person, who sold his birthright for a single meal. You know that later, when he wanted to inherit the blessing, he was rejected, for he found no chance to repent, even though he sought the blessing with tears.

If a Eucharist:
Hear the gospel of our Lord Jesus Christ according to Luke. *(12.32-40)*

Jesus said to his disciples, 'Do not be afraid, little flock, for it is your Father's good pleasure to give you the kingdom. Sell your possessions, and give alms. Make purses for yourselves that do not wear out, an unfailing treasure in heaven, where no thief comes near and no moth destroys. For where your treasure is, there your heart will be also.

'Be dressed for action and have your lamps lit; be like those who are waiting for their master to return from the wedding banquet, so that they may open the door for him as soon as he comes and knocks. Blessèd are those slaves whom the master finds alert when he comes; truly I tell you, he will fasten his belt and have them sit down to eat, and he will come and serve them. If he comes during the middle of the night, or near dawn, and finds them so, blessèd are those slaves.

'But know this: if the owner of the house had known at what hour the thief was coming, he would not have let his house be broken into. You also must be ready, for the Son of Man is coming at an unexpected hour.'

This is the gospel of the Lord.

Third Service
Ps 90; Song of Solomon 8.5-7 *or* 1 Maccabees 14.4-15;
2 Peter 3.8-13

A reading from the Song of Solomon. *(8.5-7)*

Who is that coming up from the wilderness,
  leaning upon her belovèd?

Under the apple tree I awakened you.
There your mother was in labour with you;
  there she who bore you was in labour.

Set me as a seal upon your heart,
  as a seal upon your arm;
for love is strong as death,
  passion fierce as the grave.
Its flashes are flashes of fire,
  a raging flame.
Many waters cannot quench love,
  neither can floods drown it.
If one offered for love all the wealth of one's house,
  it would be utterly scorned.

Or:

A reading from the First Book of the Maccabees. *(14.4-15)*

The land had rest all the days of Simon. He sought the good of his
nation; his rule was pleasing to them, as was the honour shown him,
all his days. To crown all his honours he took Joppa for a harbour,
and opened a way to the isles of the sea. He extended the borders of
his nation, and gained full control of the country. He gathered a host
of captives; he ruled over Gazara and Beth-zur and the citadel, and
he removed its uncleanness from it; and there was none to oppose
him. They tilled their land in peace; the ground gave its increase,
and the trees of the plains their fruit. Old men sat in the streets; they
all talked together of good things, and the youths put on splendid
military attire. He supplied the towns with food, and furnished
them with the means of defence, until his renown spread to the ends
of the earth. He established peace in the land, and Israel rejoiced
with great joy. All the people sat under their own vines and fig trees,
and there was none to make them afraid. No one was left in the land
to fight them, and the kings were crushed in those days. He gave
help to all the humble among his people; he sought out the law, and
did away with all the renegades and outlaws. He made the sanctuary glorious, and added to the vessels of the sanctuary.

A reading from the Second Letter of Peter. (3.8-13)

Do not ignore this one fact, belovèd, that with the Lord one day is like a thousand years, and a thousand years are like one day. The Lord is not slow about his promise, as some think of slowness, but is patient with you, not wanting any to perish, but all to come to repentance. But the day of the Lord will come like a thief, and then the heavens will pass away with a loud noise, and the elements will be dissolved with fire, and the earth and everything that is done on it will be disclosed.

Since all these things are to be dissolved in this way, what sort of people ought you to be in leading lives of holiness and godliness, waiting for and hastening the coming of the day of God, because of which the heavens will be set ablaze and dissolved, and the elements will melt with fire? But, in accordance with his promise, we wait for new heavens and a new earth, where righteousness is at home.

Proper 15

Sunday between 14 & 20 August inclusive

Principal Service

Continuous
1 Kings 2.10-12 & 3.3-14
Ps 111

Related
Proverbs 9.1-6
Ps 34.9-14

Ephesians 5.15-20
John 6.51-58

A reading from the First Book of the Kings. (2.10-12 & 3.3-14)

David slept with his ancestors, and was buried in the city of David. The time that David reigned over Israel was forty years; he reigned for seven years in Hebron, and thirty-three years in Jerusalem. So Solomon sat on the throne of his father David; and his kingdom was firmly established.
3.3 Solomon loved the Lord, walking in the statutes of his father David; only he sacrificed and offered incense at the high places. The king went to Gibeon to sacrifice there, for that was the principal high place; Solomon used to offer a thousand burnt-offerings on that altar. At Gibeon the Lord appeared to Solomon in a dream by night; and God said, 'Ask what I should give you.' And Solomon said, 'You have shown great and steadfast love to your servant my father David, because he walked before you in faithfulness, in righteousness, and in uprightness of heart towards you; and you have kept for

him this great and steadfast love, and have given him a son to sit on his throne today. And now, O Lord my God, you have made your servant king in place of my father David, although I am only a little child; I do not know how to go out or come in. And your servant is in the midst of the people whom you have chosen, a great people, so numerous they cannot be numbered or counted. Give your servant therefore an understanding mind to govern your people, able to discern between good and evil; for who can govern this your great people?'

It pleased the Lord that Solomon had asked this. God said to him, 'Because you have asked this, and have not asked for yourself long life or riches, or for the life of your enemies, but have asked for yourself understanding to discern what is right, I now do according to your word. Indeed I give you a wise and discerning mind; no one like you has been before you and no one like you shall arise after you. I give you also what you have not asked, both riches and honour all your life; no other king shall compare with you. If you will walk in my ways, keeping my statutes and my commandments, as your father David walked, then I will lengthen your life.'

This is the word of the Lord.

Or:

A reading from the book Proverbs. (9.1-6)

Wisdom has built her house,
　　she has hewn her seven pillars.
She has slaughtered her animals, she has mixed her wine,
　　she has also set her table.
She has sent out her servant-girls,
　　she calls from the highest places in the town,
'You that are simple, turn in here!'
　　To those without sense she says,
'Come, eat of my bread
　　and drink of the wine I have mixed.
Lay aside immaturity, and live,
　　and walk in the way of insight.'

This is the word of the Lord.

A reading from the Letter of Paul to the Ephesians. (5.15-20)

Be careful then how you live, not as unwise people but as wise, making the most of the time, because the days are evil. So do not be foolish, but understand what the will of the Lord is. Do not get drunk with wine, for that is debauchery; but be filled with the Spirit, as you sing psalms and hymns and spiritual songs among yourselves, singing and making melody to the Lord in your hearts, giving thanks to God the Father at all times and for everything in the name of our Lord Jesus Christ.

This is the word of the Lord.

Hear the gospel of our Lord Jesus Christ according to John. (6.51-58)

Jesus said to the Jews, 'I am the living bread that came down from heaven. Whoever eats of this bread will live for ever; and the bread that I will give for the life of the world is my flesh.'

The Jews then disputed among themselves, saying, 'How can this man give us his flesh to eat?' So Jesus said to them, 'Very truly, I tell you, unless you eat the flesh of the Son of Man and drink his blood, you have no life in you. Those who eat my flesh and drink my blood have eternal life, and I will raise them up on the last day; for my flesh is true food and my blood is true drink. Those who eat my flesh and drink my blood abide in me, and I in them. Just as the living Father sent me, and I live because of the Father, so whoever eats me will live because of me. This is the bread that came down from heaven, not like that which your ancestors ate, and they died. But the one who eats this bread will live for ever.'

This is the gospel of the Lord.

Second Service
Pss [92] 100; Exodus 2.23 - 3.10;
Hebrews 13.1-15; *if a Eucharist:* Luke 12.49-56

A reading from the Book of the Exodus. (2.23 -3.10)

After a long time the king of Egypt died. The Israelites groaned under their slavery, and cried out. Out of the slavery their cry for help rose up to God. God heard their groaning, and God remembered his covenant with Abraham, Isaac, and Jacob. God looked upon the Israelites, and God took notice of them.

Moses was keeping the flock of his father-in-law Jethro, the priest of Midian; he led his flock beyond the wilderness, and came to Horeb, the mountain of God. There the angel of the Lord appeared to him in a flame of fire out of a bush; he looked, and the bush was blazing, yet it was not consumed. Then Moses said, 'I must turn aside and look at this great sight, and see why the bush is not burned up.' When the Lord saw that he had turned aside to see, God called to him out of the bush, 'Moses, Moses!' And he said, 'Here I am.' Then he said, 'Come no closer! Remove the sandals from your feet, for the place on which you are standing is holy ground.' He said further,

'I am the God of your father, the God of Abraham, the God of Isaac, and the God of Jacob.' And Moses hid his face, for he was afraid to look at God.

Then the Lord said, 'I have observed the misery of my people who are in Egypt; I have heard their cry on account of their taskmasters. Indeed, I know their sufferings, and I have come down to deliver them from the Egyptians, and to bring them up out of that land to a good and broad land, a land flowing with milk and honey, to the country of the Canaanites, the Hittites, the Amorites, the Perizzites, the Hivites, and the Jebusites. The cry of the Israelites has now come to me; I have also seen how the Egyptians oppress them. So come, I will send you to Pharaoh to bring my people, the Israelites, out of Egypt.'

A reading from the Letter to the Hebrews. (13.1-15)

Let mutual love continue. Do not neglect to show hospitality to strangers, for by doing that some have entertained angels without knowing it. Remember those who are in prison, as though you were in prison with them; those who are being tortured, as though you yourselves were being tortured. Let marriage be held in honour by all, and let the marriage bed be kept undefiled; for God will judge fornicators and adulterers. Keep your lives free from the love of money, and be content with what you have; for he has said, 'I will never leave you or forsake you.' So we can say with confidence,

'The Lord is my helper;
I will not be afraid.
What can anyone do to me?'

Remember your leaders, those who spoke the word of God to you; consider the outcome of their way of life, and imitate their faith. Jesus Christ is the same yesterday and today and for ever. Do not be carried away by all kinds of strange teachings; for it is well for the heart to be strengthened by grace, not by regulations about food, which have not benefited those who observe them. We have an altar from which those who officiate in the tent have no right to eat. For the bodies of those animals whose blood is brought into the sanctuary by the high priest as a sacrifice for sin are burned outside the camp. Therefore Jesus also suffered outside the city gate in order to sanctify the people by his own blood. Let us then go to him outside the camp and bear the abuse he endured. For here we have no lasting city, but we are looking for the city that is to come. Through him, then, let us continually offer a sacrifice of praise to God, that is, the fruit of lips that confess his name.

If a Eucharist:
Hear the gospel of our Lord Jesus Christ according to Luke. *(12.49-56)*

Jesus said to his disciples, 'I came to bring fire to the earth, and how I wish it were already kindled! I have a baptism with which to be baptized, and what stress I am under until it is completed! Do you think that I have come to bring peace to the earth? No, I tell you, but rather division! From now on, five in one household will be divided, three against two and two against three; they will be divided:
> father against son
>> and son against father,
> mother against daughter
>> and daughter against mother,
> mother-in-law against her daughter-in-law
>> and daughter-in-law against mother-in-law.'

He also said to the crowds, 'When you see a cloud rising in the west, you immediately say, "It is going to rain"; and so it happens. And when you see the south wind blowing, you say, "There will be scorching heat"; and it happens. You hypocrites! You know how to interpret the appearance of earth and sky, but why do you not know how to interpret the present time?'

This is the gospel of the Lord.

Third Service
Ps 106.1-10; Jonah 1 *or* Ecclesiasticus 3.1-15; 2 Peter 3.14-18

A reading from the Book of Jonah. *(Chapter 1)*

Now the word of the Lord came to Jonah son of Amittai, saying, 'Go at once to Nineveh, that great city, and cry out against it; for their wickedness has come up before me.' But Jonah set out to flee to Tarshish from the presence of the Lord. He went down to Joppa and found a ship going to Tarshish; so he paid his fare and went on board, to go with them to Tarshish, away from the presence of the Lord.

But the Lord hurled a great wind upon the sea, and such a mighty storm came upon the sea that the ship threatened to break up. Then the mariners were afraid, and each cried to his god. They threw the cargo that was in the ship into the sea, to lighten it for them. Jonah, meanwhile, had gone down into the hold of the ship and had lain down, and was fast asleep. The captain came and said to him, 'What are you doing sound asleep? Get up, call on your god! Perhaps the god will spare us a thought so that we do not perish.'

The sailors said to one another, 'Come, let us cast lots, so that we may know on whose account this calamity has come upon us.' So they cast lots, and the lot fell on Jonah. Then they said to him, 'Tell us why this calamity has come upon us. What is your occupation? Where do you come from? What is your country? And of what people are you?' 'I am a Hebrew,' he replied. 'I worship the Lord, the God of heaven, who made the sea and the dry land.' Then the men were even more afraid, and said to him, 'What is this that you have done!' For the men knew that he was fleeing from the presence of the Lord, because he had told them so.

Then they said to him, 'What shall we do to you, that the sea may quieten down for us?' For the sea was growing more and more tempestuous. He said to them, 'Pick me up and throw me into the sea; then the sea will quieten down for you; for I know it is because of me that this great storm has come upon you.' Nevertheless, the men rowed hard to bring the ship back to land, but they could not, for the sea grew more and more stormy against them. Then they cried out to the Lord, 'Please, O Lord, we pray, do not let us perish on account of this man's life. Do not make us guilty of innocent blood; for you, O Lord, have done as it pleased you.' So they picked Jonah up and threw him into the sea; and the sea ceased from its raging. Then the men feared the Lord even more, and they offered a sacrifice to the Lord and made vows.

But the Lord provided a large fish to swallow up Jonah; and Jonah was in the belly of the fish for three days and three nights.

Or:

A reading from the book Ecclesiasticus. (3.1-15)

Listen to me your father, O children;
     act accordingly, that you may be kept in safety.
For the Lord honours a father above his children,
     and he confirms a mother's right over her children.
Those who honour their father atone for sins,
     and those who respect their mother
     are like those who lay up treasure.
Those who honour their father
     will have joy in their own children,
and when they pray
     they will be heard.
Those who respect their father will have long life,
     and those who honour their mother obey the Lord;
     they will serve their parents as their masters.

Honour your father by word and deed,
    that his blessing may come upon you.
For a father's blessing strengthens the houses of the children,
    but a mother's curse uproots their foundations.
Do not glorify yourself by dishonouring your father,
    for your father's dishonour is no glory to you.
The glory of one's father is one's own glory,
    and it is a disgrace for children not to respect their mother.

My child, help your father in his old age,
    and do not grieve him as long as he lives;
even if his mind fails, be patient with him;
    because you have all your faculties do not despise him.
For kindness to a father will not be forgotten,
    and will be credited to you against your sins;
in the day of your distress
    it will be remembered in your favour;
like frost in fair weather,
    your sins will melt away.

A reading from the Second Letter of Peter. (3.14-18)

Belovèd, while you are waiting for new heavens and a new earth, strive to be found by God at peace, without spot or blemish; and regard the patience of our Lord as salvation.   So also our belovèd brother Paul wrote to you according to the wisdom given to him, speaking of this as he does in all his letters.   There are some things in them hard to understand, which the ignorant and unstable twist to their own destruction, as they do the other scriptures.   You therefore, belovèd, since you are forewarned, beware that you are not carried away with the error of the lawless and lose your own stability.   But grow in the grace and knowledge of our Lord and Saviour Jesus Christ.   To him be the glory both now and to the day of eternity. Amen.

Proper 16

Sunday between 21 & 27 August inclusive

Principal Service

Continuous	*Related*
1 Kings 8.[1,6,10-11]22-30,41-43	Joshua 24.1-2a,14-18
Ps 84	Ps 34.15-22
Ephesians 6.10-20	
John 6.56-69	

A reading from the First Book of the Kings. *(8.[1,6,10-11] 22-30,41-43)*

[Solomon assembled the elders of Israel and all the heads of the tribes, the leaders of the ancestral houses of the Israelites, before King Solomon in Jerusalem, to bring up the ark of the covenant of the Lord out of the city of David, which is Zion.

[6] Then the priests brought the ark of the covenant of the Lord to its place, in the inner sanctuary of the house, in the most holy place, underneath the wings of the cherubim.

[10] And when the priests came out of the holy place, a cloud filled the house of the Lord, so that the priests could not stand to minister because of the cloud; for the glory of the Lord filled the house of the Lord.]

[22] Then Solomon stood before the altar of the Lord in the presence of all the assembly of Israel, and spread out his hands to heaven. He said, 'O Lord, God of Israel, there is no God like you in heaven above or on earth beneath, keeping covenant and steadfast love for your servants who walk before you with all their heart, the covenant that you kept for your servant my father David as you declared to him; you promised with your mouth and have this day fulfilled with your hand. Therefore, O Lord, God of Israel, keep for your servant my father David that which you promised him, saying, "There shall never fail you a successor before me to sit on the throne of Israel, if only your children look to their way, to walk before me as you have walked before me." Therefore, O God of Israel, let your word be confirmed, which you promised to your servant my father David.

'But will God indeed dwell on the earth? Even heaven and the highest heaven cannot contain you, much less this house that I have built! Have regard to your servant's prayer and his plea, O Lord my God, heeding the cry and the prayer that your servant prays to you today; that your eyes may be open night and day towards this house, the place of which you said, "My name shall be there", that you may heed the prayer that your servant prays towards this place. Hear the plea of your servant and of your people Israel when they pray towards this place; O hear in heaven your dwelling-place; heed and forgive.

[41] 'Likewise when a foreigner, who is not of your people Israel, comes from a distant land because of your name – for they shall hear of your great name, your mighty hand, and your outstretched arm – when a foreigner comes and prays towards this house, then hear in heaven your dwelling-place, and do according to all that the foreigner calls to you, so that all the peoples of the earth may know your name and fear you, as do your people Israel, and so that they may know that your name has been invoked on this house that I have built.'

This is the word of the Lord.

Or:

A reading from the Book of Joshua. (24.1-2a,14-18)

Joshua gathered all the tribes of Israel to Shechem, and summoned the elders, the heads, the judges, and the officers of Israel; and they presented themselves before God. And Joshua said to all the people, [14] 'Revere the Lord, and serve him in sincerity and in faithfulness; put away the gods that your ancestors served beyond the River and in Egypt, and serve the Lord. Now if you are unwilling to serve the Lord, choose this day whom you will serve, whether the gods your ancestors served in the region beyond the River or the gods of the Amorites in whose land you are living; but as for me and my household, we will serve the Lord.'

Then the people answered, 'Far be it from us that we should forsake the Lord to serve other gods; for it is the Lord our God who brought us and our ancestors up from the land of Egypt, out of the house of slavery, and who did those great signs in our sight. He protected us along all the way that we went, and among all the peoples through whom we passed; and the Lord drove out before us all the peoples, the Amorites who lived in the land. Therefore we also will serve the Lord, for he is our God.'

This is the word of the Lord.

A reading from the Letter of Paul to the Ephesians. (6.10-20)

Be strong in the Lord and in the strength of his power. Put on the whole armour of God, so that you may be able to stand against the wiles of the devil. For our struggle is not against enemies of blood and flesh, but against the rulers, against the authorities, against the cosmic powers of this present darkness, against the spiritual forces of evil in the heavenly places. Therefore take up the whole armour of God, so that you may be able to withstand on that evil day, and having done everything, to stand firm. Stand therefore, and fasten the belt of truth around your waist, and put on the breastplate of righteousness. As shoes for your feet put on whatever will make you ready to proclaim the gospel of peace. With all of these, take the shield of faith, with which you will be able to quench all the flaming arrows of the evil one. Take the helmet of salvation, and the sword of the Spirit, which is the word of God.

Pray in the Spirit at all times in every prayer and supplication. To that end keep alert and always persevere in supplication for all the saints. Pray also for me, so that when I speak, a message may be given to me to make known with boldness the mystery of the gospel, for which I am an ambassador in chains. Pray that I may declare it boldly, as I must speak.

This is the word of the Lord.

Hear the gospel of our Lord Jesus Christ according to John. (6.56-69)

Jesus said to the Jews, 'Those who eat my flesh and drink my blood abide in me, and I in them. Just as the living Father sent me, and I live because of the Father, so whoever eats me will live because of me. This is the bread that came down from heaven, not like that which your ancestors ate, and they died. But the one who eats this bread will live for ever.' He said these things while he was teaching in the synagogue at Capernaum.

When many of his disciples heard it, they said, 'This teaching is difficult; who can accept it?' But Jesus, being aware that his disciples were complaining about it, said to them, 'Does this offend you? Then what if you were to see the Son of Man ascending to where he was before? It is the spirit that gives life; the flesh is useless. The words that I have spoken to you are spirit and life. But among you there are some who do not believe.' For Jesus knew from the first who were the ones that did not believe, and who was the one that would betray him. And he said, 'For this reason I have told you that no one can come to me unless it is granted by the Father.'

Because of this many of his disciples turned back and no longer went about with him. So Jesus asked the twelve, 'Do you also wish to go away?' Simon Peter answered him, 'Lord, to whom can we go? You have the words of eternal life. We have come to believe and know that you are the Holy One of God.'

This is the gospel of the Lord.

Second Service
Ps 116 *or* 116.12-19; Exodus 4.27 - 5.1;
Hebrews 13.16-21; *if a Eucharist:* Luke 13.10-17

A reading from the Book of the Exodus. *(4.27 - 5.1)*

The Lord said to Aaron, 'Go into the wilderness to meet Moses.' So
he went; and he met him at the mountain of God and kissed him.
Moses told Aaron all the words of the Lord with which he had sent
him, and all the signs with which he had charged him. Then Moses
and Aaron went and assembled all the elders of the Israelites. Aaron
spoke all the words that the Lord had spoken to Moses, and performed the signs in the sight of the people. The people believed; and
when they heard that the Lord had given heed to the Israelites and
that he had seen their misery, they bowed down and worshipped.

Afterwards Moses and Aaron went to Pharaoh and said, 'Thus says
the Lord, the God of Israel, "Let my people go, so that they may
celebrate a festival to me in the wilderness."'

A reading from the Letter to the Hebrews. *(13.16-21)*

Do not neglect to do good and to share what you have, for such
sacrifices are pleasing to God.

Obey your leaders and submit to them, for they are keeping watch
over your souls and will give an account. Let them do this with joy
and not with sighing – for that would be harmful to you.

Pray for us; we are sure that we have a clear conscience, desiring to
act honourably in all things. I urge you all the more to do this, so that
I may be restored to you very soon.

Now may the God of peace, who brought back from the dead our
Lord Jesus, the great shepherd of the sheep, by the blood of the eternal covenant, make you complete in everything good so that you
may do his will, working among us that which is pleasing in his
sight, through Jesus Christ, to whom be the glory for ever and ever.
Amen.

If a Eucharist:
Hear the gospel of our Lord Jesus Christ according to Luke. *(13.10-17)*

Jesus was teaching in one of the synagogues on the sabbath. And just
then there appeared a woman with a spirit that had crippled her for
eighteen years. She was bent over and was quite unable to stand up
straight. When Jesus saw her, he called her over and said, 'Woman,
you are set free from your ailment.' When he laid his hands on her,
immediately she stood up straight and began praising God. But the

leader of the synagogue, indignant because Jesus had cured on the sabbath, kept saying to the crowd, 'There are six days on which work ought to be done; come on those days and be cured, and not on the sabbath day.' But the Lord answered him and said, 'You hypocrites! Does not each of you on the sabbath untie his ox or his donkey from the manger, and lead it away to give it water? And ought not this woman, a daughter of Abraham whom Satan bound for eighteen long years, be set free from this bondage on the sabbath day?' When he said this, all his opponents were put to shame; and the entire crowd was rejoicing at all the wonderful things that he was doing.

This is the gospel of the Lord.

Third Service

Ps 115; Jonah 2 *or* Ecclesiasticus 3.17-29; Revelation 1

A reading from the Book of Jonah. (Chapter 2)

Jonah prayed to the Lord his God from the belly of the fish, saying,
  'I called to the Lord out of my distress,
    and he answered me;
  out of the belly of Sheol I cried,
    and you heard my voice.
  You cast me into the deep, into the heart of the seas,
    and the flood surrounded me;
  all your waves and your billows
    passed over me.
  Then I said, "I am driven away from your sight;
    how shall I look again upon your holy temple?"
  The waters closed in over me;
    the deep surrounded me;
  weeds were wrapped around my head
    at the roots of the mountains.
  I went down to the land whose bars closed upon me for ever;
    yet you brought up my life from the Pit, O Lord my God.
  As my life was ebbing away, I remembered the Lord;
    and my prayer came to you, into your holy temple.
  Those who worship vain idols
    forsake their true loyalty.
  But I with the voice of thanksgiving will sacrifice to you;
    what I have vowed I will pay.
  Deliverance belongs to the Lord!'
Then the Lord spoke to the fish, and it spewed Jonah out upon the dry land.

Or:

A reading from the book Ecclesiasticus. *(3.17-29)*

My child, perform your tasks with humility;
   then you will be loved by those whom God accepts.
The greater you are, the more you must humble yourself;
   so you will find favour in the sight of the Lord.
For great is the might of the Lord;
   but by the humble he is glorified.
Neither seek what is too difficult for you,
   nor investigate what is beyond your power.
Reflect upon what you have been commanded,
   for what is hidden is not your concern.
Do not meddle in matters that are beyond you,
   for more than you can understand has been shown to you.
For their conceit has led many astray,
   and wrong opinion has impaired their judgement.

Without eyes there is no light;
   without knowledge there is no wisdom.
A stubborn mind will fare badly at the end,
   and whoever loves danger will perish in it.
A stubborn mind will be burdened by troubles,
   and the sinner adds sin to sins.
When calamity befalls the proud, there is no healing,
   for an evil plant has taken root in him.
The mind of the intelligent appreciates proverbs,
   and an attentive ear is the desire of the wise.

A reading from the Revelation to John. *(Chapter 1)*

The revelation of Jesus Christ, which God gave him to show his servants what must soon take place; he made it known by sending his angel to his servant John, who testified to the word of God and to the testimony of Jesus Christ, even to all that he saw.

Blessèd is the one who reads aloud the words of the prophecy, and blessèd are those who hear and who keep what is written in it; for the time is near.

John to the seven churches that are in Asia:

Grace to you and peace from him who is and who was and who is to come, and from the seven spirits who are before his throne, and from Jesus Christ, the faithful witness, the firstborn of the dead, and the ruler of the kings of the earth.

To him who loves us and freed us from our sins by his blood, and made us to be a kingdom, priests serving his God and Father, to him be glory and dominion for ever and ever. Amen.

Look! He is coming with the clouds;
every eye will see him, even those who pierced him;
and on his account all the tribes of the earth will wail.
So it is to be. Amen.

'I am the Alpha and the Omega', says the Lord God, who is and who was and who is to come, the Almighty.

I, John, your brother who share with you in Jesus the persecution and the kingdom and the patient endurance, was on the island called Patmos because of the word of God and the testimony of Jesus. I was in the spirit on the Lord's day, and I heard behind me a loud voice like a trumpet saying, 'Write in a book what you see and send it to the seven churches, to Ephesus, to Smyrna, to Pergamum, to Thyatira, to Sardis, to Philadelphia, and to Laodicea.'

Then I turned to see whose voice it was that spoke to me, and on turning I saw seven golden lampstands, and in the midst of the lampstands I saw one like the Son of Man, clothed with a long robe and with a golden sash across his chest. His head and his hair were white as white wool, white as snow; his eyes were like a flame of fire, his feet were like burnished bronze, refined as in a furnace, and his voice was like the sound of many waters. In his right hand he held seven stars, and from his mouth came a sharp, two-edged sword, and his face was like the sun shining with full force.

When I saw him, I fell at his feet as though dead. But he placed his right hand on me, saying, 'Do not be afraid; I am the first and the last, and the living one. I was dead, and see, I am alive for ever and ever; and I have the keys of Death and of Hades. Now write what you have seen, what is, and what is to take place after this. As for the mystery of the seven stars that you saw in my right hand, and the seven golden lampstands: the seven stars are the angels of the seven churches, and the seven lampstands are the seven churches.

Proper 17

Sunday between 28 August & 3 September inclusive

Principal Service

Continuous   *Related*
Song of Solomon 2.8-13   Deuteronomy 4.1-2,6-9
Ps 45.1-2,6-9 *or* 1-7   Ps 15
                    James 1.17-27
                    Mark 7.1-8,14-15,21-23

A reading from the Song of Solomon. (2.8-13)

> The voice of my belovèd!
> > Look, he comes,
> leaping upon the mountains,
> > bounding over the hills.
> My belovèd is like a gazelle
> > or a young stag.
> Look, there he stands
> > behind our wall,
> gazing in at the windows,
> > looking through the lattice.
> My belovèd speaks and says to me:
> 'Arise, my love, my fair one,
> > and come away;
> for now the winter is past,
> > the rain is over and gone.
> The flowers appear on the earth;
> > the time of singing has come,
> and the voice of the turtle-dove
> > is heard in our land.
> The fig tree puts forth its figs,
> > and the vines are in blossom;
> > they give forth fragrance.
> Arise, my love, my fair one,
> > and come away.

This is the word of the Lord.

Or:

A reading from the book Deuteronomy. (4.1-2,6-9)

Moses said: So now, Israel, give heed to the statutes and ordinances that I am teaching you to observe, so that you may live to enter and occupy the land that the Lord, the God of your ancestors, is giving you. You must neither add anything to what I command you nor take away anything from it, but keep the commandments of the Lord your God with which I am charging you.

⁶ You must observe them diligently, for this will show your wisdom and discernment to the peoples, who, when they hear all these statutes, will say, 'Surely this great nation is a wise and discerning people!' For what other great nation has a god so near to it as the Lord our God is whenever we call to him? And what other great nation has statutes and ordinances as just as this entire law that I am setting before you today?

But take care and watch yourselves closely, so as neither to forget the things that your eyes have seen nor to let them slip from your mind all the days of your life; make them known to your children and your children's children.

This is the word of the Lord.

A reading from the Letter of James. (1.17-27)

Every generous act of giving, with every perfect gift, is from above, coming down from the Father of lights, with whom there is no variation or shadow due to change. In fulfilment of his own purpose he gave us birth by the word of truth, so that we would become a kind of first fruits of his creatures.

You must understand this, my belovèd: let everyone be quick to listen, slow to speak, slow to anger; for your anger does not produce God's righteousness. Therefore rid yourselves of all sordidness and rank growth of wickedness, and welcome with meekness the implanted word that has the power to save your souls.

But be doers of the word, and not merely hearers who deceive themselves. For if any are hearers of the word and not doers, they are like those who look at themselves in a mirror; for they look at themselves and, on going away, immediately forget what they were like. But those who look into the perfect law, the law of liberty, and persevere, being not hearers who forget but doers who act – they will be blessed in their doing.

If any think they are religious, and do not bridle their tongues but deceive their hearts, their religion is worthless. Religion that is pure and undefiled before God, the Father, is this: to care for orphans and widows in their distress, and to keep oneself unstained by the world.

This is the word of the Lord.

Hear the gospel of our Lord Jesus Christ according to Mark.
(7.1-8,14-15,21-23)

When the Pharisees and some of the scribes who had come from Jerusalem gathered around Jesus, they noticed that some of his disciples were eating with defiled hands, that is, without washing them (for the Pharisees, and all the Jews, do not eat unless they thoroughly wash their hands, thus observing the tradition of the elders; and they do not eat anything from the market unless they wash it; and there are also many other traditions that they observe, the washing of cups, pots, and bronze kettles). So the Pharisees and the scribes asked him, 'Why do your disciples not live according to the tradition of the elders, but eat with defiled hands?' He said to them, 'Isaiah prophesied rightly about you hypocrites, as it is written,

> "This people honours me with their lips,
>> but their hearts are far from me;
> in vain do they worship me,
>> teaching human precepts as doctrines."

You abandon the commandment of God and hold to human tradition.'

[14] Then he called the crowd again and said to them, 'Listen to me, all of you, and understand: there is nothing outside a person that by going in can defile, but the things that come out are what defile.'

[21] 'For it is from within, from the human heart, that evil intentions come: fornication, theft, murder, adultery, avarice, wickedness, deceit, licentiousness, envy, slander, pride, folly. All these evil things come from within, and they defile a person.'

This is the gospel of the Lord.

Second Service
Ps 119.1-16 *or* 9-16; Exodus 12.21-27; Matthew 4.23 - 5.20

A reading from the Book of the Exodus. (12.21-27)

Moses called all the elders of Israel and said to them, 'Go, select lambs for your families, and slaughter the passover lamb. Take a bunch of hyssop, dip it in the blood that is in the basin, and touch the lintel and the two doorposts with the blood in the basin. None of you shall go outside the door of your house until morning. For the Lord will pass through to strike down the Egyptians; when he sees the blood on the lintel and on the two doorposts, the Lord will pass over that door and will not allow the destroyer to enter your houses to strike you down. You shall observe this rite as a perpetual ordinance for you and your children. When you come to the land that the Lord will give you, as he has promised, you shall keep this observance. And when your children ask you, "What do you mean by this observance?" you shall say, "It is the passover sacrifice to the Lord, for he passed over the houses of the Israelites in Egypt, when he struck down the Egyptians but spared our houses."' And the people bowed down and worshipped.

A reading from the gospel according to Matthew. (4.23 - 5.20)

Jesus went throughout Galilee, teaching in their synagogues and proclaiming the good news of the kingdom and curing every disease and every sickness among the people. So his fame spread throughout all Syria, and they brought to him all the sick, those who were afflicted with various diseases and pains, demoniacs, epileptics, and paralytics, and he cured them. And great crowds followed him from Galilee, the Decapolis, Jerusalem, Judea, and from beyond the Jordan.

When Jesus saw the crowds, he went up the mountain; and after he sat down, his disciples came to him. Then he began to speak, and taught them, saying:

'Blessèd are the poor in spirit, for theirs is the kingdom of heaven.

'Blessèd are those who mourn, for they will be comforted.

'Blessèd are the meek, for they will inherit the earth.

'Blessèd are those who hunger and thirst for righteousness, for they will be filled.

'Blessèd are the merciful, for they will receive mercy.

'Blessèd are the pure in heart, for they will see God.

'Blessèd are the peacemakers, for they will be called children of God.

'Blessèd are those who are persecuted for righteousness' sake, for theirs is the kingdom of heaven.

'Blessèd are you when people revile you and persecute you and utter all kinds of evil against you falsely on my account. Rejoice and be glad, for your reward is great in heaven, for in the same way they persecuted the prophets who were before you.

'You are the salt of the earth; but if salt has lost its taste, how can its saltiness be restored? It is no longer good for anything, but is thrown out and trampled under foot.

'You are the light of the world. A city built on a hill cannot be hidden. No one after lighting a lamp puts it under the bushel basket, but on the lampstand, and it gives light to all in the house. In the same way, let your light shine before others, so that they may see your good works and give glory to your Father in heaven.

'Do not think that I have come to abolish the law or the prophets;

I have come not to abolish but to fulfil. For truly I tell you, until heaven and earth pass away, not one letter, not one stroke of a letter, will pass from the law until all is accomplished. Therefore, whoever breaks one of the least of these commandments, and teaches others to do the same, will be called least in the kingdom of heaven; but whoever does them and teaches them will be called great in the kingdom of heaven. For I tell you, unless your righteousness exceeds that of the scribes and Pharisees, you will never enter the kingdom of heaven.'

Third Service

Ps 119.17-40; Jonah 3.1-9 *or* Ecclesiasticus 11.7-28 *or* 19-28; Revelation 3.14-22

A reading from the Book of Jonah. (3.1-9)

The word of the Lord came to Jonah a second time, saying, 'Get up, go to Nineveh, that great city, and proclaim to it the message that I tell you.'   So Jonah set out and went to Nineveh, according to the word of the Lord.   Now Nineveh was an exceedingly large city, a three days' walk across.   Jonah began to go into the city, going a day's walk.   And he cried out, 'Forty days more, and Nineveh shall be overthrown!' And the people of Nineveh believed God; they proclaimed a fast, and everyone, great and small, put on sackcloth.

When the news reached the king of Nineveh, he rose from his throne, removed his robe, covered himself with sackcloth, and sat in ashes.   Then he had a proclamation made in Nineveh: 'By the decree of the king and his nobles: No human being or animal, no herd or flock, shall taste anything.   They shall not feed, nor shall they drink water.   Human beings and animals shall be covered with sackcloth, and they shall cry mightily to God.   All shall turn from their evil ways and from the violence that is in their hands. Who knows? God may relent and change his mind; he may turn from his fierce anger, so that we do not perish.'

Or:

A reading from the book Ecclesiasticus. (11.7-28 or 19-28)

Do not find fault before you investigate;
    examine first, and then criticize.
Do not answer before you listen,
    and do not interrupt when another is speaking.
Do not argue about a matter that does not concern you,
    and do not sit with sinners when they judge a case.

My child, do not busy yourself with many matters;

if you multiply activities, you will not be held blameless.
If you pursue, you will not overtake,
    and by fleeing you will not escape.
There are those who work and struggle and hurry,
    but are so much the more in want.
There are others who are slow and need help,
    who lack strength and abound in poverty;
but the eyes of the Lord look kindly upon them;
    he lifts them out of their lowly condition
    and raises up their heads to the amazement of many.

Good things and bad, life and death, poverty and wealth,
    come from the Lord.
Wisdom, understanding, and knowledge of the law
    come from the Lord;
affection and the ways of good works
    come from him.
Error and darkness were created with sinners;
    evil grows old with those who take pride in malice.
The Lord's gift remains with the devout,
    and his favour brings lasting success.
One becomes rich through diligence and self-denial,
    and the reward allotted to him is this:
19 when he says, 'I have found rest,
    and now I shall feast on my goods!'
he does not know how long it will be
    until he leaves them to others and dies.

Stand by your agreement and attend to it,
    and grow old in your work.
Do not wonder at the works of a sinner,
    but trust in the Lord and keep at your job;
for it is easy in the sight of the Lord
    to make the poor rich suddenly, in an instant.
The blessing of the Lord is the reward of the pious,
    and quickly God causes his blessing to flourish.
Do not say, 'What do I need,
    and what further benefit can be mine?'
Do not say, 'I have enough,
    and what harm can come to me now?'
In the day of prosperity, adversity is forgotten,
    and in the day of adversity, prosperity is not remembered.
For it is easy for the Lord on the day of death
    to reward individuals according to their conduct.

An hour's misery makes one forget past delights,
  and at the close of one's life one's deeds are revealed.
Call no one happy before his death;
  by how he ends, a person becomes known.

A reading from the Revelation to John. (3.14-22)

'To the angel of the church in Laodicea write: The words of the Amen, the faithful and true witness, the origin of God's creation: 'I know your works; you are neither cold nor hot. I wish that you were either cold or hot. So, because you are lukewarm, and neither cold nor hot, I am about to spit you out of my mouth. For you say, "I am rich, I have prospered, and I need nothing." You do not realize that you are wretched, pitiable, poor, blind, and naked. Therefore I counsel you to buy from me gold refined by fire so that you may be rich; and white robes to clothe you and to keep the shame of your nakedness from being seen; and salve to anoint your eyes so that you may see. I reprove and discipline those whom I love. Be earnest, therefore, and repent. Listen! I am standing at the door, knocking; if you hear my voice and open the door, I will come in to you and eat with you, and you with me. To the one who conquers I will give a place with me on my throne, just as I myself conquered and sat down with my Father on his throne. Let anyone who has an ear listen to what the Spirit is saying to the churches.'

Proper 18

Sunday between 4 & 10 September inclusive

Principal Service

Continuous	*Related*
Proverbs 22.1-2,8-9,22-23	Isaiah 35.4-7a
Ps 125	Ps 146

James 2.1-10 [11-13] 14-17
Mark 7.24-37

A reading from the book Proverbs. (22.1-2,8-9,22-23)

A good name is to be chosen rather than great riches,
  and favour is better than silver or gold.
The rich and the poor have this in common:
  the Lord is the maker of them all.
⁸ Whoever sows injustice will reap calamity,
  and the rod of anger will fail.
Those who are generous are blessed,

for they share their bread with the poor.
22 Do not rob the poor because they are poor,
    or crush the afflicted at the gate;
for the Lord pleads their cause
    and despoils of life those who despoil them.

This is the word of the Lord.

Or:

A reading from the prophecy of Isaiah. *(35.4-7a)*

Say to those who are of a fearful heart,
    'Be strong, do not fear!
Here is your God.
    He will come with vengeance,
with terrible recompense.
    He will come and save you.'
Then the eyes of the blind shall be opened,
    and the ears of the deaf unstopped;
then the lame shall leap like a deer,
    and the tongue of the speechless sing for joy.
For waters shall break forth in the wilderness,
    and streams in the desert;
the burning sand shall become a pool,
and the thirsty ground springs of water.

This is the word of the Lord.

A reading from the Letter of James. *(2.1-10 [11-13] 14-17)*

My brothers and sisters, do you with your acts of favouritism really believe in our glorious Lord Jesus Christ? For if a person with gold rings and in fine clothes comes into your assembly, and if a poor person in dirty clothes also comes in, and if you take notice of the one wearing the fine clothes and say, 'Have a seat here, please', while to the one who is poor you say, 'Stand there', or, 'Sit at my feet', have you not made distinctions among yourselves, and become judges with evil thoughts? Listen, my belovèd brothers and sisters. Has not God chosen the poor in the world to be rich in faith and to be heirs of the kingdom that he has promised to those who love him? But you have dishonoured the poor. Is it not the rich who oppress you? Is it not they who drag you into court? Is it not they who blaspheme the excellent name that was invoked over you?

You do well if you really fulfil the royal law according to the scripture, 'You shall love your neighbour as yourself.' But if you show partiality, you commit sin and are convicted by the law as transgressors. For whoever keeps the whole law but fails in one point has become accountable for all of it. [11 For the one who said, 'You shall not commit adultery', also said, 'You shall not murder.' Now if you do not commit adultery but if you murder, you have become a transgressor of the law. So speak and so act as those who are to be judged by the law of liberty. For judgement will be without mercy to anyone who has shown no mercy; mercy triumphs over judgement.]

14 What good is it, my brothers and sisters, if you say you have faith but do not have works? Can faith save you? If a brother or sister is naked and lacks daily food, and one of you says to them, 'Go in peace; keep warm and eat your fill', and yet you do not supply their bodily needs, what is the good of that? So faith by itself, if it has no works, is dead.

This is the word of the Lord.

Hear the gospel of our Lord Jesus Christ according to Mark. (7.24-37)

From the land of Gennesaret, Jesus set out and went away to the region of Tyre. He entered a house and did not want anyone to know he was there. Yet he could not escape notice, but a woman whose little daughter had an unclean spirit immediately heard about him, and she came and bowed down at his feet. Now the woman was a Gentile, of Syrophoenician origin. She begged him to cast the demon out of her daughter. He said to her, 'Let the children be fed first, for it is not fair to take the children's food and throw it to the dogs.' But she answered him, 'Sir, even the dogs under the table eat the children's crumbs.' Then he said to her, 'For saying that, you may go – the demon has left your daughter.' So she went home, found the child lying on the bed, and the demon gone.

Then he returned from the region of Tyre, and went by way of Sidon towards the Sea of Galilee, in the region of the Decapolis. They brought to him a deaf man who had an impediment in his speech; and they begged him to lay his hand on him. He took him aside in private, away from the crowd, and put his fingers into his ears, and he spat and touched his tongue. Then looking up to heaven, he sighed and said to him, 'Ephphatha', that is, 'Be opened.' And immediately his ears were opened, his tongue was released, and he spoke plainly. Then Jesus ordered them to tell no one; but the more he ordered them, the more zealously they proclaimed it. They were astounded beyond measure, saying, 'He has done everything well; he even makes the deaf to hear and the mute to speak.'

This is the gospel of the Lord.

Second Service

Ps 119.41-56 *or* 49-56; Exodus 14.5-31; Matthew 6.1-18

A reading from the Book of the Exodus. (14.5-31)

When the king of Egypt was told that the people had fled, the minds of Pharaoh and his officials were changed towards the people, and they said, 'What have we done, letting Israel leave our service?' So he had his chariot made ready, and took his army with him; he took six hundred picked chariots and all the other chariots of Egypt with officers over all of them. The Lord hardened the heart of Pharaoh king of Egypt and he pursued the Israelites, who were going out boldly. The Egyptians pursued them, all Pharaoh's horses and chariots, his chariot drivers and his army; they overtook them camped by the sea, by Pi-hahiroth, in front of Baal-zephon.

As Pharaoh drew near, the Israelites looked back, and there were the Egyptians advancing on them. In great fear the Israelites cried out to the Lord. They said to Moses, 'Was it because there were no graves in Egypt that you have taken us away to die in the wilderness? What have you done to us, bringing us out of Egypt? Is this not the very thing we told you in Egypt, "Let us alone and let us serve the Egyptians"? For it would have been better for us to serve the Egyptians than to die in the wilderness.' But Moses said to the people, 'Do not be afraid, stand firm, and see the deliverance that the Lord will accomplish for you today; for the Egyptians whom you see today you shall never see again. The Lord will fight for you, and you have only to keep still.'

Then the Lord said to Moses, 'Why do you cry out to me? Tell the Israelites to go forward. But you lift up your staff, and stretch out your hand over the sea and divide it, that the Israelites may go into the sea on dry ground. Then I will harden the hearts of the Egyptians so that they will go in after them; and so I will gain glory for myself over Pharaoh and all his army, his chariots, and his chariot drivers. And the Egyptians shall know that I am the Lord, when I have gained glory for myself over Pharaoh, his chariots, and his chariot drivers.'

The angel of God who was going before the Israelite army moved and went behind them; and the pillar of cloud moved from in front of them and took its place behind them. It came between the army of Egypt and the army of Israel. And so the cloud was there with the darkness, and it lit up the night; one did not come near the other all night.

Then Moses stretched out his hand over the sea. The Lord drove the sea back by a strong east wind all night, and turned the sea into dry land; and the waters were divided. The Israelites went into the sea on dry ground, the waters forming a wall for them on their right and on their left. The Egyptians pursued, and went into the sea after them, all of Pharaoh's horses, chariots, and chariot drivers. At the morning watch the Lord in the pillar of fire and cloud looked down upon the Egyptian army, and threw the Egyptian army into panic. He clogged their chariot wheels so that they turned with difficulty. The Egyptians said, 'Let us flee from the Israelites, for the Lord is fighting for them against Egypt.'

Then the Lord said to Moses, 'Stretch out your hand over the sea, so that the water may come back upon the Egyptians, upon their chariots and chariot drivers.' So Moses stretched out his hand over the sea, and at dawn the sea returned to its normal depth. As the Egyptians fled before it, the Lord tossed the Egyptians into the sea. The waters returned and covered the chariots and the chariot drivers, the entire army of Pharaoh that had followed them into the sea; not one of them remained. But the Israelites walked on dry ground through the sea, the waters forming a wall for them on their right and on their left.

Thus the Lord saved Israel that day from the Egyptians; and Israel saw the Egyptians dead on the seashore. Israel saw the great work that the Lord did against the Egyptians. So the people feared the Lord and believed in the Lord and in his servant Moses.

A reading from the gospel according to Matthew. (6.1-18)

Jesus said to his disciples and the crowds, 'Beware of practising your piety before others in order to be seen by them; for then you have no reward from your Father in heaven.

'So whenever you give alms, do not sound a trumpet before you, as the hypocrites do in the synagogues and in the streets, so that they may be praised by others. Truly I tell you, they have received their reward. But when you give alms, do not let your left hand know what your right hand is doing, so that your alms may be done in secret; and your Father who sees in secret will reward you.

'And whenever you pray, do not be like the hypocrites; for they love to stand and pray in the synagogues and at the street corners, so that they may be seen by others. Truly I tell you, they have received their reward. But whenever you pray, go into your room and shut the door and pray to your Father who is in secret; and your Father who sees in secret will reward you.

'When you are praying, do not heap up empty phrases as the Gentiles do; for they think that they will be heard because of their many words. Do not be like them, for your Father knows what you need before you ask him.

'Pray then in this way:

Our Father in heaven,
    hallowed be your name.
    Your kingdom come.
    Your will be done,
        on earth as it is in heaven.
    Give us this day our daily bread.
    And forgive us our debts,
        as we also have forgiven our debtors.
    And do not bring us to the time of trial,
        but rescue us from the evil one.

For if you forgive others their trespasses, your heavenly Father will also forgive you; but if you do not forgive others, neither will your Father forgive your trespasses.

'And whenever you fast, do not look dismal, like the hypocrites, for they disfigure their faces so as to show others that they are fasting. Truly I tell you, they have received their reward. But when you fast, put oil on your head and wash your face, so that your fasting may be seen not by others but by your Father who is in secret; and your Father who sees in secret will reward you.'

Third Service

Ps 119.57-72; Jonah 3.10 - 4.11 *or* Ecclesiasticus 27.30 - 28.9;
Revelation 8.1-5

A reading from the Book of Jonah. (3.10 - 4.11)

When God saw what the people of Nineveh did, how they turned from their evil ways, God changed his mind about the calamity that he had said he would bring upon them; and he did not do it.

But this was very displeasing to Jonah, and he became angry. He prayed to the Lord and said, 'O Lord! Is not this what I said while I was still in my own country? That is why I fled to Tarshish at the beginning; for I knew that you are a gracious God and merciful, slow to anger, and abounding in steadfast love, and ready to relent from punishing. And now, O Lord, please take my life from me, for it is better for me to die than to live.' And the Lord said, 'Is it right for you to be angry?' Then Jonah went out of the city and sat down east of the city, and made a booth for himself there. He sat under it in the shade, waiting to see what would become of the city.

The Lord God appointed a bush, and made it come up over Jonah, to give shade over his head, to save him from his discomfort; so Jonah was very happy about the bush. But when dawn came up the next day, God appointed a worm that attacked the bush, so that it withered. When the sun rose, God prepared a sultry east wind, and the sun beat down on the head of Jonah so that he was faint and asked that he might die. He said, 'It is better for me to die than to live.'

But God said to Jonah, 'Is it right for you to be angry about the bush?' And he said, 'Yes, angry enough to die.' Then the Lord said, 'You are concerned about the bush, for which you did not labour and which you did not grow; it came into being in a night and perished in a night. And should I not be concerned about Nineveh, that great city, in which there are more than a hundred and twenty thousand persons who do not know their right hand from their left, and also many animals?'

Or:

A reading from the book Ecclesiasticus. *(27.30 - 28.9)*

Anger and wrath, these also are abominations,
    yet a sinner holds on to them.
The vengeful will face the Lord's vengeance,
    for he keeps a strict account of their sins.
Forgive your neighbour the wrong he has done,
    and then your sins will be pardoned when you pray.
Does anyone harbour anger against another,
    and expect healing from the Lord?
If someone has no mercy towards another like himself,
    can he then seek pardon for his own sins?
If a mere mortal harbours wrath,
    who will make an atoning sacrifice for his sins?
Remember the end of your life,
    and set enmity aside;
remember corruption and death,
    and be true to the commandments.
Remember the commandments,
    and do not be angry with your neighbour;
remember the covenant of the Most High,
    and overlook faults.

Refrain from strife, and your sins will be fewer;
    for the hot-tempered kindle strife,
and the sinner disrupts friendships
    and sows discord among those who are at peace.

A reading from the Revelation to John. (8.1-5)

When the Lamb opened the seventh seal, there was silence in heaven for about half an hour. And I saw the seven angels who stand before God, and seven trumpets were given to them.

Another angel with a golden censer came and stood at the altar; he was given a great quantity of incense to offer with the prayers of all the saints on the golden altar that is before the throne. And the smoke of the incense, with the prayers of the saints, rose before God from the hand of the angel. Then the angel took the censer and filled it with fire from the altar and threw it on the earth; and there were peals of thunder, rumblings, flashes of lightning, and an earthquake.

Proper 19

Sunday between 11 & 17 September inclusive

Principal Service

Continuous	*Related*
Proverbs 1.20-33	Isaiah 50.4-9*a*
Ps 19 *or* 19.1-6	Ps 116.1-9
or Canticle:	
Wisdom of Solomon 7.26 - 8.1	
James 3.1-12	
Mark 8.27-38	

A reading from the book Proverbs. (1.20-33)

Wisdom cries out in the street;
    in the squares she raises her voice.
At the busiest corner she cries out;
    at the entrance of the city gates she speaks:
'How long, O simple ones, will you love being simple?
How long will scoffers delight in their scoffing
    and fools hate knowledge?
Give heed to my reproof;
I will pour out my thoughts to you;
    I will make my words known to you.
Because I have called and you refused,
    have stretched out my hand and no one heeded,
and because you have ignored all my counsel
    and would have none of my reproof,
I also will laugh at your calamity;
    I will mock when panic strikes you,
when panic strikes you like a storm,

and your calamity comes like a whirlwind,
    when distress and anguish come upon you.
Then they will call upon me, but I will not answer;
    they will seek me diligently, but will not find me.
Because they hated knowledge
    and did not choose the fear of the Lord,
would have none of my counsel,
    and despised all my reproof,
therefore they shall eat the fruit of their way
    and be sated with their own devices.
For waywardness kills the simple,
    and the complacency of fools destroys them;
but those who listen to me will be secure
    and will live at ease, without dread of disaster.'

This is the word of the Lord.

Or:

A reading from the prophecy of Isaiah. *(50.4-9a)*

The Lord God has given me
    the tongue of a teacher,
that I may know how to sustain the weary with a word.
Morning by morning he wakens – wakens my ear
    to listen as those who are taught.
The Lord God has opened my ear,
    and I was not rebellious,
    I did not turn backwards.
I gave my back to those who struck me,
    and my cheeks to those who pulled out the beard;
I did not hide my face
    from insult and spitting.

The Lord God helps me;
    therefore I have not been disgraced;
therefore I have set my face like flint,
    and I know that I shall not be put to shame;
    he who vindicates me is near.
Who will contend with me?
    Let us stand up together.
Who are my adversaries?
    Let them confront me.
It is the Lord God who helps me;
    who will declare me guilty?

This is the word of the Lord.

A reading from the Letter of James. (3.1-12)

Not many of you should become teachers, my brothers and sisters, for you know that we who teach will be judged with greater strictness. For all of us make many mistakes. Anyone who makes no mistakes in speaking is perfect, able to keep the whole body in check with a bridle. If we put bits into the mouths of horses to make them obey us, we guide their whole bodies. Or look at ships: though they are so large that it takes strong winds to drive them, yet they are guided by a very small rudder wherever the will of the pilot directs. So also the tongue is a small member, yet it boasts of great exploits.

How great a forest is set ablaze by a small fire! And the tongue is a fire. The tongue is placed among our members as a world of iniquity; it stains the whole body, sets on fire the cycle of nature, and is itself set on fire by hell. For every species of beast and bird, of reptile and sea creature, can be tamed and has been tamed by the human species, but no one can tame the tongue – a restless evil, full of deadly poison. With it we bless the Lord and Father, and with it we curse those who are made in the likeness of God. From the same mouth come blessing and cursing. My brothers and sisters, this ought not to be so. Does a spring pour forth from the same opening both fresh and brackish water? Can a fig tree, my brothers and sisters, yield olives, or a grapevine figs? No more can salt water yield fresh.

This is the word of the Lord.

Hear the gospel of our Lord Jesus Christ according to Mark. (8.27-38)

Jesus went on with his disciples to the villages of Caesarea Philippi; and on the way he asked his disciples, 'Who do people say that I am?' And they answered him, 'John the Baptist; and others, Elijah; and still others, one of the prophets.' He asked them, 'But who do you say that I am?' Peter answered him, 'You are the Messiah.' And he sternly ordered them not to tell anyone about him.

Then he began to teach them that the Son of Man must undergo great suffering, and be rejected by the elders, the chief priests, and the scribes, and be killed, and after three days rise again. He said all this quite openly. And Peter took him aside and began to rebuke him. But turning and looking at his disciples, he rebuked Peter and said, 'Get behind me, Satan! For you are setting your mind not on divine things but on human things.'

He called the crowd with his disciples, and said to them, 'If any want to become my followers, let them deny themselves and take up their cross and follow me. For those who want to save their life will lose it, and those who lose their life for my sake, and for the sake of the gospel, will save it. For what will it profit them to gain the whole world and forfeit their life? Indeed, what can they give in return for their life? Those who are ashamed of me and of my words in this adulterous and sinful generation, of them the Son of Man will also be ashamed when he comes in the glory of his Father with the holy angels.'

This is the gospel of the Lord.

Second Service
Ps 119.73-80 [81-88]; Exodus 18.13-26; Matthew 7.1-14

A reading from the Book of the Exodus. *(18.13-26)*

Moses sat as judge for the people, while the people stood around him from morning until evening. When Moses' father-in-law saw all that he was doing for the people, he said, 'What is this that you are doing for the people? Why do you sit alone, while all the people stand around you from morning until evening?' Moses said to his father-in-law, 'Because the people come to me to inquire of God. When they have a dispute, they come to me and I decide between one person and another, and I make known to them the statutes and instructions of God.' Moses' father-in-law said to him, 'What you are doing is not good. You will surely wear yourself out, both you and these people with you. For the task is too heavy for you; you cannot do it alone. Now listen to me. I will give you counsel, and God be with you! You should represent the people before God, and you should bring their cases before God; teach them the statutes and instructions and make known to them the way they are to go and the things they are to do. You should also look for able men among all the people, men who fear God, are trustworthy, and hate dishonest gain; set such men over them as officers over thousands, hundreds, fifties and tens. Let them sit as judges for the people at all times; let them bring every important case to you, but decide every minor case themselves. So it will be easier for you, and they will bear the burden with you. If you do this, and God so commands you, then you will be able to endure, and all these people will go to their home in peace.'

So Moses listened to his father-in-law and did all that he had said. Moses chose able men from all Israel and appointed them as heads over the people, as officers over thousands, hundreds, fifties, and tens. And they judged the people at all times; hard cases they brought to Moses, but any minor case they decided themselves.

A reading from the gospel according to Matthew. (7.1-14)

Jesus said to his disciples and the crowds, 'Do not judge, so that you may not be judged. For with the judgement you make you will be judged, and the measure you give will be the measure you get. Why do you see the speck in your neighbour's eye, but do not notice the log in your own eye? Or how can you say to your neighbour, "Let me take the speck out of your eye", while the log is in your own eye? You hypocrite, first take the log out of your own eye, and then you will see clearly to take the speck out of your neighbour's eye.

'Do not give what is holy to dogs; and do not throw your pearls before swine, or they will trample them under foot and turn and maul you.

'Ask, and it will be given to you; search, and you will find; knock, and the door will be opened for you. For everyone who asks receives, and everyone who searches finds, and for everyone who knocks, the door will be opened. Is there anyone among you who, if your child asks for bread, will give a stone? Or if the child asks for a fish, will give a snake? If you then, who are evil, know how to give good gifts to your children, how much more will your Father in heaven give good things to those who ask him!

'In everything do to others as you would have them do to you; for this is the law and the prophets.

'Enter through the narrow gate; for the gate is wide and the road is easy that leads to destruction, and there are many who take it. For the gate is narrow and the road is hard that leads to life, and there are few who find it.'

Third Service
Ps 119.105-120; Isaiah 44.24 - 45.8; Revelation 12.1-12

A reading from the prophecy of Isaiah. (44.24 - 45.8)

> Thus says the Lord, your Redeemer,
>   who formed you in the womb:
> I am the Lord, who made all things,
>   who alone stretched out the heavens,
>   who by myself spread out the earth;
> who frustrates the omens of liars,
>   and makes fools of diviners;
> who turns back the wise,
>   and makes their knowledge foolish;
> who confirms the word of his servant,
>   and fulfils the prediction of his messengers;

who says of Jerusalem, 'It shall be inhabited',
    and of the cities of Judah,
    'They shall be rebuilt, and I will raise up their ruins';
who says to the deep,
    'Be dry – I will dry up your rivers';
who says of Cyrus, 'He is my shepherd,
    and he shall carry out all my purpose';
and who says of Jerusalem,
    'It shall be rebuilt',
and of the temple,
    'Your foundation shall be laid.'

Thus says the Lord to his anointed, to Cyrus, whose right hand I have grasped to subdue nations before him and strip kings of their robes, to open doors before him – and the gates shall not be closed:
I will go before you
    and level the mountains,
I will break in pieces the doors of bronze
    and cut through the bars of iron,
I will give you the treasures of darkness
    and riches hidden in secret places,
so that you may know that it is I, the Lord,
    the God of Israel, who call you by your name.
For the sake of my servant Jacob,
    and Israel my chosen,
I call you by your name,
    I surname you, though you do not know me.
I am the Lord, and there is no other;
    besides me there is no god.
    I arm you, though you do not know me,
so that they may know, from the rising of the sun
    and from the west, that there is no one besides me;
I am the Lord, and there is no other.
I form light and create darkness,
    I make weal and create woe; I the Lord do all these things.

Shower, O heavens, from above,
    and let the skies rain down righteousness;
let the earth open, that salvation may spring up,
    and let it cause righteousness to sprout up also;
I the Lord have created it.

A reading from the Revelation to John. (12.1-12)

A great portent appeared in heaven: a woman clothed with the sun, with the moon under her feet, and on her head a crown of twelve stars. She was pregnant and was crying out in birth pangs, in the agony of giving birth. Then another portent appeared in heaven: a great red dragon, with seven heads and ten horns, and seven diadems on his heads. His tail swept down a third of the stars of heaven and threw them to the earth. Then the dragon stood before the woman who was about to bear a child, so that he might devour her child as soon as it was born. And she gave birth to a son, a male child, who is to rule all the nations with a rod of iron. But her child was snatched away and taken to God and to his throne; and the woman fled into the wilderness, where she has a place prepared by God, so that there she can be nourished for one thousand two hundred and sixty days.

And war broke out in heaven; Michael and his angels fought against the dragon. The dragon and his angels fought back, but they were defeated, and there was no longer any place for them in heaven. The great dragon was thrown down, that ancient serpent, who is called the Devil and Satan, the deceiver of the whole world – he was thrown down to the earth, and his angels were thrown down with him.

Then I heard a loud voice in heaven, proclaiming,
'Now have come the salvation and the power
    and the kingdom of our God
    and the authority of his Messiah,
for the accuser of our comrades has been thrown down,
    who accuses them day and night before our God.
But they have conquered him by the blood of the Lamb
    and by the word of their testimony,
for they did not cling to life even in the face of death.
Rejoice then, you heavens
    and those who dwell in them!
But woe to the earth and the sea,
    for the devil has come down to you
with great wrath,
    because he knows that his time is short!'

Proper 20

Sunday between 18 & 24 September inclusive

Principal Service

Continuous	*Related*
Proverbs 31.10-31	Wisdom of Solomon 1.16 - 2.1,12-22
Ps 1	*or* Jeremiah 11.18-20
	Ps 54

James 3.13 - 4.3,7-8*a*
Mark 9.30-37

A reading from the book Proverbs. (31.10-31)

A capable wife who can find?
    She is far more precious than jewels.
The heart of her husband trusts in her,
    and he will have no lack of gain.
She does him good, and not harm,
    all the days of her life.
She seeks wool and flax,
    and works with willing hands.
She is like the ships of the merchant,
    she brings her food from far away.
She rises while it is still night
    and provides food for her household
    and tasks for her servant-girls.
She considers a field and buys it;
    with the fruit of her hands she plants a vineyard.
She girds herself with strength,
    and makes her arms strong.
She perceives that her merchandise is profitable.
    Her lamp does not go out at night.
She puts her hands to the distaff,
    and her hands hold the spindle.
She opens her hand to the poor,
    and reaches out her hands to the needy.
She is not afraid for her household when it snows,
    for all her household are clothed in crimson.
She makes herself coverings;
    her clothing is fine linen and purple.
Her husband is known in the city gates,
    taking his seat among the elders of the land.
She makes linen garments and sells them;

she supplies the merchant with sashes.
Strength and dignity are her clothing,
  and she laughs at the time to come.
She opens her mouth with wisdom,
  and the teaching of kindness is on her tongue.
She looks well to the ways of her household,
  and does not eat the bread of idleness.
Her children rise up and call her happy;
  her husband too, and he praises her:
'Many women have done excellently,
  but you surpass them all.'
Charm is deceitful, and beauty is vain,
  but a woman who fears the Lord is to be praised.
Give her a share in the fruit of her hands,
  and let her works praise her in the city gates.

This is the word of the Lord.

Or:

A reading from the Wisdom of Solomon. *(1.16 - 2.1,12-22)*

The ungodly by their words and deeds summoned death;
considering him a friend, they pined away
and made a covenant with him,
because they are fit to belong to his company.
For they reasoned unsoundly, saying to themselves,
'Short and sorrowful is our life,
and there is no remedy when a life comes to its end,
and no one has been known to return from Hades.

¹² 'Let us lie in wait for the righteous man,
because he is inconvenient to us and opposes our actions;
he reproaches us for sins against the law,
and accuses us of sins against our training.
He professes to have knowledge of God,
and calls himself a child of the Lord.
He became to us a reproof of our thoughts;
the very sight of him is a burden to us,
because his manner of life is unlike that of others,
and his ways are strange.
We are considered by him as something base,
and he avoids our ways as unclean;
he calls the last end of the righteous happy,
and boasts that God is his father.
Let us see if his words are true,

and let us test what will happen at the end of his life;
for if the righteous man is God's child, he will help him,
and will deliver him from the hand of his adversaries.
Let us test him with insult and torture,
so that we may find out how gentle he is,
and make trial of his forbearance.
Let us condemn him to a shameful death,
for, according to what he says, he will be protected.'

Thus they reasoned, but they were led astray,
for their wickedness blinded them,
and they did not know the secret purposes of God,
nor hoped for the wages of holiness,
nor discerned the prize for blameless souls.

This is the word of the Lord.

Or:

A reading from the prophecy of Jeremiah. (11.18-20)

It was the Lord who made it known to me, and I knew;
    then you showed me their evil deeds.
But I was like a gentle lamb
    led to the slaughter.
And I did not know it was against me
    that they devised schemes, saying,
'Let us destroy the tree with its fruit,
    let us cut him off from the land of the living,
    so that his name will no longer be remembered!'
But you, O Lord of hosts, who judge righteously,
    who try the heart and the mind,
let me see your retribution upon them,
    for to you I have committed my cause.

This is the word of the Lord.

A reading from the Letter of James. (3.13 - 4.3,7-8a)

Who is wise and understanding among you? Show by your good life that your works are done with gentleness born of wisdom. But if you have bitter envy and selfish ambition in your hearts, do not be boastful and false to the truth. Such wisdom does not come down from above, but is earthly, unspiritual, devilish. For where there is envy and selfish ambition, there will also be disorder and wickedness of every kind. But the wisdom from above is first pure, then peaceable, gentle, willing to yield, full of mercy and good fruits, without a trace of partiality or hypocrisy. And a harvest of righteousness is sown in peace for those who make peace.

Those conflicts and disputes among you, where do they come from? Do they not come from your cravings that are at war within you? You want something and do not have it; so you commit murder. And you covet something and cannot obtain it; so you engage in disputes and conflicts. You do not have, because you do not ask. You ask and do not receive, because you ask wrongly, in order to spend what you get on your pleasures.

⁷ Submit yourselves therefore to God. Resist the devil, and he will flee from you. Draw near to God, and he will draw near to you.

This is the word of the Lord.

Hear the gospel of our Lord Jesus Christ according to Mark. (9.30-37)

Jesus and his disciples went on from there and passed through Galilee. He did not want anyone to know it; for he was teaching his disciples, saying to them, 'The Son of Man is to be betrayed into human hands, and they will kill him, and three days after being killed, he will rise again.' But they did not understand what he was saying and were afraid to ask him.

Then they came to Capernaum; and when he was in the house he asked them, 'What were you arguing about on the way?' But they were silent, for on the way they had argued with one another about who was the greatest. He sat down, called the twelve, and said to them, 'Whoever wants to be first must be last of all and servant of all.' Then he took a little child and put it among them; and taking it in his arms, he said to them, 'Whoever welcomes one such child in my name welcomes me, and whoever welcomes me welcomes not me but the one who sent me.'

This is the gospel of the Lord.

Second Service
Ps 119.137-144 [145-152]; Exodus 19.10-25; Matthew 8.23-34

A reading from the Book of the Exodus. (19.10-25)

The Lord said to Moses, 'Go to the people and consecrate them today and tomorrow. Have them wash their clothes and prepare for the third day, because on the third day the Lord will come down upon Mount Sinai in the sight of all the people. You shall set limits for the people all around, saying, "Be careful not to go up the mountain or to touch the edge of it. Any who touch the mountain shall be put to death. No hand shall touch them, but they shall be stoned or shot with arrows; whether animal or human being, they shall not live." When the trumpet sounds a long blast, they may go up on the mountain.' So Moses went down from the mountain to the people. He consecrated the people, and they washed their clothes. And he said to the people, 'Prepare for the third day; do not go near a woman.'

On the morning of the third day there was thunder and lightning, as well as a thick cloud on the mountain, and a blast of a trumpet so loud that all the people who were in the camp trembled. Moses brought the people out of the camp to meet God. They took their stand at the foot of the mountain. Now Mount Sinai was wrapped in smoke, because the Lord had descended upon it in fire; the smoke went up like the smoke of a kiln, while the whole mountain shook violently. As the blast of the trumpet grew louder and louder, Moses would speak and God would answer him in thunder. When the Lord descended upon Mount Sinai, to the top of the mountain, the Lord summoned Moses to the top of the mountain, and Moses went up. Then the Lord said to Moses, 'Go down and warn the people not to break through to the Lord to look; otherwise many of them will perish. Even the priests who approach the Lord must consecrate themselves or the Lord will break out against them.' Moses said to the Lord, 'The people are not permitted to come up to Mount Sinai; for you yourself warned us, saying, "Set limits around the mountain and keep it holy."' The Lord said to him, 'Go down, and come up bringing Aaron with you; but do not let either the priests or the people break through to come up to the Lord; otherwise he will break out against them.' So Moses went down to the people and told them.

A reading from the gospel according to Matthew. (8.23-34)

When Jesus got into the boat, his disciples followed him. A gale arose on the lake, so great that the boat was being swamped by the waves; but he was asleep. And they went and woke him up, saying, 'Lord, save us! We are perishing!' And he said to them, 'Why are you afraid, you of little faith?' Then he got up and rebuked the winds and the sea; and there was a dead calm. They were amazed, saying, 'What sort of man is this, that even the winds and the sea obey him?'

When he came to the other side, to the country of the Gadarenes, two demoniacs coming out of the tombs met him. They were so fierce that no one could pass that way. Suddenly they shouted, 'What have you to do with us, Son of God? Have you come here to torment us before the time?' Now a large herd of swine was feeding at some distance from them. The demons begged him, 'If you cast us

out, send us into the herd of swine.' And he said to them, 'Go!' So
they came out and entered the swine; and suddenly, the whole herd
rushed down the steep bank into the lake and perished in the water.
The swineherds ran off, and on going into the town, they told the
whole story about what had happened to the demoniacs. Then the
whole town came out to meet Jesus; and when they saw him, they
begged him to leave their neighbourhood.

Third Service
Ps 119.153-176; Isaiah 45.9-22; Revelation 14.1-5

A reading from the prophecy of Isaiah. (45.9-22)

Woe to you who strive with your Maker,
  earthen vessels with the potter!
Does the clay say to the one who fashions it,
  'What are you making?' or 'Your work has no handles'?
Woe to anyone who says to a father, 'What are you begetting?'
  or to a woman, 'With what are you in labour?'
Thus says the Lord,
  the Holy One of Israel, and its Maker:
Will you question me about my children,
  or command me concerning the work of my hands?
I made the earth,
  and created humankind upon it;
it was my hands that stretched out the heavens,
  and I commanded all their host.
I have aroused Cyrus in righteousness,
  and I will make all his paths straight;
he shall build my city and set my exiles free,
  not for price or reward, says the Lord of hosts.
Thus says the Lord:
  The wealth of Egypt and the merchandise of Ethiopia,
  and the Sabeans, tall of stature,
shall come over to you and be yours,
  they shall follow you;
  they shall come over in chains and bow down to you.
They will make supplication to you, saying,
  'God is with you alone, and there is no other;
  there is no god besides him.'
Truly, you are a God who hides himself,
  O God of Israel, the Saviour.
All of them are put to shame and confounded,

the makers of idols go in confusion together.
But Israel is saved by the Lord with everlasting salvation;
    you shall not be put to shame or confounded to all eternity.

For thus says the Lord,
    who created the heavens (he is God!),
who formed the earth and made it
    (he established it;
    he did not create it a chaos, he formed it to be inhabited!):
I am the Lord, and there is no other.
I did not speak in secret,
    in a land of darkness;
I did not say to the offspring of Jacob,
    'Seek me in chaos.'
I the Lord speak the truth,
    I declare what is right.

Assemble yourselves and come together,
    draw near, you survivors of the nations!
They have no knowledge –
    those who carry about their wooden idols,
    and keep on praying to a god that cannot save.
Declare and present your case;
    let them take counsel together!
Who told this long ago?
    Who declared it of old?
Was it not I, the Lord?
    There is no other god besides me,
a righteous God and a Saviour;
    there is no one besides me.

Turn to me and be saved,
    all the ends of the earth!
For I am God, and there is no other.

A reading from the Revelation to John. (14.1-5)

I looked, and there was the Lamb, standing on Mount Zion! And with him were one hundred and forty-four thousand who had his name and his Father's name written on their foreheads. And I heard a voice from heaven like the sound of many waters and like the sound of loud thunder; the voice I heard was like the sound of harpists playing on their harps, and they sing a new song before the throne and before the four living creatures and before the elders. No one could learn that song except the one hundred and forty-four thousand who have been redeemed from the earth. It is these who have not defiled themselves with women, for they are virgins; these follow the Lamb wherever he goes. They have been redeemed from humankind as first fruits for God and the Lamb, and in their mouth no lie was found; they are blameless.

Proper 21

Sunday between 25 September & 1 October inclusive

Principal Service

Continuous	*Related*
Esther 7.1-6,9-10 & 9.20-22	Numbers 11.4-6,10-16,24-29
Ps 124	Ps 19.7-14

James 5.13-20
Mark 9.38-50

A reading from the Book of Esther. *(7.1-6,9-10 & 9.20-22)*

King Ahasuerus and Haman went in to feast with Queen Esther. On the second day, as they were drinking wine, the king again said to Esther, 'What is your petition, Queen Esther? It shall be granted you. And what is your request? Even to the half of my kingdom, it shall be fulfilled.' Then Queen Esther answered, 'If I have won your favour, O king, and if it pleases the king, let my life be given me – that is my petition – and the lives of my people – that is my request. For we have been sold, I and my people, to be destroyed, to be killed, and to be annihilated. If we had been sold merely as slaves, men and women, I would have held my peace; but no enemy can compensate for this damage to the king.' Then King Ahasuerus said to Queen Esther, 'Who is he, and where is he, who has presumed to do this?' Esther said, 'A foe and enemy, this wicked Haman!' Then Haman was terrified before the king and the queen.

[9] Then Harbona, one of the eunuchs in attendance on the king, said, 'Look, the very gallows that Haman has prepared for Mordecai, whose word saved the king, stands at Haman's house, fifty cubits high.' And the king said, 'Hang him on that.' So they hanged Haman on the gallows that he had prepared for Mordecai. Then the anger of the king abated.

[9.20] Mordecai recorded these things, and sent letters to all the Jews who were in all the provinces of King Ahasuerus, both near and far, enjoining them that they should keep the fourteenth day of the month Adar and also the fifteenth day of the same month, year by year, as the days on which the Jews gained relief from their enemies, and as the month that had been turned for them from sorrow into gladness and from mourning into a holiday; that they should make them days of feasting and gladness, days for sending gifts of food to one another and presents to the poor.

This is the word of the Lord.

Or:

A reading from the book Numbers. *(11.4-6,10-16,24-29)*

In the second year after the Israelites had come out of the land of Egypt, the rabble among them had a strong craving; and the Israelites also wept again, and said, 'If only we had meat to eat! We remember the fish we used to eat in Egypt for nothing, the cucumbers, the melons, the leeks, the onions, and the garlic; but now our strength is dried up, and there is nothing at all but this manna to look at.'
[10] Moses heard the people weeping throughout their families, all at the entrances of their tents. Then the Lord became very angry, and Moses was displeased. So Moses said to the Lord, 'Why have you treated your servant so badly? Why have I not found favour in your sight, that you lay the burden of all this people on me? Did I conceive all this people? Did I give birth to them, that you should say to me, "Carry them in your bosom, as a nurse carries a sucking child", to the land that you promised on oath to their ancestors? Where am I to get meat to give to all this people? For they come weeping to me and say, "Give us meat to eat!" I am not able to carry all this people alone, for they are too heavy for me. If this is the way you are going to treat me, put me to death at once – if I have found favour in your sight – and do not let me see my misery.'

So the Lord said to Moses, 'Gather for me seventy of the elders of Israel, whom you know to be the elders of the people and officers over them; bring them to the tent of meeting, and have them take their place there with you.'
[24] So Moses went out and told the people the words of the Lord; and he gathered seventy elders of the people, and placed them all around the tent. Then the Lord came down in the cloud and spoke to him, and took some of the spirit that was on him and put it on the seventy elders; and when the spirit rested upon them, they prophesied. But they did not do so again.

Two men remained in the camp, one named Eldad, and the other named Medad, and the spirit rested on them; they were among those registered, but they had not gone out to the tent, and so they prophesied in the camp. And a young man ran and told Moses, 'Eldad and

Medad are prophesying in the camp.' And Joshua son of Nun, the assistant of Moses, one of his chosen men, said, 'My lord Moses, stop them!' But Moses said to him, 'Are you jealous for my sake? Would that all the Lord's people were prophets, and that the Lord would put his spirit on them!'

This is the word of the Lord.

A reading from the Letter of James. (5.13-20)

Are any among you suffering? They should pray. Are any cheerful? They should sing songs of praise. Are any among you sick? They should call for the elders of the church and have them pray over them, anointing them with oil in the name of the Lord. The prayer of faith will save the sick, and the Lord will raise them up; and anyone who has committed sins will be forgiven. Therefore confess your sins to one another, and pray for one another, so that you may be healed. The prayer of the righteous is powerful and effective. Elijah was a human being like us, and he prayed fervently that it might not rain, and for three years and six months it did not rain on the earth. Then he prayed again, and the heaven gave rain and the earth yielded its harvest.

My brothers and sisters, if anyone among you wanders from the truth and is brought back by another, you should know that who-ever brings back a sinner from wandering will save the sinner's soul from death and will cover a multitude of sins.

This is the word of the Lord.

Hear the gospel of our Lord Jesus Christ according to Mark. (9.38-50)

John said to Jesus, 'Teacher, we saw someone casting out demons in your name, and we tried to stop him, because he was not following us.' But Jesus said, 'Do not stop him; for no one who does a deed of power in my name will be able soon afterwards to speak evil of me. Whoever is not against us is for us. For truly I tell you, whoever gives you a cup of water to drink because you bear the name of Christ will by no means lose the reward.

'If any of you put a stumbling-block before one of these little ones who believe in me, it would be better for you if a great millstone were hung around your neck and you were thrown into the sea. If your hand causes you to stumble, cut it off; it is better for you to enter life maimed than to have two hands and to go to hell, to the unquench-able fire. And if your foot causes you to stumble, cut it off; it is better for you to enter life lame than to have two feet and to be thrown into hell. And if your eye causes you to stumble, tear it out; it is better for you to enter the kingdom of God with one eye than to have two eyes and to be thrown into hell, where their worm never dies, and the fire is never quenched.

'For everyone will be salted with fire. Salt is good; but if salt has lost its saltiness, how can you season it? Have salt in yourselves, and be at peace with one another.'

This is the gospel of the Lord.

Second Service
Pss 120,121; Exodus 24; Matthew 9.1-8

A reading from the Book of the Exodus. (Chapter 24)

God said to Moses, 'Come up to the Lord, you and Aaron, Nadab, and Abihu, and seventy of the elders of Israel, and worship at a distance. Moses alone shall come near the Lord; but the others shall not come near, and the people shall not come up with him.'

Moses came and told the people all the words of the Lord and all the ordinances; and all the people answered with one voice, and said, 'All the words that the Lord has spoken we will do.' And Moses wrote down all the words of the Lord. He rose early in the morning, and built an altar at the foot of the mountain, and set up twelve pillars, corresponding to the twelve tribes of Israel. He sent young men of the people of Israel, who offered burnt-offerings and sacrificed oxen as offerings of well-being to the Lord. Moses took half of the blood and put it in basins, and half of the blood he dashed against the altar. Then he took the book of the covenant, and read it in the hearing of the people; and they said, 'All that the Lord has spoken we will do, and we will be obedient.' Moses took the blood and dashed it on the people, and said, 'See the blood of the covenant that the Lord has made with you in accordance with all these words.'

Then Moses and Aaron, Nadab, and Abihu, and seventy of the elders of Israel went up, and they saw the God of Israel. Under his feet there was something like a pavement of sapphire stone, like the very heaven for clearness. God did not lay his hand on the chief men of the people of Israel; also they beheld God, and they ate and drank.

The Lord said to Moses, 'Come up to me on the mountain, and wait there; and I will give you the tablets of stone, with the law and the commandment, which I have written for their instruction.' So Moses set out with his assistant Joshua, and Moses went up into the mountain of God. To the elders he had said, 'Wait here for us, until we come to you again; for Aaron and Hur are with you; whoever has a dispute may go to them.'

Then Moses went up on the mountain, and the cloud covered the mountain. The glory of the Lord settled on Mount Sinai, and the cloud covered it for six days; on the seventh day he called to Moses out of the cloud. Now the appearance of the glory of the Lord was like a devouring fire on the top of the mountain in the sight of the people of Israel. Moses entered the cloud, and went up on the mountain. Moses was on the mountain for forty days and forty nights.

A reading from the gospel according to Matthew. (9.1-8)

After getting into a boat, Jesus crossed the water and came to his own town.

And just then some people were carrying a paralysed man lying on a bed. When Jesus saw their faith, he said to the paralytic, 'Take heart, son; your sins are forgiven.' Then some of the scribes said to themselves, 'This man is blaspheming.' But Jesus, perceiving their thoughts, said, 'Why do you think evil in your hearts? For which is easier, to say, "Your sins are forgiven", or to say, "Stand up and walk"? But so that you may know that the Son of Man has authority on earth to forgive sins' – he then said to the paralytic – 'Stand up, take your bed and go to your home.' And he stood up and went to his home. When the crowds saw it, they were filled with awe, and they glorified God, who had given such authority to human beings.

Third Service
Ps 122; Isaiah 48.12-22; Luke 11.37-54

A reading from the prophecy of Isaiah. (48.12-22)

> Listen to me, O Jacob,
>   and Israel, whom I called:
> I am He; I am the first,
>   and I am the last.
> My hand laid the foundation of the earth,
>   and my right hand spread out the heavens;
> when I summon them,
>   they stand at attention.
>
> Assemble, all of you, and hear!
>   Who among them has declared these things?
> The Lord loves him;
>   he shall perform his purpose on Babylon,
>   and his arm shall be against the Chaldeans.
> I, even I, have spoken and called him,

I have brought him, and he will prosper in his way.
Draw near to me, hear this!
From the beginning I have not spoken in secret,
from the time it came to be I have been there.
And now the Lord God has sent me and his spirit.

Thus says the Lord,
your Redeemer, the Holy One of Israel:
I am the Lord your God,
who teaches you for your own good,
who leads you in the way you should go.
O that you had paid attention to my commandments!
Then your prosperity would have been like a river,
and your success like the waves of the sea;
your offspring would have been like the sand,
and your descendants like its grains;
their name would never be cut off
or destroyed from before me.

Go out from Babylon, flee from Chaldea,
declare this with a shout of joy, proclaim it,
send it forth to the end of the earth;
say, 'The Lord has redeemed his servant Jacob!'
They did not thirst when he led them through the deserts;
he made water flow for them from the rock;
he split open the rock and the water gushed out.
'There is no peace', says the Lord, 'for the wicked.'

A reading from the gospel according to Luke. (11.37-54)

While Jesus was speaking, a Pharisee invited him to dine with him; so he went in and took his place at the table.   The Pharisee was amazed to see that he did not first wash before dinner.   Then the Lord said to him, 'Now you Pharisees clean the outside of the cup and of the dish, but inside you are full of greed and wickedness. You fools!   Did not the one who made the outside make the inside also? So give for alms those things that are within; and see, everything will be clean for you.

'But woe to you Pharisees!   For you tithe mint and rue and herbs of all kinds, and neglect justice and the love of God; it is these you ought to have practised, without neglecting the others.   Woe to you Pharisees!   For you love to have the seat of honour in the synagogues and to be greeted with respect in the market-places. Woe to you! For you are like unmarked graves, and people walk over them without realizing it.'

One of the lawyers answered him, 'Teacher, when you say these things, you insult us too.' And he said, 'Woe also to you lawyers! For you load people with burdens hard to bear, and you yourselves do not lift a finger to ease them. Woe to you! For you build the tombs of the prophets whom your ancestors killed. So you are witnesses and approve of the deeds of your ancestors; for they killed them, and you build their tombs. Therefore also the Wisdom of God said, "I will send them prophets and apostles, some of whom they will kill and persecute", so that this generation may be charged with the blood of all the prophets shed since the foundation of the world, from the blood of Abel to the blood of Zechariah, who perished between the altar and the sanctuary. Yes, I tell you, it will be charged against this generation. Woe to you lawyers! For you have taken away the key of knowledge; you did not enter yourselves, and you hindered those who were entering.'

When he went outside, the scribes and the Pharisees began to be very hostile towards him and to cross-examine him about many things, lying in wait for him, to catch him in something he might say.

Dedication Festival

First Sunday in October or Last Sunday after Trinity (if date not known)

Evening Prayer on the Eve
Ps 24; 2 Chronicles 7.11-16; John 4.19-29

A reading from the Second Book of the Chronicles. (7.11-16)

Solomon finished the house of the Lord and the king's house; all that Solomon had planned to do in the house of the Lord and in his own house he successfully accomplished.

Then the Lord appeared to Solomon in the night and said to him: 'I have heard your prayer, and have chosen this place for myself as a house of sacrifice. When I shut up the heavens so that there is no rain, or command the locust to devour the land, or send pestilence among my people, if my people who are called by my name humble themselves, pray, seek my face, and turn from their wicked ways, then I will hear from heaven, and will forgive their sin and heal their land. Now my eyes will be open and my ears attentive to the prayer that is made in this place. For now I have chosen and consecrated this house so that my name may be there for ever; my eyes and my heart will be there for all time.

A reading from the gospel according to John. *(4.19-29)*

The Samaritan woman at the well said to Jesus, 'Sir, I see that you are a prophet. Our ancestors worshipped on this mountain, but you say that the place where people must worship is in Jerusalem.' Jesus said to her, 'Woman, believe me, the hour is coming when you will worship the Father neither on this mountain nor in Jerusalem. You worship what you do not know; we worship what we know, for salvation is from the Jews. But the hour is coming, and is now here, when the true worshippers will worship the Father in spirit and truth, for the Father seeks such as these to worship him. God is spirit, and those who worship him must worship in spirit and truth.' The woman said to him, 'I know that Messiah is coming' (who is called Christ). 'When he comes, he will proclaim all things to us.' Jesus said to her, 'I am he, the one who is speaking to you.'

Just then his disciples came. They were astonished that he was speaking with a woman, but no one said, 'What do you want?' or, 'Why are you speaking with her?' Then the woman left her water-jar and went back to the city. She said to the people, 'Come and see a man who told me everything I have ever done! He cannot be the Messiah, can he?'

Principal Service
Genesis 28.11-18 *or* Revelation 21.9-14; Ps 122;
1 Peter 2.1-10; John 10.22-29

A reading from the book Genesis. *(28.11-18)*

Jacob came to a certain place and stayed there for the night, because the sun had set. Taking one of the stones of the place, he put it under his head and lay down in that place. And he dreamed that there was a ladder set up on the earth, the top of it reaching to heaven; and the angels of God were ascending and descending on it. And the Lord stood beside him and said, 'I am the Lord, the God of Abraham your father and the God of Isaac; the land on which you lie I will give to you and to your offspring; and your offspring shall be like the dust of the earth, and you shall spread abroad to the west and to the east and to the north and to the south; and all the families of the earth shall be blessed in you and in your offspring. Know that I am with you and will keep you wherever you go, and will bring you back to this land; for I will not leave you until I have done what I have promised you.' Then Jacob woke from his sleep and said, 'Surely the Lord is in this place – and I did not know it!' And he was afraid, and said, 'How awesome is this place! This is none other than the house of God, and this is the gate of heaven.'

So Jacob rose early in the morning, and he took the stone that he had put under his head and set it up for a pillar and poured oil on the top of it.

This is the word of the Lord.

Or:

A reading from the Revelation to John. *(21.9-14)*

One of the seven angels who had the seven bowls full of the seven last plagues came and said to me, 'Come, I will show you the bride, the wife of the Lamb.' And in the spirit he carried me away to a great, high mountain and showed me the holy city Jerusalem coming down out of heaven from God. It has the glory of God and a radiance like a very rare jewel, like jasper, clear as crystal. It has a great, high wall with twelve gates, and at the gates twelve angels, and on the gates are inscribed the names of the twelve tribes of the Israelites; on the east three gates, on the north three gates, on the south three gates, and on the west three gates. And the wall of the city has twelve foundations, and on them are the twelve names of the twelve apostles of the Lamb.

This is the word of the Lord.

A reading from the First Letter of Peter. *(2.1-10)*

Rid yourselves of all malice, and all guile, insincerity, envy, and all slander. Like newborn infants, long for the pure, spiritual milk, so that by it you may grow into salvation – if indeed you have tasted that the Lord is good.

Come to him, a living stone, though rejected by mortals yet chosen and precious in God's sight, and like living stones, let yourselves be built into a spiritual house, to be a holy priesthood, to offer spiritual sacrifices acceptable to God through Jesus Christ. For it stands in scripture:
'See, I am laying in Zion a stone,
a cornerstone chosen and precious;
and whoever believes in him will not be put to shame.'
To you then who believe, he is precious; but for those who do not believe,
'The stone that the builders rejected
has become the very head of the corner',
and
'A stone that makes them stumble,

and a rock that makes them fall.'
They stumble because they disobey the word, as they were destined to do.

But you are a chosen race, a royal priesthood, a holy nation, God's own people, in order that you may proclaim the mighty acts of him who called you out of darkness into his marvellous light.

Once you were not a people,
  but now you are God's people;
once you had not received mercy,
  but now you have received mercy.

This is the word of the Lord.

Hear the gospel of our Lord Jesus Christ according to John.
(10.22-29)

The festival of the Dedication took place in Jerusalem. It was winter, and Jesus was walking in the temple, in the portico of Solomon. So the Jews gathered around him and said to him, 'How long will you keep us in suspense? If you are the Messiah, tell us plainly.' Jesus answered, 'I have told you, and you do not believe. The works that I do in my Father's name testify to me; but you do not believe, because you do not belong to my sheep. My sheep hear my voice. I know them, and they follow me. I give them eternal life, and they will never perish. No one will snatch them out of my hand. What my Father has given me is greater than all else, and no one can snatch it out of the Father's hand.'

This is the gospel of the Lord.

Second Service
Ps 132; Jeremiah 7.1-11; Luke 19.1-10

A reading from the prophecy of Jeremiah. *(7.1-11)*

The word that came to Jeremiah from the Lord: Stand in the gate of the Lord's house, and proclaim there this word, and say, Hear the word of the Lord, all you people of Judah, you that enter these gates to worship the Lord. Thus says the Lord of hosts, the God of Israel: Amend your ways and your doings, and let me dwell with you in this place. Do not trust in these deceptive words: 'This is the temple of the Lord, the temple of the Lord, the temple of the Lord.'

For if you truly amend your ways and your doings, if you truly act justly one with another, if you do not oppress the alien, the orphan, and the widow, or shed innocent blood in this place, and if you do not go after other gods to your own hurt, then I will dwell with you in this place, in the land that I gave of old to your ancestors for ever and ever.

Here you are, trusting in deceptive words to no avail. Will you steal, murder, commit adultery, swear falsely, make offerings to Baal, and go after other gods that you have not known, and then come and stand before me in this house, which is called by my name, and say, 'We are safe!' – only to go on doing all these abominations? Has this house, which is called by my name, become a den of robbers in your sight? You know, I too am watching, says the Lord.

A reading from the gospel according to Luke. (19.1-10)

Jesus entered Jericho and was passing through it. A man was there named Zacchæus; he was a chief tax-collector and was rich. He was trying to see who Jesus was, but on account of the crowd he could not, because he was short in stature. So he ran ahead and climbed a sycomore tree to see him, because he was going to pass that way. When Jesus came to the place, he looked up and said to him, 'Zacchæus, hurry and come down; for I must stay at your house today.' So he hurried down and was happy to welcome him. All who saw it began to grumble and said, 'He has gone to be the guest of one who is a sinner.' Zacchæus stood there and said to the Lord, 'Look, half of my possessions, Lord, I will give to the poor; and if I have defrauded anyone of anything, I will pay back four times as much.' Then Jesus said to him, 'Today salvation has come to this house, because he too is a son of Abraham. For the Son of Man came to seek out and to save the lost.'

Third Service
Ps 48; Haggai 2.6-9; Hebrews 10.19-25

A reading from the Book of Haggai. (2.6-9)

Thus says the Lord of hosts: Once again, in a little while, I will shake the heavens and the earth and the sea and the dry land; and I will shake all the nations, so that the treasure of all nations shall come, and I will fill this house with splendour, says the Lord of hosts. The silver is mine, and the gold is mine, says the Lord of hosts. The latter splendour of this house shall be greater than the former, says the Lord of hosts; and in this place I will give prosperity, says the Lord of hosts.

A reading from the Letter to the Hebrews. (10.19-25)

My friends, since we have confidence to enter the sanctuary by the blood of Jesus, by the new and living way that he opened for us through the curtain (that is, through his flesh), and since we have a great priest over the house of God, let us approach with a true heart in full assurance of faith, with our hearts sprinkled clean from an evil conscience and our bodies washed with pure water. Let us hold fast to the confession of our hope without wavering, for he who has promised is faithful. And let us consider how to provoke one another to love and good deeds, not neglecting to meet together, as is the habit of some, but encouraging one another, and all the more as you see the Day approaching.

Proper 22

Sunday between 2 & 8 October inclusive

Principal Service

Continuous	*Related*
Job 1.1; 2.1-10	Genesis 2.18-24
Ps 26	Ps 8
	Hebrews 1.1-4 & 2.5-12
	Mark 10.2-16

A reading from the book Job. (1.1 & 2.1-10)

There was once a man in the land of Uz whose name was Job. That man was blameless and upright, one who feared God and turned away from evil.

[2.1] One day, the heavenly beings came to present themselves before the Lord, and Satan also came among them to present himself before the Lord. The Lord said to Satan, 'Where have you come from?' Satan answered the Lord, 'From going to and fro on the earth, and from walking up and down on it.' The Lord said to Satan, 'Have you considered my servant Job? There is no one like him on the earth, a blameless and upright man who fears God and turns away from evil. He still persists in his integrity, although you incited me against him, to destroy him for no reason.' Then Satan answered the Lord, 'Skin for skin! All that people have they will give to save their lives. But stretch out your hand now and touch his bone and his flesh, and he will curse you to your face.' The Lord said to Satan, 'Very well, he is in your power; only spare his life.'

So Satan went out from the presence of the Lord, and inflicted loathsome sores on Job from the sole of his foot to the crown of his head. Job took a potsherd with which to scrape himself, and sat among the ashes.

Then his wife said to him, 'Do you still persist in your integrity? Curse God, and die.' But he said to her, 'You speak as any foolish woman would speak. Shall we receive the good at the hand of God, and not receive the bad?' In all this Job did not sin with his lips.

This is the word of the Lord.

Or:

A reading from the book Genesis. *(2.18-24)*

The Lord God said, 'It is not good that the man should be alone; I will make him a helper as his partner.' So out of the ground the Lord God formed every animal of the field and every bird of the air, and brought them to the man to see what he would call them; and whatever the man called each living creature, that was its name. The man gave names to all cattle, and to the birds of the air, and to every animal of the field; but for the man there was not found a helper as his partner. So the Lord God caused a deep sleep to fall upon the man, and he slept; then he took one of his ribs and closed up its place with flesh. And the rib that the Lord God had taken from the man he made into a woman and brought her to the man. Then the man said,

'This at last is bone of my bones
    and flesh of my flesh;
this one shall be called Woman,
    for out of Man this one was taken.'

Therefore a man leaves his father and his mother and clings to his wife, and they become one flesh.

This is the word of the Lord.

A reading from the Letter to the Hebrews. *(1.1-4 & 2.5-12)*

Long ago God spoke to our ancestors in many and various ways by the prophets, but in these last days he has spoken to us by a Son, whom he appointed heir of all things, through whom he also created the worlds. He is the reflection of God's glory and the exact imprint of God's very being, and he sustains all things by his powerful word. When he had made purification for sins, he sat down at the right hand of the Majesty on high, having become as much superior to angels as the name he has inherited is more excellent than theirs.
2.5 Now God did not subject the coming world, about which we are speaking, to angels. But someone has testified somewhere,

'What are human beings that you are mindful of them,

or mortals, that you care for them?
You have made them for a little while lower than the angels;
    you have crowned them with glory and honour,
    subjecting all things under their feet.'
Now in subjecting all things to them, God left nothing outside their control. As it is, we do not yet see everything in subjection to them, but we do see Jesus, who for a little while was made lower than the angels, now crowned with glory and honour because of the suffering of death, so that by the grace of God he might taste death for everyone.

It was fitting that God, for whom and through whom all things exist, in bringing many children to glory, should make the pioneer of their salvation perfect through sufferings. For the one who sanctifies and those who are sanctified all have one Father. For this reason Jesus is not ashamed to call them brothers and sisters, saying,
    'I will proclaim your name to my brothers and sisters,
      in the midst of the congregation I will praise you.'

This is the word of the Lord.

Hear the gospel of our Lord Jesus Christ according to Mark. (10.2-16)

Some Pharisees came, and to test Jesus they asked, 'Is it lawful for a man to divorce his wife?' He answered them, 'What did Moses command you?' They said, 'Moses allowed a man to write a certificate of dismissal and to divorce her.' But Jesus said to them, 'Because of your hardness of heart he wrote this commandment for you. But from the beginning of creation, "God made them male and female." "For this reason a man shall leave his father and mother and be joined to his wife, and the two shall become one flesh." So they are no longer two, but one flesh. Therefore what God has joined together, let no one separate.'

Then in the house the disciples asked him again about this matter. He said to them, 'Whoever divorces his wife and marries another commits adultery against her; and if she divorces her husband and marries another, she commits adultery.'

People were bringing little children to him in order that he might touch them; and the disciples spoke sternly to them. But when Jesus saw this, he was indignant and said to them, 'Let the little children come to me; do not stop them; for it is to such as these that the kingdom of God belongs. Truly I tell you, whoever does not receive the kingdom of God as a little child will never enter it.' And he took them up in his arms, laid his hands on them, and blessed them.

This is the gospel of the Lord.

Second Service

Pss 125,126; Joshua 3.7-17; Matthew 10.1-22

A reading from the Book of Joshua. *(3.7-17)*

The Lord said to Joshua, 'This day I will begin to exalt you in the sight of all Israel, so that they may know that I will be with you as I was with Moses. You are the one who shall command the priests who bear the ark of the covenant, "When you come to the edge of the waters of the Jordan, you shall stand still in the Jordan."' Joshua then said to the Israelites, 'Draw near and hear the words of the Lord your God.' Joshua said, 'By this you shall know that among you is the living God who without fail will drive out from before you the Canaanites, Hittites, Hivites, Perizzites, Girgashites, Amorites, and Jebusites: the ark of the covenant of the Lord of all the earth is going to pass before you into the Jordan. So now select twelve men from the tribes of Israel, one from each tribe. When the soles of the feet of the priests who bear the ark of the Lord, the Lord of all the earth, rest in the waters of the Jordan, the waters of the Jordan flowing from above shall be cut off; they shall stand in a single heap.'

When the people set out from their tents to cross over the Jordan, the priests bearing the ark of the covenant were in front of the people. Now the Jordan overflows all its banks throughout the time of harvest. So when those who bore the ark had come to the Jordan, and the feet of the priests bearing the ark were dipped in the edge of the water, the waters flowing from above stood still, rising up in a single heap far off at Adam, the city that is beside Zarethan, while those flowing towards the sea of the Arabah, the Dead Sea, were wholly cut off. Then the people crossed over opposite Jericho. While all Israel were crossing over on dry ground, the priests who bore the ark of the covenant of the Lord stood on dry ground in the middle of the Jordan, until the entire nation finished crossing over the Jordan.

A reading from the gospel according to Matthew. *(10.1-22)*

Jesus summoned his twelve disciples and gave them authority over unclean spirits, to cast them out, and to cure every disease and every sickness. These are the names of the twelve apostles: first, Simon, also known as Peter, and his brother Andrew; James son of Zebedee, and his brother John; Philip and Bartholomew; Thomas and Matthew the tax-collector; James son of Alphæus, and Thaddæus; Simon the Cananaean, and Judas Iscariot, the one who betrayed him.

These twelve Jesus sent out with the following instructions: 'Go nowhere among the Gentiles, and enter no town of the Samaritans, but go rather to the lost sheep of the house of Israel. As you go, pro-claim the good news, "The kingdom of heaven has come near." Cure the sick, raise the dead, cleanse the lepers, cast out demons. You received without payment; give without payment. Take no gold, or silver, or copper in your belts, no bag for your journey, or two tunics, or sandals, or a staff; for labourers deserve their food. Whatever town or village you enter, find out who in it is worthy, and stay there until you leave. As you enter the house, greet it. If the house is wor-thy, let your peace come upon it; but if it is not worthy, let your peace return to you. If anyone will not welcome you or listen to your words, shake off the dust from your feet as you leave that house or town. Truly I tell you, it will be more tolerable for the land of Sodom and Gomorrah on the day of judgement than for that town.

'See, I am sending you out like sheep into the midst of wolves; so be wise as serpents and innocent as doves. Beware of them, for they will hand you over to councils and flog you in their synagogues; and you will be dragged before governors and kings because of me, as a testi-mony to them and the Gentiles. When they hand you over, do not worry about how you are to speak or what you are to say; for what you are to say will be given to you at that time; for it is not you who speak, but the Spirit of your Father speaking through you. Brother will betray brother to death, and a father his child, and children will rise against parents and have them put to death; and you will be hated by all because of my name. But the one who endures to the end will be saved.'

Third Service
Pss 123,124; Isaiah 49.13-23; Luke 12.1-12

A reading from the prophecy of Isaiah. (49.13-23)

Sing for joy, O heavens, and exult, O earth;
    break forth, O mountains, into singing!
For the Lord has comforted his people,
    and will have compassion on his suffering ones.

But Zion said, 'The Lord has forsaken me,
    my Lord has forgotten me.'
Can a woman forget her nursing-child,
    or show no compassion for the child of her womb?
Even these may forget,
    yet I will not forget you.
See, I have inscribed you on the palms of my hands;
    your walls are continually before me.

Your builders outdo your destroyers,
  and those who laid you waste go away from you.
Lift up your eyes all around and see;
  they all gather, they come to you.
As I live, says the Lord,
  you shall put all of them on like an ornament,
  and like a bride you shall bind them on.

Surely your waste and your desolate places
  and your devastated land –
surely now you will be too crowded for your inhabitants,
  and those who swallowed you up will be far away.
The children born in the time of your bereavement
  will yet say in your hearing:
'The place is too crowded for me;
  make room for me to settle.'
Then you will say in your heart,
  'Who has borne me these?
I was bereaved and barren,
  exiled and put away – so who has reared these?
I was left all alone –
  where then have these come from?'

Thus says the Lord God:
I will soon lift up my hand to the nations,
  and raise my signal to the peoples;
and they shall bring your sons in their bosom,
  and your daughters shall be carried on their shoulders.
Kings shall be your foster-fathers,
  and their queens your nursing-mothers.
With their faces to the ground they shall bow down to you,
  and lick the dust of your feet.
Then you will know that I am the Lord;
  those who wait for me shall not be put to shame.

A reading from the gospel according to Luke. (12.1-12)

Jesus began to speak to his disciples: 'Beware of the yeast of the Pharisees, that is, their hypocrisy. Nothing is covered up that will not be uncovered, and nothing secret that will not become known. Therefore whatever you have said in the dark will be heard in the light, and what you have whispered behind closed doors will be proclaimed from the housetops.

 'I tell you, my friends, do not fear those who kill the body, and after that can do nothing more.   But I will warn you whom to fear: fear him who, after he has killed, has authority to cast into hell.   Yes, I tell you, fear him!   Are not five sparrows sold for two pennies?   Yet not one of them is forgotten in God's sight.   But even the hairs of your head are all counted.   Do not be afraid; you are of more value than many sparrows.

'And I tell you, everyone who acknowledges me before others, the Son of Man also will acknowledge before the angels of God; but whoever denies me before others will be denied before the angels of God. And everyone who speaks a word against the Son of Man will be forgiven; but whoever blasphemes against the Holy Spirit will not be forgiven.   When they bring you before the synagogues, the rulers, and the authorities, do not worry about how you are to defend yourselves or what you are to say; for the Holy Spirit will teach you at that very hour what you ought to say.'

Proper 23

Sunday between 9 & 15 October inclusive

Principal Service

Continuous	*Related*
Job 23.1-9,16-17	Amos 5.6-7,10-15
Ps 22.1-15	Ps 90.12-17

Hebrews 4.12-16

Mark 10.17-31

A reading from the Book of Job. (23.1-9,16-17)

Job said:
    'Today also my complaint is bitter;
        his hand is heavy despite my groaning.
    O that I knew where I might find him,
        that I might come even to his dwelling!
    I would lay my case before him,
        and fill my mouth with arguments.
    I would learn what he would answer me,
        and understand what he would say to me.
    Would he contend with me in the greatness of his power?
        No; but he would give heed to me.
    There an upright person could reason with him,
        and I should be acquitted for ever by my judge.
    'If I go forward, he is not there;

or backward, I cannot perceive him;
on the left he hides, and I cannot behold him;
I turn to the right, but I cannot see him.

16 God has made my heart faint;
the Almighty has terrified me;
If only I could vanish in darkness,
and thick darkness would cover my face!'

This is the word of the Lord.

Or:

A reading from the prophecy of Amos. (5.6-7,10-15)

Seek the Lord and live,
or he will break out against the house of Joseph like fire,
and it will devour Bethel, with no one to quench it.
Ah, you that turn justice to wormwood,
and bring righteousness to the ground!

10 They hate the one who reproves in the gate,
and they abhor the one who speaks the truth.
Therefore, because you trample on the poor
and take from them levies of grain,
you have built houses of hewn stone,
but you shall not live in them;
you have planted pleasant vineyards,
but you shall not drink their wine.
For I know how many are your transgressions,
and how great are your sins –
you who afflict the righteous, who take a bribe,
and push aside the needy in the gate.
Therefore the prudent will keep silent in such a time;
for it is an evil time.

Seek good and not evil,
that you may live;
and so the Lord, the God of hosts, will be with you,
just as you have said.
Hate evil and love good,
and establish justice in the gate;
it may be that the Lord, the God of hosts,
will be gracious to the remnant of Joseph.

This is the word of the Lord.

A reading from the Letter to the Hebrews. *(4.12-16)*

The word of God is living and active, sharper than any two-edged sword, piercing until it divides soul from spirit, joints from marrow; it is able to judge the thoughts and intentions of the heart. And before him no creature is hidden, but all are naked and laid bare to the eyes of the one to whom we must render an account.

Since, then, we have a great high priest who has passed through the heavens, Jesus, the Son of God, let us hold fast to our confession. For we do not have a high priest who is unable to sympathize with our weaknesses, but we have one who in every respect has been tested as we are, yet without sin. Let us therefore approach the throne of grace with boldness, so that we may receive mercy and find grace to help in time of need.

This is the word of the Lord.

Hear the gospel of our Lord Jesus Christ according to Mark. *(10.17-31)*

As Jesus was setting out on a journey, a man ran up and knelt before him, and asked him, 'Good Teacher, what must I do to inherit eternal life?' Jesus said to him, 'Why do you call me good? No one is good but God alone. You know the commandments: "You shall not murder; You shall not commit adultery; You shall not steal; You shall not bear false witness; You shall not defraud; Honour your father and mother."' He said to him, 'Teacher, I have kept all these since my youth.' Jesus, looking at him, loved him and said, 'You lack one thing; go, sell what you own, and give the money to the poor, and you will have treasure in heaven; then come, follow me.' When he heard this, he was shocked and went away grieving, for he had many possessions.

Then Jesus looked around and said to his disciples, 'How hard it will be for those who have wealth to enter the kingdom of God!' And the disciples were perplexed at these words. But Jesus said to them again, 'Children, how hard it is to enter the kingdom of God! It is easier for a camel to go through the eye of a needle than for someone who is rich to enter the kingdom of God.' They were greatly astounded and said to one another, 'Then who can be saved?' Jesus looked at them and said, 'For mortals it is impossible, but not for God; for God all things are possible.'

Peter began to say to him, 'Look, we have left everything and followed you.' Jesus said, 'Truly I tell you, there is no one who has left house or brothers or sisters or mother or father or children or fields, for my sake and for the sake of the good news, who will not receive a hundredfold now in this age – houses, brothers and sisters, mothers and children, and fields, with persecutions – and in the age to come eternal life. But many who are first will be last, and the last will be first.'

This is the gospel of the Lord.

Second Service
Pss 127 [128]; Joshua 5.13 - 6.20; Matthew 11.20-30

A reading from the Book of Joshua. (5.13 - 6.20)

Once when Joshua was near Jericho, he looked up and saw a man standing before him with a drawn sword in his hand. Joshua went to him and said to him, 'Are you one of us, or one of our adversaries?' He replied, 'Neither; but as commander of the army of the Lord I have now come.' And Joshua fell on his face to the earth and worshipped, and he said to him, 'What do you command your servant, my lord?' The commander of the army of the Lord said to Joshua, 'Remove the sandals from your feet, for the place where you stand is holy.' And Joshua did so.

Now Jericho was shut up inside and out because of the Israelites; no one came out and no one went in. The Lord said to Joshua, 'See, I have handed Jericho over to you, along with its king and soldiers. You shall march around the city, all the warriors circling the city once. Thus you shall do for six days, with seven priests bearing seven trumpets of rams' horns before the ark. On the seventh day you shall march around the city seven times, the priests blowing the trumpets. When they make a long blast with the ram's horn, as soon as you hear the sound of the trumpet, then all the people shall shout with a great shout; and the wall of the city will fall down flat, and all the people shall charge straight ahead.' So Joshua son of Nun summoned the priests and said to them, 'Take up the ark of the covenant, and have seven priests carry seven trumpets of rams' horns in front of the ark of the Lord.' To the people he said, 'Go forward and march around the city; have the armed men pass on before the ark of the Lord.'

As Joshua had commanded the people, the seven priests carrying the seven trumpets of rams' horns before the Lord went forward, blowing the trumpets, with the ark of the covenant of the Lord following them. And the armed men went before the priests who blew the trumpets; the rearguard came after the ark, while the trumpets blew continually. To the people Joshua gave this command: 'You shall not shout or let your voice be heard, nor shall you utter a word, until the day I tell you to shout. Then you shall shout.' So the ark of the Lord went around the city, circling it once; and they came into the camp, and spent the night in the camp.

Then Joshua rose early in the morning, and the priests took up the ark of the Lord. The seven priests carrying the seven trumpets of rams' horns before the ark of the Lord passed on, blowing the trumpets continually. The armed men went before them, and the rearguard came after the ark of the Lord, while the trumpets blew continually. On the second day they marched around the city once and then returned to the camp. They did this for six days.

On the seventh day they rose early, at dawn, and marched around the city in the same manner seven times. It was only on that day that they marched around the city seven times. And at the seventh time, when the priests had blown the trumpets, Joshua said to the people, 'Shout! For the Lord has given you the city. The city and all that is in it shall be devoted to the Lord for destruction. Only Rahab the prostitute and all who are with her in her house shall live, because she hid the messengers we sent. As for you, keep away from the things devoted to destruction, so as not to covet and take any of the devoted things and make the camp of Israel an object for destruction, bringing trouble upon it. But all silver and gold, and vessels of bronze and iron, are sacred to the Lord; they shall go into the treasury of the Lord.' So the people shouted, and the trumpets were blown. As soon as the people heard the sound of the trumpets, they raised a great shout, and the wall fell down flat; so the people charged straight ahead into the city and captured it.

A reading from the gospel according to Matthew. (11.20-30)

Jesus began to reproach the cities in which most of his deeds of power had been done, because they did not repent. 'Woe to you, Chorazin! Woe to you, Bethsaida! For if the deeds of power done in you had been done in Tyre and Sidon, they would have repented long ago in sackcloth and ashes. But I tell you, on the day of judgement it will be more tolerable for Tyre and Sidon than for you. And you, Capernaum, will you be exalted to heaven? No, you will be brought down to Hades. For if the deeds of power done in you had been done in Sodom, it would have remained until this day. But I tell you that on the day of judgement it will be more tolerable for the land of Sodom than for you.'

At that time Jesus said, 'I thank you, Father, Lord of heaven and earth, because you have hidden these things from the wise and the intelligent and have revealed them to infants; yes, Father, for such was your gracious will. All things have been handed over to me by my Father; and no one knows the Son except the Father, and no one knows the Father except the Son and anyone to whom the Son chooses to reveal him.

'Come to me, all you that are weary and are carrying heavy burdens, and I will give you rest. Take my yoke upon you, and learn from me; for I am gentle and humble in heart, and you will find rest for your souls. For my yoke is easy, and my burden is light.'

Third Service
Pss 129,130; Isaiah 50.4-10; Luke 13.22-30

A reading from the prophecy of Isaiah. (50.4-10)

> The Lord God has given me
> > the tongue of a teacher,
> that I may know how to sustain
> > the weary with a word.
> Morning by morning he wakens –
> > wakens my ear to listen as those who are taught.
> The Lord God has opened my ear,
> > and I was not rebellious, I did not turn backwards.
> I gave my back to those who struck me,
> > and my cheeks to those who pulled out the beard;
> > I did not hide my face from insult and spitting.
>
> The Lord God helps me;
> > therefore I have not been disgraced;
> therefore I have set my face like flint,
> > and I know that I shall not be put to shame;
> > he who vindicates me is near.
> Who will contend with me?
> > Let us stand up together.
> Who are my adversaries?
> > Let them confront me.
> It is the Lord God who helps me;
> > who will declare me guilty?
> All of them will wear out like a garment;
> > the moth will eat them up.
>
> Who among you fears the Lord
> > and obeys the voice of his servant,
> who walks in darkness and has no light,
> > yet trusts in the name of the Lord
> > and relies upon his God?

A reading from the gospel according to Luke. (13.22-30)

Jesus went through one town and village after another, teaching as he made his way to Jerusalem. Someone asked him, 'Lord, will only a few be saved?' He said to them, 'Strive to enter through the narrow door; for many, I tell you, will try to enter and will not be able. When once the owner of the house has got up and shut the door, and you begin to stand outside and to knock at the door, saying, "Lord, open to us", then in reply he will say to you, "I do not know where you come from." Then you will begin to say, "We ate and drank with you, and you taught in our streets." But he will say, "I do not know where you come from; go away from me, all you evildoers!" There will be weeping and gnashing of teeth when you see Abraham and Isaac and Jacob and all the prophets in the kingdom of God, and you yourselves thrown out. Then people will come from east and west, from north and south, and will eat in the kingdom of God. Indeed, some are last who will be first, and some are first who will be last.'

Proper 24
Sunday between 16 & 22 October inclusive

Principal Service

Continuous
Job 38.1-7[34-41]
Ps 104.1-9 [24,35c]

Related
Isaiah 53.4-12
Ps 91.9-16

Hebrews 5.1-10
Mark 10.35-45

A reading from the Book of Job. (38.1-7 [34-41])

The Lord answered Job out of the whirlwind:
    'Who is this that darkens counsel by words without knowledge?
    Gird up your loins like a man,
        I will question you, and you shall declare to me.

'Where were you when I laid the foundation of the earth?
        Tell me, if you have understanding.
Who determined its measurements – surely you know!
        Or who stretched the line upon it?
On what were its bases sunk,
        or who laid its cornerstone
when the morning stars sang together
        and all the heavenly beings shouted for joy?

[³⁴ 'Can you lift up your voice to the clouds,
    so that a flood of waters may cover you?
Can you send forth lightnings, so that they may go
    and say to you, "Here we are"?
Who has put wisdom in the inward parts,
    or given understanding to the mind?
Who has the wisdom to number the clouds?
    Or who can tilt the waterskins of the heavens,
when the dust runs into a mass
    and the clods cling together?

'Can you hunt the prey for the lion,
    or satisfy the appetite of the young lions,
when they crouch in their dens,
    or lie in wait in their covert?
Who provides for the raven its prey,
    when its young ones cry to God,
    and wander about for lack of food?']

This is the word of the Lord.

Or:

A reading from the prophecy of Isaiah. (53.4-12)

Surely he has borne our infirmities
    and carried our diseases;
yet we accounted him stricken,
    struck down by God, and afflicted.
But he was wounded for our transgressions,
    crushed for our iniquities;
upon him was the punishment that made us whole,
    and by his bruises we are healed.
All we like sheep have gone astray;
    we have all turned to our own way,
and the Lord has laid on him
    the iniquity of us all.

He was oppressed, and he was afflicted,
    yet he did not open his mouth;
like a lamb that is led to the slaughter,
    and like a sheep that before its shearers is silent,
    so he did not open his mouth.
By a perversion of justice he was taken away.
    Who could have imagined his future?
For he was cut off from the land of the living,

stricken for the transgression of my people.
They made his grave with the wicked
    and his tomb with the rich,
although he had done no violence,
    and there was no deceit in his mouth.

Yet it was the will of the Lord to crush him with pain.
When you make his life an offering for sin,
    he shall see his offspring, and shall prolong his days;
through him the will of the Lord shall prosper.
    Out of his anguish he shall see light;
he shall find satisfaction through his knowledge.
    The righteous one, my servant, shall make many righteous,
    and he shall bear their iniquities.
Therefore I will allot him a portion with the great,
    and he shall divide the spoil with the strong;
because he poured out himself to death,
    and was numbered with the transgressors;
yet he bore the sin of many,
    and made intercession for the transgressors.

This is the word of the Lord.

A reading from the Letter to the Hebrews. (5.1-10)

Every high priest chosen from among mortals is put in charge of things pertaining to God on their behalf, to offer gifts and sacrifices for sins. He is able to deal gently with the ignorant and wayward, since he himself is subject to weakness; and because of this he must offer sacrifice for his own sins as well as for those of the people. And one does not presume to take this honour, but takes it only when called by God, just as Aaron was.
  So also Christ did not glorify himself in becoming a high priest, but was appointed by the one who said to him,
    'You are my Son,
      today I have begotten you';
as he says also in another place,
    'You are a priest for ever,
      according to the order of Melchizedek.'
  In the days of his flesh, Jesus offered up prayers and supplications, with loud cries and tears, to the one who was able to save him from death, and he was heard because of his reverent submission. Although he was a Son, he learned obedience through what he suffered; and having been made perfect, he became the source of

eternal salvation for all who obey him, having been designated by God a high priest according to the order of Melchizedek.

This is the word of the Lord.

Hear the gospel of our Lord Jesus Christ according to Mark. *(10.35-45)*

James and John, the sons of Zebedee, came forward to Jesus and said to him, 'Teacher, we want you to do for us whatever we ask of you.' And he said to them, 'What is it you want me to do for you?' And they said to him, 'Grant us to sit, one at your right hand and one at your left, in your glory.' But Jesus said to them, 'You do not know what you are asking. Are you able to drink the cup that I drink, or be baptized with the baptism that I am baptized with?' They replied, 'We are able.' Then Jesus said to them, 'The cup that I drink you will drink; and with the baptism with which I am baptized, you will be baptized; but to sit at my right hand or at my left is not mine to grant, but it is for those for whom it has been prepared.'

When the ten heard this, they began to be angry with James and John. So Jesus called them and said to them, 'You know that among the Gentiles those whom they recognize as their rulers lord it over them, and their great ones are tyrants over them. But it is not so among you; but whoever wishes to become great among you must be your servant, and whoever wishes to be first among you must be slave of all. For the Son of Man came not to be served but to serve, and to give his life a ransom for many.'

This is the gospel of the Lord.

Second Service
Ps 141; Joshua 14.6-14; Matthew 12.1-21

A reading from the Book of Joshua. *(14.6-14)*

The people of Judah came to Joshua at Gilgal; and Caleb son of Jephunneh the Kenizzite said to him, 'You know what the Lord said to Moses the man of God in Kadesh-barnea concerning you and me. I was forty years old when Moses the servant of the Lord sent me from Kadesh-barnea to spy out the land; and I brought him an honest report. But my companions who went up with me made the heart of the people fail; yet I wholeheartedly followed the Lord my God. And Moses swore on that day, saying, "Surely the land on which your foot has trodden shall be an inheritance for you and your children for ever, because you have wholeheartedly followed the Lord my God." And now, as you see, the Lord has kept me alive, as he said, these forty-five years since the time that the Lord spoke this word to Moses, while Israel was journeying through the wilderness; and here I am today, eighty-five years old. I am still as strong today as I was on the day that Moses sent me; my strength now is as my strength was then, for war, and for going and coming. So now give me this hill country of which the Lord spoke on that day; for you heard on that day how the Anakim were there, with great fortified cities; it may be that the Lord will be with me, and I shall drive them out, as the Lord said.'

Then Joshua blessed him, and gave Hebron to Caleb son of Jephunneh for an inheritance. So Hebron became the inheritance of Caleb son of Jephunneh the Kenizzite to this day, because he wholeheartedly followed the Lord, the God of Israel.

A reading from the gospel according to Matthew. *(12.1-21)*

Jesus went through the cornfields on the sabbath; his disciples were hungry, and they began to pluck heads of grain and to eat. When the Pharisees saw it, they said to him, 'Look, your disciples are doing what is not lawful to do on the sabbath.' He said to them, 'Have you not read what David did when he and his companions were hungry? He entered the house of God and ate the bread of the Presence, which it was not lawful for him or his companions to eat, but only for the priests. Or have you not read in the law that on the sabbath the priests in the temple break the sabbath and yet are guiltless? I tell you, something greater than the temple is here. But if you had known what this means, "I desire mercy and not sacrifice", you would not have condemned the guiltless. For the Son of Man is lord of the sabbath.'

He left that place and entered their synagogue; a man was there with a withered hand, and they asked him, 'Is it lawful to cure on the sabbath?' so that they might accuse him. He said to them, 'Suppose one of you has only one sheep and it falls into a pit on the sabbath; will you not lay hold of it and lift it out? How much more valuable is a human being than a sheep! So it is lawful to do good on the sabbath.' Then he said to the man, 'Stretch out your hand.' He stretched it out, and it was restored, as sound as the other. But the Pharisees went out and conspired against him, how to destroy him.

When Jesus became aware of this, he departed. Many crowds followed him, and he cured all of them, and he ordered them not to make him known. This was to fulfil what had been spoken through the prophet Isaiah:

'Here is my servant, whom I have chosen,

my belovèd, with whom my soul is well pleased.
I will put my Spirit upon him,
  and he will proclaim justice to the Gentiles.
He will not wrangle or cry aloud,
  nor will anyone hear his voice in the streets.
He will not break a bruised reed
  or quench a smouldering wick
until he brings justice to victory.
  And in his name the Gentiles will hope.'

Third Service
Pss 133, 134, 137.1-6; Isaiah 54.1-14; Luke 13.31-35

A reading from the prophecy of Isaiah. (54.1-14)

Sing, O barren one who did not bear;
  burst into song and shout,
  you who have not been in labour!
For the children of the desolate woman
  will be more than the children of her that is married,
  says the Lord.
Enlarge the site of your tent,
  and let the curtains of your habitations be stretched out;
do not hold back;
  lengthen your cords and strengthen your stakes.
For you will spread out to the right and to the left,
  and your descendants will possess the nations
  and will settle the desolate towns.

Do not fear, for you will not be ashamed;
  do not be discouraged, for you will not suffer disgrace;
for you will forget the shame of your youth,
  and the disgrace of your widowhood
  you will remember no more.
For your Maker is your husband,
  the Lord of hosts is his name;
the Holy One of Israel is your Redeemer,
  the God of the whole earth he is called.
For the Lord has called you
  like a wife forsaken and grieved in spirit,
  like the wife of a man's youth when she is cast off,
  says your God.
For a brief moment I abandoned you,
  but with great compassion I will gather you.

In overflowing wrath for a moment
    I hid my face from you,
but with everlasting love I will have compassion on you,
    says the Lord, your Redeemer.

This is like the days of Noah to me:
Just as I swore that the waters of Noah
    would never again go over the earth,
so I have sworn that I will not be angry with you
    and will not rebuke you.
For the mountains may depart
    and the hills be removed,
but my steadfast love shall not depart from you,
    and my covenant of peace shall not be removed,
says the Lord,
    who has compassion on you.

O afflicted one, storm-tossed, and not comforted,
    I am about to set your stones in antimony,
    and lay your foundations with sapphires.
I will make your pinnacles of rubies,
    your gates of jewels, and all your wall of precious stones.
All your children shall be taught by the Lord,
    and great shall be the prosperity of your children.
In righteousness you shall be established;
    you shall be far from oppression,
for you shall not fear;
    and from terror, for it shall not come near you.

A reading from the gospel according to Luke. (13.31-35)

Some Pharisees came and said to Jesus, 'Get away from here, for Herod wants to kill you.' He said to them, 'Go and tell that fox for me, "Listen, I am casting out demons and performing cures today and tomorrow, and on the third day I finish my work. Yet today, tomorrow, and the next day I must be on my way, because it is impossible for a prophet to be killed away from Jerusalem." Jerusalem, Jerusalem, the city that kills the prophets and stones those who are sent to it! How often have I desired to gather your children together as a hen gathers her brood under her wings, and you were not willing! See, your house is left to you. And I tell you, you will not see me until the time comes when you say, "Blessèd is the one who comes in the name of the Lord."'

Proper 25

Sunday between 23 & 29 October inclusive

Principal Service

Continuous	*Related*
Job 42.1-6,10-17	Jeremiah 31.7-9
Ps 34.1-8 [19-22]	Ps 126
	Hebrews 7.23-28
	Mark 10.46-52

A reading from the Book of Job. *(42.1-6,10-17)*

Job answered the Lord:
> 'I know that you can do all things,
>> and that no purpose of yours can be thwarted.
> "Who is this that hides counsel without knowledge?"
> Therefore I have uttered what I did not understand,
>> things too wonderful for me, which I did not know.
> "Hear, and I will speak;
>> I will question you, and you declare to me."
> I had heard of you by the hearing of the ear,
>> but now my eye sees you;
> therefore I despise myself,
> and repent in dust and ashes.'

[10] And the Lord restored the fortunes of Job when he had prayed for his friends; and the Lord gave Job twice as much as he had before. Then there came to him all his brothers and sisters and all who had known him before, and they ate bread with him in his house; they showed him sympathy and comforted him for all the evil that the Lord had brought upon him; and each of them gave him a piece of money and a gold ring. The Lord blessed the latter days of Job more than his beginning; and he had fourteen thousand sheep, six thousand camels, a thousand yoke of oxen, and a thousand donkeys. He also had seven sons and three daughters. He named the first Jemimah, the second Keziah, and the third Keren-happuch. In all the land there were no women so beautiful as Job's daughters; and their father gave them an inheritance along with their brothers. After this Job lived for one hundred and forty years, and saw his children, and his children's children, four generations. And Job died, old and full of days.

This is the word of the Lord.

Or:

A reading from the prophecy of Jeremiah. *(31.7-9)*

Thus says the Lord:
> Sing aloud with gladness for Jacob,
>> and raise shouts for the chief of the nations;
> proclaim, give praise, and say,
>> 'Save, O Lord, your people,
>> the remnant of Israel.'
> See, I am going to bring them from the land of the north,
>> and gather them from the farthest parts of the earth,
> among them the blind and the lame,
>> those with child and those in labour, together;
>> a great company, they shall return here.
> With weeping they shall come,
>> and with consolations I will lead them back,
> I will let them walk by brooks of water,
>> in a straight path in which they shall not stumble;
> for I have become a father to Israel,
>> and Ephraim is my firstborn.

This is the word of the Lord.

A reading from the Letter to the Hebrews. *(7.23-28)*

The former priests were many in number, because they were prevented by death from continuing in office; but Jesus holds his priesthood permanently, because he continues for ever. Consequently he is able for all time to save those who approach God through him, since he always lives to make intercession for them.

For it was fitting that we should have such a high priest, holy, blameless, undefiled, separated from sinners, and exalted above the heavens. Unlike the other high priests, he has no need to offer sacrifices day after day, first for his own sins, and then for those of the people; this he did once for all when he offered himself. For the law appoints as high priests those who are subject to weakness, but the word of the oath, which came later than the law, appoints a Son who has been made perfect for ever.

This is the word of the Lord.

Hear the gospel of our Lord Jesus Christ according to Mark. *(10.46-52)*

Jesus and his disciples came to Jericho. As they and a large crowd were leaving Jericho, Bartimæus son of Timæus, a blind beggar, was sitting by the roadside. When he heard that it was Jesus of Nazareth, he began to shout out and say, 'Jesus, Son of David, have mercy on me!' Many sternly ordered him to be quiet, but he cried out even more loudly, 'Son of David, have mercy on me!' Jesus stood still and said, 'Call him here.' And they called the blind man, saying to him, 'Take heart; get up, he is calling you.' So throwing off his cloak, he sprang up and came to Jesus. Then Jesus said to him, 'What do you want me to do for you?' The blind man said to him, 'My teacher, let me see again.' Jesus said to him, 'Go; your faith has made you well.' Immediately he regained his sight and followed him on the way.

This is the gospel of the Lord.

Second Service
Ps 119.121-136; Ecclesiastes 11 & 12;
2 Timothy 2.1-7; *if a Eucharist:* Luke 18.9-14

A reading from the book Ecclesiastes. (*Chapters 11 & 12*)

> Send out your bread upon the waters,
>> for after many days you will get it back.
> Divide your means seven ways, or even eight,
>> for you do not know what disaster may happen on earth.
> When clouds are full,
>> they empty rain on the earth;
> whether a tree falls to the south or to the north,
>> in the place where the tree falls, there it will lie.
> Whoever observes the wind will not sow;
>> and whoever regards the clouds will not reap.

Just as you do not know how the breath comes to the bones in the mother's womb, so you do not know the work of God, who makes everything.

In the morning sow your seed, and at evening do not let your hands be idle; for you do not know which will prosper, this or that, or whether both alike will be good.

Light is sweet, and it is pleasant for the eyes to see the sun.

Even those who live for many years should rejoice in them all; yet let them remember that the days of darkness will be many. All that comes is vanity.

Rejoice, young man, while you are young, and let your heart cheer you in the days of your youth. Follow the inclination of your heart and the desire of your eyes, but know that for all these things God will bring you into judgement.

Banish anxiety from your mind, and put away pain from your body; for youth and the dawn of life are vanity.

Remember your creator in the days of your youth, before the days of trouble come, and the years draw near when you will say, 'I have no pleasure in them'; before the sun and the light and the moon and the stars are darkened and the clouds return with the rain; on the day when the guards of the house tremble, and the strong men are bent, and the women who grind cease working because they are few, and those who look through the windows see dimly; when the doors on the street are shut, and the sound of the grinding is low, and one rises up at the sound of a bird, and all the daughters of song are brought low; when one is afraid of heights, and terrors are in the road; the almond tree blossoms, the grasshopper drags itself along and desire fails; because all must go to their eternal home, and the mourners will go about the streets; before the silver cord is snapped, and the golden bowl is broken, and the pitcher is broken at the fountain, and the wheel broken at the cistern, and the dust returns to the earth as it was, and the breath returns to God who gave it. Vanity of vanities, says the Teacher; all is vanity.

Besides being wise, the Teacher also taught the people knowledge, weighing and studying and arranging many proverbs. The Teacher sought to find pleasing words, and he wrote words of truth plainly.

The sayings of the wise are like goads, and like nails firmly fixed are the collected sayings that are given by one shepherd. Of anything beyond these, my child, beware. Of making many books there is no end, and much study is a weariness of the flesh.

The end of the matter; all has been heard. Fear God, and keep his commandments; for that is the whole duty of everyone. For God will bring every deed into judgement, including every secret thing, whether good or evil.

A reading from the Second Letter of Paul to Timothy. (2.1-7)

You, my child, be strong in the grace that is in Christ Jesus; and what you have heard from me through many witnesses entrust to faithful people who will be able to teach others as well. Share in suffering like a good soldier of Christ Jesus. No one serving in the army gets entangled in everyday affairs; the soldier's aim is to please the enlisting officer. And in the case of an athlete, no one is crowned without competing according to the rules. It is the farmer who does the work who ought to have the first share of the crops. Think over what I say, for the Lord will give you understanding in all things.

If a Eucharist:
Hear the gospel of our Lord Jesus Christ according to Luke. *(18.9-14)*

Jesus told this parable to some who trusted in themselves that they were righteous and regarded others with contempt: 'Two men went up to the temple to pray, one a Pharisee and the other a tax-collector. The Pharisee, standing by himself, was praying thus, "God, I thank you that I am not like other people: thieves, rogues, adulterers, or even like this tax-collector. I fast twice a week; I give a tenth of all my income." But the tax-collector, standing far off, would not even look up to heaven, but was beating his breast and saying, "God, be merciful to me, a sinner!" I tell you, this man went down to his home justified rather than the other; for all who exalt themselves will be humbled, but all who humble themselves will be exalted.'

This is the gospel of the Lord.

Third Service
Ps 119.89-104; Isaiah 59.9-20; Luke 14.1-14

A reading from the prophecy of Isaiah. (59.9-20)

> Justice is far from us,
>> and righteousness does not reach us;
> we wait for light, and lo! there is darkness;
>> and for brightness, but we walk in gloom.
> We grope like the blind along a wall,
>> groping like those who have no eyes;
> we stumble at noon as in the twilight,
>> among the vigorous as though we were dead.
> We all growl like bears;
>> like doves we moan mournfully.
> We wait for justice, but there is none;
>> for salvation, but it is far from us.
> For our transgressions before you are many,
>> and our sins testify against us.
> Our transgressions indeed are with us,
>> and we know our iniquities:
> transgressing, and denying the Lord,
>> and turning away from following our God,
> talking oppression and revolt,
>> conceiving lying words and uttering them from the heart.
> Justice is turned back,
>> and righteousness stands at a distance;
> for truth stumbles in the public square,

and uprightness cannot enter.
Truth is lacking,
    and whoever turns from evil is despoiled.

The Lord saw it, and it displeased him
    that there was no justice.
He saw that there was no one,
    and was appalled that there was no one to intervene;
so his own arm brought him victory,
    and his righteousness upheld him.
He put on righteousness like a breastplate,
    and a helmet of salvation on his head;
he put on garments of vengeance for clothing,
    and wrapped himself in fury as in a mantle.
According to their deeds, so will he repay;
    wrath to his adversaries, requital to his enemies;
    to the coastlands he will render requital.
So those in the west shall fear the name of the Lord,
    and those in the east, his glory;
for he will come like a pent-up stream
    that the wind of the Lord drives on.

And he will come to Zion as Redeemer,
    to those in Jacob who turn from transgression, says the Lord.

A reading from the gospel according to Luke. (14.1-14)

On one occasion when Jesus was going to the house of a leader of the Pharisees to eat a meal on the sabbath, they were watching him closely. Just then, in front of him, there was a man who had dropsy.   And Jesus asked the lawyers and Pharisees, 'Is it lawful to cure people on the sabbath, or not?' But they were silent.   So Jesus took him and healed him, and sent him away.   Then he said to them, 'If one of you has a child or an ox that has fallen into a well, will you not immediately pull it out on a sabbath day?' And they could not reply to this.

  When he noticed how the guests chose the places of honour, he told them a parable.   'When you are invited by someone to a wedding banquet, do not sit down at the place of honour, in case someone more distinguished than you has been invited by your host; and the host who invited both of you may come and say to you, "Give this person your place", and then in disgrace you would start to take the lowest place.   But when you are invited, go and sit down at the lowest place, so that when your host comes, he may say to you, "Friend, move up higher"; then you will be honoured in the presence of all

                              Proper 25 – Third Service

who sit at the table with you.   For all who exalt themselves will be humbled, and those who humble themselves will be exalted.'

He said also to the one who had invited him, 'When you give a luncheon or a dinner, do not invite your friends or your brothers or your relatives or rich neighbours, in case they may invite you in return, and you would be repaid.   But when you give a banquet, invite the poor, the crippled, the lame, and the blind.   And you will be blessed, because they cannot repay you, for you will be repaid at the resurrection of the righteous.'

Bible Sunday

Principal Service
Isaiah 55.1-11; Ps 19.7-14; 2 Timothy 3.14 - 4.5; John 5.36*b*-47

A reading from the prophecy of Isaiah. *(55.1-11)*

Ho, everyone who thirsts,
    come to the waters;
and you that have no money,
    come, buy and eat!
Come, buy wine and milk
    without money and without price.
Why do you spend your money for that which is not bread,
    and your labour for that which does not satisfy?
Listen carefully to me, and eat what is good,
    and delight yourselves in rich food.
Incline your ear, and come to me;
    listen, so that you may live.
I will make with you an everlasting covenant,
    my steadfast, sure love for David.
See, I made him a witness to the peoples,
    a leader and commander for the peoples.
See, you shall call nations that you do not know,
    and nations that do not know you shall run to you,
because of the Lord your God, the Holy One of Israel,
for he has glorified you.

Seek the Lord while he may be found,
    call upon him while he is near;
let the wicked forsake their way,
    and the unrighteous their thoughts;
let them return to the Lord, that he may have mercy on them,

and to our God, for he will abundantly pardon.
For my thoughts are not your thoughts,
>   nor are your ways my ways, says the Lord.
For as the heavens are higher than the earth,
>   so are my ways higher than your ways
>   and my thoughts than your thoughts.

For as the rain and the snow come down from heaven,
>   and do not return there until they have watered the earth,
making it bring forth and sprout,
>   giving seed to the sower and bread to the eater,
so shall my word be that goes out from my mouth;
>   it shall not return to me empty,
but it shall accomplish that which I purpose,
>   and succeed in the thing for which I sent it.

This is the word of the Lord.

A reading from the Second Letter of Paul to Timothy. *(3.14 - 4.5)*

As for you, continue in what you have learned and firmly believed, knowing from whom you learned it, and how from childhood you have known the sacred writings that are able to instruct you for salvation through faith in Christ Jesus. All scripture is inspired by God and is useful for teaching, for reproof, for correction, and for training in righteousness, so that everyone who belongs to God may be proficient, equipped for every good work.

In the presence of God and of Christ Jesus, who is to judge the living and the dead, and in view of his appearing and his kingdom, I solemnly urge you: proclaim the message; be persistent whether the time is favourable or unfavourable; convince, rebuke, and encourage, with the utmost patience in teaching. For the time is coming when people will not put up with sound doctrine, but having itching ears, they will accumulate for themselves teachers to suit their own desires, and will turn away from listening to the truth and wander away to myths. As for you, always be sober, endure suffering, do the work of an evangelist, carry out your ministry fully.

This is the word of the Lord.

Hear the gospel of our Lord Jesus Christ according to John. *(5.36b-47)*

Jesus said to the Jews, 'The works that the Father has given me to complete, the very works that I am doing, testify on my behalf that the Father has sent me. And the Father who sent me has himself testified on my behalf. You have never heard his voice or seen his form, and you do not have his word abiding in you, because you do not believe him whom he has sent.

'You search the scriptures because you think that in them you have eternal life; and it is they that testify on my behalf. Yet you refuse to come to me to have life. I do not accept glory from human beings. But I know that you do not have the love of God in you. I have come in my Father's name, and you do not accept me; if another comes in his own name, you will accept him. How can you believe when you accept glory from one another and do not seek the glory that comes from the one who alone is God? Do not think that I will accuse you before the Father; your accuser is Moses, on whom you have set your hope. If you believed Moses, you would believe me, for he wrote about me. But if you do not believe what he wrote, how will you believe what I say?'

This is the gospel of the Lord.

Second Service
Ps 119.1-16; 2 Kings 22; Colossians 3.12-17

A reading from the Second Book of the Kings. (Chapter 22)

Josiah was eight years old when he began to reign; he reigned for thirty-one years in Jerusalem. His mother's name was Jedidah daughter of Adaiah of Bozkath. He did what was right in the sight of the Lord, and walked in all the way of his father David; he did not turn aside to the right or to the left.

In the eighteenth year of King Josiah, the king sent Shaphan son of Azaliah, son of Meshullam, the secretary, to the house of the Lord, saying, 'Go up to the high priest Hilkiah, and have him count the entire sum of the money that has been brought into the house of the Lord, which the keepers of the threshold have collected from the people; let it be given into the hand of the workers who have the oversight of the house of the Lord; let them give it to the workers who are at the house of the Lord, repairing the house, that is, to the carpenters, to the builders, to the masons; and let them use it to buy timber and quarried stone to repair the house. But no account shall be asked from them for the money that is delivered into their hand, for they deal honestly.'

The high priest Hilkiah said to Shaphan the secretary, 'I have found the book of the law in the house of the Lord.' When Hilkiah gave the book to Shaphan, he read it. Then Shaphan the secretary came to the king, and reported to the king, 'Your servants have emptied out the money that was found in the house, and have delivered it into the hand of the workers who have oversight of the house of the Lord.' Shaphan the secretary informed the king, 'The priest Hilkiah has given me a book.' Shaphan then read it aloud to the king.

When the king heard the words of the book of the law, he tore his clothes. Then the king commanded the priest Hilkiah, Ahikam son of Shaphan, Achbor son of Micaiah, Shaphan the secretary, and the king's servant Asaiah, saying, 'Go, inquire of the Lord for me, for the people, and for all Judah, concerning the words of this book that has been found; for great is the wrath of the Lord that is kindled against us, because our ancestors did not obey the words of this book, to do according to all that is written concerning us.'

So the priest Hilkiah, Ahikam, Achbor, Shaphan, and Asaiah went to the prophetess Huldah the wife of Shallum son of Tikvah, son of Harhas, keeper of the wardrobe; she resided in Jerusalem in the Second Quarter, where they consulted her. She declared to them, 'Thus says the Lord, the God of Israel: Tell the man who sent you to me, Thus says the Lord, I will indeed bring disaster on this place and on its inhabitants – all the words of the book that the king of Judah has read. Because they have abandoned me and have made offerings to other gods, so that they have provoked me to anger with all the work of their hands, therefore my wrath will be kindled against this place, and it will not be quenched. But as to the king of Judah, who sent you to inquire of the Lord, thus shall you say to him, Thus says the Lord, the God of Israel: Regarding the words that you have heard, because your heart was penitent, and you humbled yourself before the Lord, when you heard how I spoke against this place, and against its inhabitants, that they should become a desolation and a curse, and because you have torn your clothes and wept before me, I also have heard you, says the Lord. Therefore, I will gather you to your ancestors, and you shall be gathered to your grave in peace; your eyes shall not see all the disaster that I will bring on this place.' They took the message back to the king.

A reading from the Letter of Paul to the Colossians. (3.12-17)

As God's chosen ones, holy and belovèd, clothe yourselves with compassion, kindness, humility, meekness, and patience. Bear with one another and, if anyone has a complaint against another, forgive each other; just as the Lord has forgiven you, so you also must forgive. Above all, clothe yourselves with love, which binds everything together in perfect harmony. And let the peace of Christ rule in your hearts, to which indeed you were called in the one body. And be thankful. Let the word of Christ dwell in you richly; teach and admonish one another in all wisdom; and with gratitude in your hearts sing psalms, hymns, and spiritual songs to God. And whatever you do, in word or deed, do everything in the name of the Lord Jesus, giving thanks to God the Father through him.

Third Service
Ps 119.89-104; Isaiah 45.22-25; Matthew 24.30-35 *or* Luke 14.1-14

A reading from the prophecy of Isaiah. (45.22-25)

Turn to me and be saved,
    all the ends of the earth!
    For I am God, and there is no other.
By myself I have sworn,
    from my mouth has gone forth in righteousness
    a word that shall not return:
'To me every knee shall bow,
    every tongue shall swear.'

Only in the Lord, it shall be said of me,
    are righteousness and strength;
all who were incensed against him
    shall come to him and be ashamed.
In the Lord all the offspring of Israel
    shall triumph and glory.

A reading from the gospel according to Matthew. (24.30-35)

Jesus said to his disciples, 'The sign of the Son of Man will appear in heaven, and then all the tribes of the earth will mourn, and they will see "the Son of Man coming on the clouds of heaven" with power and great glory. And he will send out his angels with a loud trumpet call, and they will gather his elect from the four winds, from one end of heaven to the other.

'From the fig tree learn its lesson: as soon as its branch becomes tender and puts forth its leaves, you know that summer is near. So also, when you see all these things, you know that he is near, at the very gates. Truly I tell you, this generation will not pass away until all these things have taken place. Heaven and earth will pass away, but my words will not pass away.'

Or:
A reading from the gospel according to Luke. *(14.1-14)*

On one occasion when Jesus was going to the house of a leader of the Pharisees to eat a meal on the sabbath, they were watching him closely. Just then, in front of him, there was a man who had dropsy. And Jesus asked the lawyers and Pharisees, 'Is it lawful to cure people on the sabbath, or not?' But they were silent. So Jesus took him and healed him, and sent him away. Then he said to them, 'If one of you has a child or an ox that has fallen into a well, will you not immediately pull it out on a sabbath day?' And they could not reply to this.

When he noticed how the guests chose the places of honour, he told them a parable. 'When you are invited by someone to a wedding banquet, do not sit down at the place of honour, in case someone more distinguished than you has been invited by your host; and the host who invited both of you may come and say to you, "Give this person your place", and then in disgrace you would start to take the lowest place. But when you are invited, go and sit down at the lowest place, so that when your host comes, he may say to you, "Friend, move up higher"; then you will be honoured in the presence of all who sit at the table with you. For all who exalt themselves will be humbled, and those who humble themselves will be exalted.'

He said also to the one who had invited him, 'When you give a luncheon or a dinner, do not invite your friends or your brothers or your relatives or rich neighbours, in case they may invite you in return, and you would be repaid. But when you give a banquet, invite the poor, the crippled, the lame, and the blind. And you will be blessed, because they cannot repay you, for you will be repaid at the resurrection of the righteous.'

Dedication Festival

First Sunday in October or Last Sunday after Trinity (if date not known)
See page 407.

All Saints' Sunday

All Saints' Day to the eve of Advent Sunday is observed as a time to celebrate and reflect upon the reign of Christ in earth and heaven.

The Sunday occurring between 30 October and 5 November (inclusive) may be celebrated as All Saints' Sunday.

A local decision has to be taken if All Saints' Sunday is to be observed and, if so, what celebration of All Saints is observed on 1 November, if any.

Full provision is made below for use on All Saints' Sunday and alternative readings if The Fourth Sunday before Advent is being observed (see page 450). The readings for the Eucharist on All Saints' Sunday are the Year A readings for All Saints' Day.

If All Saints' Day and All Saints' Sunday are both being observed (but on different days), alternative readings for All Saints' Day (from Years A and C) can be found in the book Exciting Holiness *on pages 373 to 382.*

Evening Prayer on the Eve
Pss 1,5; Ecclesiasticus 44.1-15 *or* Isaiah 40.27-31; Revelation 19.6-10

A reading from the book Ecclesiasticus. (44.1-15)

Let us now sing the praises of famous men, our ancestors in their generations. The Lord apportioned to them great glory, his majesty from the beginning. There were those who ruled in their kingdoms, and made a name for themselves by their valour; those who gave counsel because they were intelligent; those who spoke in prophetic oracles; those who led the people by their counsels and by their knowledge of the people's lore; they were wise in their words of instruction; those who composed musical tunes, or put verses in writing; rich men endowed with resources, living peacefully in their homes – all these were honoured in their generations, and were the pride of their times. Some of them have left behind a name, so that others declare their praise. But of others there is no memory; they have perished as though they had never existed; they have become as though they had never been born, they and their children after them. But these also were godly men, whose righteous deeds have not been forgotten; their wealth will remain with their descendants, and their inheritance with their children's children. Their descendants stand by the covenants; their children also, for their sake. Their offspring will continue for ever, and their glory will never be blotted out. Their bodies are buried in peace, but their name lives on generation after generation. The assembly declares their wisdom, and the congregation proclaims their praise.

Or:

A reading from the prophecy of Isaiah. (40.27-31)

Why do you say, O Jacob,
   and speak, O Israel,
'My way is hidden from the Lord,
   and my right is disregarded by my God'?
Have you not known?
   Have you not heard?
The Lord is the everlasting God,
   the Creator of the ends of the earth.
He does not faint or grow weary;
   his understanding is unsearchable.
He gives power to the faint,
   and strengthens the powerless.
Even youths will faint and be weary,
   and the young will fall exhausted;
but those who wait for the Lord shall renew their strength,
   they shall mount up with wings like eagles,
they shall run and not be weary,
   they shall walk and not faint.

A reading from the Revelation to John. (19.6-10)

I heard what seemed to be the voice of a great multitude, like the sound of many waters and like the sound of mighty thunder-peals, crying out,
   'Hallelujah!
For the Lord our God the Almighty reigns.
   Let us rejoice and exult
      and give him the glory,
   for the marriage of the Lamb has come,
      and his bride has made herself ready;
   to her it has been granted to be clothed
      with fine linen, bright and pure' –
for the fine linen is the righteous deeds of the saints.

And the angel said to me, 'Write this: Blessèd are those who are invited to the marriage supper of the Lamb.' And he said to me, 'These are true words of God.' Then I fell down at his feet to worship him, but he said to me, 'You must not do that! I am a fellow-servant with you and your comrades who hold the testimony of Jesus. Worship God! For the testimony of Jesus is the spirit of prophecy.'

Eucharist

Wisdom 3.1-9 *or* Isaiah 25.6-9; Ps 24.1-6; Rev 21.1-6*a*; John 11.32-44

A reading from the Wisdom of Solomon. (3.1-9)

The souls of the righteous are in the hand of God,
and no torment will ever touch them.
In the eyes of the foolish they seemed to have died,
and their departure was thought to be a disaster,
and their going from us to be their destruction;
but they are at peace.
For though in the sight of others they were punished,
their hope is full of immortality.
Having been disciplined a little, they will receive great good,
because God tested them and found them worthy of himself;
like gold in the furnace he tried them,
and like a sacrificial burnt-offering he accepted them.
In the time of their visitation they will shine forth,
and will run like sparks through the stubble.
They will govern nations and rule over peoples,
and the Lord will reign over them for ever.
Those who trust in him will understand truth,
and the faithful will abide with him in love,
because grace and mercy are upon his holy ones,
and he watches over his elect.

This is the word of the Lord.

Or:

A reading from the prophecy of Isaiah. (25.6-9)

On this mountain the Lord of hosts will make for all peoples
a feast of rich food, a feast of well-matured wines,
of rich food filled with marrow,
of well-matured wines strained clear.
And he will destroy on this mountain
the shroud that is cast over all peoples,
the sheet that is spread over all nations;
he will swallow up death for ever.
Then the Lord God will wipe away the tears from all faces, and the disgrace of his people he will take away from all the earth, for the Lord has spoken.
It will be said on that day, Lo, this is our God; we have waited for him, so that he might save us. This is the Lord for whom we have waited; let us be glad and rejoice in his salvation.

This is the word of the Lord.

A reading from the Revelation to John. (21.1-6a)

I saw a new heaven and a new earth; for the first heaven and the first earth had passed away, and the sea was no more. And I saw the holy city, the new Jerusalem, coming down out of heaven from God, prepared as a bride adorned for her husband. And I heard a loud voice from the throne saying,

'See, the home of God is among mortals.
He will dwell with them;
they will be his peoples,
and God himself will be with them;
he will wipe every tear from their eyes.
Death will be no more;
mourning and crying and pain will be no more,
for the first things have passed away.'

And the one who was seated on the throne said, 'See, I am making all things new.' Also he said, 'Write this, for these words are trustworthy and true.' Then he said to me, 'It is done! I am the Alpha and the Omega, the beginning and the end.'

This is the word of the Lord.

Hear the gospel of our Lord Jesus Christ according to John. (11.32-44)

When Mary came where Jesus was and saw him, she knelt at his feet and said to him, 'Lord, if you had been here, my brother would not have died.' When Jesus saw her weeping, and the Jews who came with her also weeping, he was greatly disturbed in spirit and deeply moved. He said, 'Where have you laid him?' They said to him, 'Lord, come and see.' Jesus began to weep. So the Jews said, 'See how he loved him!' But some of them said, 'Could not he who opened the eyes of the blind man have kept this man from dying?'

Then Jesus, again greatly disturbed, came to the tomb. It was a cave, and a stone was lying against it. Jesus said, 'Take away the stone.' Martha, the sister of the dead man, said to him, 'Lord, already there is a stench because he has been dead for four days.' Jesus said to her, 'Did I not tell you that if you believed, you would see the glory of God?' So they took away the stone. And Jesus looked upwards and said, 'Father, I thank you for having heard me. I knew that you always hear me, but I have said this for the sake of the crowd standing here, so that they may believe that you sent me.' When he had said this, he cried with a loud voice, 'Lazarus, come out!' The dead man came out, his hands and feet bound with strips of cloth, and his face wrapped in a cloth. Jesus said to them, 'Unbind him, and let him go.'

This is the gospel of the Lord.

Morning Prayer
Pss 15,84; Isaiah 35.1-9; Luke 9.18-27

A reading from the prophecy of Isaiah. *(35.1-9)*

The wilderness and the dry land shall be glad,
    the desert shall rejoice and blossom;
like the crocus it shall blossom abundantly,
    and rejoice with joy and singing.
The glory of Lebanon shall be given to it,
    the majesty of Carmel and Sharon.
They shall see the glory of the Lord,
    the majesty of our God.

Strengthen the weak hands,
    and make firm the feeble knees.
Say to those who are of a fearful heart,
    'Be strong, do not fear!
Here is your God.
    He will come with vengeance, with terrible recompense.
He will come and save you.'

Then the eyes of the blind shall be opened,
    and the ears of the deaf unstopped;
then the lame shall leap like a deer,
    and the tongue of the speechless sing for joy.
For waters shall break forth in the wilderness,
    and streams in the desert;
the burning sand shall become a pool,
    and the thirsty ground springs of water;
the haunt of jackals shall become a swamp,
    the grass shall become reeds and rushes.

A highway shall be there,
    and it shall be called the Holy Way;
the unclean shall not travel on it,
    but it shall be for God's people;
    no traveller, not even fools, shall go astray.
No lion shall be there,
    nor shall any ravenous beast come up on it;
they shall not be found there,
    but the redeemed shall walk there.

A reading from the gospel according to Luke. (9.18-27)

Once when Jesus was praying alone, with only the disciples near him, he asked them, 'Who do the crowds say that I am?' They answered, 'John the Baptist; but others, Elijah; and still others, that one of the ancient prophets has arisen.' He said to them, 'But who do you say that I am?' Peter answered, 'The Messiah of God.'

He sternly ordered and commanded them not to tell anyone, saying, 'The Son of Man must undergo great suffering, and be rejected by the elders, chief priests, and scribes, and be killed, and on the third day be raised.'

Then he said to them all, 'If any want to become my followers, let them deny themselves and take up their cross daily and follow me. For those who want to save their life will lose it, and those who lose their life for my sake will save it. What does it profit them if they gain the whole world, but lose or forfeit themselves? Those who are ashamed of me and of my words, of them the Son of Man will be ashamed when he comes in his glory and the glory of the Father and of the holy angels. But truly I tell you, there are some standing here who will not taste death before they see the kingdom of God.'

Evening Prayer
Pss 148,150; Isaiah 65.17-25; Hebrews 11.32 - 12.2

A reading from the prophecy of Isaiah. (65.17-25)

I am about to create new heavens and a new earth;
>   the former things shall not be remembered or come to mind.
But be glad and rejoice for ever in what I am creating;
>   for I am about to create Jerusalem as a joy,
>   and its people as a delight.
I will rejoice in Jerusalem,
>   and delight in my people;
no more shall the sound of weeping be heard in it,
>   or the cry of distress.
No more shall there be in it an infant that lives but a few days,
>   or an old person who does not live out a lifetime;
for one who dies at a hundred years will be considered a youth,
>   and one who falls short of a hundred
>   will be considered accursed.
They shall build houses and inhabit them;
>   they shall plant vineyards and eat their fruit.
They shall not build and another inhabit;
>   they shall not plant and another eat;

for like the days of a tree shall the days of my people be,
    and my chosen shall long enjoy the work of their hands.
They shall not labour in vain, or bear children for calamity;
    for they shall be offspring blessed by the Lord –
    and their descendants as well.
Before they call I will answer,
    while they are yet speaking I will hear.
The wolf and the lamb shall feed together,
    the lion shall eat straw like the ox;
but the serpent –
    its food shall be dust!
They shall not hurt or destroy on all my holy mountain,
    says the Lord.

A reading from the Letter to the Hebrews. (11.32 - 12.2)

What more should I say? For time would fail me to tell of Gideon, Barak, Samson, Jephthah, of David and Samuel and the prophets – who through faith conquered kingdoms, administered justice, obtained promises, shut the mouths of lions, quenched raging fire, escaped the edge of the sword, won strength out of weakness, became mighty in war, put foreign armies to flight. Women received their dead by resurrection. Others were tortured, refusing to accept release, in order to obtain a better resurrection. Others suffered mocking and flogging, and even chains and imprisonment. They were stoned to death, they were sawn in two, they were killed by the sword; they went about in skins of sheep and goats, destitute, persecuted, tormented – of whom the world was not worthy. They wandered in deserts and mountains, and in caves and holes in the ground.

Yet all these, though they were commended for their faith, did not receive what was promised, since God had provided something better so that they would not, without us, be made perfect.

Therefore, since we are surrounded by so great a cloud of witnesses, let us also lay aside every weight and the sin that clings so closely, and let us run with perseverance the race that is set before us, looking to Jesus the pioneer and perfecter of our faith, who for the sake of the joy that was set before him endured the cross, disregarding its shame, and has taken his seat at the right hand of the throne of God.

The Fourth Sunday before Advent

Sunday between 30 October & 5 November inclusive
(see note on page 443)

Principal Service

Deuteronomy 6.1-9; Ps 119.1-8; Hebrews 9.11-14; Mark 12.28-34

A reading from the book Deuteronomy. (6.1-9)

Moses said to all Israel: Now this is the commandment – the statutes and the ordinances – that the Lord your God charged me to teach you to observe in the land that you are about to cross into and occupy, so that you and your children and your children's children may fear the Lord your God all the days of your life, and keep all his decrees and his commandments that I am commanding you, so that your days may be long. Hear therefore, O Israel, and observe them diligently, so that it may go well with you, and so that you may multiply great-ly in a land flowing with milk and honey, as the Lord, the God of your ancestors, has promised you.

  Hear, O Israel: The Lord is our God, the Lord alone. You shall love the Lord your God with all your heart, and with all your soul, and with all your might. Keep these words that I am commanding you today in your heart. Recite them to your children and talk about them when you are at home and when you are away, when you lie down and when you rise. Bind them as a sign on your hand, fix them as an emblem on your forehead, and write them on the doorposts of your house and on your gates.

This is the word of the Lord.

A reading from the Letter to the Hebrews. (9.11-14)

When Christ came as a high priest of the good things that have come, then through the greater and perfect tent (not made with hands, that is, not of this creation), he entered once for all into the Holy Place, not with the blood of goats and calves, but with his own blood, thus obtaining eternal redemption. For if the blood of goats and bulls, with the sprinkling of the ashes of a heifer, sanctifies those who have been defiled so that their flesh is purified, how much more will the blood of Christ, who through the eternal Spirit offered himself with-out blemish to God, purify our conscience from dead works to wor-ship the living God!

This is the word of the Lord.

Hear the gospel of our Lord Jesus Christ according to Mark. (12.28-34)

One of the scribes came near to Jesus and the Sadducees and heard them disputing with one another, and seeing that he answered them well, he asked him, 'Which commandment is the first of all?' Jesus answered, 'The first is, "Hear, O Israel: the Lord our God, the Lord is one; you shall love the Lord your God with all your heart, and with all your soul, and with all your mind, and with all your strength." The second is this, "You shall love your neighbour as yourself." There is no other commandment greater than these.' Then the scribe said to him, 'You are right, Teacher; you have truly said that "he is one, and besides him there is no other"; and "to love him with all the heart, and with all the understanding, and with all the strength", and "to love one's neighbour as oneself", – this is much more important than all whole burnt-offerings and sacrifices.' When Jesus saw that he answered wisely, he said to him, 'You are not far from the kingdom of God.' After that no one dared to ask him any question.

This is the gospel of the Lord.

Second Service
Ps 145 *or* 145.1-9; Daniel 2.1-48 (*or* 1-11,25-48); Revelation 7.9-17; *if a Eucharist:* Matthew 5.1-12

A reading from the Book of Daniel. (2.1-48; or 2.1-11,25-48)

In the second year of Nebuchadnezzar's reign, Nebuchadnezzar dreamed such dreams that his spirit was troubled and his sleep left him. So the king commanded that the magicians, the enchanters, the sorcerers, and the Chaldeans be summoned to tell the king his dreams. When they came in and stood before the king, he said to them, 'I have had such a dream that my spirit is troubled by the desire to understand it.' The Chaldeans said to the king (in Aramaic), 'O king, live for ever! Tell your servants the dream, and we will reveal the interpretation.' The king answered the Chaldeans, 'This is a public decree: if you do not tell me both the dream and its interpretation, you shall be torn limb from limb, and your houses shall be laid in ruins. But if you do tell me the dream and its interpretation, you shall receive from me gifts and rewards and great honour. Therefore tell me the dream and its interpretation.' They answered a second time, 'Let the king first tell his servants the dream, then we can give its interpretation.' The king answered, 'I know with certainty that you are trying to gain time, because you see I have firmly decreed: if you do not tell me the dream, there is but one verdict for you. You have agreed to speak lying and misleading words to me until things take a turn. Therefore, tell me the dream, and I shall know that you can give me its interpretation.' The Chaldeans answered the king, 'There is no one on earth who can reveal what the king demands! In fact no king, however great and powerful, has ever asked such a thing of any magician or enchanter or Chaldean. The thing that the king is asking is too difficult, and no one can reveal it to the king except the gods, whose dwelling is not with mortals.'

[12 Because of this the king flew into a violent rage and commanded that all the wise men of Babylon be destroyed. The decree was issued, and the wise men were about to be executed; and they looked for Daniel and his companions, to execute them. Then Daniel responded with prudence and discretion to Arioch, the king's chief executioner, who had gone out to execute the wise men of Babylon; he asked Arioch, the royal official, 'Why is the decree of the king so urgent?' Arioch then explained the matter to Daniel. So Daniel went in and requested that the king give him time and he would tell the king the interpretation.

Then Daniel went to his home and informed his companions, Hananiah, Mishael, and Azariah, and told them to seek mercy from the God of heaven concerning this mystery, so that Daniel and his companions with the rest of the wise men of Babylon might not perish. Then the mystery was revealed to Daniel in a vision of the night, and Daniel blessed the God of heaven.

Daniel said:

'Blessèd be the name of God from age to age,
    for wisdom and power are his.
He changes times and seasons,
    deposes kings and sets up kings;
he gives wisdom to the wise and knowledge
    to those who have understanding.
He reveals deep and hidden things;
    he knows what is in the darkness,
    and light dwells with him.
To you, O God of my ancestors,
    I give thanks and praise,
for you have given me wisdom and power,
    and have now revealed to me what we asked of you,
    for you have revealed to us what the king ordered.'

Therefore Daniel went to Arioch, whom the king had appointed to destroy the wise men of Babylon, and said to him, 'Do not destroy the wise men of Babylon; bring me in before the king, and I will give the king the interpretation.']

²⁵ Then Arioch quickly brought Daniel before the king and said to him: 'I have found among the exiles from Judah a man who can tell the king the interpretation.' The king said to Daniel, whose name was Belteshazzar, 'Are you able to tell me the dream that I have seen and its interpretation?' Daniel answered the king, 'No wise men, enchanters, magicians, or diviners can show to the king the mystery that the king is asking, but there is a God in heaven who reveals mysteries, and he has disclosed to King Nebuchadnezzar what will happen at the end of days. Your dream and the visions of your head as you lay in bed were these: To you, O king, as you lay in bed, came thoughts of what would be hereafter, and the revealer of mysteries disclosed to you what is to be. But as for me, this mystery has not been revealed to me because of any wisdom that I have more than any other living being, but in order that the interpretation may be known to the king and that you may understand the thoughts of your mind.

'You were looking, O king, and lo! there was a great statue. This statue was huge, its brilliance extraordinary; it was standing before you, and its appearance was frightening. The head of that statue was of fine gold, its chest and arms of silver, its middle and thighs of bronze, its legs of iron, its feet partly of iron and partly of clay. As you looked on, a stone was cut out, not by human hands, and it struck the statue on its feet of iron and clay and broke them in pieces. Then the iron, the clay, the bronze, the silver, and the gold, were all broken in pieces and became like the chaff of the summer threshing-floors; and the wind carried them away, so that not a trace of them could be found. But the stone that struck the statue became a great mountain and filled the whole earth.

'This was the dream; now we will tell the king its interpretation. You, O king, the king of kings – to whom the God of heaven has given the kingdom, the power, the might, and the glory, into whose hand he has given human beings, wherever they live, the wild animals of the field, and the birds of the air, and whom he has established as ruler over them all – you are the head of gold. After you shall arise another kingdom inferior to yours, and yet a third kingdom of bronze, which shall rule over the whole earth. And there shall be a fourth kingdom, strong as iron; just as iron crushes and smashes everything, it shall crush and shatter all these. As you saw the feet and toes partly of potter's clay and partly of iron, it shall be a divided kingdom; but some of the strength of iron shall be in it, as you saw the iron mixed with the clay. As the toes of the feet were part iron and part clay, so the kingdom shall be partly strong and partly brittle. As you saw the iron mixed with clay, so will they mix with one another in marriage, but they will not hold together, just as iron does not mix with clay. And in the days of those kings the God of heaven will set up a kingdom that shall never be destroyed, nor shall this kingdom be left to another people. It shall crush all these kingdoms and bring them to an end, and it shall stand for ever; just as you saw that a stone was cut from the mountain not by hands, and that it crushed the iron, the bronze, the clay, the silver, and the gold. The great God has informed the king what shall be hereafter. The dream is certain, and its interpretation trustworthy.'

Then King Nebuchadnezzar fell on his face, worshipped Daniel, and commanded that a grain-offering and incense be offered to him. The king said to Daniel, 'Truly, your God is God of gods and Lord of kings and a revealer of mysteries, for you have been able to reveal this mystery!' Then the king promoted Daniel, gave him many great gifts, and made him ruler over the whole province of Babylon and chief prefect over all the wise men of Babylon.

A reading from the Revelation to John. (7.9-17)

I looked, and there was a great multitude that no one could count, from every nation, from all tribes and peoples and languages, standing before the throne and before the Lamb, robed in white, with palm branches in their hands. They cried out in a loud voice, saying,
  'Salvation belongs to our God who is seated on the throne,
    and to the Lamb!'
And all the angels stood around the throne and around the elders and the four living creatures, and they fell on their faces before the throne and worshipped God, singing,
  'Amen! Blessing and glory and wisdom
    and thanksgiving and honour and power and might
    be to our God for ever and ever! Amen.'
  Then one of the elders addressed me, saying, 'Who are these, robed in white, and where have they come from?' I said to him, 'Sir, you are the one that knows.' Then he said to me, 'These are they who have come out of the great ordeal; they have washed their robes and made them white in the blood of the Lamb.
  For this reason they are before the throne of God,
    and worship him day and night within his temple,
    and the one who is seated on the throne will shelter them.
  They will hunger no more, and thirst no more;
    the sun will not strike them, nor any scorching heat;

for the Lamb at the centre of the throne will be their shepherd,
  and he will guide them to springs of the water of life,
  and God will wipe away every tear from their eyes.'

If a Eucharist:
Hear the gospel of our Lord Jesus Christ according to Matthew. *(5.1-12)*

When Jesus saw the crowds, he went up the mountain; and after he sat down, his disciples came to him. Then he began to speak, and taught them, saying:
 'Blessèd are the poor in spirit, for theirs is the kingdom of heaven.
 'Blessèd are those who mourn, for they will be comforted.
 'Blessèd are the meek, for they will inherit the earth.
 'Blessèd are those who hunger and thirst for righteousness, for they will be filled.
 'Blessèd are the merciful, for they will receive mercy.
 'Blessèd are the pure in heart, for they will see God.
 'Blessèd are the peacemakers, for they will be called children of God.
 'Blessèd are those who are persecuted for righteousness' sake, for theirs is the kingdom of heaven.
 'Blessèd are you when people revile you and persecute you and utter all kinds of evil against you falsely on my account. Rejoice and be glad, for your reward is great in heaven, for in the same way they persecuted the prophets who were before you.'

This is the gospel of the Lord.

Third Service
Pss 112,149; Jeremiah 31.31-34; 1 John 3.1-3

A reading from the prophecy of Jeremiah. (31.31-34)

The days are surely coming, says the Lord, when I will make a new covenant with the house of Israel and the house of Judah. It will not be like the covenant that I made with their ancestors when I took them by the hand to bring them out of the land of Egypt – a covenant that they broke, though I was their husband, says the Lord. But this is the covenant that I will make with the house of Israel after those days, says the Lord: I will put my law within them, and I will write it on their hearts; and I will be their God, and they shall be my people. No longer shall they teach one another, or say to each other, 'Know the Lord', for they shall all know me, from the least of them to the greatest, says the Lord; for I will forgive their iniquity, and remember their sin no more.

A reading from the First Letter of John. (3.1-3)

See what love the Father has given us, that we should be called children of God; and that is what we are. The reason the world does not know us is that it did not know him. Belovèd, we are God's children now; what we will be has not yet been revealed. What we do know is this: when he is revealed, we will be like him, for we will see him as he is. And all who have this hope in him purify themselves, just as he is pure.

The Third Sunday before Advent
Sunday between 6 & 12 November inclusive

Principal Service
Jonah 3.1-5,10; Ps 62.5-12; Hebrews 9.24-28; Mark 1.14-20

A reading from the Book of Jonah. (3.1-5,10)

The word of the Lord came to Jonah a second time, saying, 'Get up, go to Nineveh, that great city, and proclaim to it the message that I tell you.' So Jonah set out and went to Nineveh, according to the word of the Lord. Now Nineveh was an exceedingly large city, a three days' walk across. Jonah began to go into the city, going a day's walk. And he cried out, 'Forty days more, and Nineveh shall be overthrown!' And the people of Nineveh believed God; they proclaimed a fast, and everyone, great and small, put on sackcloth.
¹⁰ When God saw what they did, how they turned from their evil ways, God changed his mind about the calamity that he had said he would bring upon them; and he did not do it.

This is the word of the Lord.

A reading from the Letter to the Hebrews. (9.24-28)

Christ did not enter a sanctuary made by human hands, a mere copy of the true one, but he entered into heaven itself, now to appear in the presence of God on our behalf. Nor was it to offer himself again and again, as the high priest enters the Holy Place year after year with blood that is not his own; for then he would have had to suffer again and again since the foundation of the world. But as it is, he has appeared once for all at the end of the age to remove sin by the sacrifice of himself. And just as it is appointed for mortals to die once, and after that the judgement, so Christ, having been offered once to bear the sins of many, will appear a second time, not to deal with sin, but to save those who are eagerly waiting for him.

This is the word of the Lord.

Hear the gospel of our Lord Jesus Christ according to Mark. (1.14-20)

After John was arrested, Jesus came to Galilee, proclaiming the good news of God, and saying, 'The time is fulfilled, and the kingdom of God has come near; repent, and believe in the good news.'

As Jesus passed along the Sea of Galilee, he saw Simon and his brother Andrew casting a net into the lake – for they were fishermen. And Jesus said to them, 'Follow me and I will make you fish for people.' And immediately they left their nets and followed him. As he went a little farther, he saw James son of Zebedee and his brother John, who were in their boat mending the nets. Immediately he called them; and they left their father Zebedee in the boat with the hired men, and followed him.

This is the gospel of the Lord.

Second Service
Pss 46 [82]; Isaiah 10.33 - 11.9; John 14.1-29 (*or* 23-29)

A reading from the prophecy of Isaiah. (10.33 - 11.9)

Look, the Sovereign, the Lord of hosts,
　　will lop the boughs with terrifying power;
the tallest trees will be cut down,
　　and the lofty will be brought low.
He will hack down the thickets of the forest with an axe,
　　and Lebanon with its majestic trees will fall.
A shoot shall come out from the stock of Jesse,
　　and a branch shall grow out of his roots.
The spirit of the Lord shall rest on him,
　　the spirit of wisdom and understanding,
　　the spirit of counsel and might,
　　the spirit of knowledge and the fear of the Lord.
His delight shall be in the fear of the Lord.

He shall not judge by what his eyes see,
　　or decide by what his ears hear;
but with righteousness he shall judge the poor,
　　and decide with equity for the meek of the earth;
he shall strike the earth with the rod of his mouth,
　　and with the breath of his lips he shall kill the wicked.
Righteousness shall be the belt around his waist,
　　and faithfulness the belt around his loins.
The wolf shall live with the lamb,
　　the leopard shall lie down with the kid,

the calf and the lion and the fatling together,
    and a little child shall lead them.
The cow and the bear shall graze,
    their young shall lie down together;
    and the lion shall eat straw like the ox.
The nursing child shall play over the hole of the asp,
    and the weaned child shall put its hand on the adder's den.
They will not hurt or destroy
    on all my holy mountain;
for the earth will be full of the knowledge of the Lord
    as the waters cover the sea.

A reading from the gospel according to John. (14.1-29; or 23-29)

[Jesus said to his disciples, 'Do not let your hearts be troubled. Believe in God, believe also in me. In my Father's house there are many dwelling-places. If it were not so, would I have told you that I go to prepare a place for you? And if I go and prepare a place for you, I will come again and will take you to myself, so that where I am, there you may be also. And you know the way to the place where I am going.' Thomas said to him, 'Lord, we do not know where you are going. How can we know the way?' Jesus said to him, 'I am the way, and the truth, and the life. No one comes to the Father except through me. If you know me, you will know my Father also. From now on you do know him and have seen him.'

Philip said to him, 'Lord, show us the Father, and we will be satisfied.' Jesus said to him, 'Have I been with you all this time, Philip, and you still do not know me? Whoever has seen me has seen the Father. How can you say, "Show us the Father"? Do you not believe that I am in the Father and the Father is in me? The words that I say to you I do not speak on my own; but the Father who dwells in me does his works. Believe me that I am in the Father and the Father is in me; but if you do not, then believe me because of the works themselves. Very truly, I tell you, the one who believes in me will also do the works that I do and, in fact, will do greater works than these, because I am going to the Father. I will do whatever you ask in my name, so that the Father may be glorified in the Son. If in my name you ask me for anything, I will do it.

'If you love me, you will keep my commandments. And I will ask the Father, and he will give you another Advocate, to be with you for ever. This is the Spirit of truth, whom the world cannot receive, because it neither sees him nor knows him. You know him, because he abides with you, and he will be in you.

'I will not leave you orphaned; I am coming to you. In a little while the world will no longer see me, but you will see me; because I live, you also will live. On that day you will know that I am in my Father, and you in me, and I in you. They who have my commandments and keep them are those who love me; and those who love me will be loved by my Father, and I will love them and reveal myself to them.' Judas (not Iscariot) said to him, 'Lord, how is it that you will reveal yourself to us, and not to the world?']

[23] Jesus said, 'Those who love me will keep my word, and my Father will love them, and we will come to them and make our home with them. Whoever does not love me does not keep my words; and the word that you hear is not mine, but is from the Father who sent me.

'I have said these things to you while I am still with you. But the Advocate, the Holy Spirit, whom the Father will send in my name, will teach you everything, and remind you of all that I have said to you. Peace I leave with you; my peace I give to you. I do not give to you as the world gives. Do not let your hearts be troubled, and do not let them be afraid. You heard me say to you, "I am going away, and I am coming to you." If you loved me, you would rejoice that I am going to the Father, because the Father is greater than I. And now I have told you this before it occurs, so that when it does occur, you may believe.'

Third Service
Ps 136; Micah 4.1-5; Philippians 4.6-9

A reading from the prophecy of Micah. (4.1-5)

In days to come
    the mountain of the Lord's house
shall be established as the highest of the mountains,
    and shall be raised up above the hills.
Peoples shall stream to it,
    and many nations shall come and say:
'Come, let us go up to the mountain of the Lord,
    to the house of the God of Jacob;
that he may teach us his ways
    and that we may walk in his paths.'
For out of Zion shall go forth instruction,
    and the word of the Lord from Jerusalem.
He shall judge between many peoples,
    and shall arbitrate between strong nations far away;
they shall beat their swords into ploughshares,

and their spears into pruning-hooks;
nation shall not lift up sword against nation,
neither shall they learn war any more;
but they shall all sit under their own vines
and under their own fig trees,
and no one shall make them afraid;
for the mouth of the Lord of hosts has spoken.

For all the peoples walk,
each in the name of its god,
but we will walk in the name of the Lord our God
for ever and ever.

A reading from the Letter of Paul to the Philippians. (4.6-9)

Do not worry about anything, but in everything by prayer and sup-plication with thanksgiving let your requests be made known to God. And the peace of God, which surpasses all understanding, will guard your hearts and your minds in Christ Jesus.

Finally, belovèd, whatever is true, whatever is honourable, what-ever is just, whatever is pure, whatever is pleasing, whatever is com-mendable, if there is any excellence and if there is anything worthy of praise, think about these things. Keep on doing the things that you have learned and received and heard and seen in me, and the God of peace will be with you.

The Second Sunday before Advent

Sunday between 13 & 19 November inclusive

Principal Service

Daniel 12.1-3; Ps 16; Hebrews 10.11-14 [15-18] 19-25; Mark 13.1-8

A reading from the Book of Daniel. (12.1-3)

Daniel continued his prophecy:
'At that time Michael, the great prince, the protector of your people, shall arise. There shall be a time of anguish, such as has never occurred since nations first came into existence. But at that time your people shall be delivered, everyone who is found written in the book. Many of those who sleep in the dust of the earth shall awake, some to everlasting life, and some to shame and everlasting contempt. Those who are wise shall shine like the brightness of the sky, and those who lead many to righteousness, like the stars for ever and ever.

This is the word of the Lord.

A reading from the Letter to the Hebrews. (10.11-14 [15-18] 19-25)

Every priest stands day after day at his service, offering again and again the same sacrifices that can never take away sins. But when Christ had offered for all time a single sacrifice for sins, 'he sat down at the right hand of God', and since then has been waiting 'until his enemies would be made a footstool for his feet.' For by a single offering he has perfected for all time those who are sanctified.
[15 And the Holy Spirit also testifies to us, for after saying,
   'This is the covenant that I will make with them
      after those days, says the Lord:
   I will put my laws in their hearts,
      and I will write them on their minds',
he also adds,
   'I will remember their sins
      and their lawless deeds no more.'
Where there is forgiveness of these, there is no longer any offering for sin.]
   Therefore, my friends, since we have confidence to enter the sanctuary by the blood of Jesus, by the new and living way that he opened for us through the curtain (that is, through his flesh), and since we have a great priest over the house of God, let us approach with a true heart in full assurance of faith, with our hearts sprinkled clean from an evil conscience and our bodies washed with pure water. Let us hold fast to the confession of our hope without wavering, for he who has promised is faithful. And let us consider how to provoke one another to love and good deeds, not neglecting to meet together, as is the habit of some, but encouraging one another, and all the more as you see the Day approaching.

This is the word of the Lord.

Hear the gospel of our Lord Jesus Christ according to Mark. (13.1-8)

As Jesus came out of the temple, one of his disciples said to him, 'Look, Teacher, what large stones and what large buildings!' Then Jesus asked him, 'Do you see these great buildings? Not one stone will be left here upon another; all will be thrown down.'
   When he was sitting on the Mount of Olives opposite the temple, Peter, James, John, and Andrew asked him privately, 'Tell us, when will this be, and what will be the sign that all these things are about to be accomplished?' Then Jesus began to say to them, 'Beware that no one leads you astray. Many will come in my name and say, "I am he!" and they will lead many astray. When you hear of wars and

rumours of wars, do not be alarmed; this must take place, but the end is still to come. For nation will rise against nation, and kingdom against kingdom; there will be earthquakes in various places; there will be famines. This is but the beginning of the birth pangs.'

This is the gospel of the Lord.

Second Service
Ps 95; Daniel 3 (*or* 3.13-30); Matthew 13.24-30,36-43

A reading from the Book of Daniel. (Chapter 3 or 3.13-30)

[King Nebuchadnezzar made a golden statue whose height was sixty cubits and whose width was six cubits; he set it up on the plain of Dura in the province of Babylon. Then King Nebuchadnezzar sent for the satraps, the prefects, and the governors, the counsellors, the treasurers, the justices, the magistrates, and all the officials of the provinces, to assemble and come to the dedication of the statue that King Nebuchadnezzar had set up. So the satraps, the prefects, and the governors, the counsellors, the treasurers, the justices, the magistrates, and all the officials of the provinces, assembled for the dedication of the statue that King Nebuchadnezzar had set up. When they were standing before the statue that Nebuchadnezzar had set up, the herald proclaimed aloud, 'You are commanded, O peoples, nations, and languages, that when you hear the sound of the horn, pipe, lyre, trigon, harp, drum, and entire musical ensemble, you are to fall down and worship the golden statue that King Nebuchadnezzar has set up. Whoever does not fall down and worship shall immediately be thrown into a furnace of blazing fire.' Therefore, as soon as all the peoples heard the sound of the horn, pipe, lyre, trigon, harp, drum, and entire musical ensemble, all the peoples, nations, and languages fell down and worshipped the golden statue that King Nebuchadnezzar had set up.

Accordingly, at this time certain Chaldeans came forward and denounced the Jews. They said to King Nebuchadnezzar, 'O king, live for ever! You, O king, have made a decree, that everyone who hears the sound of the horn, pipe, lyre, trigon, harp, drum, and entire musical ensemble, shall fall down and worship the golden statue, and whoever does not fall down and worship shall be thrown into a furnace of blazing fire. There are certain Jews whom you have appointed over the affairs of the province of Babylon: Shadrach, Meshach, and Abednego. These pay no heed to you, O king. They do not serve your gods and they do not worship the golden statue that you have set up.'

[13] Then] Nebuchadnezzar in furious rage commanded that Shadrach, Meshach, and Abednego be brought in; so they brought those men before the king. Nebuchadnezzar said to them, 'Is it true, O Shadrach, Meshach, and Abednego, that you do not serve my gods and you do not worship the golden statue that I have set up? Now if you are ready when you hear the sound of the horn, pipe, lyre, trigon, harp, drum, and entire musical ensemble to fall down and worship the statue that I have made, well and good. But if you do not worship, you shall immediately be thrown into a furnace of blazing fire, and who is the god that will deliver you out of my hands?'

Shadrach, Meshach, and Abednego answered the king,
'O Nebuchadnezzar, we have no need to present a defence to you in this matter. If our God whom we serve is able to deliver us from the furnace of blazing fire and out of your hand, O king, let him deliver us. But if not, be it known to you, O king, that we will not serve your gods and we will not worship the golden statue that you have set up.'

Then Nebuchadnezzar was so filled with rage against Shadrach, Meshach, and Abednego that his face was distorted. He ordered the furnace to be heated up seven times more than was customary, and ordered some of the strongest guards in his army to bind Shadrach, Meshach, and Abednego and to throw them into the furnace of blazing fire. So the men were bound, still wearing their tunics, their trousers, their hats, and their other garments, and they were thrown into the furnace of blazing fire. Because the king's command was urgent and the furnace was so overheated, the raging flames killed the men who lifted Shadrach, Meshach, and Abednego. But the three men, Shadrach, Meshach, and Abednego, fell down, bound, into the furnace of blazing fire.

Then King Nebuchadnezzar was astonished and rose up quickly. He said to his counsellors, 'Was it not three men that we threw bound into the fire?' They answered the king, 'True, O king.' He replied, 'But I see four men unbound, walking in the middle of the fire, and they are not hurt; and the fourth has the appearance of a god.' Nebuchadnezzar then approached the door of the furnace of blazing fire and said, 'Shadrach, Meshach, and Abednego, servants of the Most High God, come out! Come here!' So Shadrach, Meshach, and Abednego came out from the fire. And the satraps, the prefects, the governors, and the king's counsellors gathered together and saw that the fire had not had any power over the bodies of those men; the hair of their heads was not singed, their tunics were not harmed, and not even the smell of fire came from them. Nebuchadnezzar said, 'Blessèd be the God of Shadrach, Meshach, and Abednego, who has sent his angel and delivered his servants who trusted in him. They disobeyed the king's command and yielded up their bodies rather than serve and worship any god except their own God. Therefore I make a decree: Any people, nation, or language that utters blasphemy against the God of Shadrach, Meshach, and Abednego shall be torn limb from limb, and their houses laid in ruins; for there is no other god who is able to deliver in this way.' Then the king promoted Shadrach, Meshach, and Abednego in the province of Babylon.

A reading from the gospel according to Matthew. (13.24-30,36-43)

Jesus put before his disciples another parable: 'The kingdom of heaven may be compared to someone who sowed good seed in his field; but while everybody was asleep, an enemy came and sowed weeds among the wheat, and then went away. So when the plants came up and bore grain, then the weeds appeared as well. And the slaves of the householder came and said to him, "Master, did you not sow good seed in your field? Where, then, did these weeds come from?" He answered, "An enemy has done this." The slaves said to him, "Then do you want us to go and gather them?" But he replied, "No; for in gathering the weeds you would uproot the wheat along with them. Let both of them grow together until the harvest; and at harvest time I will tell the reapers, Collect the weeds first and bind them in bundles to be burned, but gather the wheat into my barn."'
[36] Then he left the crowds and went into the house. And his disciples approached him, saying, 'Explain to us the parable of the weeds of the field.' He answered, 'The one who sows the good seed is the Son of Man; the field is the world, and the good seed are the children of the kingdom; the weeds are the children of the evil one, and the enemy who sowed them is the devil; the harvest is the end of the age, and the reapers are angels. Just as the weeds are collected and burned up with fire, so will it be at the end of the age. The Son of Man will send his angels, and they will collect out of his kingdom all causes of sin and all evildoers, and they will throw them into the furnace of fire, where there will be weeping and gnashing of teeth. Then the righteous will shine like the sun in the kingdom of their Father. Let anyone with ears listen!'

Third Service

Ps 96; 1 Samuel 9.27 - 10.2*a* & 10.17-26; Matthew 13.31-35

A reading from the First Book of Samuel. *(9.27 - 10.2a & 10.17-26)*

As they were going down to the outskirts of the town, Samuel said to Saul, 'Tell the boy to go on before us, and when he has passed on, stop here yourself for a while, that I may make known to you the word of God.' Samuel took a phial of oil and poured it on his head, and kissed him; he said, 'The Lord has anointed you ruler over his people Israel. You shall reign over the people of the Lord and you will save them from the hand of their enemies all around. Now this shall be the sign to you that the Lord has anointed you ruler over his heritage: When you depart from me today you will meet two men by Rachel's tomb in the territory of Benjamin at Zelzah.'

[10.17] Samuel summoned the people to the Lord at Mizpah and said to them, 'Thus says the Lord, the God of Israel, "I brought up Israel out of Egypt, and I rescued you from the hand of the Egyptians and from the hand of all the kingdoms that were oppressing you." But today you have rejected your God, who saves you from all your calamities and your distresses; and you have said, "No! but set a king over us." Now therefore present yourselves before the Lord by your tribes and by your clans.'

Then Samuel brought all the tribes of Israel near, and the tribe of Benjamin was taken by lot. He brought the tribe of Benjamin near by its families, and the family of the Matrites was taken by lot. Finally he brought the family of the Matrites near man by man, and Saul the son of Kish was taken by lot. But when they sought him, he could not be found. So they inquired again of the Lord, 'Did the man come here?' and the Lord said, 'See, he has hidden himself among the baggage.' Then they ran and brought him from there. When he took his stand among the people, he was head and shoulders taller than any of them. Samuel said to all the people, 'Do you see the one whom the Lord has chosen? There is no one like him among all the people.' And all the people shouted, 'Long live the king!'

Samuel told the people the rights and duties of the kingship; and he wrote them in a book and laid it up before the Lord. Then Samuel sent all the people back to their homes. Saul also went to his home at Gibeah, and with him went warriors whose hearts God had touched.

A reading from the gospel according to Matthew. (13.31-35)

Jesus put before the crowds another parable: 'The kingdom of heaven is like a mustard seed that someone took and sowed in his field; it is the smallest of all the seeds, but when it has grown it is the greatest of shrubs and becomes a tree, so that the birds of the air come and make nests in its branches.'

He told them another parable: 'The kingdom of heaven is like yeast that a woman took and mixed in with three measures of flour until all of it was leavened.'

Jesus told the crowds all these things in parables; without a parable he told them nothing. This was to fulfil what had been spoken through the prophet: 'I will open my mouth to speak in parables; I will proclaim what has been hidden from the foundation of the world.'

Christ the King
The Sunday next before Advent
Sunday between 20 & 26 November inclusive

Evening Prayer on the Eve
Pss 99,100; Isaiah 10.33 - 11.9; 1 Timothy 6.11-16

A reading from the prophecy of Isaiah. (10.33 - 11.9)

Look, the Sovereign, the Lord of hosts,
 will lop the boughs with terrifying power;
the tallest trees will be cut down,
 and the lofty will be brought low.
He will hack down the thickets of the forest with an axe,
 and Lebanon with its majestic trees will fall.

A shoot shall come out from the stock of Jesse,
 and a branch shall grow out of his roots.
The spirit of the Lord shall rest on him,
 the spirit of wisdom and understanding,
 the spirit of counsel and might,
 the spirit of knowledge and the fear of the Lord.
His delight shall be in the fear of the Lord.

He shall not judge by what his eyes see,
 or decide by what his ears hear;
but with righteousness he shall judge the poor,
 and decide with equity for the meek of the earth;

he shall strike the earth with the rod of his mouth,
    and with the breath of his lips he shall kill the wicked.
Righteousness shall be the belt around his waist,
    and faithfulness the belt around his loins.

The wolf shall live with the lamb,
    the leopard shall lie down with the kid,
the calf and the lion and the fatling together,
    and a little child shall lead them.
The cow and the bear shall graze,
    their young shall lie down together;
    and the lion shall eat straw like the ox.
The nursing child shall play over the hole of the asp,
    and the weaned child shall put its hand on the adder's den.
They will not hurt or destroy on all my holy mountain;
    for the earth will be full of the knowledge of the Lord
    as the waters cover the sea.

A reading from the First Letter of Paul to Timothy. (6.11-16)

As for you, man of God, shun all this; pursue righteousness, godli-ness, faith, love, endurance, gentleness. Fight the good fight of the faith; take hold of the eternal life, to which you were called and for which you made the good confession in the presence of many wit-nesses. In the presence of God, who gives life to all things, and of Christ Jesus, who in his testimony before Pontius Pilate made the good confession, I charge you to keep the commandment without spot or blame until the manifestation of our Lord Jesus Christ, which he will bring about at the right time – he who is the blessèd and only Sovereign, the King of kings and Lord of lords. It is he alone who has immortality and dwells in unapproachable light, whom no one has ever seen or can see; to him be honour and eternal dominion. Amen.

Principal Service
Daniel 7.9-10,13-14; Ps 93; Revelation 1.4b-8; John 18.33-37

A reading from the Book of Daniel. (7.9-10)

As I watched,
    thrones were set in place,
        and an Ancient One took his throne;
    his clothing was white as snow,
        and the hair of his head like pure wool;
    his throne was fiery flames,
        and its wheels were burning fire.

A stream of fire issued
    and flowed out from his presence.
A thousand thousand served him,
    and ten thousand times ten thousand stood attending him.
The court sat in judgement,
    and the books were opened.

[13] As I watched in the night visions,
    I saw one like a human being
        coming with the clouds of heaven.
And he came to the Ancient One
    and was presented before him.
To him was given dominion
    and glory and kingship,
that all peoples, nations, and languages
    should serve him.
His dominion is an everlasting dominion
    that shall not pass away,
and his kingship is one
    that shall never be destroyed.

This is the word of the Lord.

A reading from the Revelation to John. (1.4b-8)

Grace to you and peace from him who is and who was and who is to come, and from the seven spirits who are before his throne, and from Jesus Christ, the faithful witness, the firstborn of the dead, and the ruler of the kings of the earth.

   To him who loves us and freed us from our sins by his blood, and made us to be a kingdom, priests serving his God and Father, to him be glory and dominion for ever and ever. Amen.

    Look! He is coming with the clouds;
        every eye will see him,
    even those who pierced him;
        and on his account all the tribes of the earth will wail.
    So it is to be. Amen.
'I am the Alpha and the Omega', says the Lord God, who is and who was and who is to come, the Almighty.

This is the word of the Lord.

Hear the gospel of our Lord Jesus Christ according to John. (18.33-37)

Pilate entered the headquarters, summoned Jesus, and asked him, 'Are you the King of the Jews?' Jesus answered, 'Do you ask this on your own, or did others tell you about me?' Pilate replied, 'I am not a Jew, am I? Your own nation and the chief priests have handed you over to me. What have you done?' Jesus answered, 'My kingdom is not from this world. If my kingdom were from this world, my followers would be fighting to keep me from being handed over to the Jews. But as it is, my kingdom is not from here.' Pilate asked him, 'So you are a king?' Jesus answered, 'You say that I am a king. For this I was born, and for this I came into the world, to testify to the truth. Everyone who belongs to the truth listens to my voice.'

This is the gospel of the Lord.

Second Service
Ps 72 *or* 72.1-7; Daniel 5; John 6.1-15

A reading from the Book of Daniel. (Chapter 5)

King Belshazzar made a great festival for a thousand of his lords, and he was drinking wine in the presence of the thousand.

Under the influence of the wine, Belshazzar commanded that they bring in the vessels of gold and silver that his father Nebuchadnezzar had taken out of the temple in Jerusalem, so that the king and his lords, his wives, and his concubines might drink from them. So they brought in the vessels of gold and silver that had been taken out of the temple, the house of God in Jerusalem, and the king and his lords, his wives, and his concubines drank from them. They drank the wine and praised the gods of gold and silver, bronze, iron, wood, and stone.

Immediately the fingers of a human hand appeared and began writing on the plaster of the wall of the royal palace, next to the lampstand. The king was watching the hand as it wrote. Then the king's face turned pale, and his thoughts terrified him. His limbs gave way, and his knees knocked together. The king cried aloud to bring in the enchanters, the Chaldeans, and the diviners; and the king said to the wise men of Babylon, 'Whoever can read this writing and tell me its interpretation shall be clothed in purple, have a chain of gold around his neck, and rank third in the kingdom.' Then all the king's wise men came in, but they could not read the writing or tell the king the interpretation. Then King Belshazzar became greatly terrified and his face turned pale, and his lords were perplexed.

The queen, when she heard the discussion of the king and his lords, came into the banqueting-hall. The queen said, 'O king, live for ever! Do not let your thoughts terrify you or your face grow pale. There is a man in your kingdom who is endowed with a spirit of the holy gods. In the days of your father he was found to have enlightenment, understanding, and wisdom like the wisdom of the gods. Your father, King Nebuchadnezzar, made him chief of the magicians, enchanters, Chaldeans, and diviners, because an excellent spirit, knowledge, and understanding to interpret dreams, explain riddles, and solve problems were found in this Daniel, whom the king named Belteshazzar. Now let Daniel be called, and he will give the interpretation.'

Then Daniel was brought in before the king. The king said to Daniel, 'So you are Daniel, one of the exiles of Judah, whom my father the king brought from Judah? I have heard of you that a spirit of the gods is in you, and that enlightenment, understanding, and excellent wisdom are found in you. Now the wise men, the enchanters, have been brought in before me to read this writing and tell me its interpretation, but they were not able to give the interpretation of the matter. But I have heard that you can give interpretations and solve problems. Now if you are able to read the writing and tell me its interpretation, you shall be clothed in purple, have a chain of gold around your neck, and rank third in the kingdom.'

Then Daniel answered in the presence of the king, 'Let your gifts be for yourself, or give your rewards to someone else! Nevertheless, I will read the writing to the king and let him know the interpretation. O king, the Most High God gave your father Nebuchadnezzar kingship, greatness, glory, and majesty. And because of the greatness that he gave him, all peoples, nations, and languages trembled and feared before him. He killed those he wanted to kill, kept alive those he wanted to keep alive, honoured those he wanted to honour, and degraded those he wanted to degrade. But when his heart was lifted up and his spirit was hardened so that he acted proudly, he was deposed from his kingly throne, and his glory was stripped from him. He was driven from human society, and his mind was made like that of an animal. His dwelling was with the wild asses, he was fed grass like oxen, and his body was bathed with the dew of heaven, until he learned that the Most High God has sovereignty over the kingdom of mortals, and sets over it whomsoever he will. And you, Belshazzar his son, have not humbled your heart, even though you knew all this! You have exalted yourself against the Lord of heaven! The vessels of his temple have been brought in before you, and you and your lords, your wives and your concubines have been drinking wine from them. You have praised the gods of silver and gold, of bronze, iron, wood, and stone, which do not see or hear or know; but the God in whose power is your very breath, and to whom belong all your ways, you have not honoured.

'So from his presence the hand was sent and this writing was inscribed. And this is the writing that was inscribed: MENE, MENE, TEKEL, and PARSIN. This is the interpretation of the matter: MENE, God has numbered the days of your kingdom and brought it to an end; TEKEL, you have been weighed on the scales and found wanting; PERES, your kingdom is divided and given to the Medes and Persians.'

Then Belshazzar gave the command, and Daniel was clothed in purple, a chain of gold was put around his neck, and a proclamation was made concerning him that he should rank third in the kingdom.

That very night Belshazzar, the Chaldean king, was killed. And Darius the Mede received the kingdom, being about sixty-two years old.

A reading from the gospel according to John. (6.1-15)

Jesus went to the other side of the Sea of Galilee, also called the Sea of Tiberias. A large crowd kept following him, because they saw the signs that he was doing for the sick. Jesus went up the mountain and sat down there with his disciples. Now the Passover, the festival of the Jews, was near. When he looked up and saw a large crowd coming towards him, Jesus said to Philip, 'Where are we to buy bread for these people to eat?' He said this to test him, for he himself knew what he was going to do. Philip answered him, 'Six months' wages would not buy enough bread for each of them to get a little.' One of his disciples, Andrew, Simon Peter's brother, said to him, 'There is a boy here who has five barley loaves and two fish. But what are they among so many people?' Jesus said, 'Make the people sit down.' Now there was a great deal of grass in the place; so they sat down, about five thousand in all. Then Jesus took the loaves, and when he had given thanks, he distributed them to those who were seated; so also the fish, as much as they wanted. When they were satisfied, he told his disciples, 'Gather up the fragments left over, so that nothing may be lost.' So they gathered them up, and from the fragments of the five barley loaves, left by those who had eaten, they filled twelve baskets. When the people saw the sign that he had done, they began to say, 'This is indeed the prophet who is to come into the world.'

When Jesus realized that they were about to come and take him by force to make him king, he withdrew again to the mountain by himself.

Third Service

Pss 29,110; Isaiah 32.1-8; Revelation 3.7-22

A reading from the prophecy of Isaiah. (32.1-8)

See, a king will reign in righteousness,
    and princes will rule with justice.
Each will be like a hiding-place from the wind,
    a covert from the tempest,
like streams of water in a dry place,
    like the shade of a great rock in a weary land.
Then the eyes of those who have sight will not be closed,
    and the ears of those who have hearing will listen.
The minds of the rash will have good judgement,
    and the tongues of stammerers
        will speak readily and distinctly.
A fool will no longer be called noble,
    nor a villain be said to be honourable.
For fools speak folly,
    and their minds plot iniquity:
to practise ungodliness,
    to utter error concerning the Lord,
to leave the craving of the hungry unsatisfied,
    and to deprive the thirsty of drink.
The villainies of villains are evil;
    they devise wicked devices
to ruin the poor with lying words,
    even when the plea of the needy is right.
But those who are noble plan noble things,
    and by noble things they stand.

A reading from the Revelation to John. (3.7-22)

'To the angel of the church in Philadelphia write:
    These are the words of the holy one, the true one,
        who has the key of David,
        who opens and no one will shut, who shuts and no one opens:
    'I know your works. Look, I have set before you an open door,
which no one is able to shut. I know that you have but little power,
and yet you have kept my word and have not denied my name. I will
make those of the synagogue of Satan who say that they are Jews and
are not, but are lying – I will make them come and bow down before
your feet, and they will learn that I have loved you. Because you
have kept my word of patient endurance, I will keep you from the

hour of trial that is coming on the whole world to test the inhabitants of the earth. I am coming soon; hold fast to what you have, so that no one may seize your crown. If you conquer, I will make you a pillar in the temple of my God; you will never go out of it. I will write on you the name of my God, and the name of the city of my God, the new Jerusalem that comes down from my God out of heaven, and my own new name.

Let anyone who has an ear listen to what the Spirit is saying to the churches.

'And to the angel of the church in Laodicea write: The words of the Amen, the faithful and true witness, the origin of God's creation:

'I know your works; you are neither cold nor hot. I wish that you were either cold or hot. So, because you are lukewarm, and neither cold nor hot, I am about to spit you out of my mouth. For you say, "I am rich, I have prospered, and I need nothing." You do not realize that you are wretched, pitiable, poor, blind, and naked. Therefore I counsel you to buy from me gold refined by fire so that you may be rich; and white robes to clothe you and to keep the shame of your nakedness from being seen; and salve to anoint your eyes so that you may see. I reprove and discipline those whom I love. Be earnest, therefore, and repent. Listen! I am standing at the door, knocking; if you hear my voice and open the door, I will come in to you and eat with you, and you with me. To the one who conquers I will give a place with me on my throne, just as I myself conquered and sat down with my Father on his throne. Let anyone who has an ear listen to what the Spirit is saying to the churches.'